Willmington's
COMPLETE GUIDE TO
BIBLE KNOWLEDGE
The Life of Christ

The Life of Christ

Willmington's
Complete
GUIDE
to
BIBLE
KNOWLEDGE

HAROLD L. WILLMINGTON

Tyndale House Publishers, Inc.

WHEATON, ILLINOIS

This book, the third in the series

Willmington's Complete Guide to Bible Knowledge,

is dedicated to my first grandchild,

NATHANAEL PAUL WILLMINGTON,

who was born the very day this manuscript was completed,

October 28, 1989

Cover illustration copyright © 1991 by Zev Radovan

Scriptures, unless otherwise noted, are from the King
James Version of the Bible. Scripture quotations marked
NIV are from the *Holy Bible,* New International Version.
Copyright © 1973, 1978, 1984 International Bible
Society. Used by permission of Zondervan Bible
Publishers.

Library of Congress Catalog Card Number: 91-65396
ISBN 0-8423-8163-5
Copyright © 1991 by Harold L. Willmington
All rights reserved
Printed in the United States of America

99 98 97 96 95 94 93 92 91
9   8   7   6   5   4   3   2   1

CONTENTS

FOREWORD

I don't know of any man who is more qualified to write an accurate account of the life of Christ than Harold Willmington. We have been friends for more than twenty-five years, and I know that he loves the Word of God. Quite often when we drink coffee together (his office is down the hall from mine), we talk about Bible content.

With other friends I discuss golf, sports, or church growth; but with Harold Willmington, we always discuss Bible content.

During the first year at Regent University (called Lynchburg Baptist College in those days, and until recently was called Liberty University), I was the Academic Dean with the difficult task of infusing academic quality into the life of a new college. I invited Harold Willmington to give a week-long lecture series on the life of Christ. The other classes were canceled during that week, and Dr. Willmington taught all 154 students of this new college in one room. He gave focus to the students and laid a foundation for the future of the college.

When he told me he was writing another volume of *Willmington's Complete Guide to Bible Knowledge,* this one on the life of Christ, I joked with him that it should really be "Christ's Guide to the Life of Willmington." We both laughed. Then I realized that the reversed title I suggested is actually the Bible itself. God has given the Bible as a guide to the life of Harold Willmington—and to all the rest of us as well.

Jesus Christ is the focus of all Christian writing. Yet there has not been a significant work on the life of Christ published in the past few years. It is time for this volume. We need to know Jesus Christ better, and this volume will accomplish that. Since we need this book, and since Harold Willmington is the best person to write it, I highly recommend this work to you.

DR. ELMER L. TOWNS, Vice-President of Regent University and Dean of the School of Religion.

INTRODUCTION

It has been estimated that since the time of Adam some 40 billion people have lived on earth. Of this number more than 5 billion are living at the present time. Sociologists and anthropologists have separated these 40 billion into endless categories—those of race, geography, religion, politics, economics, etc.

The sobering truth is, however, that their Creator has placed this mass of humanity into one of two categories, the saved and the lost. Furthermore, the eternal destiny of each of the 40 billion depends totally upon his or her relationship with one Man. Who is this amazing individual? His official name and title read *The Lord Jesus Christ.*

What a marvelous and mysterious book is the Bible!

The Old Testament opens up with man made in the image of God (Gen. 1:26). The New Testament begins with God made in the image of man (Matt. 1:23). In the Old Testament we see the sheep dying for the shepherd (Gen. 4:2, 4). In the New Testament we read of the Shepherd dying for the sheep (John 10:11).

The following is an overview of Christ's earthly ministry, from his touchdown in a manger to his liftoff from a mountain.

This glory story begins with his arrival as the Lamb of Jehovah and concludes with his ascension as the Lion of Judah.

The life of Christ will be considered here both chronologically and topically. The chronological approach briefly overviews those key events such as Christ's birth, baptism, temptation, and transfiguration. The topical approach summarizes such subjects as his miracles, parables, sermons, and prayers.

FIRST STUDY: *Statistics on the Life of Christ*

Heavenly Father: The first Person in the Trinity (Luke 2:49);
Earthly father: The Holy Spirit (Luke 1:35; Matt. 1:20)
His mother: Mary (Luke 2:7)
His half brothers: James, Joseph, Simon, and Judas (Matt. 13:55)
His half sisters: Unnamed (Matt. 13:56)
His famous ancestors: Abraham and David (Matt. 1:1)
First mention: The seed of the woman (Gen. 3:15)
Final mention: The Lord Jesus Christ (Rev. 22:21)
Meaning of his name:
    Jesus means "Savior";
    Christ means "The Anointed One."
Frequency of his name: These three key names and titles, "Jesus," "Christ," and "Lord," appear nearly 2,000 times in the New Testament. In addition, there are literally hundreds of other names and titles found throughout the entire Bible.
Biblical books mentioning him: He is referred to in every one of the sixty-six books.
Occupation: Creator (John 1:3); Redeemer (1 Pet. 1:18-19); Prophet (Matt. 13:57); Priest (Heb. 3:1; 4:14); King (Rev. 19:16); Shepherd (John 10:11); Judge (John 5:22)
Place of birth: Bethlehem (Luke 2:4-7)
Place of death: Outside Jerusalem, on a hill (Matt. 27:33)
Manner of death: Crucifixion (John 19:18)
Age at death: Approximately thirty-four years old
Place of resurrection: From a garden tomb (John 19:41; 20:11-17)
Important fact about his life: He was (and is) the Son of God who became the sinless Son of Man, that sinful sons of men might become the sons of God.

FINAL STUDY: *Summary of the Life of Christ*

PART ONE: A CHRONOLOGICAL OVERVIEW
A CHRONOLOGICAL OVERVIEW
 I. An Introduction to the Ministry of Christ
   ONE: The four biographers (Matthew, Mark, Luke, John)
   TWO: The two genealogies
   THREE: The two prefaces
   FOUR: The three announcements
   FIVE: The three songs of praise
 II. The Manifestation of the Ministry of Christ
   ONE: Christ's birth
   TWO: Christ's circumcision
   THREE: Christ's dedication
   FOUR: Christ's visit by the Wise Men
   FIVE: Christ's flight into Egypt
   SIX: Christ's early years in Nazareth
   SEVEN: Christ's temple visit at age twelve
   EIGHT: Christ's forerunner
   NINE: Christ's baptism
   TEN: Christ's temptations
   ELEVEN: Christ is presented as the Lamb of God.
   TWELVE: Christ meets his first five disciples.
   THIRTEEN: Christ performs his first miracle while attending a wedding in Cana of
      Galilee.
   FOURTEEN: Christ performs the first temple cleansing.
   FIFTEEN: Christ meets with Nicodemus.
   SIXTEEN: Christ meets with the Samaritan woman.
   SEVENTEEN: Christ's first preaching tour of Galilee
   EIGHTEEN: Christ's first return trip to Nazareth
   NINETEEN: Christ moves into Capernaum and makes this city his northern headquarters.
   TWENTY: Christ extends a call to four fishermen.
   TWENTY-ONE: Christ's second preaching tour of Galilee
   TWENTY-TWO: Christ extends a call to Matthew.
   TWENTY-THREE: Christ's first meeting with John's disciples
   TWENTY-FOUR: Christ heals a man who has been an invalid for thirty-eight years.
   TWENTY-FIVE: Christ's first Sabbath controversy with the Pharisees
   TWENTY-SIX: Christ officially selects the twelve apostles.
   TWENTY-SEVEN: Christ delivers his Sermon on the Mount.
   TWENTY-EIGHT: Christ's third preaching tour of Galilee
   TWENTY-NINE: Christ sends out the twelve apostles.
   THIRTY: Christ's fourth preaching tour of Galilee

THIRTY-ONE: Christ denounces some key cities in Galilee.

THIRTY-TWO: Christ issues a universal invitation.

THIRTY-THREE: Christ is anointed in Simon's house.

THIRTY-FOUR: Christ's fifth preaching tour of Galilee

THIRTY-FIVE: Christ refuses on two occasions to show the Pharisees a sign.

THIRTY-SIX: Christ is misunderstood by his family on several occasions.

THIRTY-SEVEN: Christ explains who his real family is.

THIRTY-EIGHT: Christ relates his parable on the nature of the kingdom of heaven.

THIRTY-NINE: Christ rebukes the stormy Galilean Sea.

FORTY: Christ heals the maniac of Gadara.

FORTY-ONE: Christ's second return trip to Nazareth

FORTY-TWO: Christ's forerunner, John, is murdered by Herod.

FORTY-THREE: Christ feeds the five thousand.

FORTY-FOUR: Christ refuses the offer of the people he fed to crown him king.

FORTY-FIVE: Christ walks on the water.

FORTY-SIX: Christ preaches his sermon on the bread of life.

FORTY-SEVEN: Christ hears Peter's confession and promises to build Jesus' church.

FORTY-EIGHT: Christ rebukes Peter.

FORTY-NINE: Christ is transfigured.

FIFTY: Christ heals a demon-possessed boy.

FIFTY-ONE: Christ performs the miracle of the fish with a coin in its mouth.

FIFTY-TWO: Christ rebukes James and John on three occasions.

FIFTY-THREE: Christ answers the apostles' argument concerning who was the greatest among them.

FIFTY-FOUR: Christ warns about mistreating a little child.

FIFTY-FIVE: Christ is approached by three would-be disciples.

FIFTY-SIX: Christ is rebuked by his unbelieving half brothers.

FIFTY-SEVEN: Christ forgives a woman taken in the act of adultery.

FIFTY-EIGHT: Christ heals a man born blind.

FIFTY-NINE: Christ preaches his Good Shepherd sermon.

SIXTY: Christ sends out seventy disciples.

SIXTY-ONE: Christ visits with Mary and Martha.

SIXTY-TWO: Christ commands people to repent.

SIXTY-THREE: Christ relates the parable of the Good Samaritan.

SIXTY-FOUR: Christ relates the parable of the rich fool.

SIXTY-FIVE: Christ relates the parables of the lost sheep, coin, and son.

SIXTY-SIX: Christ relates the parable of the rich man and Lazarus.

SIXTY-SEVEN: Christ raises Lazarus from the dead.

SIXTY-EIGHT: Christ teaches on the subject of discipleship.

SIXTY-NINE: Christ teaches on the subject of forgiveness.

SEVENTY: Christ teaches on the subject of hell.

SEVENTY-ONE: Christ teaches on the subject of church discipline.

SEVENTY-TWO: Christ teaches on the subject of divorce.

SEVENTY-THREE: Christ teaches on the subject of rewards.

SEVENTY-FOUR: Christ teaches on the subject of faith.

SEVENTY-FIVE: Christ attends the Feast of Tabernacles.

SEVENTY-SIX: Christ attends the Feast of Dedication.

SEVENTY-SEVEN: Christ relates his overall purpose for coming to earth.

SEVENTY-EIGHT: Christ blesses some little children.

SEVENTY-NINE: Christ is approached by a rich young ruler.

EIGHTY: Christ heals blind Bartimaeus.

EIGHTY-ONE: Christ saves Zacchaeus.

III. The Completion of the Ministry of Christ

The Eight-day Period:

Day One: Saturday

One: Christ is plotted against by Caiaphas, the high priest.

Two: Christ is anointed by Mary in the home of Simon the leper.

Day Two: Sunday—Christ makes his triumphal entry into Jerusalem.

Day Three: Monday

One: Christ pronounces judgment upon a fruitless fig tree.

Two: Christ performs the second temple cleansing.

Three: Christ is sought after by some Gentile Greeks.

Day Four: Tuesday

One: Christ confronts the Pharisees and Sadducees.

Two: Tuesday (Passion Week) confrontations

Three: Christ observes the widow and her mite.

Four: Christ weeps over Jerusalem for the final time.

Five: Christ preaches the Mount Olivet Discourse.

Six: Christ relates the parables of the ten virgins, the talents, and the sheep and goats.

Day Five: Wednesday—Christ is secretly betrayed by Judas.

Day Six: Thursday

One: Christ sends Peter and John from Bethany into Jerusalem.

Two: Christ meets with his disciples in the Upper Room.

Three: Christ preaches his sermon on the Father's house.

Day Seven: Friday

One: Christ preaches his sermon on fruitbearing, en route to the Mount of Olives.

Two: Christ prays his great high priestly prayer at the Mount of Olives.

Three: Christ arrives in the Garden of Gethsemane.

Four: Christ suffers his first unfair trial—The appearance before Annas.

Five: Christ suffers his second unfair trial—The appearance before Caiaphas.

Six: Christ is denied by Simon Peter.

Seven: Christ suffers his third unfair trial—The appearance before the Sanhedrin.

Eight: Christ's betrayer shows remorse and commits suicide.

Nine: Christ suffers his fourth unfair trial—The first appearance before Pilate.

Ten: Christ suffers his fifth unfair trial—His appearance before Herod Antipas.

Eleven: Christ suffers his sixth unfair trial—The final appearance before Pilate.

Twelve: Christ suffers his seventh unfair trial—The appearance before the Roman soldiers.

Thirteen: Christ walks the road to Calvary.

Fourteen: Christ is crucified on the cross.

Fifteen: Christ's death introduces some supernatural events.

Sixteen: Christ's body is removed from the cross and placed in a tomb.

Day Eight: Saturday—Christ's tomb is officially sealed.

The Final Forty-day Period:

One: Christ is risen from the dead.

Two: Christ is ascended into heaven.

PART ONE: A CHRONOLOGICAL OVERVIEW

I. An Introduction to the Ministry of Christ

ONE: The four biographers (Matthew, Mark, Luke, John, each present a different aspect of the Savior.

A. Matthew, the teacher—He presents Christ as the King, and lionlike; emphasizes his sermons; writes to the Jews.

B. Mark, the preacher—He presents Christ as the Servant, and oxlike; emphasizes his miracles; writes to the Romans.

C. Luke, the historian—He presents Christ as the perfect man, and manlike; emphasizes his parables; writes to the Greeks.

D. John, the theologian—He presents Christ as the mighty God, and eagle-like; emphasizes his doctrine; writes to the world.

TWO: The two genealogies—There is a genealogy in Matthew, for a king must have one. There is a genealogy in Luke, for a perfect man should have one. There is no genealogy in Mark, for a servant does not need one. There is no genealogy in John, for the mighty God does not have one.

A. Matthew's genealogy (Matt. 1:1-17)—"The book of the generation of Jesus Christ, the son of David, the son of Abraham" (1:1).

---

†*These three names, Abraham, David, and Christ, are referred to by Matthew both here at the beginning of his genealogy and at the end. Note: "So all the generations from Abraham to David are fourteen generations; and from David until the carrying away into Babylon are fourteen generations; and from the carrying away into Babylon unto Christ are fourteen generations" (Matt. 1:17).*

It can be seen that his genealogy records 41 generations consisting of three groups of 14 each:

A. From Abraham to David

B. From David to the Babylonian Captivity

C. From the Babylonian Captivity to Christ

To make these three groups of 14 each, Matthew omitted three generations, those of Ahaziah, Joash, and Amaziah. Chronologically they should appear between the two names, "Jehoram begat Uzziah" in Matthew 1:8. There were probably several reasons why Matthew used this approach:

A. As a memory device

B. The number 14 is twice seven, the number of perfection.

C. The name David, Israel's greatest king, has a numerical value in the Hebrew language which totals 14.

1. He begins with Abraham and goes forward in time to Joseph.
2. He gives the royal line of Joseph.
3. He traces this line through Solomon, David's first son.
4. His list includes forty-one names, four of which are women.
   a. Tamar
   b. Rahab
   c. Ruth
   d. Bath-sheba

---

†*This genealogy is remarkable for several reasons:*
  A. It contains the names of four women—Oriental and Mideastern genealogies rarely do this.
  B. All four women had questionable backgrounds.
    1. Tamar was an ex-harlot (Matt. 1:3; Gen. 38:13-30).
    2. Rahab was an ex-harlot (Matt.1:5; Josh. 2:1).
    3. Ruth was a former pagan (Matt. 1:5; Ruth 1:4).
    4. Bath-sheba was a former adulteress (Matt. 1:6; 2 Sam. 11:1-5).
  But through the manifold and marvelous grace of God, the first of these women (Tamar) became the distantly removed grandmother of King David; the second (Rahab) became his great-great-grandmother; the third (Ruth) was his great-grandmother; and the fourth (Bath-sheba) became his beloved wife and mother of Solomon. (See Ruth 4:18-22.)

  B. Luke's genealogy (Luke 3:23-38)
    1. He begins with Joseph and goes backward in time to Adam.
    2. He gives the racial line of Mary.
    3. He traces this line through Nathan, David's second son.
    4. His list includes seventy-four names.

---

†*Several problems are involved in both of these genealogies.*
  A. Joseph's father is said by Matthew to be Jacob (Matt. 1:16), while Luke says he was Heli's son (Luke 3:23). The ancient world often referred to their sons-in-law as their own sons. Thus it is possible that Heli was actually the father of Mary and the father-in-law of Joseph.
  B. Satan was keenly aware of the fact that the line leading to Christ would go through David's seed. He thus apparently attempted to break a link in the royal chain. With the advent of King Jeconiah (the 19th "link" from David), it appeared that the devil had succeeded, for God pronounced the following curse upon this wicked young ruler: "Thus saith the Lord, write ye this man childless, a man that shall not prosper in his days; for no man of his seed shall prosper, sitting upon the throne of David, and ruling any more in Judah" (Jer. 22:30).
  This declaration did not mean he would have no children, for in 1 Chronicles 3:17-18, some are named. (See also Matt. 1:12.) What it did mean is that by divine judgment this king would be considered childless as far as the throne of Judah was concerned. Whatever it meant, it seemed the royal line of David and Solomon had ground to a stop with Jeconiah (also called Coniah and Jehoiachin in the Old Testament). (See Jer. 22:24; 2 Kings 24:8.) But what a rude shock when the devil learned that God was not limited to one line. David had another son named Nathan, and it was through this line that Mary, the mother of Jesus, came.

THREE: The two prefaces
A. Luke's preface (Luke 1:1-4)
　1. Many had already drawn up a narrative of Christ's life.
　2. Luke proposed to do the same, obtaining his facts from various eyewitnesses.
　3. He then planned to forward his narrative to his friend Theophilus.
B. John's preface (John 1:1-5)—"In the beginning was the Word, and the Word was with God, and the Word was God. The same was in the beginning with God. All things were made by him; and without him was not any thing made that was made. In him was life; and the life was the light of men. And the light shineth in darkness; and the darkness comprehended it not" (John 1:1-5).

---

†*These first five verses in John are the most profound in the Bible and are worthy to have been written in gold. In fact, the first verse affirms three great truths concerning Christ:*
　A. His eternality—"In the beginning was the Word."
　B. His personality—"And the Word was with God."
　C. His deity—"And the Word was God."

---

　1. Jesus Christ was with the Father in eternity past.
　2. He was the Creator of all things.
　3. He is both the light and life of all people.
　4. He shone in the darkness, which could not extinguish him. Luke concerns himself with the details in Christ's life, while John is interested in the deity of Christ's Person.
FOUR: The three announcements
A. To Zacharias, about the birth of John, the Messiah's forerunner (Luke 1:5-25)

---

†*This old couple doubtless had many things going for them.*
　A. Both had experienced the new birth.
　B. Both were walking in the will of God.
　C. Each was apparently enjoying good health.
　But there was an unanswered prayer need which had burdened their hearts for a number of decades: "And they had no child, because that Elisabeth was barren, and they both were now well stricken in years" (Luke 1:7).

---

　1. His devotion to God—Both he and his wife Elisabeth loved the Lord—"And they were both righteous before God, walking in all the commandments and ordinances of the Lord blameless" (Luke 1:6).
　2. His duties for God

---

†*We are informed in Luke 1:5 that Zacharias was from the course (or division) of Abijah. Because the priests became so numerous, and they could not all officiate at the altar, David divided them into twenty-four courses or classes. This act is described in 1 Chronicles 24, which mentions the curse of Abia (Abijah in Hebrew) as the eighth one. Josephus says that in his day there were about 20,000 priests. The Talmud says there were even more.*

At Passover, Pentecost, and the Feast of Tabernacles, all of the priests served, but the rest of the year was divided up among the courses. Since there were so many in each course (an average of nearly 850, if Josephus' figure is accurate), the various duties were assigned by the casting of lots.

      a. Zacharias and the altar of the Lord—"And it came to pass, that while he executed the priest's office before God in the order of his course, according to the custom of the priest's office, his lot was to burn incense when he went into the temple of the Lord. And the whole multitude of the people were praying without at the time of incense" (Luke 1:8-10).

      b. Zacharias and the angel of the Lord

        (1) The reassurance—"And there appeared unto him an angel of the Lord standing on the right side of the altar of incense. And when Zacharias saw him, he was troubled, and fear fell upon him. But the angel said unto him, Fear not, Zacharias: for thy prayer is heard" (Luke 1:11-13).

† A. *The archangel Gabriel appeared to Zacharias the priest as he burned incense at the golden altar in the Jerusalem temple. (See Exod. 30:7; 2 Chron. 29:11.)*

  B. *This is the first spoken message from heaven in more than 400 years.*

  C. *The last person before Zacharias to receive a message given by angels was named Zechariah (see Zech. 1–6).*

        (2) The revelation—He heard a sixfold prophecy from this heavenly angel, whose name was Gabriel (Luke 1:19): He and Elisabeth would have a son (Luke 1:13); his name would be John (Luke 1:13); he would become a Spirit-filled Nazarite (Luke 1:15); he would have a successful ministry (Luke 1:16); he would prepare the way for the Messiah (Luke 1:17); and his style would be similar to that of Elijah (Luke 1:17).

† A. *This is the eighth of nine biblical births in which God himself intervened. They are:*

    1. The birth of Isaac to Abraham and Sarah (Gen. 21:1)

    2. The birth of Jacob and Esau to Isaac and Rebekah (Gen. 25:21)

    3. The birth of Reuben to Jacob and Leah (Gen. 29:31)

    4. The birth of Issachar to Jacob and Leah (Gen 30:17-18)

    5. The birth of Joseph to Jacob and Rachel (Gen. 30:22-24)

    6. The birth of Samuel to Elkanah and Hannah (1 Sam. 1:19)

    7. The birth of Samson to Manoah and his wife (Judg. 13:1-2)

    8. The birth of John to Zacharias and Elisabeth (Luke 1:57)

    9. The birth of Jesus to Mary (Luke 2:7)

  B. *The child was to be called John, which means "the grace of Jehovah." The name Zacharias means "God remembers," and the name Elisabeth means "his oath." Thus, at the birth of John the Baptist, God was remembering his covenant of grace made in Psalm 89:34-37 concerning David's seed, Jesus, to which John would serve as a forerunner. Note: "My covenant will I not break, nor alter the thing that is gone out of my lips. Once have I sworn by my holiness that I will not lie unto David. His seed shall endure for ever, and his throne as the sun before me. It shall be established for ever as the moon, and as a faithful witness in heaven" (Psa. 89:34-37). "And he [John] shall go before him [Jesus] in the spirit and power of Elijah . . . to make ready a people for the Lord" (Luke 1:17).*

C. John was to function as a Nazarite (Luke 1:15). There is a difference between a Nazarite and a Nazarene:
   1. A Nazarite *had to do with vocation. This is to say that the Nazarite took upon him a threefold vow (Num. 6:2-6).*
      a. *He would abstain from wine.*
      b. *He would not have his hair cut.*
      c. *He would not come in contact with a dead body.*
   2. A Nazarene *had to do with location. This is to say that if one lived in the city of Nazareth, he was known as a Nazarene. Thus, while John was a Nazarite, Jesus became a Nazarene (Matt. 2:23). In fact, our Lord did not observe any of the three Nazarite vows.*
      a. *He did partake of the fruit of the vine. He both created it (John 2:1-10) and served it (Matt. 26:26-29).*
      b. *He did cut his hair. Jesus was often looked upon as a Jewish rabbi, and it is known that they did cut their hair (John 3:2).*
      c. *He did come in contact with dead bodies. In fact, our Lord broke up every funeral he ever attended by raising the corpse (Luke 7:14; 8:54; John 11:43).*
D. *John would be filled with the Holy Spirit from his mother's womb. This is said also about two other men:*
   1. *Jeremiah (Jer. 1:5)*
   2. *Paul (Gal. 1:15)*
E. *He would turn many Israelites to the Lord. This he did at the Lord's first coming, as Elijah will someday do at Christ's second coming (Mal. 4:5-6).*

---

(3) The response—"And Zacharias said unto the angel, Whereby shall I know this? for I am an old man, and my wife well stricken in years" (Luke 1:18).

---

†*As both he and his wife were advanced in years, Zacharias had some difficulty believing all this (as once did Abraham and Sarah; see Gen. 17:17; 18:12).*

---

(4) The rebuke—"And the angel answering said unto him, I am Gabriel, that stand in the presence of God; and am sent to speak unto thee, and to shew thee these glad tidings. And, behold, thou shalt be dumb, and not able to speak, until the day that these things shall be performed, because thou believest not my words, which shall be fulfilled in their season" (Luke 1:19-20).

---

†*The name Gabriel means "God's hero," or "mighty man of God." He is one of the two most powerful and important good angels in the entire Bible. The other is Michael (Dan. 10:13, 21; Jude 9; Rev. 12:7). Both probably hold the title of archangel. How thrilling to realize that even in the birth announcement of Christ's forerunner, God chose the very best.*

(5) The results—"And the people waited for Zacharias, and marvelled that he tarried so long in the temple. And when he came out, he could not speak unto them: and they perceived that he had seen a vision in the temple: for he beckoned unto them, and remained speechless" (Luke 1:21-22).

† *A. The waiting crowd soon realized that something very strange had happened to Zacharias and that he could not pronounce the expected blessing upon them. No doubt many in that waiting crowd were there to help Zacharias celebrate a very special event, the burning of incense upon the golden altar. A priest could do this only once in his entire life. Others in the multitude were expecting to hear him pronounce the great Levitical blessing. In Numbers 6:22-27 we read: "And the Lord spoke unto Moses, saying, Speak unto Aaron and unto his sons, saying, On this wise ye shall bless the children of Israel, saying unto them, the Lord bless thee, and keep thee; the Lord make his face shine upon thee, and be gracious unto thee; the Lord lift up his countenance upon thee, and give thee peace. And they shall put my name upon the children of Israel; and I will bless them."*

B. But on that day there was no celebration or benediction. Something far more exciting and eternal was about to happen. Zacharias returned home and soon his old and barren wife conceived a child.

(6) The rejoicing—"And it came to pass, that, as soon as the days of his ministration were accomplished, he departed to his own house. And after those days his wife Elisabeth conceived, and hid herself five months, saying, Thus hath the Lord dealt with me in the days wherein he looked on me, to take away my reproach among men" (Luke 1:23-25).

B. To Mary, about the birth of Jesus (Luke 1:26-38)
  1. The salutation—"And in the sixth month the angel Gabriel was sent from God unto a city of Galilee, named Nazareth, to a virgin espoused to a man whose name was Joseph, of the house of David; and the virgin's name was Mary. And the angel came in unto her, and said, Hail, thou that art highly favoured, the Lord is with thee: blessed art thou among women. And when she saw him, she was troubled at his saying, and cast in her mind what manner of salutation this should be" (Luke 1:26-29).

†*The angel did not say Mary was to be blessed* above *women, but* among *women. Note also that Luke tells us the first recorded person to call Jesus Savior was Mary. "And Mary said, My soul doth magnify the Lord, and my spirit hath rejoiced in God my Saviour" (Luke 1:46-47). Mary needed salvation, as did all others (see Rom. 3:23).*

a. Concerning the birth of Jesus
  (1) The choice of Mary—"And the angel said unto her, Fear not, Mary: for thou hast found favour with God" (Luke 1:30).
  (2) The child in Mary—"And, behold, thou shalt conceive in thy womb, and bring forth a son, and shalt call his name JESUS. He shall be

great, and shall be called the Son of the Highest: and the Lord God shall give unto him the throne of his father David: And he shall reign over the house of Jacob for ever; and of his kingdom there shall be no end" (Luke 1:31-33).

(3) The concern of Mary—"Then said Mary unto the angel, How shall this be, seeing I know not a man?" (Luke 1:34).

(4) The clarification to Mary—"And the angel answered and said unto her, The Holy Ghost shall come upon thee, and the power of the Highest shall overshadow thee: therefore also that holy thing which shall be born of thee shall be called the Son of God" (Luke 1:35).

---

†*At this point, two questions can be raised:*

A. *What was the real mystery involved in the incarnation and where did it take place? The supernatural element in the incarnation was not the birth of Christ, but rather his conception. He was born as all humans are born. It is vital to make this distinction, for he was not only as completely God as though he had never been man; he was also as completely man as though he had never been God. Thus, the actual miracle occurred not at Bethlehem, but in Nazareth.*

B. *Why did the angel Gabriel rebuke Zacharias for his question and not rebuke Mary for her question?*

   1. *Zacharias: "Whereby shall I know this? For I am an old man, and my wife well stricken in years" (Luke 1:18).*

   2. *Mary: "How shall this be, seeing I know not a man?" (Luke 1:34).*

C. *Answer: Zacharias had for many years been praying for a son (Luke 1:13), but when the announcement came, he doubted God's power to do this. When something wonderful happens sometimes the most surprised individual on earth is that very Christian who has been fervently praying for it to happen. However, there is no reason to believe that Mary had been praying to become the mother of Jesus.*

Another classic example is found in the book of Acts. Peter was in prison awaiting execution, and when the Jerusalem believers heard of it, "prayer was made without ceasing of the church unto God for him" (Acts 12:5). At God's command an angel staged a spectacular jailbreak. Upon being set free, Peter hurried to the prayer meeting to announce the good news. Note the amusing account: "And when he had considered the thing, he came to the house of Mary the mother of John, whose surname was Mark; where many were gathered together praying. And as Peter knocked at the door of the gate, a damsel came to hearken, named Rhoda. And when she knew Peter's voice, she opened not the gate for gladness, but ran in and told how Peter stood before the gate. And they said unto her, thou art mad. But she constantly affirmed that it was even so. Then said they, It is his angel. But Peter continued knocking: and when they had opened the door, and saw him, they were astonished" (Acts 12:12-16). Peter had a harder time getting into that prayer meeting then he had had getting out of prison.

---

   b. Concerning the birth of John—"And, behold, thy cousin Elisabeth, she hath also conceived a son in her old age: and this is the sixth month with her, who was called barren. For with God nothing shall be impossible" (Luke 1:36-37).

†Some twenty centuries previous to this, another woman had heard similar words: "Is any thing too hard for the Lord? At the time appointed I will return unto thee, according to the time of life, and Sarah shall have a son" (Gen. 18:14).

2. The submission—"And Mary said, Behold the handmaid of the Lord; be it unto me according to thy word. And the angel departed from her" (Luke 1:38).

C. To Joseph about the purity of Mary (Matt. 1:18-25)

1. The distress of Joseph—"Now the birth of Jesus Christ was on this wise: When as his mother Mary was espoused to Joseph, before they came together, she was found with child of the Holy Ghost" (Matt. 1:18).

2. The decision of Joseph—"Then Joseph her husband, being a just man, and not willing to make her a publick example, was minded to put her away privily" (Matt. 1:19).

3. The dream of Joseph

a. The message in the dream

(1) Concerning the purity of Mary—"But while he thought on these things, behold, the angel of the Lord appeared unto him in a dream, saying, Joseph, thou son of David, fear not to take unto thee Mary thy wife: for that which is conceived in her is of the Holy Ghost" (Matt. 1:20).

(2) Concerning the person within Mary—"And she shall bring forth a son, and thou shalt call his name JESUS: for he shall save his people from their sins" (Matt. 1:21).

(3) Concerning the prophecy about Mary—"Now all this was done, that it might be fulfilled which was spoken of the Lord by the prophet, saying, Behold, a virgin shall be with child, and shall bring forth a son, and they shall call his name Emmanuel, which being interpreted is, God with us" (Matt. 1:22-23).

†This prophecy was of course a fulfillment of Isaiah 7:14 (see Matt. 1:23). Some have questioned (unsuccessfully) the Hebrew word Almah in Isaiah 7:14, saying it does not always mean virgin. However, there is absolutely no doubt whatsoever about the Greek word for virgin, which is parthenos *and always, without exception, refers to a young girl totally devoid of sexual experience.*

b. The marriage following the dream—"Then Joseph being raised from sleep did as the angel of the Lord had bidden him, and took unto him his wife: and knew her not till she had brought forth her firstborn son: and he called his name JESUS" (Matt. 1:24-25).

†Joseph arranged to make Mary his full, legal wife. Joseph must be considered by all standards of measurement a truly just man, with the spiritual maturity of a David, Moses, or Paul. In fact, the New Testament Joseph may be favorably compared to the Old Testament Joseph. Both had fathers named Jacob. Both had amazing maturity. Both received visions from God. Both were in Egypt. One was a type of Christ; the other was his legal guardian. In fact, had

it not been for Judah's sin, Joseph would have been ruling from Jerusalem as the rightful king when Christ was born. It was he and not Herod who had the proper credentials to sit upon the throne of Israel.

FIVE: The three songs of praise
  A. The praise of Elisabeth to Mary (Luke 1:39-45)—"And Mary arose in those days, and went into the hill country with haste, into a city of Juda; and entered into the house of Zacharias, and saluted Elisabeth" (Luke 1:39-40).

---

†*Never in the history of childbirth did two expectant mothers have more to talk about than these two women.*
  A. Here was Elisabeth, well past the childbearing years, but anticipating a baby.
  B. Here was Mary, a young virgin, but now with child. This was the case because "with God nothing shall be impossible" (Luke 1:37).
  It should be noted that Elisabeth's unborn child is referred to twice as "the babe" (Luke 1:41, 44), indicating Scripture's position on abortion. From the beginning, John was not looked upon as a developing mass of human tissue or a fetus, but as "the babe."
  But what about a therapeutic abortion? Consider the following: A therapeutic abortion occurs when a pregnant woman is persuaded (often by her doctor) that her unborn child presents an emotional or mental threat to her general well-being. Therefore, the most practical and painless solution (for the mother at least) is simply to kill the offending baby. There are two well-known instances in history in which this attitude toward unborn human life could certainly have been applied.
  The first case involved that of an older woman, the wife of a respected religious leader, living in a large southern city. Present-day advice to her would have been: "Do you really feel it wise to complete this birth? Consider your age. The psychological strain upon you will be much greater than it would be on a younger woman. Then too, as an older parent, don't you think you'll have real problems adjusting to this infant? I mean, it might even affect your relationship with your husband. No, all things considered, it would be far better to terminate the potential problem right now."
  The second case had to do with a teenage girl, engaged to a struggling young tradesman, living in a small northern town. Here there could be no doubt. A quick abortion would immediately solve the embarrassment and downright hostility which would certainly develop if the unborn baby was not destroyed.
  Two simple and clear-cut cases for therapeutic abortion. Not quite. Could even the most calloused present-day abortion mill operator stomach the thought of Elisabeth (the older woman) and Mary (the teenager) with trembling hands and hearts awaiting the sharp instrument of some ancient abortionist?

---

    1. The babe in Elisabeth—"And it came to pass, that, when Elisabeth heard the salutation of Mary, the babe leaped in her womb; and Elisabeth was filled with the Holy Ghost" (Luke 1:41).
    2. The blessing from Elisabeth—"And she spake out with a loud voice, and said, Blessed art thou among women, and blessed is the fruit of thy womb. And whence is this to me, that the mother of my Lord should come to me? For, lo, as soon as the voice of thy salutation sounded in mine ears, the babe leaped in

my womb for joy. And blessed is she that believed: for there shall be a performance of those things which were told her from the Lord" (Luke 1:42-45).

B. The praise of Mary to God (Luke 1:46-56)—In these verses Mary quotes from at least fifteen Old Testament sources and praises God for his manifold characteristics.
  1. His grace (Luke 1:46-48)
  2. His power (1:51)
  3. His mercy (1:50)
  4. His holiness (1:49)
  5. His goodness (1:53)
  6. His faithfulness (1:54-56)

C. The praise of Zacharias to God (Luke 1:57-59)—Zacharias is able to speak on the day of John's circumcision.
  1. Zacharias, the parent
    a. Writing—The silent words of Zacharias
      (1) The celebration—"Now Elisabeth's full time came that she should be delivered; and she brought forth a son. And her neighbours and her cousins heard how the Lord had shewed great mercy upon her; and they rejoiced with her" (Luke 1:57-58).
      (2) The circumcision—"And it came to pass, that on the eighth day they came to circumcise the child; and they called him Zacharias, after the name of his father" (Luke 1:59).
      (3) The confusion—"And his mother answered and said, Not so; but he shall be called John. And they said unto her, There is none of thy kindred that is called by this name" (Luke 1:60-61).
      (4) The confirmation—"And they made signs to his father, how he would have him called. And he asked for a writing table, and wrote, saying, His name is John. And they marvelled all" (Luke 1:62-63).
    b. Worshiping—The spoken words of Zacharias—"And his mouth was opened immediately, and his tongue loosed, and he spake, and praised God" (Luke 1:64).
  2. Zacharias, the prophet
    a. His words to his Savior—"And his father Zacharias was filled with the Holy Ghost, and prophesied, saying, Blessed be the Lord God of Israel; for he hath visited and redeemed his people, and hath raised up an horn of salvation for us in the house of his servant David. . . . The oath which he sware to our father Abraham" (Luke 1:67-69, 73).

---

†*These immutable Old Testament covenants included the following features:*
  A. *The Abrahamic Covenant had to do with seed and soil. God promised Abraham he would father a great nation (seed) and be given a special land (soil). (See Gen. 12—15.)*
  B. *The Davidic Covenant had to do with a Sovereign. God promised David that a male descendant from his line (Christ) would someday rule over that seed upon that soil. (See 2 Sam. 7.) "He shall be great, and shall be called the Son of the Highest: and the Lord God shall give unto him the throne of his father David: and he shall reign over the house of Jacob for ever; and of his kingdom there shall be no end" (Luke 1:32-33).*

b. His words to his son—"And thou, child, shalt be called the prophet of the Highest: for thou shalt go before the face of the Lord to prepare his ways; to give knowledge of salvation unto his people by the remission of their sins, through the tender mercy of our God; whereby the dayspring from on high hath visited us, to give light to them that sit in darkness and in the shadow of death, to guide our feet into the way of peace" (Luke 1:76-79).

---

†*Zacharias predicted that his son would be called "the prophet of the Highest," as contrasted to Gabriel, who referred to Jesus as "the Son of the Highest!"*

II. The Manifestation of the Ministry of Christ—"The former treatise have I made, O Theophilus, of all that Jesus began both to do and teach" (Acts 1:1). Luke begins the book of Acts with these words. The following outline presents some one hundred-plus key events that our Lord began both to do and teach during his earthly ministry. (Note: It should be kept in mind that this is a *Chronological Overview.* While some of the more well-known miracles, sermons, and parables are mentioned here, they are summarized under the *Topical Overview.*)
ONE: Christ's birth (Luke 2:1-20)
A. The Son of Jehovah (Luke 2:1-7)
    1. The circumstances—"And it came to pass in those days, that there went out a decree from Caesar Augustus, that all the world should be taxed. . . . And all went to be taxed, every one into his own city. And Joseph also went up from Galilee, out of the city of Nazareth, into Judaea, unto the city of David, which is called Bethlehem; (because he was of the house and lineage of David)" (Luke 2:1, 3-4).

---

†*Joseph and Mary were brought to Bethlehem because of an enrollment decree which commanded each Hebrew citizen to be counted from that town where he or she was born. Note: This is the third all-important trip made to Bethlehem. Ruth and Naomi made the first journey. (See Ruth 1:22.) Samuel the prophet made the second. (See 1 Sam. 16.)*

---

    2. The channel—"To be taxed with Mary his espoused wife, being great with child. And so it was, that, while they were there, the days were accomplished that she should be delivered. And she brought forth her firstborn son, and wrapped him in swaddling clothes, and laid him in a manger; because there was no room for them in the inn" (Luke 2:5-7).

---

† *A. Mary gave birth to the Savior and "wrapped him in swaddling clothes, and laid him in a manger; because there was no room for them in the inn" (Luke 2:7).*
    1. This was the fourth greatest day in human history.
    2. The third greatest day in human history occurred some thirty-four years later when this Babe grew into glorious manhood, only to be put to death between a pair of thieves on Calvary's cross. "And when they were come to the place, which is called Calvary, there they

crucified him, and the malefactors, one on the right hand, and the other on the left" (Luke 23:33).

3. *The second greatest day in human history occurred three days later, when an angel told some sorrowing women: "Fear not ye; for I know that ye seek Jesus, which was crucified. He is not here; for he is risen as he said. Come, see the place where the Lord lay" (Matt. 28:5-6).*

4. *The greatest day in human history is yet to happen. The Apostle John tells us of this: "And the seventh angel sounded; and there were great voices in heaven, saying, The kingdoms of this world are become the kingdoms of our Lord, and of his Christ, and he shall reign forever and ever" (Rev. 11:15).*

B. *One may favorably contrast Matthew 2:7 with Daniel 2:11. In this Old Testament passage King Nebuchadnezzar had just ordered the death of his wise men because of their inability to relate a dream he had just experienced. These astrologers thereupon protested, exclaiming: "And it is a rare thing that the king requireth, and there is no other that can shew it before the king, except the gods, whose dwelling is not with flesh." But at the advent of the fourth greatest day in history all this would change.*

C. *In John 1:14 we read that the Word was made flesh. One of the most glorious truths of the incarnation was its eternality. This simply means that the results of the fourth day will last forever. He still has and always will have a body of flesh and bone (see Luke 24:39).*

D. *In the 1960s an American astronaut wrote a book entitled* **Moon Walk.** *In it he related how he had left a pleasant, familiar, and safe place called earth and had landed on an alien, dangerous, and unfamiliar planet known as the moon. When rightly understood, Luke 2:7 is the divine account of* **Earth Walk,** *for it begins the story of how God's Son left the beauty and safety of heaven to dwell upon an alien and sin-cursed planet, the wicked world of mankind.*

E. *To rephrase the familiar nursery rhyme:*

> *Mary had a little Lamb, His life was pure as snow.*
> *And everywhere the Father led, the Lamb was sure to go.*
> *He followed Him to Calvary, one dark and dreadful day,*
> *And there the Lamb that Mary had washed all my sins away.*

B. The shepherds of Judah (Luke 2:8-20)
   1. Watching—"And there were in the same country shepherds abiding in the field, keeping watch over their flock by night" (Luke 2:8).
   2. Wondering
      a. The reassurance by the angel of the Lord—"And, lo, the angel of the Lord came upon them, and the glory of the Lord shone round about them: and they were sore afraid. And the angel said unto them, Fear not: for, behold, I bring you good tidings of great joy, which shall be to all people" (Luke 2:9-10).
      b. The revelation by the angel of the Lord
         (1) Concerning the Son of God—"For unto you is born this day in the city of David a Saviour, which is Christ the Lord" (Luke 2:11).

---

†*He is called a Savior—not an example, or a teacher, but a Savior. Consider:*

If our greatest need had been information
God would have sent us an educator.
If our greatest need had been technology
God would have sent us a scientist.
If our greatest need had been money
God would have sent us an economist.
If our greatest need had been pleasure
God would have sent us an entertainer.
But, alas, our greatest need was forgiveness and redemption
So . . . God sent us a Savior.

---

(2) Concerning the sign from God—"And this shall be a sign unto you; Ye shall find the babe wrapped in swaddling clothes, lying in a manger" (Luke 2:12).

c. The rejoicing by the angels of the Lord—"And suddenly there was with the angel a multitude of the heavenly host praising God, and saying, Glory to God in the highest, and on earth peace, good will toward men" (Luke 2:13-14).

3. Worshiping
   a. The decision of the shepherds—"And it came to pass, as the angels were gone away from them into heaven, the shepherds said one to another, Let us now go even unto Bethlehem, and see this thing which is come to pass, which the Lord hath made known unto us" (Luke 2:15)
   b. The devotion of the shepherds—"And they came with haste, and found Mary, and Joseph, and the babe lying in a manger" (Luke 2:16).

4. Witnessing—"And when they had seen it, they made known abroad the saying which was told them concerning this child. And all they that heard it wondered at those things which were told them by the shepherds. But Mary kept all these things, and pondered them in her heart. And the shepherds returned, glorifying and praising God for all the things that they had heard and seen, as it was told unto them" (Luke 2:17-20).

A. *Observe how the shepherds came, and how they left.*
   1. *They "came with haste" (Luke 2:16).*
   2. *They left and "made known abroad . . . concerning this child" (Luke 2:17).*
B. *Luke tells us Mary "pondered" all this in her heart (Luke 2:19). Without doubt, this young mother had more to ponder than did any other human in history. Consider:*
   1. *As she held the newly born baby, she knew he was already infinitely older than his mother and as old as his Father.*
   2. *As she fed the tiny infant, she realized she was nursing the One who had once fed the animals in the Garden of Eden, and her ancestors in the wilderness of Sinai. In essence, she was providing food for the Bread of Life.*
C. *At this point, let us stop and consider several questions that may be raised concerning those events leading up to the birth of the Savior.*
   1. *Why did Joseph and Mary wait so long before coming to Bethlehem? We know that both believed the angel's message about the Babe in Mary's womb, and they doubtless were well aware of the prophecy in Micah 5:2 which stated that Christ was to be born in Bethlehem.*

Why did they wait until the last moment to come? In fact, one is somewhat led to believe that had it not been for the decree of Caesar Augustus they might not have come at all. Answer: No satisfactory answer has been found by this author. It is best to conclude that Joseph (man of God that he was) had good reasons for acting in the manner that he did. The reader may desire to explore this further.

2. *Why didn't Mary and Joseph stay with their relatives in Bethlehem? The inns of those days were rather notorious, and Joseph must have been desperate to subject his pregnant wife to the sin and noise of such a place. But, of course, they were denied even this. Answer: It would have been too difficult to explain (or to expect them to understand) the nature of the virgin birth. Every gossip in town doubtless knew by this time that Joseph and Mary had been married only six months, and there she was, expecting a baby at any moment. Was the father Joseph? Did the child belong to some stranger? Thus, to spare his beloved wife all this, Joseph did not call upon their relatives.*

3. *Why was Jesus born in a place which apparently housed animals? Answer: Because lambs are usually born in barns. This was God's Lamb.*

4. *Why did the angels appear to the shepherds first? Answer: What other earthly group than shepherds would better understand what God had just accomplished? These were men who raised lambs and later sold them for sacrificial purposes in the temple. (See John 1:29; 10:11.) Note: They would eventually understand that in the past the sheep had died for the shepherd, but soon the Shepherd planned to die for the sheep. (See John 10:11.)*

5. *Why did God use the angels in the first place? Answer:*
   a. *Because angels are interested in the things of salvation. (See 1 Pet. 1:12; Exod. 25:20; Dan. 12:5-6; Luke 15:10; Eph. 3:10.)*
   b. *Because they were present at the creation of this world and shouted for joy (Job 38:7). It is only logical, therefore, that God would allow them to be on hand at the presentation of the Savior of this world.*

TWO: Christ's circumcision—"And when eight days were accomplished for the circumcising of the child, his name was called JESUS, which was so named of the angel before he was conceived in the womb" (Luke 2:21).

THREE: Christ's dedication (Luke 2:22-38)—"And when the days of her purification according to the law of Moses were accomplished, they brought him to Jerusalem, to present him to the Lord; (As it is written in the law of the Lord, Every male that openeth the womb shall be called holy to the Lord;) And to offer a sacrifice according to that which is said in the law of the Lord, a pair of turtledoves, or two young pigeons" (Luke 2:22-24).

---

†*Jesus was brought to the temple to be dedicated to the Lord.*
   A. *He was at least forty days old at this time, for Mary would have been considered ceremonially impure until forty days had elapsed following childbirth. (See Lev. 12:2-4; Exod. 13:2.)*
   B. *Two offerings were to be brought (Lev. 12:6).*
      1. *A yearling lamb as a burnt offering*
      2. *A young pigeon or turtledove as a sin offering*
   C. *However, if the family was poor, God would accept two birds (Lev. 12:8).*
   D. *Joseph and Mary offered these birds in place of the lamb.*

A. The testimony of Simeon (2:25-35)
   1. The righteousness of Simeon—"And, behold, there was a man in Jerusalem, whose name was Simeon; and the same man was just and devout, waiting for the consolation of Israel: and the Holy Ghost was upon him" (Luke 2:25).
   2. The revelation to Simeon—"And it was revealed unto him by the Holy Ghost, that he should not see death, before he had seen the Lord's Christ" (Luke 2:26).
   3. The recognition by Simeon
      a. Simeon and the Messiah
         (1) Who he was—"And he came by the Spirit into the temple: and when the parents brought in the child Jesus, to do for him after the custom of the law, then took he him up in his arms, and blessed God, and said, Lord, now lettest thou thy servant depart in peace, according to thy word: For mine eyes have seen thy salvation" (Luke 2:27-30).
         (2) What he would do—"Which thou hast prepared before the face of all people; a light to lighten the Gentiles, and the glory of thy people Israel" (Luke 2:31-32).
      b. Simeon and the mother—"And Joseph and his mother marvelled at those things which were spoken of him. And Simeon blessed them, and said unto Mary his mother, Behold, this child is set for the fall and rising again of many in Israel; and for a sign which shall be spoken against; (Yea, a sword shall pierce through thy own soul also,) that the thoughts of many hearts may be revealed" (Luke 2:33-35).

---

†*Some thirty-four years later, Mary would stand at the foot of a hideous Roman cross outside the city of Jerusalem, watching her firstborn Son die in agony. Surely at that awful moment the full significance of Simeon's strange words would fall with crushing weight upon her soul.*

B. The testimony of Anna
   1. Her widowhood—"And there was one Anna, a prophetess, the daughter of Phanuel, of the tribe of Aser: she was of a great age, and had lived with an husband seven years from her virginity" (Luke 2:36).
   2. Her worship—"And she was a widow of about fourscore and four years, which departed not from the temple, but served God with fastings and prayers night and day" (Luke 2:37).
   3. Her witness—"And she coming in that instant gave thanks likewise unto the Lord, and spake of him to all them that looked for redemption in Jerusalem" (Luke 2:38).
FOUR: Christ's visit by the Wise Men (Matt. 2:1-12)
A. The Wise Men—Their frustration in Jerusalem
   1. Their public meeting
      a. The request of the Magi—"Now when Jesus was born in Bethlehem of Judaea in the days of Herod the king, behold, there came wise men from the east to Jerusalem, Saying, Where is he that is born King of the Jews? for we have seen his star in the east, and are come to worship him" (Matt. 2:1-2).

†*Herod (known as Herod the Great) was the second son of Antipater, and a descendant of Esau. His mother was from Cyprus, an Arabian.*

    A. *Herod the brutal—He became King of the Jews through the favor of the Romans. Able and courageous, but jealous and cruel, he became half-insane toward the close of his life and tried to murder everybody who seemed to threaten his throne. He killed his wife Mariamne and three of his sons. He killed his son Antipater just five days before his own death. He commanded a large group of the nobles among the Jews to be assembled and killed at his death in order that there should be a sufficient amount of mourning.*

    B. *Herod the builder—Josephus, the Jewish historian, writes:*

> To conciliate the Jews, who had been alienated by his cruelties, he with much address proposed to reconstruct their ancient temple which Solomon had originally built, though it has been shrewdly suspected that he entertained the sinister motive to possess himself of the public genealogies collected there, especially those relating to the priestly families, unto whom they were of paramount importance and interest. It is said that he thereby hoped to destroy the genealogy of the expected Messiah, lest he should come and usurp his kingdom. However that may be, he endeavored to make the Jewish nation understand that he was doing them a great kindness without cost to them, and he promised that he would not attempt to build them a new temple, but merely restore to its ancient magnificence the one originally built by David's son. For the restoration made by Zerubbabel upon the return of Israel from the captivity of Babylon seems to have fallen short in architectural measurement, in height some sixty cubits, and the whole was becoming marked with decay. To this end Herod took down the old temple to its very foundations, and engaged one thousand wagons to draw stones and ten thousand skilled workmen to teach the priests the art of stonecutting and carpentering.
>
> The temple proper which he erected was one hundred cubits in length and twenty cubits in height. It was constructed of white stone, each one being twenty-five cubits long and eight in height. Surmounting this structure was a great white dome adorned with a pinnacle of gold, suggestive of a mountain of snow as seen from afar.
>
> The Jewish tradition holds that the temple itself was built by the priests in one year and six months, when they celebrated its completion with Jewish feasts and sacrifices; but that the cloisters and outer inclosures were eight years in building. However that may be, additions were made continuously from year to year; so that though Herod began the rebuilding in 20 B.C., as a whole it was literally true that the temple was built in forty and six years, when the Jews so asserted to Jesus (John 2:20).
>
> But the end was not yet, for the work was really continued until A.D. 64, just six years before the final destruction of the temple (Ant. XV. Ch. 11).

        b. The reaction of the monarch
           (1) His concern—"When Herod the king had heard these things, he was troubled, and all Jerusalem with him" (Matt. 2:3).

(2) His command—"And when he had gathered all the chief priests and scribes of the people together, he demanded of them where Christ should be born" (Matt. 2:4).

    c. The reply of the ministers—"And they said unto him, In Bethlehem of Judaea: for thus it is written by the prophet, And thou Bethlehem, in the land of Juda, art not the least among the princes of Juda: for out of thee shall come a Governor, that shall rule my people Israel" (Matt. 2:5-6).

  2. Their private meeting

    a. The king's demand—"Then Herod, when he had privily called the wise men, enquired of them diligently what time the star appeared" (Matt. 2:7).

    b. The king's deception—"And he sent them to Bethlehem, and said, Go and search diligently for the young child; and when ye have found him, bring me word again, that I may come and worship him also" (Matt. 2:8).

B. The Wise Men—Their celebration in Bethlehem

  1. The witness of the star—"When they had heard the king, they departed; and, lo, the star, which they saw in the east, went before them, till it came and stood over where the young child was" (Matt. 2:9).

  2. The worship of the Magi

    a. Their gladness—"When they saw the star, they rejoiced with exceeding great joy" (Matt. 2:10).

    b. Their gifts—"And when they were come into the house, they saw the young child with Mary his mother, and fell down, and worshipped him: and when they had opened their treasures, they presented unto him gifts; gold, and frankincense, and myrrh" (Matt. 2:11).

  3. The warning from the Lord—"And being warned of God in a dream that they should not return to Herod, they departed into their own country another way" (Matt. 2:12).

---

†*A brief summary of the Wise Men's visit is appropriate at this point.*

  A. *Who were these wise men? It is thought that they were perhaps a group of religious astronomers living in the Mesopotamian area.*

  B. *How did they associate the star with Christ? There are several possibilities. In the fourteenth century, B.C., a prophet from their area named Balaam had spoken of this star. (See Num. 24:17.) They also had the writings of Daniel, who had been prime minister of both Babylon and Persia some six centuries before Christ. Daniel, of course, wrote much about the second coming.*

  C. *Why did they come? These men were doubtless acquainted with the various religions of the East and knew the emptiness of them all. It would seem that they followed this star to find peace and purpose for their lives.*

  D. *When did they arrive in Bethlehem? It was perhaps not until some two years after the angels announced his birth to the shepherds. He is referred to as "the young child" (Matt. 2:9, 11, 13-14), and is not a tiny babe at this time. When Herod later attempted to destroy this unknown Babe, he had all children in the Bethlehem area two years and under slain (Matt. 2:16).*

  E. *How many wise men came? There is no evidence that there were three. On the contrary, the group may have numbered from two to several hundred or more. Tradition, however, claims that there were but three and that their names were Caspar, Melchior, and Balthazar.*

F. *Why did the star, after leading the wise men to Jerusalem, apparently disappear for a brief time and then reappear, taking them directly to Bethlehem? It may be that God intended this visit for the sake of the Jewish leaders. However, they had degenerated to such a level that they were unwilling to travel down the road a few miles from Jerusalem to Bethlehem to see if their Messiah had really come. But here was a group of sincere Gentiles who had traveled across a hostile and extended desert to find him.*

G. *Was the star a regular one? The astronomer Kepler said there was a conjunction of the planets Jupiter and Saturn about this time in history. However, by no stretch of the imagination could a planet or star located thousands of millions of miles from earth function in the precise way this star did as recorded by Matthew: "The star . . . came and stood over where the young child was" (Matt. 2:9). It is not at all unreasonable, however, to suggest that the star was actually a New Testament appearance of that Old Testament Shekinah Glory cloud that led Israel across the desert.*

H. *What gifts did they offer him?*

1. *They gave him gold, which spoke of his deity.*

2. *They gave him frankincense, which spoke of his humanity.*

3. *They gave him myrrh, which spoke of his future sufferings. Reg Grant writes: "During her life, Mary would see Jesus receive the gift of myrrh on five occasions; twice from Gentiles and three times from Jews.*

   a. *On the first occasion, the Magi brought myrrh from the east in honor of Jesus as King of Kings (Matt. 2:11). This event anticipated the worship Christ will receive from the Gentile nations in the future kingdom.*

   b. *The second occasion found Jesus in the home of Simon the Pharisee receiving myrrh from the loving hand of a contrite woman who approached Jesus as her great High Priest, the One who could forgive her many sins (Luke 7:36-50).*

   c. *The third offering of myrrh came from the devout Mary of Bethany as she anointed Christ for his burial prior to his death. This showed that she understood the sacrificial nature of his ministry in a way that even his closest disciples had failed to grasp.*

   d. *Just before the crucifixion, the Roman soldiers offered Christ a fourth 'gift' of myrrh mixed with wine—a kind of narcotic to dull the pain—but he refused it.*

   e. *The fifth and final offering came from the hand of Nicodemus when he provided a mixture of myrrh and aloes for anointing Christ's body following his crucifixion (John 19:39)." (Kindred Spirit, Winter 1988, pp. 13-14.)*

FIVE: Christ's flight into Egypt (Matt. 2:13-20)

A. The reason for this trip: Herod's wrath (2:13-18)—"And when they were departed, behold, the angel of the Lord appeareth to Joseph in a dream, saying, Arise, and take the young child and his mother, and flee into Egypt, and be thou there until I bring thee word: for Herod will seek the young child to destroy him. When he arose, he took the young child and his mother by night, and departed into Egypt. . . . Then Herod, when he saw that he was mocked of the wise men, was exceeding wroth, and sent forth, and slew all the children that were in Bethlehem, and in all the coasts thereof, from two years old and under, according to the time which he had diligently enquired of the wise men" (Matt. 2:13-14, 16).

†*A divine irony is seen here. In the Old Testament God led his chosen people out of Egypt to escape Satan's wrath, but in the New Testament he leads his beloved Son into Egypt to escape this same wrath.*

B. The return from this trip—Herod's death
1. The messenger from God—"But when Herod was dead, behold, an angel of the Lord appeareth in a dream to Joseph in Egypt" (Matt. 2:19).
2. The message from God—"Saying, Arise, and take the young child and his mother, and go into the land of Israel: for they are dead which sought the young child's life" (Matt. 2:20).

SIX: Christ's early years in Nazareth
A. The city of Jesus—"And he arose, and took the young child and his mother, and came into the land of Israel. . . . And he came and dwelt in a city called Nazareth: that it might be fulfilled which was spoken by the prophets, He shall be called a Nazarene" (Matt. 2:21, 23).
B. The childhood of Jesus—"And the child grew, and waxed strong in spirit, filled with wisdom: and the grace of God was upon him. . . . And Jesus increased in wisdom and stature, and in favour with God and man" (Luke 2:40, 52).

---

† *A. How did Jesus develop as a human being?*
1. He increased in wisdom (mental maturity).
2. He increased in stature (physical maturity).
3. He increased in favor with God (spiritual maturity).
4. He increased in favor with man (social maturity).
B. Did he go to school? Some would say no, based on these verses in John's Gospel: "Now about the midst of the feast Jesus went up into the temple, and taught. And the Jews marvelled, saying, How knoweth this man letters, having never learned? Jesus answered them, and said, My doctrine is not mine, but his that sent me" (John 7:14-16).

However, the phrase "having never learned" may have referred to the learning offered in a rabbinical school. In other words, the Jewish leaders were amazed that Christ could speak with such spiritual knowledge and authority, since he had never been enrolled in their religious schools.

Jesus as a boy had doubtless learned Hebrew, Aramaic, and Greek. He later would read from a Hebrew scroll in Nazareth (Luke 4), teach the multitudes in Aramaic, and converse with Pilate in Greek. He may have read the Testaments of the Twelve Patriarchs, *which was a noncanonical account relating the testimony of Jacob's twelve sons. He surely also would have been familiar with well-known Jewish books on the sacred Law and writings.*

C. Do we know anything concerning his early years? In reality we possess no hard facts whatsoever about Jesus from age two to age twelve. However, E. F. Harrison has suggested the following: "Jesus' Boyhood—This hamlet of Nazareth in northern Palestine was a miniature of the whole country in the sense that its situation afforded ready contact with the outside world, yet considerable separation from it, the very features Israel historically had enjoyed. Their land lay at the crossroads of the world but was detached by its peculiar topography, which confined the flow of travel largely to the lowlands, passing by the plateau where the life of the nation centered.

"From the hill back of Nazareth, Jesus as a boy must often have scanned the horizon in all directions. Travelers attest to the magnificence of the view from this spot. The panorama would include the Mediterranean Sea to the west, Mount Carmel and the plain of Sharon

south of it, the broad valley of Esdraelon, with Mount Tabor on the north, the hill of Moreh and Mount Gilboa on the south, and Samaria beyond—all of these in an almost perfect line north and south. To the east, beyond the depression made by the Sea of Galilee and the Jordan, rose the hills that marked the beginning of the Bashan-Gilead country. To the north lay the somewhat broken terrain of Galilee, rising to plateau proportions in the distance, with glistening Mount Hermon to the northeast capping the scene.

"No patriotic son of Israel could allow his eye to sweep these vistas without being reminded of the stirring events of history that would forever be associated with them: Elijah's triumph over the prophets of Baal, the victory of Deborah and Barak, the crushing of the Midianites by Gideon and his band, the lamented death of Saul and Jonathan—these and other episodes would easily rise out of the past and in fancy be reenacted. Yes, Nazareth was secluded, but just beyond its sheltering quiet lay the world of affairs. Its immediate gift to Jesus was an opportunity to live a life of simplicity. More remotely, it provided a door of entrance to the busier and more complex life in which he would minister.

"Nazareth depended for its livelihood upon the tillage of its grainfields and the cultivation of its vineyards and groves, which ranged up and down the neighboring hills. Though his labor kept him in the village, Jesus loved the out-of-doors, and must have often tramped through the countryside enjoying its sights and sounds. Years later, when he chose to slip away from human companionship to commune with the Father, he was remaining true to the influence of the environment of the early days.

"Judging from his parables Jesus must have cultivated early in life the habit of observing what went on around him. He saw that not all the sower's seed fell on good ground. He knew that a good tree was needed to insure good fruit.

"He had many times stuffed dried grass into his mother's stove to heat it for baking, grass that only a short time before had been growing in the field. Perchance he had watched Mary light a lamp and look carefully for the coin that had slipped from her hand and rolled out of view. Whether indoors or out he was alert to all that was going on. This panorama of early days furnished him with many a true-to-life illustration as he stood before the multitude and taught." (Everett F. Harrison, A Short Life of Christ, *pp. 56-57)*

D. Do we have any fictitious accounts of his early childhood? *There are a number of Apocryphal Gospels (apocryphal means "hidden") that attempt to "fill us in" on the details, but their accounts are nonsensical.*

    Foster writes: *"In order to give an idea of the character of stories told in these Apocryphal Gospels, the following summary is offered of the records given in the* First Gospel of the Infancy of Jesus Christ. *The author pretends to have his information from Caiaphas, the High Priest. As Joseph and Mary are going to Bethlehem to be taxed they stop outside the town in a cave. Joseph goes in search of a Hebrew woman to act as midwife, but returns to find the cave filled with great lights and the Infant in the arms of His mother. The old Hebrew woman is cured by touching the child. The shepherds come and make a fire ready for the family. The heavenly hosts appear and sing. As an infant in the cradle, Jesus informs Mary that He is the Son of God. The Wise Men preserve one of His swaddling clothes, which proves indestructible. When Jesus is presented in the temple, He shines like a pillar of light and the angels stand around adoring Him. When the family flees to Egypt, they stop in a city, a great idol falls from its pedestal, and the son of the priest is healed of infirmity. They flee to the haunts of robbers who are frightened away by a miraculous noise. Water is supplied by springs bursting forth. All sorts of cures are performed by the afflicted touching the child, his clothing, or by being sprinkled with the water in which he has been bathed. A young man who had been bewitched and turned into a mule is miraculously cured by the infant's being placed upon his back, and is married to a girl who had just been cured of leprosy. Joseph and Mary pass through a country infested by robbers. Titus, a humane thief, offers Dumachus, his comrade, forty groats to let Joseph and Mary pass without giving the alarm. The Infant prophesies that the two thieves shall be crucified and that Titus shall go before Him into Paradise. Jesus works miracles in Memphis and they return to Nazareth. Here Jesus and other boys play together and make clay figures of animals, Jesus causes them to walk and also makes clay birds which he causes to fly, eat, and drink. He goes to a dyer's shop and throws all the clothes into the furnace, but brings them forth again unharmed and miraculously dyed. The king of Jerusalem gives Joseph an order for a throne. Joseph works on it for two years in the king's palace and makes it two spans too short. Jesus lengthens it by a miracle. He miraculously widens or contracts the gates, milk pails, or boxes not properly made by Joseph."* (The Youth of Jesus in the Apocryphal Gospels, *Foster, pp. 286-288*)

SEVEN: Christ's temple visit at age twelve (Luke 2:41-51)—Jesus is found missing on the way back from Jerusalem to Nazareth and is finally located in the temple discussing theology with the priests. "And all that heard him were astonished at his understanding and answers" (Luke 2:47).
  A. The rebuke by Mary—"And when they saw him, they were amazed: and his mother said unto him, Son, why hast thou thus dealt with us? behold, thy father and I have sought thee sorrowing" (Luke 2:48).
  B. The reminder by Jesus—"And he said unto them, How is it that ye sought me? wist ye not that I must be about my Father's business? And they understood not the saying which he spake unto them. And he went down with them, and came to Nazareth, and was subject unto them: but his mother kept all these sayings in her heart. And Jesus increased in wisdom and stature, and in favour with God and man" (Luke 2:49-52).

---

†*This is but the first of many incidents in which people were astonished at the words and wisdom of Christ. This is recorded:*
  A. Following his Sermon on the Mount (Matt. 7:28)
  B. At the end of his lecture in Nazareth (Matt. 13:54)
  C. During his debate with the Pharisees in Jerusalem (Matt. 22:33)
  Note also that Jesus spoke his first recorded words: "I must be about my Father's business." Compare these with the words he spoke en route from heaven's glory to Bethlehem's manger: "Wherefore when he cometh into the world, he saith, Sacrifice and offering thou wouldest not, but a body hast thou prepared me. . . . Then said I, Lo, I come (in the volume of the book it is written of me,) to do thy will, O God" (Heb. 10:5, 7).

EIGHT: Christ's forerunner—The ministry of John the Baptist (Matt. 3:1-12; Mark 1:1-8; Luke 1:80; 3:1-18; John 1:6-34).—"And the child grew, and waxed strong in spirit, and was in the deserts till the day of his shewing unto Israel" (Luke 1:80). Upon reaching maturity, John begins his ministry as a Nazarite evangelist: "There was a man sent from God, whose name was John. The same came for a witness, to bear witness of the Light, that all men through him might believe. He was not that Light, but was sent to bear witness of the Light. That was the true Light, which lighteth every man that cometh into the world. He was in the world, and the world was made by him, and the world knew him not. He came unto his own, and his own received him not. But as many as received him, to them gave he power to become the sons of God, even to them that believe on his name: Which were born, not of the blood, nor of the will of the flesh, nor of the will of man, but of God. And the Word was made flesh, and dwelt among us, (and we beheld his glory, the glory as of the only begotten of the Father,) full of grace and truth" (John 1:6-14).

† A. *The words "which lighteth every man that cometh into the world" (John 1:9) do not indicate universal salvation or inner illumination. Instead, they refer to Christ as the Light that shines (photizei) on each person either in salvation or in illuminating that person with regard to sin and coming judgment (3:18-21; 9:39-41; compare 16:8-11)* (Bible Knowledge Commentary, Victor Books, p. 272).

B. *It has been said that John 1:11 is the "saddest" verse in the Bible, and that 1:12 is the "gladdest." "He came unto his own, and his own received him not." "But as many as received him, to them gave he power to become the sons of God, even to them that believe on his name."*

C. *This Light, in human flesh, full of grace and truth, would turn into sons of God all repenting sinners. Thus, the Son of God became the Son of man, that sons of men might become sons of God (John 1:11-14). We note from 1:13 that salvation is not of generation (not of blood), reformation (nor of the will of the flesh), nor confirmation (nor of the will of man), but regeneration (of God).*

A. The message of John
   1. As predicted by Isaiah and Malachi
      a. Isaiah's prophecy (Isa. 40:3-5)—"In those days came John the Baptist, preaching in the wilderness of Judea" (Matt. 3:1). "And the same John had his raiment of camel's hair, and a leathern girdle about his loins; and his meat was locusts and wild honey" (Matt. 3:4). "And he came into all the country about Jordan, preaching the baptism of repentance for the remission of sins; as it is written in the book of the words of Esaias the prophet, saying, The voice of one crying in the wilderness, Prepare ye the way of the Lord, make his paths straight. Every valley shall be filled, and every mountain and hill shall be brought low; and the crooked shall be made straight, and the rough ways shall be made smooth; and all flesh shall see the salvation of God" (Luke 3:3-6).

A. *Some have attempted to show that the word* locust *here does not refer to the insect but rather to a Judean fruit or plant. However, the Greek word for locust,* akris, *is used but four times in the New Testament, two times in relation to John's diet (Matt. 3:4; Mark 1:6), and the remaining two times in the book of Revelation. Here the author John definitely has a literal locust in mind (see Rev. 9:3, 7).*

B. *The eating of locusts was permitted under the Levitical Law (see Lev. 11:22).*

b. Malachi's prophecy (Mal. 3:1)—"For this is he, of whom it is written, Behold, I send my messenger before thy face, which shall prepare thy way before thee" (Matt. 11:10).

---

†*John thus became the last of the great biblical prophets, as Samuel in the Old Testament was the first. Samuel introduced Israel's first king, Saul (1 Sam. 10), while John would present its eternal King, Jesus (John 1:29).*

---

2. As proclaimed by John
   a. To the crowds
      (1) His message to their hearts—"Repent; for the kingdom of heaven is at hand" (Matt. 3:2). "Prepare ye the way of the Lord, make his paths straight" (Matt. 3:3b).
      (2) His message to their hands—"And the people asked him, saying, What shall we do then? He answereth and saith unto them, He that hath two coats, let him impart to him that hath none; and he that hath meat, let him do likewise" (Luke 3:10-11).
   b. To the Pharisees and Sadducees—"But when he saw many of the Pharisees and Sadducees come to his baptism, he said unto them, O generation of vipers, who hath warned you to flee from the wrath to come? Bring forth therefore fruits meet for repentance: And think not to say within yourselves, We have Abraham to our father: for I say unto you, that God is able of these stones to raise up children unto Abraham. And now also the axe is laid unto the root of the trees: therefore every tree which bringeth not forth good fruit is hewn down, and cast into the fire" (Matt. 3:7-10).
   c. To the tax collectors—"Then came also publicans to be baptized, and said unto him, Master, what shall we do? And he said unto them, Exact no more than that which is appointed you" (Luke 3:12-13).
   d. To the soldiers—"And the soldiers likewise demanded of him, saying, And what shall we do? And he said unto them, Do violence to no man, neither accuse any falsely; and be content with your wages" (Luke 3:14).
   e. To the world—"The next day John seeth Jesus coming unto him, and saith, Behold the Lamb of God, which taketh away the sin of the world" (John 1:29).
B. The ministry of John
   1. He baptized the converts of Israel—"Then went out to him Jerusalem, and all Judea, and all the region round about Jordan, and were baptized of him in Jordan, confessing their sins" (Matt. 3:5-6).
   2. He baptized the Christ of Israel (Matt. 3:13-17).
C. The Messiah of John
   1. John's loyalty to Christ
      a. He correctly described his Savior to the public—"John bare witness of him, and cried, saying, This was he of whom I spake, He that cometh after me is preferred before me: for he was before me. And of his fulness have all we received, and grace for grace. For the law was given by Moses, but grace and truth came by Jesus Christ. No man hath seen God at any time; the only begotten Son, which is in the bosom of the Father, he hath declared him" (John 1:15-18).

†*Some have imagined a contradiction here in John 1:18 when compared with the prophet Isaiah's testimony: "In the year that King Uzziah died I saw also the Lord sitting upon a throne, high and lifted up, and his train filled the temple" (Isa. 6:1).*

However, the answer is that no one has ever seen God's essential nature. His inner being is disclosed only in and through Jesus. The Savior made this clear in the Upper Room: "Philip saith unto him, Lord, shew us the Father, and it sufficeth us. Jesus saith unto him, Have I been so long time with you, and yet hast thou not known me, Philip? he that hath seen me hath seen the Father; and how sayest thou then, Shew us the father" (John 14:8-9). (See also 1 Tim. 1:17; 6:16.)

All this is indicated by Solomon, as he wrote of Christ: "The Lord possessed me in the beginning of his way, before his works of old. I was set up from everlasting, from the beginning, or ever the earth was. When there were no depths, I was brought forth; when there were no fountains abounding with water. Before the mountains were settled, before the hills was I brought forth: while as yet he had not made the earth, nor the fields, nor the highest part of the dust of the world. When he prepared the heavens, I was there: when he set a compass upon the face of the depth: when he established the clouds above: when he strengthened the fountains of the deep: when he gave to the sea his decree, that the waters should not pass his commandment: when he appointed the foundations of the earth: then I was by him, as one brought up with him: and I was daily his delight, rejoicing always before him" (Prov. 8:22-30).

---

     b. He correctly described himself to the Pharisees—"And this is the record of John, when the Jews sent priests and Levites from Jerusalem to ask him, Who art thou? And he confessed, and denied not; but confessed, I am not the Christ. And they asked him, What then? Art thou Elias? And he saith, I am not. Art thou that prophet? And he answered, No. Then said they unto him, Who art thou? that we may give an answer to them that sent us. What sayest thou of thyself? He said, I am the voice of one crying in the wilderness, Make straight the way of the Lord, as said the prophet Esaias. And they which were sent were of the Pharisees. And they asked him, and said unto him, Why baptizest thou then, if thou be not that Christ, nor Elias, neither that prophet? John answered them, saying, I baptize with water: but there standeth one among you, whom ye know not; he it is, who coming after me is preferred before me, whose shoe's latchet I am not worthy to unloose" (John 1:19-27).

2. John's love for Christ—"Then there arose a question between some of John's disciples and the Jews about purifying. And they came unto John, and said unto him, Rabbi, he that was with thee beyond Jordan, to whom thou barest witness, behold, the same baptizeth, and all men come to him. John answered and said, A man can receive nothing, except it be given him from heaven. Ye yourselves bear me witness, that I said, I am not the Christ, but that I am sent before him. He that hath the bride is the bridegroom: but the friend of the bridegroom, which standeth and heareth him, rejoiceth greatly because of the bridegroom's voice: this my joy therefore is fulfilled. He must increase, but I must decrease" (John 3:25-30).

NINE: Christ's baptism (Matt. 3:13-17; Mark 1:9-11; Luke 3:21-22; John 1:32-33)
  A. Jesus and John—The acquiescence

    1. John's objection—"Then cometh Jesus from Galilee to Jordan unto John, to be baptized of him. But John forbad him, saying, I have need to be baptized of thee, and comest thou to me?" (Matt. 3:13-14).

    2. John's obedience—"And Jesus answering said unto him, Suffer it to be so now: for thus it becometh us to fulfil all righteousness. Then he suffered him" (Matt. 3:15).

  B. Jesus and the Spirit—The anointing: "And Jesus, when he was baptized, went up straightway out of the water: and, lo, the heavens were opened unto him, and he saw the Spirit of God descending like a dove, and lighting upon him" (Matt. 3:16).

  C. Jesus and the Father—The approval: "And lo a voice from heaven, saying, This is my beloved Son, in whom I am well pleased" (Matt. 3:17).

---

† A. *This is the clearest illustration of the doctrine of the Trinity in the entire Bible.*

    1. *The Father speaks from heaven.*

    2. *The Son stands in the water.*

    3. *The Holy Spirit descends.*

  B. *This marks the first of three occasions on which the Father orally expressed his approval of the Son.*

    1. *Here at the baptism*

    2. *On the Mount of Transfiguration (Matt. 17:5)*

    3. *In Jerusalem (John 12:28)*

  C. *This event gives us the first reference to Christ's prayer life. "Now when all the people were baptized, it came to pass, that Jesus also being baptized, and praying, the heaven was opened" (Luke 3:21).*

  D. *Why was Christ baptized? Here it may be stated that his baptism totally refutes that false doctrine of baptismal regeneration, that is, the claim that one must be baptized to be saved. The Savior of all people did not need to be saved himself. But why, then, was he baptized?*

    1. *He was baptized in order to identify with the message of John the Baptist. Actually, there were two aspects to John's message:*

      a. *"God's kingdom is at hand! The Messiah is here!"*

      b. *"Repent therefore of your sin and be baptized to demonstrate this repentance."*

      Thus Christ was baptized to identify with the first part of John's message, while the rest fulfilled the second aspect.

    2. *He was baptized so that John would know that Jesus was the true Messiah. "And I knew him not: but he that sent me to baptize with water, the same said unto me, Upon whom thou shalt see the Spirit descending, and remaining on him, the same is he which baptizeth with the Holy Ghost" (John 1:33).*

    3. *He was baptized to signal the beginning of his work as the Messiah. This was similar to the Old Testament minister who began his ministry at age thirty after a special ordination service.*

    4. *He was baptized to identify himself with the office of the prophet, priest, and king. In the Old Testament, all three were anointed in connection with their office. In Leviticus 8 is described the threefold anointing of a priest. He was first washed with water, then anointed with oil, then finally with blood. Christ submitted to the first two of these (water baptism and the oil of the Spirit), but not to the third.*

    5. *He was baptized to show that he had the total approval and support of both other members of the Trinity, the Father and Holy Spirit.*

E. *This is the first of various baptisms mentioned in the Gospel accounts. The word baptism means "to identify with."*
   1. *The baptism of John the Baptist—This was national baptism. (See Mark 1:4.)*
   2. *The baptism of Jesus*
      a. *With water by John (Matt. 3:15)*
      b. *With the Holy Spirit by the Father (Matt. 3:16)*
   3. *The baptism of sin upon Christ at Calvary (Luke 12:50; Matt. 20:22)*
   4. *The baptism of the Holy Spirit upon believers at Pentecost (Matt. 3:11b)*
   5. *The baptism of God's wrath upon sinners during the tribulation (Matt. 3:11b; 3:12; 13:30)*
   6. *The baptism of believers (Matt. 28:19)*

TEN: Christ's temptations (Matt. 4:1-11; Mark 1:12-13; Luke 4:1-13)—"Then was Jesus led up of the Spirit into the wilderness to be tempted of the devil. And when he had fasted forty days and forty nights, he was afterward an hungred" (Matt. 4:1-2).
A. Round One
   1. The temptation—"And when the tempter came to him, he said, If thou be the Son of God, command that these stones be made bread" (Matt. 4:3).
   2. The triumph—"Jesus said unto him, It is written again, Thou shalt not tempt the Lord thy God" (Matt. 4:7).
B. Round Two
   1. The temptation—"Then the devil taketh him up into the holy city, and setteth him on a pinnacle of the temple, and saith unto him, If thou be the Son of God, cast thyself down: for it is written, He shall give his angels charge concerning thee: and in their hands they shall bear thee up, lest at any time thou dash thy foot against a stone" (Matt. 4:5-6).
   2. The triumph—"But he answered and said, It is written, Man shall not live by bread alone, but by every word that proceedeth out of the mouth of God" (Matt. 4:4).
C. Round Three
   1. The temptation—"Again, the devil taketh him up into an exceeding high mountain, and sheweth him all the kingdoms of the world, and the glory of them; and saith unto him, All these things will I give thee, if thou wilt fall down and worship me" (Matt. 4:8-9).
   2. The triumph—"Then saith Jesus unto him, Get thee hence, Satan: for it is written, Thou shalt worship the Lord thy God, and him only shalt thou serve. Then the devil leaveth him, and, behold, angels came and ministered unto him" (Matt. 4:10-11). "And when the devil had ended all the temptation, he departed from him for a season" (Luke 4:13).

---

†*Here are some questions and answers concerning the temptations of Christ.*
   A. *In what ways can the temptations experienced by the first Adam and the second Adam be compared and contrasted?*
      1. *The comparison—In his first epistle, John separated all temptations into three general categories or groups (1 John 2:16). These are: the lust of the flesh, the lust of the eyes, and the pride of life.*

        a. *The first Adam was tempted in each area (Gen. 3:6).*
           (1) *"The tree was good for food" (the lust of the flesh).*
           (2) *"It was pleasant to the eyes" (the lust of the eyes).*
           (3) *"A tree desired to make one wise" (the pride of life)*
        b. *The second Adam was tempted in each area.*
           (1) *"Command that these stones be made bread" (the lust of the flesh).*
           (2) *"The devil . . . showeth him all the kingdoms of the world and the glory of them" (the lust of the eyes).*
           (3) *"Cast thyself down: for . . . he shall give his angels charge concerning thee" (the pride of life).*
    2. *The contrast*
        a. *The first Adam was tempted in a beautiful garden, while the second Adam met Satan in a desolate wilderness.*
        b. *The first Adam experienced total failure, while the second Adam was completely victorious.*
B. *Did Satan know whom he was tempting? He did indeed. The account in Matthew 4:3 and 4:6 is in the indicative mode in the Greek and should be rendered, "Since you are the Son of God."*
C. *What benefits did Satan offer him?*
    1. *First temptation: To fill his stomach (and thus depend upon his own resources)*
    2. *Second temptation: To jump off the temple (and thus force the hand of the Father)*
    3. *Third temptation: To grasp the kingdoms of this world (and thus refuse Calvary)*
D. *What method did Satan use during the second temptation? He attempted to confuse Christ by quoting Scripture out of context. (Compare Matt. 4:6 with Psa. 91:11-12.) In essence, he did the same thing in dealing with the first Adam (Gen. 3:1).*
E. *Why are Jesus' temptations associated with a period of forty days? This number is often one of tempting or testing as found in the Bible. Examples would be:*
    1. *Moses (Exod. 24:18; 34:28)*
    2. *Israel (Deut. 8:2-3)*
    3. *Elijah (1 Kings 19:8)*
    4. *Goliath (1 Sam. 17:16)*
F. *Did Satan really have the right to offer Christ "all the kingdoms of the world and the glory of them" (Matt. 4:8)?*
    1. *In a shallow and temporary sense, yes. (See John 14:30; Eph. 2:2; 6:12; 1 John 5:19; Rev. 13:7.)*
    2. *In the deepest and most eternal sense, no. "Yet have I set my king upon my holy hill of Zion. I will declare the decree: the Lord hath said unto me, Thou art my Son; this day have I begotten thee. Ask of me, and I shall give thee the heathen for thine inheritance, and the uttermost parts of the earth for thy possession. Thou shalt break them with a rod of iron; thou shalt dash them in pieces like a potter's vessel" (Psa. 2:6-9). "And the seventh angel sounded; and there were great voices in heaven, saying, The kingdoms of this world are become the kingdoms of our Lord, and of his Christ; and he shall reign for ever and ever" (Rev. 11:15).*
G. *How did Christ answer Satan? By the Word of God.*
    1. *First temptation: "It is written, man shall not live by bread alone, but by every word that proceedeth out of the mouth of God." (Compare Matt. 4:4 with Deut. 8:3.)*
    2. *Second temptation: "It is written again, Thou shalt not tempt the Lord thy God." (Compare Matt. 4:7 with Deut. 6:16.)*

This temptation was probably an attempt for him to prematurely (and wrongly) fulfill Malachi 3:1: "Behold, I will send my messenger, and he shall prepare the way before me; and the Lord, whom ye seek, shall suddenly come to his temple, even the messenger of the covenant, whom ye delight in; behold, he shall come, saith the Lord of hosts."

Satan's supreme object in the temptation ordeal was to cause Christ to act by himself, independent of the Father. Just what does it mean to tempt God? Israel is said to have tempted God on ten specific occasions en route to the promised land. (See Num. 14:11, 22; Heb. 3:9.) It means simply to presume upon the goodness of God. It refers to using this goodness in a selfish way. It means to force God's hand on something. Had Christ actually jumped from this temple pinnacle, God would have been forced to step in and save Christ from smashing his physical body on the ground below.

3. *Third temptation: "Get thee hence, Satan: for it is written, thou shalt worship the Lord thy God, and him only shalt thou serve." (Compare Matt. 4:10 with Deut. 6:13. See also James 4:7.)*

   Dr. Everett F. Harrison writes the following about the third temptation: "In this final episode Satan is unmasked. Gone is any suggestion that he is working for the best interests of the Son of God. No citation from Scripture is offered. Satan reveals the inmost secret of his being. Much as he enjoys the distinction of being the prince of this world, a distinction only sin has enabled him to achieve, he covets something else infinitely more. He would be like the Most High. He would receive to himself what is most characteristically and exclusively the prerogative of God, namely, worship. A true angel abhors the very thought of being worshiped (Rev. 22: 8-9), but this fallen angel fiercely, cravenly covets it. That such an offer was extended to Jesus is a testimony to his greatness. The stakes are high. When Satan made Judas his victim, his bait was a mere thirty pieces of silver. Indeed Satan could not well offer a lesser inducement to our Lord, for the nations were the promised inheritance of the Messiah and the uttermost parts of the earth were his anticipated possession (Psa. 2:8). In Psalm 2 this passage follows immediately the divine recognition of the sonship of the Messiah, the focal point of the temptation. 'Ask of me,' says God, but Satan brazenly usurps the place of the Almighty." (A Short Life of Christ, p. 90)

   As can be seen, Christ quotes from the book of Deuteronomy each time. It is no accident that higher criticism in Germany began with Deuteronomy in its vicious attack against the Bible.

H. Is this the only time Satan tempted Christ? No. In Luke 4:13 we are told: *"And when the devil had ended all the temptation, he departed from him for a season."* Note especially the last three words. Satan tempted Christ all through his ministry. At least three specific instances come to mind here in which, at a later date, Satan continued his tempting work against Christ.

   1. *As expressed by the 5,000 men Christ fed—"When Jesus therefore perceived that they would come and take him by force, to make him a king, he departed again into a mountain himself alone" (John 6:15). "Bypass the cross and grab the crown!"*

   2. *As expressed by Simon Peter—"From that time forth began Jesus to shew unto his disciples, how that he must go unto Jerusalem, and suffer many things of the elders and chief priests and scribes, and be killed, and be raised again the third day. Then Peter took him, and began to rebuke him, saying, Be it far from thee, Lord: this shall not be unto thee. But he turned, and said unto Peter, Get thee behind me, Satan: thou art an offence unto me: for thou savourest not the things that be of God, but those that be of men" (Matt. 16:21-23). "Don't even talk about the Cross!"*

3. *As expressed by the mob at Calvary—"And they that passed by reviled him, wagging their heads, and saying, Thou that destroyest the temple, and buildest it in three days, save thyself. If thou be the Son of God, come down from the cross" (Matt. 27:39-40). "Come down from the cross!"*

I. *What happened after the wilderness temptation? "Then the devil leaveth him, and behold, angels came and ministered unto him" (Matt. 4:11). Heaven's angels played an important part in the earthly ministry of Christ.*

   1. *They announced his birth (Luke 1–2; Matt. 1).*

   2. *They later ministered to him in Gethsemane (Luke 22:43).*

   3. *They announced his resurrection (Matt. 28:6).*

J. *Could Christ have sinned during the temptation experience? He could not; God cannot sin. The Bible declares:*

   1. *He knew no sin (2 Cor. 5:21).*

   2. *He did no sin (1 Pet. 2:22; Heb. 4:15).*

   3. *He had no sin (1 John 3:5; John 14:30). (See also Heb. 7:26.)*

K. *What then was the purpose for the temptation? The purpose was not to see if he would, but to prove that he could not sin. During the settling of the West a railroad company faced a problem. A bridge spanning a deep chasm gained the reputation of being unsafe. Careful examination by railroad officials showed this to be totally unfounded, but the rumor persisted. Finally, a train was formed made up of only heavy locomotives. For an entire day as hundreds watched, this train crossed and recrossed the bridge. Why was this done? Did the railroad engineers arrange the experiment to see if the bridge would hold, or did they do it to prove it would hold? The obvious answer here may be applied to the purpose of Christ's temptations. The purpose was to provide the believer with an experienced high priest. (See Heb. 4:15; 2:18.)*

L. *Were both God and Satan involved in the temptation of Christ? Is this the case also, when we are tempted? The answer to both questions is yes. The reason for this is seen in the twofold meaning of the word temptation.*

   1. *First meaning—To test in a good sense with the goal of confirming one in matters of righteousness*

      a. *As experienced by Jesus—"Then was Jesus led of the Spirit into the wilderness to be tempted of the devil" (Matt. 4:1). "For we have not an high priest which cannot be touched with the feeling of our infirmities; but was in all points tempted like as we are, yet without sin" (Heb. 4:15).*

      b. *As experienced by believers—"And it came to pass after these things, that God did tempt Abraham, and said unto him, Abraham: and he said, Behold, here I am" (Gen. 22:1). "My brethren, count it all joy when ye fall into divers temptations. . . . Blessed is the man that endureth temptation: for when he is tried, he shall receive the crown of life, which the Lord hath promised to them that love him" (James 1: 2, 12).*

   2. *Second meaning*

      a. *As experienced by Jesus—Satan made a desperate attempt to entice Jesus into evil.*

      b. *As experienced by believers—"And Satan stood up against Israel, and provoked David to number Israel" (1 Chron. 21:1). "Let no man say when he is tempted, I am tempted of God: for God cannot be tempted with evil, neither tempteth he any man: But every man is tempted, when he is drawn away of his own lust, and enticed" (James 1:13-14).*

ELEVEN: Christ is presented as the Lamb of God—"The next day John seeth Jesus coming unto him, and saith, Behold the Lamb of God, which taketh away the sin of the world" (John 1:29).

---

† A. *Perhaps without being fully aware of it, John was here answering the question asked by a young boy some twenty centuries earlier. "And Isaac spoke unto Abraham, his father, and said, My father: and he said, Here am I, my son. And he said, Behold the fire and the wood: but where is the lamb for a burnt offering?" (Gen. 22:7).*

For the glorious conclusion of this wonderful theme, hear the cry of heaven's angels who exclaim: "Worthy is the Lamb that was slain to receive power and riches, and wisdom, and strength, and honor and glory and blessing" (Rev. 5:12). Thus we see a threefold summary of the entire Bible which is, in reality, a book about God's Lamb:

1. *"Where is the Lamb?"*
2. *"Behold, the Lamb!"*
3. *"Worthy is the Lamb!"*

B. *Note also the awesome protective and purifying power of the bleeding lamb as revealed in the Scriptures:*

1. *A lamb provides for the needs of a man—"And Abel, he also brought of the firstlings of his flock and of the fat thereof. And the LORD had respect unto Abel and to his offering" (Gen. 4:4).*
2. *A lamb provides for the needs of a family—"Speak ye unto all the congregation of Israel, saying, In the tenth day of this month they shall take to them every man a lamb, according to the house of their fathers, a lamb for an house" (Exod. 12:3).*
3. *A lamb provides for the needs of a nation—"Now this is that which thou shalt offer upon the altar; two lambs of the first year day by day continually. The one lamb thou shalt offer in the morning; and the other lamb thou shalt offer at even. . . . and there I will meet with the children of Israel, and the tabernacle shall be sanctified by my glory. . . . And I will dwell among the children of Israel, and will be their God" (Exod. 29:38-39, 43, 45).*
4. *A lamb provides for the needs of the world—"The next day John seeth Jesus coming unto him, and saith, Behold the Lamb of God, which taketh away the sin of the world" (John 1:29).*

TWELVE: Christ meets his first five disciples
A. The first meeting with Andrew, John, and Peter (John 1:35-42)
   1. John, son of Zebedee, and Andrew, two disciples of John the Baptist, leave their master to follow Christ.
   2. Andrew then brings his brother Peter to Christ. Andrew to Peter: "We have found the Messias, which is, being interpreted, the Christ" (1:41b). Christ to Peter: "Thou art Simon . . . thou shalt be called Cephas, which is by interpretation, a stone" (1:42).

---

† A. *Andrew called Jesus "Messias" [Messiah] (John 1:41). This title is found only three other times in the entire Bible.*
   1. *As used (twice) by the angel Gabriel (Dan. 9:25-26)*
   2. *As used by the Samaritan woman (John 4:25)*

B. *Jesus calls Peter "Cephas," which is translated, "a stone." God's purpose is to change people's names (and character). (See Rev. 3:12.)*
  1. *He changed Abram to Abraham (Gen. 17:5).*
  2. *He changed Sarai to Sarah (Gen. 17:15).*
  3. *He changed Jacob to Israel (Gen. 32:28).*
  4. *He changed Saul to Paul (Acts 13:9).*
      Note, however, that Peter at this point was anything but a rock. He was, in fact, in a practical sense, "tossed to and fro, and carried about with every wind of doctrine" (Eph. 4:14). Actually, Jesus' description of Peter here can be compared to the one he once gave the timid Gideon in the Old Testament, referring to him as "thou mighty man of valour" (Judg. 6:12). But for Peter, all this would change after Pentecost.
C. *Without realizing it, Andrew answered Job's perplexing question:*
  1. *Job: "Oh that I knew where I might find him!" (23:3).*
  2. *Andrew (to Peter): "We have found the Messias, which is, being interpreted, the Christ" (John 1:41).*

B. The first meeting with Philip and Nathanael (John 1:43-51).
  1. Philip's willingness—"The day following Jesus would go forth into Galilee, and findeth Philip, and saith unto him, Follow me" (John 1:43).
  2. Philip's witness—"Philip findeth Nathanael, and saith unto him, We have found him, of whom Moses in the law, and the prophets, did write, Jesus of Nazareth, the son of Joseph" (John 1:45).
  3. Philip's wisdom—"And Nathanael said unto him, Can there any good thing come out of Nazareth? Philip saith unto him, Come and see" (John 1:46).

---

† A. *We note that Philip, a new convert, did not have a full understanding of the virgin birth, but he was still an effective witness. (He refers to Jesus as "the son of Joseph.") Nathanael was bothered by Philip's "Jesus of Nazareth" title. He doubtless realized that the Messiah would be born in Bethlehem. In addition, he probably had a low view of Galileans. Nazareth was the town which housed the Roman garrison for the northern regions of Galilee. In light of this, most Jews would have little to do with that city. In fact, those who lived there were looked down upon as compromisers. Thus, to call one a "Nazarene" was to use a term of utter contempt.*
  B. *Philip wisely refused to argue, but invited him to "come and see." His approach was the one suggested in the Psalms: "O taste and see that the Lord is good: blessed is the man that trusteth in him" (Psa. 34:8).*

---

  4. The surprise of Nathanael—"Jesus saw Nathanael coming to him, and saith of him, Behold an Israelite indeed, in whom is no guile! Nathanael saith unto him, Whence knowest thou me? Jesus answered and said unto him, Before that Philip called thee, when thou wast under the fig tree, I saw thee" (John 1:47-48).

---

†*He was amazed that Jesus knew he had been sitting under a fig tree when Philip talked to him. The Savior always dealt with people on their own level.*
  A. *He dealt with Nathanael under a fig tree (John 1:48).*

B. He dealt with Zacchaeus up a sycamore tree (Luke 19:4-5).
C. He dealt with a dying thief on a cruel tree (Luke 23:39-43).

---

5. The salvation of Nathanael
   a. His faith— "Nathanael answered and saith unto him, Rabbi, thou art the Son of God; thou art the King of Israel" (John 1:49).
   b. His future— "Jesus answered and said unto him, Because I said unto thee, I saw thee under the fig tree, believest thou? thou shalt see greater things than these. And he saith unto him, Verily, verily, I say unto you, Hereafter ye shall see heaven open, and the angels of God ascending and descending upon the Son of man" (John 1:50-51).

---

† *A. Nathanael was promised he would someday see heaven open and the angels ascending and descending upon Christ. This happened at the ascension. (See Acts 1:9-11.)*
  B. Although Nathanael addressed him as the Son of God and King of Israel (1:49), our Lord referred to himself as the Son of man (1:51). This was by far his favorite title for himself. He used it more times than any other name. Nathanael and Philip are the first to hear it.
  C. Note: It is thrilling to observe that our Lord's first recorded prediction was not concerning his suffering, death, or even resurrection, but the promise that he would someday ascend. As Isaiah once declared of God: "Remember the former things of old: for I am God, and there is none else; I am God, and there is none like me, declaring the end from the beginning, and from ancient times the things that are not yet done, saying, my counsel shall stand, and I will do all my pleasure" (46:9-10).

THIRTEEN: Christ performs his first miracle while attending a wedding in Cana of Galilee (John 2:1-11). (Note: For a fuller discussion, find this miracle under the *Topical Overview.*)
FOURTEEN: Christ performs the first temple cleansing (John 2:13-25).
A. Purging the corruption from his Father's temple (John 2:13-17).
   1. Cleansing the temple—"And the Jews' passover was at hand, and Jesus went up to Jerusalem, and found in the temple those that sold oxen and sheep and doves, and the changers of money sitting: And when he had made a scourge of small cords, he drove them all out of the temple, and the sheep, and the oxen; and poured out the changers' money, and overthrew the tables" (John 2:13-15).
   2. Condemning the thieves—"And said unto them that sold doves, Take these things hence; make not my Father's house an house of merchandise" (John 2:16).

---

† *A. This marks the second recorded temple visit by our Lord. Both can be favorably compared and contrasted.*
   1. Contrasted

      a. The boy Jesus displayed his wisdom during the first visit—"And all that heard him were astonished at his understanding and answers" (Luke 2:47).

      b. The man Jesus displayed his wrath during the second visit.

    2. Compared—On each occasion, he spoke of his Father.

      a. First visit—"And he said unto them, How is it that ye sought me? wist ye not that I must be about my Father's business?" (Luke 2:49).

      b. Second visit—"And said unto them that sold doves, Take these things hence; make not my Father's house an house of merchandise" (John 2:16).

  B. Several factors no doubt invoked his wrath at this time:

    1. They were selling cattle, sheep, and doves in the court of the Gentiles, the only place where non-Jews could come and pray.

    2. They may have been selling blemished animals.

    3. They could have been overcharging.

    4. They were obviously filled with greed.

  B. Predicting the resurrection of his fleshly temple (John 2:18-25)

    1. The ignorance of the Jewish leaders

      a. The sign demanded—"Then answered the Jews and said unto him, What sign shewest thou unto us, seeing that thou doest these things?" (John 2:18).

---

† *A. This is the first of at least three instances in which the Jewish leaders demanded a sign from Christ to prove his claims. On all three occasions our Lord referred to his future resurrection (Matt. 12:38-40; 16:1-4). For example: "For as Jonas was three days and three nights in the whale's belly; so shall the Son of man be three days and three nights in the heart of the earth" (Matt. 12:40).*

B. In this present generation there are still many professing Christians who continue to seek after divine signs and wonders to establish their faith. But what is the New Testament position on this? Consider: "Jesus saith unto him, Thomas, because thou hast seen me, thou hast believed: blessed are they that have not seen, and yet have believed" (John 20:29). "For the Jews require a sign, and the Greeks seek after wisdom" (1 Cor. 1:22). "(For we walk by faith, not by sight)" (2 Cor. 5:7).

---

      b. The sign described—"Jesus answered and said unto them, Destroy this temple, and in three days I will raise it up" (John 2:19).

      c. The sign distorted—"Then said the Jews, Forty and six years was this temple in building, and wilt thou rear it up in three days? But he spake of the temple of his body" (John 2:20-21).

---

†*The Jews thought he spoke of Herod's temple, which took forty-six years to build. Later they would twist this statement completely out of context during Jesus' trial, and even while he was on the cross. (See Matt. 26:61; 27:40; Mark 15:29.) He was, of course, referring to his body. (See 1 Cor. 3:16; 6:19; 2 Cor. 6:16.) The Jews should have known this, for Jesus used two separate words here. He used the word* hieron *when referring to the temple of Herod, and the word* naos *when describing his body.*

2. The insincerity of the Jewish leaders—"Now when he was in Jerusalem at the passover, in the feast day, many believed in his name, when they saw the miracles which he did. But Jesus did not commit himself unto them, because he knew all men" (John 2:23-24)

FIFTEEN: Christ meets with Nicodemus (John 3:1-21)
A. The character of Nicodemus
    1. He was a Jewish religious leader (John 3:1).
    2. He was a member of the Pharisees (John 3:1).
    3. He was a well-known teacher (John 3:10).
B. The confession of Nicodemus—"The same came to Jesus by night, and said unto him, Rabbi, we know that thou art a teacher come from God: for no man can do these miracles that thou doest, except God be with him" (John 3:2).

---

†*Several questions may be raised here:*
    A. Why did he come by night? We do not know, and it is unfair to brand him a coward. Perhaps the heavy schedules of both men required this.
    B. What did Nicodemus know about Jesus? He knew he was from God because of his supernatural miracles. (Compare John 3:2 with 20:30-31.)

C. The concern of Nicodemus—He probably scheduled the meeting with Jesus to learn more about the new birth. This is indicated by Jesus' opening statement: "Jesus answered and said unto him, Verily, verily, I say unto thee, Except a man be born again, he cannot see the kingdom of God" (John 3:3).

---

†*This is the first of but three occasions on which the term "born again" is found in the Word of God. (See John 3:3, 7; 1 Pet. 1:23.) However, John often uses the phrase "born of God." (See John 1:13; 1 John 3:9; 4:7; 5:18.)*

D. The confusion of Nicodemus
    1. The ruler's ignorance—"Nicodemus saith unto him, How can a man be born when he is old? can he enter the second time into his mother's womb, and be born?" (John 3:4).
        a. His rank may have confused him (John 3:1).
        b. His religion may have confused him (John 3:1, 10).
    2. The Redeemer's illustrations—Jesus offers three illustrations to help Nicodemus understand the new birth.
        a. A physical illustration—"Jesus answered, Verily, verily, I say unto thee, Except a man be born of water and of the Spirit, he cannot enter into the kingdom of God. That which is born of the flesh is flesh; and that which is born of the Spirit is spirit" (John 3:5-6).

---

†*What did Jesus mean by his expression, "Except a man be born of water and of the Spirit, he cannot enter into the Kingdom of God" (John 3:5)? Here five main views have been offered:*

A. *He was referring to baptismal regeneration. This, of course, is totally refuted by other biblical passages. (See Eph. 2:8-9; 1 Cor. 1:17; Rom. 5:1.)*
B. *He was referring to that watery sac, the placenta, which accompanies physical birth. Thus he contrasted physical birth with spiritual birth.*
C. *He was saying that the one requirement to live on this earth is to have had a physical birthday; and likewise, the one requirement to someday live in heaven is to have a spiritual birthday. Those who hold this view point to 3:6 where they feel Jesus clarifies his position.*
D. *He was referring to John's baptism of repentance in the Jordan, which baptism the Pharisees had rejected. (Compare Luke 3:3 with 7:30.)*
E. *He was referring to the Word of God (the water) and the Spirit of God (Spirit), without which no man can ever be saved. (See John 16:8-11; Rom. 11:6-15.) Advocates of this position point out that water in the Bible is often the recognized symbol for the Word of God. (See Psa. 119:9; John 4:14; Eph. 5:25-26; Titus 3:5.)*

---

b. A natural illustration—"The wind bloweth where it listeth, and thou hearest the sound thereof, but canst not tell whence it cometh, and whither it goeth: so is every one that is born of the Spirit" (John 3:8).
c. A scriptural illustration—"And as Moses lifted up the serpent in the wilderness, even so must the Son of man be lifted up" (John 3:14).

---

† A. *Jesus illustrated his visitor's need by referring to Moses and the brazen serpent. (Compare John 3:14 with Num. 21:9.) On this occasion in the Old Testament account, God had sent poisonous serpents to punish rebellious Israel. The people repented and a cure was provided. A serpent of brass was placed atop a wooden pole where all could view it. Anyone bitten needed only to look upon the brass serpent to be healed.*

To paraphrase, here is what Jesus told Nicodemus: "Nicodemus, like those Old Testament Israelites, you have been bitten by a serpent—the serpent of sin. It is an incurable and fatal bite. But soon God is going to erect a crosslike pole just outside Jerusalem. And on that cross he will place a Savior."
B. *It may be said that one cannot fully grasp the most famous verse in the Bible, John 3:16, unless he has some understanding of its background, which is found in John 3:14: "And as Moses lifted up the serpent in the wilderness, even so must the Son of man be lifted up."*

E. The chastisement of Nicodemus—"Jesus answered and said unto him, Art thou a master of Israel, and knowest not these things? If I have told you earthly things, and ye believe not, how shall ye believe, if I tell you of heavenly things?" (John 3:10, 12).

---

† A. *Although this man was both a ruler and a religious leader, he needed the new birth. Note Jesus' question in 3:10, "Art thou a master of Israel, and knoweth not these things?" In the Greek the definite article is used, meaning, "Are you the teacher in Israel?" Nicodemus may have been the most famous teacher of his day.*
B. *In John 3:12 Jesus connects earthly things with heavenly things, indicating that a right view of the second is based squarely on a right view of the first. This only serves to emphasize the supreme importance of accepting at face value the historical words of Moses concerning creation (Gen. 1–2), as one would do with Christ's words concerning redemption.*

F. The conversion of Nicodemus—The evidence strongly suggests that Nicodemus accepted Christ at this time, perhaps after hearing the most important verse in the Bible: "For God so loved the world, that he gave his only begotten Son, that whosoever believeth in him should not perish, but have everlasting life" (John 3:16).

† *A. It is the most important verse, because it contains the gospel in a nutshell.*
  B. It is the greatest verse, because it contains nine of the most profound truths ever recorded:
  1. *"For God"—The greatest Person*
  2. *"So loved the world"—The greatest truth*
  3. *"That he gave"—The greatest act*
  4. *"His only begotten Son"—The greatest gift*
  5. *"That whosoever"—The greatest number*
  6. *"Believeth in him"—The greatest invitation*
  7. *"Should not perish"—The greatest promise*
  8. *"But have"—The greatest certainty*
  9. *"Everlasting life"—The greatest destiny*

SIXTEEN: Christ meets with the Samaritan woman (John 4:1-42)—"When therefore the Lord knew how the Pharisees had heard that Jesus made and baptized more disciples than John, (Though Jesus himself baptized not, but his disciples,) He left Judaea and departed again into Galilee. And he must needs go through Samaria" (John 4:1-4).

† *A. After realizing that the Pharisees were pitting him against John in a baptismal contest, Jesus quickly left the Judean area. Our Lord did not come to compete with John, but rather to be crucified for him, along with all other sinners.*
  B. Note the phrase, "He must needs go through Samaria." H. A. Ironsides observed: "An orthodox Jew would cross the Jordan near Jericho and make his way up through Perea, and then cross back near the Sea of Galilee in the north. But the Lord Jesus Christ did not take that route. A stern legalist would not go through Samaria; but the Lord Jesus Christ took that direct road because of the very fact that He was anxious to meet these poor Samaritan sinners that He might reveal the truth to them. 'He must needs go through Samaria.' Long before the creation of the world it had been settled in the counsels of eternity that he was to meet a poor, sinful, Samaritan woman that day. He could not forego that appointment." (Gospel of John, John Loizeaux Brothers, N.Y., 1954, p. 138.)

A. The Sinner of Sychar
  1. The contact—"Then cometh he to a city of Samaria, which is called Sychar, near to the parcel of ground that Jacob gave to his son Joseph. Now Jacob's well was there. Jesus therefore, being wearied with his journey, sat thus on the well: and it was about the sixth hour" (John 4:5-6).
    a. His request—"There cometh a woman of Samaria to draw water: Jesus saith unto her, Give me to drink. (For his disciples were gone away unto the city to buy meat)" (John 4:7-8).

b. Her response—"Then saith the woman of Samaria unto him, How is it that thou, being a Jew, askest drink of me, which am a woman of Samaria? for the Jews have no dealings with the Samaritans" (John 4:9).

2. The contrasts

a. Jesus contrasts living water with liquid water.

(1) Living water

(a) His revelation—"Jesus answered and said unto her, If thou knewest the gift of God, and who it is that saith to thee, Give me to drink; thou wouldest have asked of him, and he would have given thee living water" (John 4:10).

(b) Her reaction—"The woman saith unto him, Sir, thou hast nothing to draw with, and the well is deep: from whence then hast thou that living water? Art thou greater than our father Jacob, which gave us the well, and drank thereof himself, and his children, and his cattle?" (John 4:11-12).

✝ A. *"The well is deep"—When this well was cleaned out in 1935 it was found to be almost 150 feet deep.*

B. *"Art thou greater than . . . Jacob?" He was (and is), also greater than:*

1. Abraham (John 8:53, 58)

2. Moses (Heb. 3:3)

3. Aaron (Heb. 5:1-10)

4. Joshua (Heb. 4:8)

5. Solomon (Matt. 12:42)

6. Jonah (Matt. 12:41)

7. The angels (Heb. 1:4)

---

(2) Liquid water

(a) His revelation—"Jesus answered and said unto her, Whosoever drinketh of this water shall thirst again: But whosoever drinketh of the water that I shall give him shall never thirst; but the water that I shall give him shall be in him a well of water springing up into everlasting life" (John 4:13-14).

(b) Her reaction—"The woman saith unto him, Sir, give me this water, that I thirst not, neither come hither to draw" (John 4:15).

b. Jesus contrasts real worship with ritual worship.

(1) The command—"Jesus saith unto her, Go, call thy husband, and come hither" (John 4:16).

(2) The concealment—"The woman answered and said, I have no husband. Jesus said unto her, Thou hast well said, I have no husband: For thou hast had five husbands; and he whom thou now hast is not thy husband: in that saidst thou truly" (John 4:17-18).

(3) The cleverness—she attempts to change the subject by complimenting Jesus—"The woman saith unto him, Sir, I perceive that thou art a prophet" (John 4:19).

(4) The confusion—"Our fathers worshipped in this mountain; and ye say, that in Jerusalem is the place where men ought to worship" (John 4:20).

†*The mountain referred to here was Mount Gerizim, especially sacred to the Samaritans.*
  A. Abraham and Jacob had built altars in that general vicinity (Gen. 12:7; 33:20).
  B. The people of Israel had been blessed from this mountain (Deut. 11:29; 27:12).
  C. The Samaritans had built a temple on Mount Gerizim around 400 B.C., which had later
  been destroyed by the Jews.

> (5) The correction—"Jesus saith unto her, Woman, believe me, the hour cometh, when ye shall neither in this mountain, nor yet at Jerusalem, worship the Father. . . . But the hour cometh, and now is, when the true worshippers shall worship the Father in spirit and in truth: for the Father seeketh such to worship him. God is a Spirit: and they that worship him must worship him in spirit and in truth" (John 4:21, 23-24).
> (6) The conversion—"The woman saith unto him, I know that Messias cometh, which is called Christ: when he is come, he will tell us all things. Jesus saith unto her, I that speak unto thee am he" (John 4:25-26).

† *A. It was at this time that Christ made the first recorded announcement that he indeed was the anticipated Messiah. This revelation was given to an immoral woman (John 4:26).*
  B. Later, the Savior would make the first resurrection appearance in his new body before another woman, who had been possessed of devils—Mary Magdalene (John 20:11-18).

A. The Soul-winner of Sychar
  1. The faithfulness of the woman
    a. As seen by the message she proclaimed—"The woman then left her waterpot, and went her way into the city, and saith to the men, Come, see a man, which told me all things that ever I did: is not this the Christ? Then they went out of the city, and came unto him" (John 4:28-30).
    b. As seen by the model she presented. Jesus used this woman as an illustration to the disciples on the subject of soul-winning.
      (1) He talks about the real food—"In the mean while his disciples prayed him, saying, Master, eat. But he said unto them, I have meat to eat that ye know not of. Therefore said the disciples one to another, Hath any man brought him ought to eat? Jesus saith unto them, My meat is to do the will of him that sent me, and to finish his work" (John 4:31-34).
      (2) He talks about the real fields—"Say not ye, There are yet four months, and then cometh harvest? behold, I say unto you, Lift up your eyes, and look on the fields; for they are white already to harvest. And he that reapeth receiveth wages, and gathereth fruit unto life eternal: that both he that soweth and he that reapeth may rejoice together. And herein is that saying true, One soweth, and another reapeth. I sent you to reap that whereon ye bestowed no labour: other men laboured, and ye are entered into their labours" (John 4:35-38).
  2. The fruit of the woman
    a. The conversions in Samaria—"And many of the Samaritans of that city believed on him for the saying of the woman, which testified, He told me all that ever I did" (John 4:39).

b. The crusade in Samaria—"So when the Samaritans were come unto him, they besought him that he would tarry with them: and he abode there two days. And many more believed because of his own word; and said unto the woman, Now we believe, not because of thy saying: for we have heard him ourselves, and know that this is indeed the Christ, the Saviour of the world" (John 4:40-42).

---

† *A. The title "Savior of the world" is found only here and in 1 John 4:14.*
   B. This passage contains one of the greatest examples for soul winners in the entire Bible. Note a few of its practical points:
   1. Jesus refused to argue with the woman.
   2. He avoided getting entangled by various theological concepts.
   3. He never browbeat her, even though she was a great sinner.
   4. He repeatedly spoke of the living water, which was the real (and only) issue.
   5. He concluded by pointing her to himself (4:26).
   6. The Christian has only to lift up his eyes to see the bountiful harvest of lost souls all around him.
   7. Christians sometimes sow seed that will be reaped by others, but they often reap seed planted by another. God alone gives the increase. (See 1 Cor. 3:5-9.)

SEVENTEEN: Christ's first preaching tour of Galilee (Matt. 4:17; Mark 1:15; Luke 4:14-15)—"And Jesus returned in the power of the Spirit into Galilee: and there went out a fame of him through all the region round about. And he taught in their synagogues, being glorified of all" (Luke 4:14-15).

EIGHTEEN: Christ's first return trip to Nazareth (Luke 4:16-30)—"And he came to Nazareth, where he had been brought up: and, as his custom was, he went into the synagogue on the sabbath day, and stood up for to read" (Luke 4:16). (Note: For a fuller discussion, see the outline of the sermon he preached at this time under the *Topical Overview*.)

NINETEEN: Christ moves into Capernaum and makes this city his northern headquarters (Matt. 4:13-16).
   A. The fulfillment of Isaiah's prophecy—"And leaving Nazareth, he came and dwelt in Capernaum, which is upon the sea coast, in the borders of Zabulon and Nephthalim: That it might be fulfilled which was spoken by Esaias the prophet, saying, The land of Zabulon, and the land of Nephthalim, by the way of the sea, beyond Jordan, Galilee of the Gentiles" (Matt. 4:13-15).
   B. The fruits of Isaiah's prophecy—"The people which sat in darkness saw great light; and to them which sat in the region and shadow of death light is sprung up. From that time Jesus began to preach, and to say, Repent: for the kingdom of heaven is at hand" (Matt. 4:16-17).

TWENTY: Christ extends a call to four fishermen (Matt. 4:18-22; Mark 1:16-20; Luke 5:1-11).
   A. The call to Simon and Andrew—"And Jesus, walking by the sea of Galilee, saw two brethren, Simon called Peter, and Andrew his brother, casting a net into the sea: for they were fishers. And he saith unto them, Follow me, and I will make you fishers of men. And they straightway left their nets, and followed him" (Matt. 4:18-20).

B. The call to James and John—"And going on from thence, he saw other two brethren, James the son of Zebedee, and John his brother, in a ship with Zebedee their father, mending their nets; and he called them. And they immediately left the ship and their father, and followed him" (Matt. 4:21-22).

TWENTY-ONE: Christ's second preaching tour of Galilee (Matt. 4:23-25; Mark 1:35-39; Luke 4:42-44)

A. The ministry he accomplished—"And Jesus went about all Galilee, teaching in their synagogues, and preaching the gospel of the kingdom, and healing all manner of sickness and all manner of disease among the people. And his fame went throughout all Syria: and they brought unto him all sick people that were taken with divers diseases and torments, and those which were possessed with devils, and those which were lunatick, and those that had the palsy; and he healed them" (Matt. 4:23-24).

B. The multitudes he attracted—"And there followed him great multitudes of people from Galilee, and from Decapolis, and from Jerusalem, and from Judaea, and from beyond Jordan" (Matt. 4:25).

TWENTY-TWO: Christ extends a call to Matthew (Matt. 9:9-13; Mark 2:13-17; Luke 5:27-32).

A. The conversion of Levi—"And after these things he went forth, and saw a publican, named Levi, sitting at the receipt of custom: and he said unto him, Follow me. And he left all, rose up, and followed him" (Luke 5:27-28).

B. The celebration of Levi—"And Levi made him a great feast in his own house: and there was a great company of publicans and of others that sat down with them" (Luke 5:29).

TWENTY-THREE: Christ's first meeting with John's disciples (Matt. 9:14-17; Mark 2:18-22; Luke 5:33-39)

A. Their confusion—"Then came to him the disciples of John, saying, Why do we and the Pharisees fast oft, but thy disciples fast not?" (Matt. 9:14).

B. His correction—"And Jesus said unto them, Can the children of the bridechamber mourn, as long as the bridegroom is with them? but the days will come, when the bridegroom shall be taken from them, and then shall they fast" (Matt. 9:15).

TWENTY-FOUR: Christ heals a man who had been an invalid for thirty-eight years (John 5:1-14). (Note: For a fuller discussion, find this miracle under the *Topical Overview*.)

TWENTY-FIVE: Christ's first Sabbath controversy with the Pharisees (Matt. 12:1-8; Mark 2:23-28; Luke 6:1-5)

A. The action of the disciples—"And it came to pass on the second sabbath after the first, that he went through the corn fields; and his disciples plucked the ears of corn, and did eat, rubbing them in their hands" (Luke 6:1).

B. The accusation of the Pharisees—"And certain of the Pharisees said unto them, Why do ye that which is not lawful to do on the sabbath days?" (Luke 6:2).

C. The answer of the Savior—"And Jesus answering them said, Have ye not read so much as this, what David did, when himself was an hungred, and they which were with him; how he went into the house of God, and did take and eat the shewbread, and gave also to them that were with him; which it is not lawful to eat but for the priests alone? And he said unto them, That the Son of man is Lord also of the sabbath" (Luke 6:3-5).

TWENTY-SIX: Christ officially selects the twelve apostles (Matt. 10:2-4; Mark 3:13-19; Luke 6:12-16).
  A. The prayer involved—"And it came to pass in those days, that he went out into a mountain to pray, and continued all night in prayer to God" (Luke 6:12).
  B. The personalities involved—"And when it was day, he called unto him his disciples: and of them he chose twelve, whom also he named apostles; Simon, (whom he also named Peter,) and Andrew his brother, James and John, Philip and Bartholomew, Matthew and Thomas, James the son of Alphaeus, and Simon called Zelotes, and Judas the brother of James, and Judas Iscariot, which also was the traitor" (Luke 6:13-16).
TWENTY-SEVEN: Christ delivers his Sermon on the Mount (Matt. 5:1—7:29; Luke 6:17-49)—"And seeing the multitudes, he went up into a mountain: and when he was set, his disciples came unto him: And he opened his mouth, and taught them, saying. . . . And it came to pass, when Jesus had ended these sayings, the people were astonished at his doctrine: For he taught them as one having authority, and not as the scribes" (Matt. 5:1-2; 7:28-29). (Note: For a fuller discussion, see the outline of this sermon under the *Topical Overview.)*
TWENTY-EIGHT: Christ's third preaching tour of Galilee (Matt. 9:35-38)
  A. The great healer
    1. Whom he healed—"And Jesus went about all the cities and villages, teaching in their synagogues, and preaching the gospel of the kingdom, and healing every sickness and every disease among the people" (Matt. 9:35).
    2. Why he healed—"But when he saw the multitudes, he was moved with compassion on them, because they fainted, and were scattered abroad, as sheep having no shepherd" (Matt. 9:36).

---

†*The Greek word for* fainted, *used here to describe the multitude, means "skinned, flayed, rent, mangled, vexed, annoyed; hence, fatigued, suffering violence, distressed." The Greek word for* scattered *means "cast down and prostrate on the ground, mentally dejected; hence, harassed, importuned, bewildered." These two Greek words describe vividly the picture of sheep being driven in terror, falling exhausted and helpless, torn and mangled by the wild beasts that are chasing and devouring them.* (Studies in the Life of Christ, *R. C. Foster. Baker Books, Grand Rapids, Mich., 1979, p. 615)*

  B. The great harvest—"Then saith he unto his disciples, The harvest truly is plenteous, but the labourers are few; Pray ye therefore the Lord of the harvest, that he will send forth labourers into his harvest" (Matt. 9:37-38).
TWENTY-NINE: Christ sends out the twelve apostles (Matt. 10:1-42; Mark 6:7-13; Luke 9:1-6). In these verses Christ gives instruction to three kinds of disciples.
  A. To those former disciples, living in the time of Christ (the twelve) (Matt. 10:1-15; Mark 6:7-11; Luke 9:1-5)
    1. Their mission—"These twelve Jesus sent forth, and commanded them, saying, Go not into the way of the Gentiles, and into any city of the Samaritans enter ye not: But go rather to the lost sheep of the house of Israel" (Matt. 10:5-6).
    2. Their message—"And as ye go, preach, saying, The kingdom of heaven is at hand" (Matt. 10:7).

3. Their methodology—"Heal the sick, cleanse the lepers, raise the dead, cast out devils: freely ye have received, freely give" (Matt. 10:8).

4. Their mobility—"Provide neither gold, nor silver, nor brass in your purses, nor scrip for your journey, neither two coats, neither shoes, nor yet staves: for the workman is worthy of his meat" (Matt. 10:9-10).

5. Their militancy—"And whosoever shall not receive you, nor hear your words, when ye depart out of that house or city, shake off the dust of your feet" (Matt. 10:14). "And they went out, and preached that men should repent" (Mark 6:12).

6. Their miracles—"And they cast out many devils, and anointed with oil many that were sick, and healed them" (Mark 6:13).

B. To those future disciples, living during the tribulation (perhaps the 144,000) (Matt. 10:16-23)

1. To be hated by the enemies of God

a. Religious persecution—"But beware of men: for they will deliver you up to the councils, and they will scourge you in their synagogues" (Matt. 10:17).

b. Government persecution—"And ye shall be brought before governors and kings for my sake, for a testimony against them and the Gentiles" (Matt. 10:18).

c. Family persecution—"And the brother shall deliver up the brother to death, and the father the child: and the children shall rise up against their parents, and cause them to be put to death" (Matt. 10:21).

2. To be helped by the Spirit of God—"But when they deliver you up, take no thought how or what ye shall speak: for it shall be given you in that same hour what ye shall speak. For it is not ye that speak, but the Spirit of your Father which speaketh in you" (Matt. 10:19-20).

3. To be honored by the Son of God—"But when they persecute you in this city, flee ye into another: for verily I say unto you, Ye shall not have gone over the cities of Israel, till the Son of man be come. Whosoever therefore shall confess me before men, him will I confess also before my Father which is in heaven" (Matt. 10:23, 32).

C. To those faithful disciples, living throughout church history (Matt. 10:24-42)

1. The cost of true discipleship

a. It demands suffering for Christ.

(1) The persecution of Christ warns of this—"The disciple is not above his master, nor the servant above his lord. It is enough for the disciple that he be as his master, and the servant as his lord. If they have called the master of the house Beelzebub, how much more shall they call them of his household?" (Matt. 10:24-25).

(2) The preaching of Christ warns of this—"Think not that I am come to send peace on earth: I came not to send peace, but a sword. For I am come to set a man at variance against his father, and the daughter against her mother, and the daughter in law against her mother in law" (Matt. 10:34-35).

b. It demands single-mindedness to Christ—"He that loveth father or mother more than me is not worthy of me: and he that loveth son or daughter more than me is not worthy of me. And he that taketh not his cross, and followeth after me, is not worthy of me" (Matt. 10:37-38).

2. The compensation of true discipleship—"Are not two sparrows sold for a farthing? and one of them shall not fall on the ground without your Father. But the very hairs of your head are all numbered. Fear ye not therefore, ye are of more value than many sparrows. Whosoever therefore shall confess me before men, him will I confess also before my Father which is in heaven. He that findeth his life shall lose it: and he that loseth his life for my sake shall find it" (Matt. 10:29-32, 39).

THIRTY: Christ's fourth preaching tour of Galilee—"And it came to pass, when Jesus had made an end of commanding his twelve disciples, he departed thence to teach and to preach in their cities" (Matt. 11:1).

THIRTY-ONE: Christ denounces some key cities in Galilee (Matt. 11:20-24)
A. Chorazin and Bethsaida
   1. Their great privilege—"Woe unto thee, Chorazin! woe unto thee, Bethsaida! for if the mighty works, which were done in you, had been done in Tyre and Sidon, they would have repented long ago in sackcloth and ashes" (Matt. 11:21).
   2. Their grievous punishment—"But I say unto you, It shall be more tolerable for Tyre and Sidon at the day of judgment, than for you" (Matt. 11:22).
B. Capernaum
   1. The great privilege—"And thou, Capernaum, which art exalted unto heaven, shalt be brought down to hell: for if the mighty works, which have been done in thee, had been done in Sodom, it would have remained until this day" (Matt. 11:23).

---

†*These verses illustrate the amazing omniscience of Jesus. He not only knows what has been, and what will be, but also what might have been.*

---

2. Its grievous punishment—"But I say unto you, That it shall be more tolerable for the land of Sodom in the day of judgment, than for thee" (Matt. 11:24).

THIRTY-TWO: Christ issues a universal invitation—"Come unto me, all ye that labour and are heavy laden, and I will give you rest. Take my yoke upon you, and learn of me; for I am meek and lowly in heart: and ye shall find rest unto your souls. For my yoke is easy, and my burden is light" (Matt. 11:28-30).

---

†*This is the only self-description of Christ found in the Bible. Author R. C. Foster observes: "The Shakespearean actor Thomas Keene was once being entertained at a banquet in his honor by a large group of admirers. Someone at the banquet table suggested that each person present should stand and quote his favorite passage from the literature of the world. A buzz of excited whispers went around the table as all tried to speculate what Mr. Keene would quote. Some felt sure it would be something from* Hamlet, As You Like It, *or* King Lear. *But when Thomas Keene arose he quoted with simplicity and humility these matchless words, 'Come unto me, all ye that labor and are heavy laden, and I will give you rest.'"* (Studies in the Life of Christ, *Baker Books, Grand Rapids, Mich., 1979*)

THIRTY-THREE: Christ is anointed in Simon's house (Luke 7:36-39)
A. The brokenhearted sinful woman—"And, behold, a woman in the city, which was a sinner, when she knew that Jesus sat at meat in the Pharisee's house,

brought an alabaster box of ointment, and stood at his feet behind him weeping, and began to wash his feet with tears, and did wipe them with the hairs of her head, and kissed his feet, and anointed them with the ointment" (Luke 7:37-38).

B. The hard-hearted Pharisee—"Now when the Pharisee which had bidden him saw it, he spake within himself, saying, This man, if he were a prophet, would have known who and what manner of woman this is that toucheth him: for she is a sinner" (Luke 7:39). (Note: For a fuller discussion, see the parable Jesus related at this time, entitled "Forgiving the 50 and the 500," under the *Topical Overview.)*

THIRTY-FOUR: Christ's fifth preaching tour of Galilee

A. Those ministering with Christ—"And it came to pass afterward, that he went throughout every city and village, preaching and shewing the glad tidings of the kingdom of God: and the twelve were with him" (Luke 8:1).

B. Those ministering to Christ—"And certain women, which had been healed of evil spirits and infirmities, Mary called Magdalene, out of whom went seven devils, and Joanna the wife of Chuza Herod's steward, and Susanna, and many others, which ministered unto him of their substance" (Luke 8:2-3).

THIRTY-FIVE: Christ refuses on two occasions to show the Pharisees a sign (Matt. 12:38).

A. First occasion

1. He refers to Jonah and the men of Nineveh—"But he answered and said unto them, An evil and adulterous generation seeketh after a sign; and there shall no sign be given to it, but the sign of the prophet Jonas: For as Jonas was three days and three nights in the whale's belly; so shall the Son of man be three days and three nights in the heart of the earth. The men of Nineveh shall rise in judgment with this generation, and shall condemn it: because they repented at the preaching of Jonas; and, behold, a greater than Jonas is here" (Matt. 12:39-41).

2. He refers to Solomon and the Queen of Sheba—"The queen of the south shall rise up in the judgment with this generation, and shall condemn it: for she came from the uttermost parts of the earth to hear the wisdom of Solomon; and, behold, a greater than Solomon is here" (Matt. 12:42).

B. Second occasion (Matt. 16:1-4; Mark 8:11-12)—"The Pharisees also with the Sadducees came, and tempting desired him that he would shew them a sign from heaven. He answered and said unto them, When it is evening, ye say, It will be fair weather: for the sky is red. And in the morning, It will be foul weather to day: for the sky is red and lowring. O ye hypocrites, ye can discern the face of the sky; but can ye not discern the signs of the times?" (Matt. 16:1-3).

THIRTY-SIX: Christ is misunderstood by his family on several occasions (Matt. 13:54-56; Mark 6:1-6; John 6:42)

A. First occasion (Matt. 13:57)—"And they were offended in him. But Jesus said unto them, A prophet is not without honour, save in his own country, and in his own house" (Matt. 13:57).

B. Second occasion (John 7:3-9)—"For neither did his brethren believe in him" (John 7:5).

THIRTY-SEVEN: Christ explains who his real family is (Matt. 12:46-50; Mark. 3:31-35; Luke 8:19-21).

A. His earthly kin—"While he yet talked to the people, behold, his mother and his brethren stood without, desiring to speak with him. Then one said unto him,

Behold, thy mother and thy brethren stand without, desiring to speak with thee" (Matt. 12:46-47).
B. His eternal kin—"But he answered and said unto him that told him, Who is my mother? and who are my brethren? And he stretched forth his hand toward his disciples, and said, Behold my mother and my brethren! For whosoever shall do the will of my Father which is in heaven, the same is my brother, and sister, and mother" (Matt. 12:48-50).

---

†*Two of Jesus' half brothers (James and Jude) later took this to heart, as seen in their epistles.*
  A. Both describe themselves as "servants of Jesus Christ" (see James 1:1; Jude 1:1).
  B. James also added the following admonition: "But be ye doers of the word, and not hearers only, deceiving your own selves. For if any be a hearer of the word, and not a doer, he is like unto a man beholding his natural face in a glass" (James 1:22-23).

THIRTY-EIGHT: Christ relates his parable on the nature of the kingdom of heaven (Matt. 13:1-53; Mark 4:1-34; Luke 8:4-18)—"He answered and said unto them, Because it is given unto you to know the mysteries of the kingdom of heaven, but to them it is not given" (Matt. 13:11). (Note: For a fuller discussion see the section on miracles under the *Topical Overview.*)
THIRTY-NINE: Christ rebukes the stormy Galilean Sea (Matt. 8:18, 23-27; Mark 5:1-20; Luke 8:26-39). (Note: For a fuller discussion, see the section on miracles under the *Topical Overview.*)
FORTY: Christ heals the maniac of Gadara (Matt. 8:28-34; Mark 5:1-20; Luke 8:26-39). (Note: For a fuller discussion, see the section on miracles under the *Topical Overview.*)
FORTY-ONE: Christ's second return trip to Nazareth (Matt. 13:54-58; Mark 6:1-6)
A. What the citizens would not do: accept his messiahship—"Is not this the carpenter's son? is not his mother called Mary? and his brethren, James, and Joses, and Simon, and Judas? And his sisters, are they not all with us? Whence then hath this man all these things?" (Matt. 13:55-56).

---

†*This title, "son of Mary," as recorded in Mark 6:3 and indicated here in Matthew's account, was a derogatory phrase, since a man was never referred to as his mother's son in Jewish usage, even if she was a widow. See Judges 11:1-2; John 8:41; 9:29. By not mentioning Mary's husband Joseph, i.e., "the son of Joseph," they were cruelly and crudely intimating that there was a real question concerning who the father was.*

B. What the Savior could not do: accomplish his miracles—"And they were offended in him. But Jesus said unto them, A prophet is not without honour, save in his own country, and in his own house. And he did not many mighty works there because of their unbelief" (Matt. 13:57-58).
FORTY-TWO: Christ's forerunner is murdered by Herod (Matt. 14:1-12; Mark 6:14-29; Luke 9:7-9).
A. The martyrdom of John
    1. The detainment of John—John is cast into prison.
        a. The who of the matter—"For Herod himself had sent forth and laid

hold upon John, and bound him in prison for Herodias' sake, his brother Philip's wife: for he had married her" (Mark 6:17).

    b. The why of the matter—"For John had said unto Herod, It is not lawful for thee to have thy brother's wife. Therefore Herodias had a quarrel against him, and would have killed him; but she could not: For Herod feared John, knowing that he was a just man and an holy, and observed him; and when he heard him, he did many things, and heard him gladly" (Mark 6:18-20).

2. The doubts of John

    a. His request to the Savior—"Now when John had heard in the prison the works of Christ, he sent two of his disciples, and said unto him, Art thou he that should come, or do we look for another?" (Matt. 11:2-3).

---

†*John had by this time spent many long weeks chained in a dungeon located near the Dead Sea, one of the most desolate and depressing places in the entire Middle East. He probably was allowed very little food and water, kept in darkness, and may have been tortured.*

---

    b. His reassurance from the Savior—"And in that same hour he cured many of their infirmities and plagues, and of evil spirits; and unto many that were blind he gave sight. Then Jesus answering said unto them, Go your way, and tell John what things ye have seen and heard; how that the blind see, the lame walk, the lepers are cleansed, the deaf hear, the dead are raised, to the poor the gospel is preached" (Luke 7:21-22).

---

†*We note that Jesus' answer contained only reassurance, and not one word of rebuke. Our Lord knew that John harbored no disbelief or denial in his heart, but only that element of painful doubt, as is on occasion experienced by all redeemed people. As the psalmist once wrote: "Like as a father pitieth his children, so the Lord pitieth them that fear him. For he knoweth our frame; he remembereth that we are dust" (Psa. 103:13-14).*

---

3. The death of John

    a. The party—"And when a convenient day was come, that Herod on his birthday made a supper to his lords, high captains, and chief estates of Galilee" (Mark 6:21).

    b. The performance—"And the daughter of the said Herodias came in, and danced, and pleased Herod and them that sat with him, the king said unto the damsel, Ask of me whatsoever thou wilt, and I will give it thee. And he sware unto her, Whatsoever thou shalt ask of me, I will give it thee, unto the half of my kingdom" (Mark 6:22-23).

    c. The plot—"And she went forth, and said unto her mother, What shall I ask? And she said, The head of John the Baptist. And she came in straightway with haste unto the king, and asked, saying, I will that thou give me by and by in a charger the head of John the Baptist" (Mark 6:24-25).

    d. The platter—"And the king was exceeding sorry; yet for his oath's sake, and for their sakes which sat with him, he would not reject her. And immediately the king sent an executioner, and commanded his head to be brought: and he went and beheaded him in the prison. And brought his head in a charger, and gave it to the damsel, and the damsel gave it to her mother" (Mark 6:26-28).

B. The magnificence of John—"And as they departed, Jesus began to say unto the multitudes concerning John, What went ye out into the wilderness to see? A reed shaken with the wind? But what went ye out for to see? A man clothed in soft raiment? behold, they that wear soft clothing are in kings' houses. But what went ye out for to see? A prophet? yea, I say unto you, and more than a prophet. . . . Verily I say unto you, Among them that are born of women there hath not risen a greater than John the Baptist: notwithstanding he that is least in the kingdom of heaven is greater than he" (Matt. 11:7-9, 11). "Ye sent unto John, and he bare witness unto the truth. . . . He was a burning and a shining light: and ye were willing for a season to rejoice in his light" (John 5:33, 35).

---

†*To whom did Jesus refer by his statement, "least in the Kingdom . . . is greater"? Two theories have been offered:*

   A. That he had the Apostle Paul in mind. (See Eph. 3:8; 1 Cor. 15:9.)

   B. That he had the Millennium in mind, when the least citizen of that glorious kingdom would experience more of God's majesty than any prophet, priest, or king had previously done. In other words, that citizen would be positionally—not morally—greater than John.

---

1. Jesus said John came with the sermon of Malachi (compare Matt. 11:10 with Mal. 3:1)—"For this is he, of whom it is written, Behold, I send my messenger before thy face, which shall prepare thy way before thee" (Matt. 11:10).

---

†*Why did Jesus leave out the last phrase of Malachi 3:1 when he quoted that verse? He omitted the words, "And the Lord whom ye shall seek, shall suddenly come to his temple." According to Habakkuk 2:20, when this happens, Christ comes to judge. However, his first coming was marked by grace; thus the final part was omitted.*

---

2. Jesus said John came in the spirit of Elijah—"And if ye will receive it, this is Elias, which was for to come" (Matt. 11:14).

FORTY-THREE: Christ feeds the 5,000 (Matt. 14:13-22; Mark 6:30-44; Luke 9:10-17; John 6:1-13).

FORTY-FOUR: Christ refuses the offer of the people he fed to crown him king (Matt. 14:22-23; Mark 6:45-46; John 6:14-15)—"Then those men, when they had seen the miracle that Jesus did, said, This is of a truth that prophet that should come into the world. When Jesus therefore perceived that they would come and take him by force, to make him a king, he departed again into a mountain himself alone" (John 6:14-15).

FORTY-FIVE: Christ walks on the water (Matt. 14:24-33; Mark 6:47-52; John 6:16-21). (Note: For a fuller discussion, see the section on miracles under the *Topical Overview*.)

FORTY-SIX: Christ preaches his sermon on the bread of life (John 6:22-71). (Note: For a fuller discussion, see the section on his sermons under the *Topical Overview*.)

FORTY-SEVEN: Christ hears Peter's confession and promises to build Jesus' church (Matt. 16:13-21; Mark 8:27-31; Luke 9:18-22).
A. The probing of Christ—"When Jesus came into the coasts of Caesarea Philippi, he asked his disciples, saying, Whom do men say that I the Son of man am?" (Matt. 16:13).
   1. The rumors—"And they said, Some say that thou art John the Baptist: some, Elias; and others, Jeremias, or one of the prophets. He saith unto them, But whom say ye that I am?" (Matt. 16:14-15).

---

† A. *How are we to account for the various rumors concerning Jesus' identity? Some, influenced by Herod Antipas, confused Jesus with John the Baptist, whom they felt had been raised from the dead (Matt. 14:2). Others identified Jesus with the prophet Elijah, whose coming had been predicted by Malachi (4:5-6). The apocryphal book 2 Esdras predicted the return of Isaiah and Jeremiah (2:18). It was commonly believed among the Jews that at the Messiah's coming the prophets would rise again. "The nearer still the 'kingdom of heaven' came, by so much the more did they dream of the resurrection of the prophets."*
   B. *Note the phrase, "But whom say ye?" Jesus both was, and is now, far more interested in what his people think about him than what the world might say about him.*

---

   2. The recognition—"And Simon Peter answered and said, Thou art the Christ, the Son of the living God" (Matt. 16:16).
   3. The revelation—"And Jesus answered and said unto him, Blessed art thou, Simon-Barjona: for flesh and blood hath not revealed it unto thee, but my Father which is in heaven" (Matt. 16:17).

---

†*Luke provides for us the reason for this timely revelation, namely, the request of Christ to his Father. "And it came to pass, as he was alone praying, his disciples were with him: and he asked them, saying, Whom say the people that I am?" (Luke 9:18).*

   B. The promise of Christ
   1. What he would do for his disciples—"And I say also unto thee, That thou art Peter, and upon this rock I will build my church; and the gates of hell shall not prevail against it" (Matt. 16:18).
   2. What he would give to his disciples—"And I will give unto thee the keys of the kingdom of heaven: and whatsoever thou shalt bind on earth shall be bound in heaven: and whatsoever thou shalt loose on earth shall be loosed in heaven" (Matt. 16:19).

---

† A. *Was Jesus building his church upon Peter and planning to make him its first Pope? It may be clearly stated that he was not, for the following reasons:*
   1. *Christ later gave the same responsibilities to the other apostles which he here gives to Peter. (Compare Matt. 16:19 with John 20:22-23.)*
   2. *The New Testament clearly presents Christ and Christ only as the foundation of his Church. (See Acts 4:11-12; 1 Cor. 3:11; 1 Pet. 2:4-8.)*

3. *The New Testament clearly presents Christ and Christ only as the Head of his Church. (See Eph. 1:20-23; 5:23; Col. 1:18; 2:18-19.)*

4. *In the Greek language, there is a play upon words in this verse. Jesus said, "Thou art Peter [*petros, *a little stone,] and upon this rock [*petra, *massive cliff or rock] I will build my church."*

5. *Peter's testimony denies it (see 1 Pet. 5:1-4).*

6. *James and not Peter later officiated at the Jerusalem church (see Acts 15:13, 19).*

B. *What then, was Christ doing? The answer is given in Ephesians. "Now therefore ye are no more strangers and foreigners, but fellow-citizens with the saints, and of the household of God; and are built upon the foundation of the apostles and prophets, Jesus Christ himself being the chief corner stone; in whom all the building fitly framed together groweth unto an holy temple in the Lord: in whom ye also are builded together for an habitation of God through the Spirit" (Eph. 2:19-22).*

C. *What did he mean by "the gates of hell shall not prevail against it"? J. Vernon McGee wrote: "The gates of hell refer to the 'gates of death.' The word used here is the hades and sheol of the Old Testament, which refers to the unseen world and means death. The gates of death shall not prevail against Christ's church" (Matthew, Vol. II, p. 23). This glorious event is called the rapture. (See 1 Thess. 4:13-18; 1 Cor. 15:51-57.)*

D. *What were the "keys of the kingdom of heaven" that Jesus gave Peter? A key, of course, unlocks doors and makes available something which was previously closed. Jesus here predicts that Peter would be given the privilege of opening the door of salvation to various peoples. This he later did.*

1. *He opened the door of Christian opportunity to Israel at Pentecost (Acts 2:38-42).*

2. *He did the same thing for the Samaritans (Acts 8:14-17).*

3. *He performed this ministry to the Gentiles at Cornelius' house at Caesarea (Acts 10).*

E. *What did Christ mean by the binding and loosing of Matthew 16:19? This authority was given to all the apostles as well as to other believers. (See Matt. 18:18; John 20:22-23.) W. A. Criswell writes: "In Greek the future perfect tense is used to express the double notion of an action terminated in the past but whose effects are still existing in the present. 'Having been bound and still bound,' and 'having been loosed and still loosed.' The meaning is: if the disciples act in their proper capacity as stewards, they will be acting in accordance with the principles and elective purposes ordained beforehand in heaven." (Expository Notes on Matthew, p. 101)*

In other words, all the actions of the Spirit-filled believer, whether positive or negative in nature, will carry with them the awesome authority of heaven itself.

C. The passion of Christ—"From that time forth began Jesus to shew unto his disciples, how that he must go unto Jerusalem, and suffer many things of the elders and chief priests and scribes, and be killed, and be raised again the third day" (Matt. 16:21).

---

†*This shocking and sobering truth would be hammered home repeatedly by the Savior. Examples: "And while they abode in Galilee, Jesus said unto them, The Son of man shall be betrayed into the hands of men: and they shall kill him, and the third day he shall be raised again. And they were exceeding sorry" (Matt. 17:22-23). "Behold, we go up to Jerusalem; and the Son of man shall be betrayed unto the chief priests and unto the scribes, and they shall condemn him to death, and shall deliver him to the Gentiles to mock, and to scourge, and to crucify him: and the third day he shall rise again" (Matt. 20:18-19).*

FORTY-EIGHT: Christ rebukes Peter (Matt. 16:22-23)—"Then Peter took him, and began to rebuke him, saying, Be it far from thee, Lord: this shall not be unto thee. But he turned, and said unto Peter, Get thee behind me, Satan: thou art an offence unto me: for thou savourest not the things that be of God, but those that be of men" (Matt. 16:22-23).

†*Here Satan employs a familiar tactic, using a secondary source through which to spew forth his poison. The first successful attempt occurred in the Garden of Eden. "Now the serpent was more subtil than any beast of the field which the Lord God had made. And he said unto the woman, Yea, hath God said, Ye shall not eat of every tree of the garden?" (Gen. 3:1).*

FORTY-NINE: Christ is transfigured (Matt. 17:1-8; Mark 9:2-8; Luke 9:28-36).
 A. The prophecy involved—"Verily I say unto you, There be some standing here, which shall not taste of death, till they see the Son of man coming in his kingdom" (Matt. 16:28).
 B. The place involved—"An high mountain" (Matt. 17:1), probably Mount Hermon.
 C. The purpose involved—"He . . . went up into a mountain to pray" (Luke 9:28).
 D. The personalities involved
   1. Peter, James, and John (Matt. 17:1)
   2. The Savior
   3. The Father
   4. Moses and Elijah
 E. The particulars involved
   1. The transfiguration of the Son
     a. The splendor from within—"He was transfigured before them" (Mark 9:2). "The fashion of his countenance was altered" (Luke 9:29). "His face did shine as the sun" (Matt. 17:2). "And his raiment became shining, exceeding white as snow" (Mark 9:3).
     b. The spokesmen from above—"And, behold, there talked with him two men, which were Moses and Elias: Who appeared in glory, and spake of his decease which he should accomplish at Jerusalem" (Luke 9:30-31).
   2. The testimony of the Father—"While he yet spake, behold, a bright cloud overshadowed them: and behold a voice out of the cloud, which said, This is my beloved Son, in whom I am well pleased; hear ye him" (Matt. 17:5).
   3. The talk of the apostles
     a. The foolishness involved—"And it came to pass, as they departed from him, Peter said unto Jesus, Master, it is good for us to be here: and let us make three tabernacles; one for thee, and one for Moses, and one for Elias: not knowing what he said" (Luke 9:33).
     b. The fear involved—"For he wist not what to say; for they were sore afraid" (Mark 9:6).

†*Thoughts on the transfiguration:*
   A. The Scriptures suggest that this may have been a night scene, for the three disciples had just awakened from a deep sleep. (See Luke 9:32.)

B. Note that the light was from within, and not from some giant cosmic spotlight suddenly focusing down upon Jesus. His countenance was affected first, then his garments. This was the same glory that shone in both the Old Testament tabernacle (Exod. 40) and the temple (1 Kings 8). It would later be withdrawn because of Israel's sin in the days of Ezekiel (Ezek. 10–11). Later it was revealed to the shepherds (Luke 2:9), to the disciples (Acts 1:9), to Stephen (Acts 7:55), to Saul (Acts 9:3), and to John the apostle (Rev. 1:16). Finally, at Christ's second coming this glory will be revealed to the whole world. "And then shall appear the sign of the Son of man in heaven: and then shall all the tribes of the earth mourn, and they shall see the Son of man coming in the clouds of heaven with power and great glory" (Matt. 24:30).

Christ's eternal glory was not surrendered at the time of the incarnation, but rather was covered and contained by his fleshly body. The body of Christ was to the disciples what the veil of the tabernacle was to Old Testament Israel.

1. Both "veils" housed and protected the glory of God from within.
2. Both "veils" were broken at Calvary. "And he took bread, and gave thanks, and brake it, and gave unto them, saying, This is my body which is given for you: this do in remembrance of me." (Luke 22:19). "And, behold, the vail of the temple was rent in twain from the top to the bottom; and the earth did quake, and the rocks rent" (Matt. 27:51). Satan tried, unsuccessfully, to imitate this inward splendor of Christ (2 Cor. 11:14).

C. The word "transfigured" is metamorphoo in the Greek language. We get our word "metamorphosis" from it. It brings to mind a caterpillar in the cocoon coming forth as a butterfly. The transfiguration of Christ does not set forth his deity, but rather his humanity. Transformation is the goal of humanity. We shall experience this at the rapture. Adam and Eve may well have been clothed by a light of innocence proceeding from within. But all this was lost through sin.

D. Why the appearance of both Moses and Elijah?

1. Because of what they represented—The main reason for the writing of the Old Testament was to prepare us for Christ. Jesus himself testified of this: "Search the scriptures . . . they . . . testify of me" (John 5:39). "And beginning at Moses and all the prophets, he expounded unto them in all the scriptures, the things concerning himself" (Luke 24:27). While he was on earth, Jesus had a very simple way of summarizing the entire Old Testament: "Think not that I am come to destroy the law, or the prophets: I am not come to destroy, but to fulfil" (Matt. 5:17). Why then the appearance of these two men?

    a. Moses was there because he represented the Law.
    b. Elijah was there because he represented the prophets.

2. Because of who they represented—Why were Moses and Elijah, of all Old Testament people, present on this occasion? Perhaps these two men and the disciples suggest all the categories of people who will be in Jesus' coming kingdom. The disciples represent individuals who will be present in physical bodies. Moses represents saved individuals who have died or will die. Elijah represents saved individuals who will not experience death, but will be caught up to heaven alive (1 Thess. 4:17). These three groups will be present when Christ institutes his kingdom on earth. Furthermore, the Lord will be in his glory as he was at the transfiguration, and the kingdom will take place on earth, as this event obviously did. The disciples were thus enjoying a foretaste of the promised kingdom of the Lord (Matt. 16:28). (The Bible Knowledge Commentary, *Victor Books*, Wheaton, Ill., 1983, p. 59)

3. Because of their future ministry during the great tribulation—Many believe that

Moses and Elijah will be the two witnesses referred to in Revelation 11:3-12. See also Malachi 4:4-5. If this is true, the transfiguration event would thus serve as a "trial run." In fact, Jesus had suggested this very thing on the way down from the mountain: "And Jesus answered and said unto them, Elias truly shall first come, and restore all things" (Matt. 17:11).

E. *Both Moses and Elijah had previously experienced a special revelation from God (see Exod. 33:17-23 and 1 Kings 19:9-13), and at the same place (Mount Sinai/Horeb). The transfiguration answered Moses' twofold request:*
   1. *To see the glory of God (Exod. 33:18)*
   2. *To enter the promised land (Deut 3:23-25)*

F. *Peter here thoughtlessly suggests the building of three booths. It may be that at this time the Feast of Tabernacles (booths) was being celebrated in Jerusalem. This was to be a type of the coming Millennium as well as a reminder of Israel's redemption from Egypt. (See Lev. 23:34-44.) But before this (the Millennium) could happen, another feast would take place—the Passover. (See Lev. 23:4-8 and Matt. 26–27.) "For even Christ, our passover, is sacrificed for us" (1 Cor. 5:7).*

G. *Peter would never forget this great event. He later wrote about it (see 2 Pet. 1:16-18).*

H. *Jesus spoke to Moses and Elijah concerning his "decease" (Luke 9:31). The word here is actually "exodus," and is used by Peter at a later date in describing his approaching death. (See 2 Pet. 1: 13-14.)*

I. *Mark concluded the transfiguration event with the following words: "And as they came down from the mountain, he charged them that they should tell no man what things they had seen, till the Son of man were risen from the dead. And they kept that saying with themselves, questioning one with another what the rising from the dead should mean" (Mark 9:9-10). The Jews were familiar with the doctrine of the resurrection (see Job. 19:25-26; Isa. 25:8; 26:19; Hosea 13:14), but the resurrection of the Son of man astonished them, for their theology had no place for a suffering and dying Messiah. This is seen especially in John 12:32-39.*

FIFTY: Christ heals a demon-possessed boy (Matt. 17:14-21; Mark 9:14-29; Luke 9:37-43). (Note: For a fuller discussion, see the section on miracles under the *Topical Overview.*)

FIFTY-ONE: Christ performs the miracle of the fish with a coin in its mouth (Matt. 17:24-27). (Note: For a fuller discussion, see the section on miracles under the *Topical Overview.*)

FIFTY-TWO: Christ rebukes James and John on three occasions.

A. First occasion (Mark 9:28-41; Luke 9:49-50)—"And John answered and said, Master, we saw one casting out devils in thy name; and we forbad him, because he followeth not with us. And Jesus said unto him, Forbid him not: for he that is not against us is for us" (Luke 9:49-50).

---

†*The disciples may have been jealous, for this man was able to do what they had just recently failed to accomplish. "When Jesus saw that the people came running together, he rebuked the foul spirit, saying unto him, Thou dumb and deaf spirit, I charge thee, come out of him, and enter no more into him. And when he was come into the house, the disciples asked him privately,*

Why could not we cast him out? And he said unto them, This kind can come forth by nothing, but by prayer and fasting" (Mark 9:25, 28-29).

B. Second occasion (Luke 9:51-56)
   1. The refusal demonstrated by the Samaritans—"And it came to pass, when the time was come that he should be received up, he stedfastly set his face to go to Jerusalem, and sent messengers before his face: and they went, and entered into a village of the Samaritans, to make ready for him. And they did not receive him, because his face was as though he would go to Jerusalem" (Luke 9:51-53).
   2. The retaliation demanded by the brothers—"And when his disciples James and John saw this, they said, Lord, wilt thou that we command fire to come down from heaven, and consume them, even as Elias did?" (Luke 9:54).
   3. The rebuke delivered by the Lord—"But he turned, and rebuked them, and said, Ye know not what manner of spirit ye are of. For the Son of man is not come to destroy men's lives, but to save them. And they went to another village" (Luke 9:55-56).
C. Third occasion (Matt. 20:20-28; Mark 10:35-45)
   1. The request of the two—"And James and John, the sons of Zebedee, come unto him, saying, Master, we would that thou shouldest do for us whatsoever we shall desire. And he said unto them, What would ye that I should do for you? They said unto him, Grant unto us that we may sit, one on thy right hand, and the other on thy left hand, in thy glory" (Mark 10:35-37).
   2. The resentment of the ten—"And when the ten heard it, they began to be much displeased with James and John" (Mark 10:41).
   3. The response of the Lord
      a. Toward the two—"And he saith unto them, Ye shall drink indeed of my cup, and be baptized with the baptism that I am baptized with: but to sit on my right hand, and on my left, is not mine to give, but it shall be given to them for whom it is prepared of my Father" (Matt. 20:23).

---

†The "cup" phrase here is a common Jewish metaphor referring to:
   A. Joy (Psa. 23:5; 116:13)
   B. Judgment against sin (Psa. 75:7-8; Isa. 51:17-23; Jer. 25:15-28; 49:12; 51:7; Ezek. 23:31-34; Hab. 2:16; Zech. 12:2)—The judgment cup brought with it, of course, much pain and suffering. This is the cup our Lord prayed about in Gethsemane: "And he went a little farther, and fell on his face, and prayed, saying, O my Father, if it be possible, let this cup pass from me: nevertheless not as I will, but as thou wilt" (Matt. 26:39).
Jesus warned his disciples that they would indeed drink of the cup of suffering. Church history affirms that this was fulfilled, for it reports that all of his apostles experienced great trials, and many had violent deaths. Thus they were to share his sufferings, not in a redemptive sense, but as predicted by Isaiah: "But he was wounded for our transgressions, he was bruised for our iniquities: the chastisement of our peace was upon him; and with his stripes we are healed" (Isa. 53:5).

---

      b. Toward the ten—"But it shall not be so among you: but whosoever will be great among you, let him be your minister; and whosoever will be chief among you, let him be your servant: Even as the Son of man came not to be ministered unto, but to minister, and to give his life a ransom for many" (Matt. 20:26-28).

FIFTY-THREE: Christ answers the apostles' argument concerning who was the greatest among them (Matt. 18:1-5; Mark 9:33-37; Luke 9:46-48).

A. The child—"Then there arose a reasoning among them, which of them should be greatest. And Jesus, perceiving the thought of their heart, took a child, and set him by him" (Luke 9:46-47).

B. The conclusion—"And said unto them, Whosoever shall receive this child in my name receiveth me: and whosoever shall receive me receiveth him that sent me: for he that is least among you all, the same shall be great" (Luke 9:48).

FIFTY-FOUR: Christ warns about mistreating a little child (Matt. 18:6, 10; Mark 9:42).

A. The punishment involved—"But whoso shall offend one of these little ones which believe in me, it were better for him that a millstone were hanged about his neck, and that he were drowned in the depth of the sea" (Matt. 18:6).

B. The protection involved—"Take heed that ye despise not one of these little ones; for I say unto you, That in heaven their angels do always behold the face of my Father which is in heaven" (Matt. 18:10).

---

†*Do we have "guardian angels"? Consider: "The angel of the Lord encampeth round about them that fear him, and delivereth them: For he shall give his angels charge over thee, to keep thee in all thy ways" (Psa. 34:7; 91:11). "Are they not all ministering spirits, sent forth to minister for them who shall be heirs of salvation?" (Heb. 1:14).*

FIFTY-FIVE: Christ is approached by three would-be disciples (Matt. 8:19-22; Luke 9:57-62).

A. First candidate—"And it came to pass, that, as they went in the way, a certain man said unto him, Lord, I will follow thee whithersoever thou goest. And Jesus said unto him, Foxes have holes, and birds of the air have nests; but the Son of man hath not where to lay his head" (Luke 9:57-58).

B. Second candidate—"And he said unto another, Follow me. But he said, Lord, suffer me first to go and bury my father. Jesus said unto him, Let the dead bury their dead: but go thou and preach the kingdom of God" (Luke 9:59-60).

C. Third candidate—"And another also said, Lord, I will follow thee; but let me first go bid them farewell, which are at home at my house. And Jesus said unto him, No man, having put his hand to the plough, and looking back, is fit for the kingdom of God" (Luke 9:61-62).

FIFTY-SIX: Christ is rebuked by his unbelieving half brothers (John 7:2-9)—"Now the Jews' feast of tabernacles was at hand. His brethren therefore said unto him, Depart hence, and go into Judaea, that thy disciples also may see the works that thou doest. For there is no man that doeth any thing in secret, and he himself seeketh to be known openly. If thou do these things, shew thyself to the world. For neither did his brethren believe in him" (John 7:2-5).

FIFTY-SEVEN: Christ forgives a woman taken in the act of adultery (John 8:1-11).

A. The connivers—"And the scribes and Pharisees brought unto him a woman taken in adultery; and when they had set her in the midst, They say unto him, Master, this woman was taken in adultery, in the very act" (John 8:3-4).
B. The conniving
1. What they said—"Now Moses in the law commanded us, that such should be stoned: but what sayest thou?" (John 8:5).

✝ *A. Here the wicked Jewish leaders altered the Law somewhat.*
1. *The manner of execution was not prescribed unless the woman was a betrothed virgin (Deut. 22:23-24)*
2. *The Law also required both parties to be killed (Lev. 20:10; Deut. 22:22).*
B. There is only one Old Testament instance in which this law was carried out (see Num. 25:7-8).

2. Why they said it—"This they said, tempting him, that they might have to accuse him" (John 8:6a).
C. The conviction—"But Jesus stooped down, and with his finger wrote on the ground, as though he heard them not" (John 8:6b).

✝*What did he write? It has been suggested that he may have written down the names of those Pharisees standing there who had secretly committed adultery. Consider Paul's words at a later date: "Behold, thou art called a Jew, and restest in the law, and makest thy boast of God. . . . thou that sayest a man should not commit adultery, dost thou commit adultery? thou that abhorrest idols, dost thou commit sacrilege?" (Rom. 2:17, 22).*

D. The convicted—"And they which heard it, being convicted by their own conscience, went out one by one, beginning at the eldest, even unto the last: and the woman standing in the midst" (John 8:9).
E. The cleansed
1. No earthly condemnation— "When Jesus had lifted up himself, and saw none but the woman, he said unto her, Woman, where are those thine accusers? hath no man condemned thee?" (John 8:10)
2. No heavenly condemnation—"She said, No man, Lord. And Jesus said unto her, Neither do I condemn thee: go, and sin no more" (John 8:11).
FIFTY-EIGHT: Christ heals a man born blind (John 9:138). (Note: For a fuller discussion, see this miracle under the *Topical Overview.*)
FIFTY-NINE: Christ preaches his Good Shepherd sermon (John 10:1-21). (Note: For a fuller discussion, see this sermon under the *Topical Overview.*)
SIXTY: Christ sends out seventy disciples (Luke 10:1-24).

✝*Foster wrote: "About six months may have intervened since the twelve were sent forth two by two on a similar mission (see Matt. 10). One of the striking differences in the two commissions is that the prohibition against going into any way of the Gentiles or Samaritans is not repeated. Drawing around Jerusalem an imaginary circle of about fifty or sixty miles in radius, we can see that thirty-five evangelistic teams, preaching for several days in each town and village, could have reached an immense number of people. Within range would have been the cities on the seacoast, such as Joppa, and those to the southwest that bordered on the desert, such as Gaza and Beersheba, with all the intermediate places. The centers of Essene population in the wilderness of Judaea at Ain Feska and Engedi together with the military fortress at Masada could have been assigned to some of these evangelists. If these people had refused to come out of their isolation to see and hear Jesus, at least they could receive from His chosen messengers instruction, invitation, and solemn warning. To the east of the Dead Sea, Machaerus, Herod's winter resort, and the mighty fortress of Kerak would have been within reach. The populous centers of the southern Decapolis and Peraea would have offered a vast field for evangelization. Questions naturally arise as to the identity of the seventy evangelists and why seventy. Early Christian writers record different traditions about various men famous in the early church who were supposed to have been included in the seventy, but these are obviously guesses. The fact that there were twelve apostles suggests the twelve tribes of Israel and Jacob's twelve sons. Farther than this we cannot go, except to observe that twelve was a good number, not too large or too small, and that it was the express will of Christ. The seventy evangelists suggests the seventy elders of Israel appointed by Moses (Num. 11:16-17, 24-25) and the seventy members of the Sanhedrin with the high priest presiding, in imitation of the seventy elders under Moses. But no connection is stated in the Scripture. We do not know why seventy men were sent on this mission. A large number of evangelists were needed, and Jesus chose seventy of the most able men."* (Studies in the Life of Christ, R. C. Foster, Baker Books, Grand Rapids, Mich., 1979, pp. 842-43)

A. The job given to the seventy by the Savior (10:1-16)
   1. Their appointment—"After these things the Lord appointed other seventy also, and sent them two and two before his face into every city and place, whither he himself would come" (Luke 10:1).
   2. Their assignment
      a. The mission field involved—"Go your ways: behold, I send you forth as lambs among wolves" (Luke 10:3).
      b. The message involved—"And heal the sick that are therein, and say unto them, The kingdom of God is come nigh unto you" (Luke 10:9).
      c. The method involved—"But into whatsoever city ye enter, and they receive you not, go your ways out into the streets of the same, and say, Even the very dust of your city, which cleaveth on us, we do wipe off against you: notwithstanding be ye sure of this, that the kingdom of God is come nigh unto you" (Luke 10:10-11).
   3. Their authority—"He that heareth you heareth me; and he that despiseth you despiseth me; and he that despiseth me despiseth him that sent me" (Luke 10:16).
B. The joy felt by the seventy and the Savior (10:17-24)
   1. The joy of the seventy
      a. The passing joy—"And the seventy returned again with joy, saying, Lord, even the devils are subject unto us through thy name" (Luke 10:17).
      b. The permanent joy—"And he said unto them, I beheld Satan as lightning fall from heaven. Behold, I give unto you power to tread on serpents and scorpions, and over all the power of the enemy: and nothing shall by any means hurt you" (Luke 10:18-19).
         (1) Because of their heavenly position—"Notwithstanding in this rejoice not, that the spirits are subject unto you; but rather rejoice, because your names are written in heaven" (Luke 10:20).

(2) Because of their earthly privilege—"And he turned him unto his disciples, and said privately, Blessed are the eyes which see the things that ye see: For I tell you, that many prophets and kings have desired to see those things which ye see, and have not seen them; and to hear those things which ye hear, and have not heard them" (Luke 10:23-24).

†*Both Peter and the author of Hebrews speak concerning this Old Testament desire.*
  A. Peter's testimony: *"Of which salvation the prophets have inquired and searched diligently, who prophesied of the grace that should come unto you: searching what, or what manner of time the Spirit of Christ which was in them did signify, when it testified beforehand the sufferings of Christ, and the glory that should follow. Unto whom it was revealed, that not unto themselves, but unto us they did minister the things, which are now reported unto you by them that have preached the gospel unto you with the Holy Ghost sent down from heaven; which things the angels desire to look into" (1 Pet. 1:10-12).*
  B. Paul's testimony: *"And what shall I more say? for the time would fail me to tell of Gedeon, and of Barak, and of Samson, and of Jephthae; of David also, and Samuel, and of the prophets. . . . and these all, having obtained a good report through faith, received not the promise" (Heb. 11:32, 39).*

2. The joy of the Savior—"In that hour Jesus rejoiced in spirit, and said, I thank thee, O Father, Lord of heaven and earth, that thou hast hid these things from the wise and prudent, and hast revealed them unto babes: even so, Father; for so it seemed good in thy sight. All things are delivered to me of my Father: and no man knoweth who the Son is, but the Father; and who the Father is, but the Son, and he to whom the Son will reveal him" (Luke 10:21-22).
SIXTY-ONE: Christ visits with Mary and Martha (Luke 10:38-42).
  A. The complaint of Martha—"Now it came to pass, as they went, that he entered into a certain village: and a certain woman named Martha received him into her house" (Luke 10:38).
    1. The eager student— "And she had a sister called Mary, which also sat at Jesus' feet, and heard his word" (Luke 10:39).
    2. The busy servant—"But Martha was cumbered about much serving, and came to him, and said, Lord, dost thou not care that my sister hath left me to serve alone? bid her therefore that she help me" (Luke 10:40).
  B. The correction of Jesus
    1. What she had been doing—"And Jesus answered and said unto her, Martha, Martha, thou art careful and troubled about many things" (Luke 10:41).
    2. What she should be doing—"But one thing is needful: and Mary hath chosen that good part, which shall not be taken away from her" (Luke 10:41-42).

†*We are all too often so busy in ministering for the Lord, that we neglect our ministering to the Lord. Note an event in the early days of the Antioch church: "Now there were in the church that was in Antioch certain prophets and teachers. . . . As they ministered to the Lord, and fasted, the Holy Ghost said, Separate me Barnabas and Saul for the work whereunto I have called them"*

(Acts 13:1-2). Martha was simply too busy. She was allowing the good to become the enemy of the best. To rephrase this truth: Our worship of Christ is more important and must precede our work for Christ.

SIXTY-TWO: Christ commands people to repent (Luke 13:1-5). He relates two incidents.
A. First incident—"There were present at that season some that told him of the Galilaeans, whose blood Pilate had mingled with their sacrifices. And Jesus answering said unto them, Suppose ye that these Galilaeans were sinners above all the Galilaeans, because they suffered such things? I tell you, Nay: but, except ye repent, ye shall all likewise perish" (Luke 13:1-3).
B. Second incident—"Or those eighteen, upon whom the tower in Siloam fell, and slew them, think ye that they were sinners above all men that dwelt in Jerusalem? I tell you, Nay: but, except ye repent, ye shall all likewise perish" (Luke 13:4-5).

†*Here Jesus emphasizes three key truths:*
  A. *Death, like God, is impartial. To reword Romans 2:11: "For there is no respect of persons with the grim reaper."*
  B. *Death can, and often does, strike with no warning whatsoever.*
  C. *In light of this, all people, moral and immoral, need to repent, lest death overtake them and they suffer both physical and spiritual death.*

SIXTY-THREE: Christ relates the parable of the Good Samaritan (Luke 10:25-37). (Note: For a fuller discussion, see this parable under the *Topical Overview.*)
SIXTY-FOUR: Christ relates the parable of the rich fool (Luke 12:13-34). (Note: For a fuller discussion, see this parable under the *Topical Overview.*)
SIXTY-FIVE: Christ relates the parable of the lost sheep, coin, and son (Luke 15:1-32). (Note: For a fuller discussion, see this parable under the *Topical Overview.*)
SIXTY-SIX: Christ relates the parable of the rich man and Lazarus (Luke 16:19-31). (Note: For a fuller discussion, see this parable under the *Topical Overview.*)
SIXTY-SEVEN: Christ raises Lazarus from the dead (John 11:1-44). (Note: For a fuller discussion, see this parable under the *Topical Overview.*)
SIXTY-EIGHT: Christ teaches on the subject of discipleship (Matt. 16:24-27; Mark 8:34-38; Luke 9:23-26; 14:25-33).
A. Those requirements for discipleship—"And when he had called the people unto him with his disciples also, he said unto them, Whosoever will come after me, let him deny himself, and take up his cross, and follow me. For whosoever will save his life shall lose it; but whosoever shall lose his life for my sake and the gospel's, the same shall save it. For what shall it profit a man, if he shall gain the whole world, and lose his own soul? Or what shall a man give in exchange for his soul? Whosoever therefore shall be ashamed of me and of my words in this adulterous and sinful generation; of him also shall the Son of man be ashamed, when he cometh in the glory of his Father with the holy angels" (Mark 8:34-38).

† A. *"Let him deny himself." This is the exact opposite of the modern Playboy philosophy, which says, "Indulge yourself!" "If it feels good, do it twice!"*
  B. *"Whosoever shall lose his life for my sake . . . shall save it." These words are extremely important, for they are among those rare ones recorded by all four of the Gospel writers. (See Matt. 10:39; 16:25; Mark 8:35; Luke 9:24; John 12:25.) The Apostle Paul patterned his life after this statement of Jesus (see Acts 20:22-24; 21:10-13).*

B. Those rejected from discipleship
  1. First example—"If any man come to me, and hate not his father, and mother, and wife, and children, and brethren, and sisters, yea, and his own life also, he cannot be my disciple. And whosoever doth not bear his cross, and come after me, cannot be my disciple" (Luke 14:26-27).

† A. *This has bothered some people. However, it should be kept in mind that the Greek word* misco *can also mean a preference for one thing over another. Greek scholar W. E. Vine points to two other passages in which this preference meaning is obviously intended. "No man can serve two masters; for either he will hate [prefer] the one and love the other; or else he will hold to the one, and despise [count as nothing] the other. Ye cannot serve God and mammon" (Matt. 6:24). "He that loveth his life shall lose it; and he that hateth his life [counts it as less than Christ] in this world shall keep it unto life eternal" (John 12:25).*
  B. *In reality, Christ taught a man to love his family (see Eph. 5:25, 28).*

  2. Second example—"For which of you, intending to build a tower, sitteth not down first, and counteth the cost, whether he have sufficient to finish it? Lest haply, after he hath laid the foundation, and is not able to finish it, all that behold it begin to mock him, Saying, This man began to build, and was not able to finish" (Luke 14:28-30).
  3. Third example—"Or what king, going to make war against another king, sitteth not down first, and consulteth whether he be able with ten thousand to meet him that cometh against him with twenty thousand? Or else, while the other is yet a great way off, he sendeth an ambassage, and desireth conditions of peace. So likewise, whosoever he be of you that forsaketh not all that he hath, he cannot be my disciple" (Luke 14:31-33).
SIXTY-NINE: Christ teaches on the subject of forgiveness (Matt. 18:21-22)—"Then came Peter to him, and said, Lord, how oft shall my brother sin against me, and I forgive him? till seven times? Jesus saith unto him, I say not unto thee, Until seven times: but, Until seventy times seven" (Matt. 18:21-22).

†*Peter thought he was being generous here in suggesting a sevenfold forgiveness policy, for the traditional rabbinic teaching required only three times, and that was only in special cases.*

SEVENTY: Christ teaches on the subject of hell (Matt. 18:8-9; Mark 9:43-48; Luke 12:4-5).

A. "Fear the fire."

    1. First illustration— "And if thy hand offend thee, cut it off: it is better for thee to enter into life maimed, than having two hands to go into hell, into the fire that never shall be quenched: Where their worm dieth not, and the fire is not quenched" (Mark 9:43-44).

    2. Second illustration—"And if thy foot offend thee, cut it off: it is better for thee to enter halt into life, than having two feet to be cast into hell, into the fire that never shall be quenched: Where their worm dieth not, and the fire is not quenched" (Mark 9:45-46).

    3. Third illustration—"And if thine eye offend thee, pluck it out: it is better for thee to enter into the kingdom of God with one eye, than having two eyes to be cast into hell fire: Where their worm dieth not, and the fire is not quenched" (Mark 9:47-48).

B. "Fear the Father"—"And I say unto you my friends, Be not afraid of them that kill the body, and after that have no more that they can do. But I will forewarn you whom ye shall fear: Fear him, which after he hath killed hath power to cast into hell; yea, I say unto you, Fear him" (Luke 12:4-5).

SEVENTY-ONE: Christ teaches on the subject of church discipline (Matt. 18:15-20).

A. The procedure involved

    1. First step—"Moreover if thy brother shall trespass against thee, go and tell him his fault between thee and him alone: if he shall hear thee, thou hast gained thy brother" (Matt. 18:15).

    2. Second step—"But if he will not hear thee, then take with thee one or two more, that in the mouth of two or three witnesses every word may be established" (Matt. 18:16).

    3. Third step—"And if he shall neglect to hear them, tell it unto the church" (Matt. 18:17a).

B. The punishment involved—"But if he neglect to hear the church, let him be unto thee as an heathen man and a publican" (Matt. 18:17b).

C. The power involved—"Verily I say unto you, Whatsoever ye shall bind on earth shall be bound in heaven: and whatsoever ye shall loose on earth shall be loosed in heaven" (Matt. 18:18-20).

SEVENTY-TWO: Christ teaches on the subject of divorce (Matt. 19:3-12; Mark 10:2-12).

A. Jesus and his foes

    1. Round One

        a. Their question—"The Pharisees also came unto him, tempting him, and saying unto him, Is it lawful for a man to put away his wife for every cause?" (Matt. 19:3).

---

†*We are told that they came "tempting" him. Here the motive may have been to cause Christ to offend Herod Antipas, as John the Baptist had once done, and thus be arrested.*

---

        b. His answer—"And he answered and said unto them, Have ye not read, that he which made them at the beginning made them male and female, and said, For this cause shall a man leave father and mother, and shall cleave to his wife: and they twain shall be one flesh? Wherefore they are no more twain, but one flesh. What therefore God hath joined together, let not man put asunder" (Matt. 19:4-6).

2. Round Two

    a. Their question—"They say unto him, Why did Moses then command to give a writing of divorcement, and to put her away?" (Matt. 19:7).

    b. His answer—"He saith unto them, Moses because of the hardness of your hearts suffered you to put away your wives: but from the beginning it was not so. And I say unto you, Whosoever shall put away his wife, except it be for fornication, and shall marry another, committeth adultery: and whoso marrieth her which is put away doth commit adultery" (Matt. 19:8-9).

---

† A. *Few topics were more contested in the days of Jesus than the subject of divorce. There were two opposing schools of thought, each headed up by a famous and respected rabbi. They were Shammai and Hillel. The controversy centered around the interpretation of Deuteronomy 24:1-4. "When a man hath taken a wife, and married her, and it come to pass that she find no favour in his eyes, because he hath found some uncleanness in her: then let him write her a bill of divorcement, and give it in her hand, and send her out of his house. And when she is departed out of his house, she may go and be another man's wife. And if the latter husband hate her, and write her a bill of divorcement, and giveth it in her hand, and sendeth her out of his house; or if the latter husband die, which took her to be his wife; her former husband, which sent her away, may not take her again to be his wife, after that she is defiled; for that is abomination before the* LORD: *and thou shalt not cause the land to sin, which the* LORD *thy God giveth thee for an inheritance" (Deut. 24:1-4).*

    1. *The school of Shammai held that the "uncleanness" phrase meant marital unfaithfulness and that this was the only allowable cause for divorce.*

    2. *The school of Hillel emphasized the preceding clause, "She find no favour in his eyes," and would allow a man to divorce his wife if she did anything he disliked—even if she burned his food while cooking it. Our Lord clearly took the side of Shammai (see v. 9), but only after first pointing back to God's original ideal for marriage in Genesis 1:27; 2:24.*

B. *Louis Barbieri offers the following summary: "Bible scholars differ over the meaning of this 'exception clause,' found only in Matthew's Gospel. The word for 'marital unfaithfulness' is* porneia.

    1. *Some feel Jesus used this as a synonym for adultery (*moicheia*). Therefore adultery by either partner in a marriage is the only sufficient grounds for a marriage to end in divorce. Among those holding this view, some believe remarriage is possible but others believe remarriage should never occur.*

    2. *Others define* porneia *as a sexual offense that could occur only in the betrothal period when a Jewish man and woman were considered married but had not yet consummated their coming marriage with sexual intercourse. If in this period the woman was found pregnant (as was Mary; 1:18-19), a divorce could occur in order to break the contract.*

    3. *Still others believe the term* porneia *referred to illegitimate marriages within prohibited degrees of kinship, as in Leviticus 18:6-18. If a man discovered that his wife was a near relative, he would actually be involved in an incestuous marriage. Then this would be justifiable grounds for divorce. Some say this meaning of* porneia *is found in Acts 15:20, 29 (compare 1 Cor. 5:1).*

    4. *Another view is that* porneia *refers to a relentless, persistent, unrepentant life-style of sexual unfaithfulness—different from a one-time act of illicit relations. (In the New Testament* porneia *is broader than* moicheia.*) Such a continued practice would thus be*

the basis for divorce, since such unfaithful and unrelenting conduct would have broken the marriage bond. Whatever view one takes on the exception clause, Jesus obviously affirmed the permanence of marriage." (The Bible Knowledge Commentary, *Victor Books, Wheaton, Ill., 1983, pp. 63-64).*

B. Jesus and his friends
   1. Their confusion—"His disciples say unto him, If the case of the man be so with his wife, it is not good to marry" (Matt. 19:10).
   2. His clarification—"But he said unto them, All men cannot receive this saying, save they to whom it is given. For there are some eunuchs, which were so born from their mother's womb: and there are some eunuchs, which were made eunuchs of men: and there be eunuchs, which have made themselves eunuchs for the kingdom of heaven's sake. He that is able to receive it, let him receive it" (Matt. 19:11-12).
SEVENTY-THREE: Christ teaches on the subject of rewards (Matt. 19:27-30; Mark 10:28-30; Luke 18:28-30)—"Then answered Peter and said unto him, Behold, we have forsaken all, and followed thee; what shall we have therefore?" (Matt. 19:27).
   A. Faithful Christians will rule with Christ—"And Jesus said unto them, Verily I say unto you, That ye which have followed me, in the regeneration when the Son of man shall sit in the throne of his glory, ye also shall sit upon twelve thrones, judging the twelve tribes of Israel" (Matt. 19:28).
   B. Faithful Christians will receive from Christ—"And every one that hath forsaken houses, or brethren, or sisters, or father, or mother, or wife, or children, or lands, for my name's sake, shall receive an hundredfold, and shall inherit everlasting life. But many that are first shall be last; and the last shall be first" (Matt. 19:29-30).
SEVENTY-FOUR: Christ teaches on the subject of faith (Matt. 21:21-22; Mark 11:22-24)—"And Jesus answering saith unto them, Have faith in God. For verily I say unto you, That whosoever shall say unto this mountain, Be thou removed, and be thou cast into the sea; and shall not doubt in his heart, but shall believe that those things which he saith shall come to pass; he shall have whatsoever he saith. Therefore I say unto you, What things soever ye desire, when ye pray, believe that ye receive them, and ye shall have them" (Mark 11:22-24).
SEVENTY-FIVE: Christ attends the feast of tabernacles (John 7:37-39). "In the last day, that great day of the feast, Jesus stood and cried, saying, If any man thirst, let him come unto me, and drink. He that believeth on me, as the scripture hath said, out of his belly shall flow rivers of living water. (But this spake he of the Spirit, which they that believe on him should receive: for the Holy Ghost was not yet given; because that Jesus was not yet glorified)" (John 7:37-39).

---

†*John, of course, does not mean the Holy Spirit was yet to make his first appearance. The truth is, he is seen busily at work in the second verse in the Bible. "And the earth was without form, and void; and darkness was upon the face of the deep. And the Spirit of God moved upon the face of the waters" (Gen. 1:2).*

John was saying that the Holy Spirit had not yet begun his new ministry of gathering out a special spiritual body known as the Church, which he would do at Pentecost (Acts 2) after the Savior had been crucified, resurrected, and ascended, i.e., glorified.

SEVENTY-SIX: Christ attends the feast of dedication (John 10:22-23). "And it was at Jerusalem the feast of the dedication, and it was winter. And Jesus walked in the temple in Solomon's porch" (John 10:22-23).

SEVENTY-SEVEN: Christ relates his overall purpose for coming to earth (Matt. 20:28; Mark 10:45; John 10:10). "Even as the Son of man came not to be ministered unto, but to minister, and to give his life a ransom for many" (Matt. 20:28). "The thief cometh not, but for to steal, and to kill, and to destroy: I am come that they might have life, and that they might have it more abundantly" (John 10:10).

SEVENTY-EIGHT: Christ blesses some little children (Matt. 19:13-15; Mark 10:13-16; Luke 18:15-17).

A. The request of the parents—"Then were there brought unto him little children, that he should put his hands on them, and pray: and the disciples rebuked them" (Matt. 19:13).

B. The rebuke of the disciples—"And they brought young children to him, that he should touch them: and his disciples rebuked those that brought them" (Mark 10:13).

C. The reaction of the Savior—"But when Jesus saw it, he was much displeased, and said unto them, Suffer the little children to come unto me, and forbid them not: for of such is the kingdom of God. . . . And he took them up in his arms, put his hands upon them, and blessed them" (Mark 10:14, 16).

SEVENTY-NINE: Christ is approached by a rich young ruler (Matt. 19:16-26; Mark 10:17-26; Luke 18:18-27). The rich young ruler was confused concerning four things. Jesus corrects all four errors.

A. First confusion and correction
  1. The confusion: concerning the deity of Christ—"There came one running, and kneeled to him, and asked him, Good Master . . . " (Mark 10:17).
  2. The correction—"And Jesus said unto him, Why callest thou me good? there is none good but one, that is, God" (Mark 10:18).

---

†*The rabbis had no room whatsoever in their theology for the idea that the promised Old Testament Messiah would actually be God himself. Thus, Jesus may have been saying, "In light of the fact that God alone is good, are you still willing to call me good Master?"*

B. Second confusion and correction
  1. The confusion: concerning the vanity of works—"What good thing shall I do, that I might have eternal life?" (Matt. 19:16)
  2. The correction—"If thou wilt enter into life, keep the commandments" (Matt. 19:17).
     (Note: Christ then lists five of the Ten Commandments.)
     a. Honor thy father and mother (fifth)
     b. Thou shalt do no murder (sixth)
     c. Thou shalt not commit adultery (seventh)
     d. Thou shalt not steal (eighth)
     e. Thou shalt not bear false witness (ninth)
     He does not, however, list the first commandment (Thou shalt have no other gods before me), nor the tenth (Thou shalt not covet), the very two already broken by the rich young ruler. Apparently Christ wanted him to come to this conclusion himself.

C. Third confusion and correction
   1. The confusion: concerning the depravity of man—"The young man saith unto
      him, All these things have I kept from my youth up: what lack I yet?" (Matt.
      19:20).

---

†*Had he really done this? A case could be made concerning the possibility of observing the first
nine commandments, but only in an outward and external manner. However, no human could
ever even remotely keep the Tenth Commandment, which is an inward law, dealing with the
heart—"Thou shalt not covet" (Exod. 20:17).*

---

   2. The correction—"Jesus said unto him, If thou wilt be perfect, go and sell that
      thou hast, and give to the poor, and thou shalt have treasure in heaven: and
      come and follow me" (Matt. 19:21).
D. Fourth confusion and correction
   1. The confusion: concerning the captivity of riches—"But when the young man
      heard that saying, he went away sorrowful: for he had great possessions"
      (Matt. 19:22).

---

†*A rabbi once visited a miserly old man who was known far and wide for his greed. Pointing out
the window, the rabbi asked him what he saw. "Well," he said, "I see children playing and adults
walking." The rabbi then placed a mirror in front of the old man. "Now," he asked, "what do you
see?" "Oh," replied the man, "I see myself!" In a quiet tone, the rabbi observed: "I have just
shown you two pieces of glass. Concerning the first, you saw people, but concerning the second,
you saw only yourself. The reason you could not see human beings through the second was
because it has been coated with a thin layer of silver."*

---

   2. The correction—"Then said Jesus unto his disciple, Verily I say unto you, That
      a rich man shall hardly enter into the kingdom of heaven. And again I say
      unto you, It is easier for a camel to go through the eye of a needle, than for a
      rich man to enter into the kingdom of God. When his disciples heard it, they
      were exceedingly amazed, saying, Who then can be saved? But Jesus beheld
      them, and said unto them, With men this is impossible; but with God all
      things are possible" (Matt. 19:23-26).

---

†*The "eye of a needle" phrase here is often explained in terms of a small gate in the city wall of
Jerusalem through which, with great difficulty, camel herdsmen would be forced to enter the city
with their animals, after the main gates had closed for the night. There is, however, no evidence
whatsoever to support this claim. The fact is, the Greek word refers to a literal sewing needle.*

EIGHTY: Christ heals blind Bartimaeus (Matt. 20:29-34; Mark 10:46-52; Luke
18:35-43). (Note: For a fuller discussion, see this miracle under the *Topical
Overview*.)

EIGHTY-ONE: Christ saves Zacchaeus (Luke 19:1-10).
A. Zacchaeus the sinner—"And Jesus entered and passed through Jericho. And, behold, there was a man named Zacchaeus, which was the chief among the publicans, and he was rich" (Luke 19:1-2).
B. Zacchaeus the seeker—This man wanted to meet Jesus but had a problem.
  1. The source of his problem—"And he sought to see Jesus who he was; and could not for the press, because he was little of stature" (Luke 19:3).
  2. The solution to his problem—"And he ran before, and climbed up into a sycomore tree to see him: for he was to pass that way" (Luke 19:4).
C. Zacchaeus the saved
  1. The request of the Savior—"And when Jesus came to the place, he looked up, and saw him, and said unto him, Zacchaeus, make haste, and come down; for to day I must abide at thy house" (Luke 19:5).
  2. The response of the publican—"And he made haste, and came down, and received him joyfully" (Luke 19:6).
  3. The reaction of the crowd—"And when they saw it, they all murmured, saying, That he was gone to be guest with a man that is a sinner" (Luke 19:7).
D. Zacchaeus the Spirit-controlled
  1. As witnessed by his own testimony—"And Zacchaeus stood, and said unto the Lord; Behold, Lord, the half of my goods I give to the poor; and if I have taken any thing from any man by false accusation, I restore him fourfold" (Luke 19:8).
  2. As witnessed by Jesus' testimony—"And Jesus said unto him, This day is salvation come to this house, forsomuch as he also is a son of Abraham. For the Son of man is come to seek and to save that which was lost" (Luke 19:9-10).

This marks the end of the Christ's public ministry.

III. The Completion of the Ministry of Christ—We now consider the final forty-eight days our Lord spent upon this earth beginning with his anointing in Bethany and concluding with his ascension from the Mount of Olives. This time period will be summarized as follows:
  First, the eight days from his anointing on Saturday until the sealing of his grave on the following Saturday.
  Second, the forty days from his glorious resurrection until his ascension.

---

†*There are a total of 89 chapters in the four Gospel accounts of Matthew, Mark, Luke, and John. Of these 89, only four record the first 30 years of Jesus' earthly ministry. However, of the remaining 85, no less than 23 describe the final eight days of his life. In other words, as measured by the scriptural space given it, the last week or so of our Lord's ministry was some eight times more important than the first 30 years. These eight "dreadful days of divine destiny" began with a conspiracy by sinners. They would end with a crucifixion for sinners.*

THE EIGHT-DAY PERIOD:
Here we will use the Roman system of reckoning time as employed by the Apostle John (see John 19:14), which begins at both midnight and noon. This, of course, is

our system today. Matthew, Mark, and Luke, however, use the Hebrew system, which begins the new day at 6:00 P.M. (sunset).

Day One: Saturday

ONE: Christ is plotted against by Caiaphas, the high priest. This was the final of two occasions when the wicked Jewish leader conspired to kill Christ.

    A. First occasion (John 11:45-53)

        1. The problem—"Then gathered the chief priests and the Pharisees a council, and said, What do we? for this man doeth many miracles. If we let him thus alone, all men will believe on him: and the Romans shall come and take away both our place and nation" (John 11:47-48).

        2. The prophecy—"And one of them, named Caiaphas, being the high priest that same year, said unto them, Ye know nothing at all, Nor consider that it is expedient for us, that one man should die for the people, and that the whole nation perish not. And this spake he not of himself: but being high priest that year, he prophesied that Jesus should die for that nation; and not for that nation only, but that also he should gather together in one the children of God that were scattered abroad" (John 11:49-52).

---

†*This marks the final prophecy uttered by a high priest of Israel. The* Wycliffe Bible Commentary *observes: "The words, so to speak, were put into his mouth. Here is a Balaam (see Num. 22–24), who would curse Jesus, but out of the prophecy comes the realization of the purpose of God that Christ should die for the nation in a redemptive, vicarious sense, and even for a large group, that all the dispersed children of God (in a prospective sense) would be brought together. How fitting it was that one who filled the office of high priest should unwittingly set forth the work of Christ as the Lamb who takes away sin!" (p. 331). Note also the high priest's fear which prompted this prophecy: "If we let him thus alone, all men will believe on him: and the Romans shall come and take away both our place and nation" (John 11:48). The divine irony of history is, of course, that both things did happen. Men did believe on him and the Romans did come.*

---

        3. The plot—"Then from that day forth they took counsel together for to put him to death" (John 11:53).

    B. Second occasion (Matt. 26:3-5; Mark 14:1-2; Luke 22:2) "Then assembled together the chief priests, and the scribes, and the elders of the people, unto the palace of the high priest, who was called Caiaphas, and consulted that they might take Jesus by subtilty, and kill him. But they said, Not on the feast day, lest there be an uproar among the people" (Matt. 26:3-5).

TWO: Christ is anointed by Mary in the home of Simon the leper (Matt. 26:6-13; Mark 14:3-9; John 12:1-8).

    A. The gift of Mary

        1. Her gift was precious.

            a. The cost involved—"Then took Mary a pound of ointment of spikenard, very costly, and anointed the feet of Jesus, and wiped his feet with her hair: and the house was filled with the odour of the ointment" (John 12:3).

†*This was the only anointing his body would receive. In spite of the many times Christ had warned of his suffering and death (see Matt. 16:21; 20:18-19), apparently the only person to take him seriously was Mary. (See also John 10:11, 17-18.)*

---

      b. The criticism involved—"Then saith one of his disciples, Judas Iscariot, Simon's son, which should betray him, Why was not this ointment sold for three hundred pence, and given to the poor? This he said, not that he cared for the poor; but because he was a thief, and had the bag, and bare what was put therein" (John 12:4-6).

---

†*The 300 pence (denarii) was roughly a year's wages. In present-day finances this would have represented some 20 to 25 thousand dollars. There is a possibility that Mary inherited this, or that it represented her life's savings.*

---

    2. Her gift was prophetical.
      a. In regard to the burial of Christ—"And Jesus said, Let her alone; why trouble ye her? she hath wrought a good work on me. For ye have the poor with you always, and whensoever ye will ye may do them good: but me ye have not always. She hath done what she could: she is come aforehand to anoint my body to the burying" (Mark 14:6-8).
      b. In regard to the body of Christ (the Church)—"Verily I say unto you, Wheresoever this gospel shall be preached in the whole world, there shall also this, that this woman hath done, be told for a memorial of her" (Matt. 26:13).
  B. The gall of Judas
    1. The pretended reason—"Then saith one of his disciples, Judas Iscariot, Simon's son, which should betray him, Why was not this ointment sold for three hundred pence, and given to the poor?" (John 12:4-5).
    2. The perverted reason—"This he said, not that he cared for the poor; but because he was a thief, and had the bag, and bare what was put therein" (John 12:6).
Day Two: Sunday
Christ makes his triumphal entry into Jerusalem (Matt. 21:1-11, 14-17; Mark 11:1-11; Luke 19:29-44).
    ONE: The colt—"And it came to pass, when he was come nigh to Bethphage and Bethany, at the mount called the mount of Olives, he sent two of his disciples, Saying, Go ye into the village over against you; in the which at your entering ye shall find a colt tied, whereon yet never man sat: loose him, and bring him hither. And if any man ask you, Why do ye loose him? thus shall ye say unto him, Because the Lord hath need of him" (Luke 19:29-31). "And they brought the colt to Jesus, and cast their garments on him; and he sat upon him" (Mark 11:7).
    TWO: The crowd—"On the next day much people that were come to the feast, when they heard that Jesus was coming to Jerusalem, took branches of palm trees, and went forth to meet him, and cried, Hosanna: Blessed is the King of Israel that cometh in the name of the Lord" (John 12:12-13).

THREE: The celebration
A. They greeted him with branches of palm trees and stalks cut from the fields (Matt. 21:9; Mark 11:8; John 12:13).
B. They spread their garments in the way (Matt. 21:8; Mark 11:8; Luke 19:36).
FOUR: "Hosanna; Blessed is he that cometh in the name of the Lord" (Mark 11:9). "Hosanna to the son of David . . . Hosanna in the highest" (Matt. 21:9). "Blessed is the kingdom that cometh, the kingdom of our father David" (Mark 11:10).
FIVE: "And some of the Pharisees from among the multitude said unto him, Master, rebuke thy disciples. And he answered and said unto them, I tell you that, if these should hold their peace, the stones would immediately cry out" (Luke 19:39-40).
SIX: The children—"And when the chief priests and scribes saw the wonderful things that he did, and the children crying in the temple, and saying, Hosanna to the Son of David; they were sore displeased, and said unto him, Hearest thou what these say? And Jesus saith unto them, Yea; have ye never read, Out of the mouth of babes and sucklings thou hast perfected praise?" (Matt. 21:15-16).
SEVEN: The Christ
A. Weeping—"And when he was come near, he beheld the city, and wept over it, Saying, If thou hadst known, even thou, at least in this thy day, the things which belong unto thy peace! but now they are hid from thine eyes" (Luke 19:41-42).

---

†The famous Bible student, Sir Robert Anderson, has attached great meaning to the three words, "this thy day." According to the prophecy in Daniel 9:24-27 (often called the 70-week prophecy) God told Daniel he would deal with Israel for yet another 70 "weeks," which is usually interpreted as 490 years. The prophecy continued that after 69 of these "weeks," or 483 years, the Messiah would be "cut off" (rejected and crucified). The prophecy was to start on March 14, 445 B.C. Mr. Anderson suggests that if one begins counting forward from that day, he discovers that the 483 years (173,880 days) runs out on April 6, A.D. 32. It was on this exact day that Jesus rode into Jerusalem on the foal of an ass and, although welcomed by the masses, was officially rejected by Israel's leaders. According to Sir Robert, all this was in mind when our Lord uttered the words of this statement.

B. Warning—"For the days shall come upon thee, that thine enemies shall cast a trench about thee, and compass thee round, and keep thee in on every side, and shall lay thee even with the ground, and thy children within thee; and they shall not leave in thee one stone upon another; because thou knewest not the time of thy visitation" (Luke 19:43-44).
C. Working—"And the blind and the lame came to him in the temple; and he healed them" (Matt. 21:14).

Day Three: Monday
ONE: Christ pronounces judgment upon a fruitless fig tree (Matt. 21:18-19; Mark 11:12-14). Note: For a fuller discussion, see this miracle under the *Topical Overview.*
TWO: Christ performs the second temple cleansing (Matt. 21:12; Mark 11:15-17; Luke 19:45-46).

A. What he did—"And they come to Jerusalem: and Jesus went into the temple, and began to cast out them that sold and bought in the temple, and overthrew the tables of the moneychangers, and the seats of them that sold doves; and would not suffer that any man should carry any vessel through the temple" (Mark 11:15-16).

---

†*John Grassmick observes: "When Jesus arrived in Jerusalem, he went into the temple area, the large outer court of the Gentiles surrounding the inner sacred courts of the temple itself. No Gentile was allowed beyond this outer court. In it the high priest Caiaphas had authorized a market (probably a recent economic innovation) for the sale of ritually pure items necessary for temple sacrifice: wine, oil, salt, approved sacrificial animals and birds. Money from three sources circulated in Palestine in New Testament times: imperial money (Roman), provincial money (Greek), and local money (Jewish). Money changers provided the required Tyrian (Jewish) coinage for the annual half-shekel temple tax (Exod. 30:12-16) required of all male Jews twenty years of age and up. This was in exchange for their Greek and Roman currency, which featured human portraits considered idolatrous. Though a small surcharge was permitted in these transactions, dealings were not free from extortion and fraud. In addition (according to Mark 11:16) people loaded with merchandise were taking shortcuts through this area, making it a thoroughfare from one part of the city to another"* (The Bible Knowledge Commentary, Victor Books, Wheaton, Ill., 1983, p. 157)

B. Why he did it—"And he taught, saying unto them, Is it not written, My house shall be called of all nations the house of prayer? but ye have made it a den of thieves" (Mark 11:17).

---

†*Here Jesus quotes from Jeremiah's sermon delivered some six centuries earlier in the same temple area, condemning Israel for the same thing. "Is this house, which is called by my name, become a den of robbers in your eyes? Behold, even I have seen it, saith the Lord" (Jer. 7:11). Our Lord also refers to a prophecy of Isaiah concerning Gentile people and the temple during the Millennium. "Even them will I bring to my holy mountain, and make them joyful in my house of prayer: their burnt offerings and their sacrifices shall be accepted upon mine altar; for mine house shall be called an house of prayer for all people" (Isa. 56:7).*

THREE: Christ is sought after by some Gentile Greeks (John 12:20).
A. The request from the Greeks—"And there were certain Greeks among them that came up to worship at the feast: The same came therefore to Philip, which was of Bethsaida of Galilee, and desired him, saying, Sir, we would see Jesus. Philip cometh and telleth Andrew: and again Andrew and Philip tell Jesus" (John 12:20-22).
B. The response from the Savior—"And Jesus answered them, saying, The hour is come, that the Son of man should be glorified. Verily, verily, I say unto you, Except a corn of wheat fall into the ground and die, it abideth alone: but if it die, it bringeth forth much fruit. He that loveth his life shall lose it; and he that hateth his life in this world shall keep it unto life eternal. If any man serve me, let him follow me; and where I am, there shall also my servant be: if any man serve me,

him will my Father honour. Now is my soul troubled; and what shall I say? Father, save me from this hour: but for this cause came I unto this hour" (John 12:23-27).

C. The revelation from the Father—"Father, glorify thy name. Then came there a voice from heaven, saying, I have both glorified it, and will glorify it again. The people therefore, that stood by, and heard it, said that it thundered: others said, An angel spake to him" (John 12:28-29).

Day Four: Tuesday

ONE: Christ confronts the Pharisees and Sadducees.

A. Prior confrontations. All throughout his ministry, Christ had tangled with the Pharisees who had constantly attemped to either accuse him or ensnare him.

1. The accusations (prior confrontations)

a. That he violated the Sabbath (Matt. 12:9-12; Luke 14:3, 5; John 5:1-10; 9:1-16)—"Therefore said some of the Pharisees, This man is not of God, because he keepeth not the sabbath day. Others said, How can a man that is a sinner do such miracles? And there was a division among them" (John 9:16).

(1) He had allowed his disciples to pluck grain on the Sabbath (Mark 2:23-28).

(2) He had healed on the Sabbath (Matt. 12:10-12).

b. That he had transgressed the traditions of the Fathers (Mark 7:5-9, 13).

c. That he did not insist upon his disciples observing the many fasts (Mark 2:18-20).

d. That he ate and associated with sinners—"And it came to pass, that, as Jesus sat at meat in his house, many publicans and sinners sat also together with Jesus and his disciples: for there were many, and they followed him. And when the scribes and Pharisees saw him eat with publicans and sinners, they said unto his disciples, How is it that he eateth and drinketh with publicans and sinners? When Jesus heard it, he saith unto them, They that are whole have no need of the physician, but they that are sick: I came not to call the righteous, but sinners to repentance" (Mark 2:15-17).

e. That he was a blasphemer

(1) Because he claimed to forgive sin—"And he entered into a ship, and passed over, and came into his own city. And, behold, they brought to him a man sick of the palsy, lying on a bed: and Jesus seeing their faith said unto the sick of the palsy; Son, be of good cheer; thy sins be forgiven thee. And, behold, certain of the scribes said within them-selves, This man blasphemeth" (Matt. 9:1-3).

(2) Because he claimed to be God—"Then the Jews took up stones again to stone him. Jesus answered them, Many good works have I shewed you from my Father; for which of those works do ye stone me? The Jews answered him, saying, For a good work we stone thee not; but for blasphemy; and because that thou, being a man, makest thyself God" (John 10:31-33).

f. That he was actually energized by Satan himself—"Then was brought unto him one possessed with a devil, blind, and dumb: and he healed him, insomuch that the blind and dumb both spake and saw. But when the Pharisees heard it, they said, This fellow doth not cast out devils, but by Beelzebub the prince of the devils" (Matt. 12:22, 24).

      2. The ensnarements they attempted
         a. Demanding a sign (Matt. 12:38; 16:1)
         b. Asking about divorce (Matt. 19:3)
         c. Bringing the adulterous woman to him (John 8:3)
    B. Tuesday (Passion Week) confrontations
      1. Concerning the source of his authority (Matt. 21:23-27; Mark 11:27-33; Luke 20:1-8)
         a. The demands by the Jewish leaders—"And they come again to Jerusalem: and as he was walking in the temple, there come to him the chief priests, and the scribes, and the elders, and say unto him, By what authority doest thou these things? and who gave thee this authority to do these things?" (Mark 11:27-28).
         b. The defeat of the Jewish leaders—"And Jesus answered and said unto them, I will also ask of you one question, and answer me, and I will tell you by what authority I do these things. The baptism of John, was it from heaven, or of men? answer me. And they reasoned with themselves, saying, If we shall say, From heaven; he will say, Why then did ye not believe him? But if we shall say, Of men; they feared the people: for all men counted John, that he was a prophet indeed. And they answered and said unto Jesus, We cannot tell. And Jesus answering saith unto them, Neither do I tell you by what authority I do these things" (Mark 11:29-33).
      2. Concerning paying tribute to Caesar (Matt. 22:15-22; Mark 12:13-17; Luke 20:20-26)
         a. The deceit of the Jewish leaders—"And they asked him, saying, Master, we know that thou sayest and teachest rightly, neither acceptest thou the person of any, but teachest the way of God truly: Is it lawful for us to give tribute unto Caesar, or no?" (Luke 20:21-22).

---

†*R. C. Foster observes: "Two general types of tribute were paid to Rome: taxes and customs. For the collection of taxes, levied with the assistance of the Sanhedrin throughout the eleven districts of Judaea, the Roman procurator was responsible. Herod Antipas and Philip were responsible for the taxes in their respective tetrarchies. Much of these taxes was spent upon the upkeep of roads, harbors, public buildings, and the governments. The remainder was sent on to Rome. The right to collect customs having been purchased by senatorial corporations in Rome, these taxes were collected by them through the commissioners and the horde of publicans they employed. Customs included export and import duties, bridge and harbor tolls, market taxes, tax on salt and many similar duties. While the system of collection was full of corruption and the publicans notorious for extortion, the Romans in general had a genius for government and maintained their dominions most efficiently. They preserved law and order, permitted remarkable freedom of local rule and worship, and built such highways and buildings as have resisted the march of time in an astonishing way."* (Studies in the Life of Christ, *Baker Books, Grand Rapids, Mich., 1979, p. 1137)*

---

         b. The defeat of the Jewish leaders—"But he perceived their craftiness, and said unto them, Why tempt ye me? Shew me a penny. Whose image and superscription hath it? They answered and said, Caesar's. And he said unto them, Render therefore unto Caesar the things which be Caesar's,

and unto God the things which be God's. And they could not take hold of his words before the people: and they marvelled at his answer, and held their peace" (Luke 20:23-26).
3. Concerning the resurrection (Matt. 22:23-33; Mark 12:18-27; Luke 20:27-40)
   a. Their silly illustration—"Then came to him certain of the Sadducees, which deny that there is any resurrection; and they asked him, saying, Master, Moses wrote unto us, If any man's brother die, having a wife, and he die without children, that his brother should take his wife, and raise up seed unto his brother. There were therefore seven brethren: and the first took a wife, and died without children. And the second took her to wife, and he died childless. And the third took her; and in like manner the seven also: and they left no children, and died. Last of all the woman died also. Therefore in the resurrection whose wife of them is she? for seven had her to wife" (Luke 20:27-33).
   b. His Spirit-anointed answer—"Jesus answered and said unto them, Ye do err, not knowing the Scriptures, nor the power of God" (Matt. 22:29).

---

†*This ignorance of God's Word had always been Israel's problem. The Old Testament prophets often testified of this: "The ox knoweth his owner, and the ass his master's crib: but Israel doth not know, my people doth not consider" (Isa. 1:3). "My people are destroyed for lack of knowledge: because thou hast rejected knowledge, I will also reject thee, that thou shalt be no priest to me: seeing thou hast forgotten the law of thy God, I will also forget thy children" (Hos. 4:6). "Behold, the days come, saith the Lord GOD, that I will send a famine in the land, not a famine of bread, nor a thirst for water, but of hearing the words of the LORD: And they shall wander from sea to sea, and from the north even to the east, they shall run to and fro to seek the word of the LORD, and shall not find it" (Amos 8:11-12).*

---

   (1) They didn't understand the scriptural *fact* of the resurrection—"And as touching the dead, that they rise: have ye not read in the book of Moses, how in the bush God spake unto him, saying, I am the God of Abraham, and the God of Isaac, and the God of Jacob? He is not the God of the dead, but the God of the living: ye therefore do greatly err" (Mark 12:26-27).
   (2) They didn't understand the scriptural *nature* of the resurrection—"For in the resurrection they neither marry, nor are given in marriage, but are as the angels of God in heaven" (Matt. 22:30).
4. Concerning the greatest commandment (Matt. 22:34-40; Mark 12:28-34)—"Master, which is the great commandment in the law? Jesus said unto him, Thou shalt love the Lord thy God with all thy heart, and with all thy soul, and with all thy mind. This is the first and great commandment. And the second is like unto it, Thou shalt love thy neighbour as thyself. On these two commandments hang all the law and the prophets" (Matt. 22:36-40).

---

† *A. Mark records the full statement of Jesus concerning the first great command: "And Jesus answered him, The first of all the commandments is, Hear, O Israel; The Lord our God is one Lord" (Mark 12:99). The "Hear, O Israel" phrase is known as the* shema, *named after the first*

word of Deuteronomy 6:4 in Hebrew which means "hear." The Shema became the Jewish confession of faith, which was recited by pious Jews every morning and evening. To this day it begins every synagogue service.
B. As Jesus stated, the Ten Commandments are aptly summarized by these two statements:
   1. The first statement is vertical in nature, and covers commands 1-4 (Exod. 20:3-11).
   2. The second statement is horizontal in nature, and covers commands 5-10 (Exod. 20:12-17).

---

   5. Concerning the deity of the Messiah (Matt. 22:41-46; Mark 12:35-37; Luke 20:41-44)—"While the Pharisees were gathered together, Jesus asked them, Saying, What think ye of Christ? whose son is he? They say unto him, The Son of David. He saith unto them, How then doth David in spirit call him Lord, saying, The Lord said unto my Lord, Sit thou on my right hand, till I make thine enemies thy footstool? If David then call him Lord, how is he his son? And no man was able to answer him a word, neither durst any man from that day forth ask him any more questions" (Matt. 22:41-46).

---

†Here Jesus quoted from Psalm 110. The New Testament has more references and allusions to this Psalm than to any other Old Testament passage.

TWO: Christ condemns the Pharisees and Sadducees (Matt. 23:1-39; Mark 12:38-40; Luke 20:45-47).
A. Their words and their works were totally unrelated—"Then spake Jesus to the multitude, and to his disciples, Saying, The scribes and the Pharisees sit in Moses' seat: All therefore whatsoever they bid you observe, that observe and do; but do not ye after their works: for they say, and do not" (Matt. 23:1-3).
B. They placed grievous weights of their own vain traditions upon the shoulders of men (23:4).
C. They dressed and performed only for the praise of men.
   1. Wearing fancy prayer boxes (23:5)
   2. Displaying lavish garments (23:5)
   3. Occupying prominent places at feasts and in synagogues (23:6)
   4. Demanding to be addressed by their full titles (23:7)
D. They not only refused to enter into the kingdom of heaven, but stood in the doorway to prevent others from entering (23:13).
E. They cheated poor widows out of their homes (23:14).
F. They repeated long and insincere prayers (23:14).
G. They made converts and taught them their evil ways—"Woe unto you, scribes and Pharisees, hypocrites! for ye compass sea and land to make one proselyte, and when he is made, ye make him twofold more the child of hell than yourselves" (Matt. 23:15).
H. They uttered their oaths of promise with forked tongues (23:16-22).
I. They had, in their legalistic bondage, perverted the very Law of Moses.
   1. In their tithing—"Woe unto you, scribes and Pharisees, hypocrites! for ye pay tithe of mint and anise and cummin, and have omitted the weightier matters of the law, judgment, mercy, and faith: these ought ye to have

done, and not to leave the other undone. Ye blind guides, which strain at a gnat, and swallow a camel" (Matt. 23:23-24).

✝ *A. In their deceitful tithing practices, they had actually done violence to their own parents. Mark records Jesus' word on this: "For Moses said, Honour thy father and thy mother; and, Whoso curseth father or mother, let him die the death: But ye say, If a man shall say to his father or mother, It is Corban, that is to say, a gift, by whatsoever thou mightest be profited by me; he shall be free" (Mark 7:10-11).*

John Grassmick writes: "'Corban' is the Greek (and English) transliteration of a Hebrew term used to refer to a gift devoted to God. It was a dedicatory formula pronounced over money and property donated to the temple and its service by an inviolable vow. Such gifts could only be used for religious purposes. If a son declared that the resources needed to support his aging parents were 'Corban,' then, according to scribal tradition, he was exempt from this command of God, and his parents were legally excluded from any claim on him. The scribes emphasized that his vow was unalterable (cf. Num. 30) and held priority over his family responsibilities. So they no longer let him do anything for his parents." (The Bible Commentary, *Victor Books, Wheaton, Ill., 1983, p. 133)*

Thus, by this despicable method, the wicked Jewish leaders were deliberately violating the Fifth Commandment. Centuries before, Isaiah had written concerning this sad and sordid thing: "Wherefore the Lord said, Forasmuch as this people draw near me with their mouth, and with their lips do honour me, but have removed their heart far from me, and their fear toward me is taught by the precept of men" (Isa. 29:13).

B. Note the phrase, "swallow a camel." The strict Pharisee would carefully strain his drinking water through a cloth to make sure he did not unknowingly swallow a gnat, the smallest of unclean creatures. But, in a figurative sense, by his double standard of life, he would knowingly swallow a camel, one of the largest of unclean creatures.

---

2. In their ritual washings—"Woe unto you, scribes and Pharisees, hypocrites! for ye make clean the outside of the cup and of the platter, but within they are full of extortion and excess. Thou blind Pharisee, cleanse first that which is within the cup and platter, that the outside of them may be clean also" (Matt. 23:25-26).

J. They had polished exteriors, but polluted interiors (23:27-28)—"Woe unto you, scribes and Pharisees, hypocrites! for ye are like unto whited sepulchres, which indeed appear beautiful outward, but are within full of dead men's bones, and of all uncleanness" (Matt. 23:27).

K. They revered the memories of their murderous fathers (23:29-32).

L. They were, in fact, descendants from a race of religious snakes (23:33).

M. They would later kill God's prophets—"Wherefore, behold, I send unto you prophets, and wise men, and scribes: and some of them ye shall kill and crucify; and some of them shall ye scourge in your synagogues, and persecute them from city to city" (Matt. 23:34).

N. They had already killed God's prophets—"That upon you may come all the righteous blood shed upon the earth, from the blood of righteous Abel unto the blood of Zacharias son of Barachias, whom ye slew between the temple and the altar" (Matt. 23:35).

†*Here Jesus summarized the past cruel action of the unsaved Jewish leaders by referring to the first and last Old Testament martyrs. The killing of Abel is recorded in Genesis 4:8, in Scripture's first book; and the killing of Zechariah in 2 Chronicles 24:20-22, the final book of the Hebrew Bible.*

THREE: Christ observes the widow and her mite (Mark 12:41-44; Luke 21:1-4)—"And he looked up, and saw the rich men casting their gifts into the treasury. And he saw also a certain poor widow casting in thither two mites. And he said, Of a truth I say unto you, that this poor widow hath cast in more than they all: For all these have of their abundance cast in unto the offerings of God: but she of her penury hath cast in all the living that she had" (Luke 21:1-4).

FOUR: Christ weeps over Jerusalem for the final time.

A. The pain of the Savior—"O Jerusalem, Jerusalem, thou that killest the prophets, and stonest them which are sent unto thee, how often would I have gathered thy children together, even as a hen gathereth her chickens under her wings, and ye would not!" (Matt. 23:37).

B. The prediction of the Savior—"Behold, your house is left unto you desolate. For I say unto you, Ye shall not see me henceforth, till ye shall say, Blessed is he that cometh in the name of the Lord" (Matt. 23:38-39).

†*Note especially Jesus' reference to "your house" (the temple) here as contrasted to the "my house" statements of John 2:16 and Matthew 21:13. At this point Israel is set aside for the duration of the Church age (see Matt. 21:33-46). Jesus' statement in 23:39 will someday be gloriously fulfilled. "Blessed be he that cometh in the name of the Lord: we have blessed you out of the house of the Lord" (Psa. 118:26).*

FIVE: Christ preaches the Mount Olivet Discourse (Matt. 24:1-51; Mark 13:1-37; Luke 21:5-36). (Note: For a fuller discussion, see this sermon under the *Topical Overview*.)

SIX: Christ relates the parables of the ten virgins, the talents, and the sheep and goats (Matt. 25:1-46). Note: For a fuller discussion, see these parables under the *Topical Overview.*

Day Five: Wednesday

Christ is secretly betrayed by Judas (Matt. 26:14-16; Mark 14:10-11; Luke 22:3-6).

A. The power behind the betrayal—"Then entered Satan into Judas surnamed Iscariot, being of the number of the twelve. And he went his way, and communed with the chief priests and captains, how he might betray him unto them" (Luke 22:3-4).

†*This is the first of two recorded occasions when Satan himself entered into Judas (see also John 13:27). This can be said about no other person in the Bible.*

B. The price for the betrayal—"And said unto them, What will ye give me, and I will deliver him unto you? And they covenanted with him for thirty pieces of silver. And from that time he sought opportunity to betray him" (Matt. 26:15-16).

✝"*Why did Judas offer to betray Jesus? Various suggestions have been made, each of which may contain an element of truth: (1) Judas, the only non-Galilean member of the Twelve, may have responded to the official notice (John 11:57). (2) He was disillusioned by Jesus' failure to establish a political kingdom and his hopes for material gain seemed doomed. (3) His love for money moved him to salvage something for himself. Ultimately he came under satanic control (cf. Luke 22:3; John 13:2, 27). In Judas' life one finds an intriguing combination of divine sovereignty and human responsibility. According to God's plan Jesus must suffer and die (Rev. 13:8); yet Judas, though not compelled to be the traitor, was held responsible for submitting to Satan's directives (cf. Mark 14:21; John 13:27).*" (The Bible Knowledge Commentary, Victor Books, Wheaton, Ill., 1983, p. 175)*

Day Six: Thursday
   ONE: Christ sends Peter and John from Bethany into Jerusalem (Matt. 26:17-19; Mark 14:12-16; Luke 22:7-13).
     A. The messengers—"And he sent Peter and John, saying, Go and prepare us the passover, that we may eat. And they said unto him, Where wilt thou that we prepare?" (Luke 22:8-9).
     B. The man—"And he said unto them, Behold, when ye are entered into the city, there shall a man meet you, bearing a pitcher of water; follow him into the house where he entereth in" (Luke 22:10).
     C. The message—"And ye shall say unto the goodman of the house, The Master saith unto thee, Where is the guestchamber, where I shall eat the passover with my disciples?" (Luke 22:11).

✝*The purpose behind this somewhat strange instruction of Jesus was probably to keep the actual location of the final Passover from Judas as long as possible. Our Lord was, of course, aware of the wicked plot against him.*

     D. The meeting place—"And he shall shew you a large upper room furnished: there make ready. And they went, and found as he had said unto them: and they made ready the passover" (Luke 22:12-13).

✝*This is the first reference to the Upper Room, a place that would become very important in the life of the early church.*
     A. Jesus instituted the Lord's Supper in this room (Luke 22:14-15).
     B. He later appeared here to ten of his apostles on the first Easter Sunday night (John 20:19).
     C. He showed his nail-pierced hands to Thomas a week later (John 20:24-26).
     D. The apostles gathered for both a prayer meeting and a business meeting in this room (Acts 1:12-26).
     E. The Holy Spirit came upon them here (Acts 2:1).

   TWO: Christ meets with his disciples in the Upper Room (Matt. 26:20-35; Mark 14:17-31; Luke 22:14-38; John 13:1-14, 31)—"Now before the feast of the passover, when Jesus knew that his hour was come that he should depart out of this world unto the Father, having loved his own which were in the world, he loved them unto the end" (John 13:1).

A. The Old Covenant meal (the Passover supper)

†*This involved roasting the lamb, setting out the unleavened bread and wine, and preparing bitter herbs along with a sauce made of dried fruit moistened with vinegar and wine and combined with spices.*

1. He shares his heart—"And when the hour was come, he sat down, and the twelve apostles with him. And he said unto them, With desire I have desired to eat this passover with you before I suffer: For I say unto you, I will not any more eat thereof, until it be fulfilled in the kingdom of God" (Luke 22:14-16).
2. He answers their question—"And there was also a strife among them, which of them should be accounted the greatest" (Luke 22:24).
   a. Godless greatness—"And he said unto them, The kings of the Gentiles exercise lordship over them; and they that exercise authority upon them are called benefactors" (Luke 22:25).
   b. Godly greatness—"But ye shall not be so: but he that is greatest among you, let him be as the younger; and he that is chief, as he that doth serve. For whether is greater, he that sitteth at meat, or he that serveth? is not he that sitteth at meat? but I am among you as he that serveth" (Luke 22:26-27).
3. He describes their future roles—"Ye are they which have continued with me in my temptations. And I appoint unto you a kingdom, as my Father hath appointed unto me; That ye may eat and drink at my table in my kingdom, and sit on thrones judging the twelve tribes of Israel" (Luke 22:28-30).
4. He washes their feet (John 13:4-17)—"He riseth from supper, and laid aside his garments; and took a towel, and girded himself. After that he poureth water into a bason, and began to wash the disciples' feet, and to wipe them with the towel wherewith he was girded" (John 13:4-5).
   a. Simon Peter, lagging behind in the will of God—"Peter saith unto him, Thou shalt never wash my feet. Jesus answered him, If I wash thee not, thou hast no part with me" (John 13:8).
   b. Simon Peter, lunging ahead in the will of God—"Simon Peter saith unto him, Lord, not my feet only, but also my hands and my head. Jesus saith to him, He that is washed needeth not save to wash his feet, but is clean every whit: and ye are clean, but not all" (John 13:9-10).
5. He announces his betrayal (Matt. 26:21-22; Mark 14:18-21; Luke 22:21-22; John 13:18-21).
   a. The horror of the eleven (Matt. 26:22; Mark 14:19; Luke 22:23; John 13:22)—"And as they did eat, he said, Verily I say unto you, that one of you shall betray me. And they were exceeding sorrowful, and began every one of them to say unto him, Lord, is it I?" (Matt. 26:21-22)

†*To their credit, they did not say, "Lord, is it such and such?" or "Lord, I'm sure I know who it is."*

   b. The hypocrisy of the one—"Then Judas, which betrayed him, answered and said, Master, is it I? He said unto him, Thou hast said" (Matt. 26:25).

†Here Judas called Jesus "Rabbi" (Master), and not "Lord," as did the other apostles in the Upper Room.

      c. The hint by the Savior (Matt. 26:23-24; Mark 14:20-21; John 13:23-26a)—"And he answered and said unto them, It is one of the twelve, that dippeth with me in the dish" (Mark 14:20).
    6. He dips the sop with Judas
      a. The confirmation—"Jesus answered, He it is, to whom I shall give a sop, when I have dipped it. And when he had dipped the sop, he gave it to Judas Iscariot, the son of Simon" (John 13:26).

†Apparently Judas had played his deceitful role so well that the eleven still did not realize he was the traitor, in spite of Christ's obvious statement.

      b. The command—"And after the sop Satan entered into him. Then said Jesus unto him, That thou doest, do quickly. . . . He then having received the sop went immediately out: and it was night" (John 13:27, 30).
      c. The confusion—"Now no man at the table knew for what intent he spake this unto him. For some of them thought, because Judas had the bag, that Jesus had said unto him, Buy those things that we have need of against the feast; or, that he should give something to the poor" (John 13:28-29).
   B. The New Covenant meal (the Lord's table)
    1. The death of Christ predicted (Matt. 26:31-35; Mark 14:27-31; Luke 22:31-38; John 13:36-38).
      a. The shepherd would be smitten.
      b. The sheep would be scattered—"Then saith Jesus unto them, All ye shall be offended because of me this night: for it is written, I will smite the shepherd, and the sheep of the flock shall be scattered abroad. But after I am risen again, I will go before you into Galilee" (Matt. 26:31-32).
      c. The spokesman would be shamed—"But Peter said unto him, Although all shall be offended, yet will not I. And Jesus saith unto him, Verily I say unto thee, That this day, even in this night, before the cock crow twice, thou shalt deny me thrice. But he spake the more vehemently, If I should die with thee, I will not deny thee in any wise. Likewise also said they all" (Mark 14:29-31). "And the Lord said, Simon, Simon, behold, Satan hath desired to have you, that he may sift you as wheat: But I have prayed for thee, that thy faith fail not: and when thou art converted, strengthen thy brethren" (Luke 22:31-32).

†The devil once requested permission from God to test and torment another choice servant of God, Job (see Job 1–2). Here Satan apparently asked for the same power over Simon Peter. The apostle may have had this very event in mind when he wrote concerning the devil and the believer in one of his epistles. (See 1 Pet. 5:7-11.) At any rate, it should be a great comfort for all believers to know that the resurrected Savior is, even today, at this very moment, praying for them in glory. (See Rom. 8:34; 1 John 2:1; Heb. 7:25; 9:24.)

2. The death of Christ pictured (Matt. 26:26-29; Mark 14:22-25; Luke 22:17-20;
1 Cor. 11:23-26)
 a. The bread, a symbol for his broken body—"And he took bread, and gave
 thanks, and brake it, and gave unto them, saying, This is my body which is
 given for you: this do in remembrance of me" (Luke 22:19).
 b. The cup, a symbol for his shed blood—"And he took the cup, and gave
 thanks, and gave it to them, saying, Drink ye all of it; For this is my blood
 of the new testament, which is shed for many for the remission of sins"
 (Matt. 26:27-28).
THREE: Christ preaches his sermon on the Father's house (John 14:1-31)—"Let
not your heart be troubled: ye believe in God, believe also in me. In my
Father's house are many mansions: if it were not so, I would have told you.
I go to prepare a place for you. And if I go and prepare a place for you, I
will come again, and receive you unto myself; that where I am, there ye may
be also. . . . But that the world may know that I love the Father; and as the
Father gave me commandment, even so I do. Arise, let us go hence" (John
14:1-3, 31). (Note: For a fuller discussion, see this sermon under the *Topical
Overview.*)
Day Seven: Friday
ONE: Christ preaches his sermon on fruitbearing, en route to the Mount of Olives
(John 15–16)—"And when they had sung an hymn, they went out into the
mount of Olives" (Matt. 26:30).

---

†*Six Psalms are called the "Hallel" Psalms. These are: 113, 114, 115, 116, 117, and 118. All of
these were to be sung on the eve of the Passover. This is what Jesus and the disciples sang. Note
some of the verses in these Psalms: "The sorrows of death compassed me, and the pains of hell gat
hold upon me: I found trouble and sorrow" (116:3). "I will take the cup of salvation, and call
upon the name of the Lord" (116:13). "The stone which the builders refused is become the head
stone of the corner. This is the Lord's doing; it is marvelous in our eyes. This is the day which the
Lord hath made; we will rejoice and be glad in it" (118:22-24). "Blessed is he that cometh in the
name of the Lord . . ." (118:26).*

(Note: For a fuller discussion, see this sermon under the *Topical Overview.*) "And he came
out, and went, as he was wont, to the mount of Olives; and his disciples also followed
him" (Luke 22:39).
TWO: Christ prays his great high priestly prayer at the Mount of Olives (John 17).

---

† *A. Question: Where in the New Testament is the Lord's Prayer recorded, and what does it say?
B. Answer: Many Christians would mistakenly turn to Matthew 6 and begin reading those
familiar words: "Our Father which art in heaven, Hallowed be thy name" (Matt. 6:9).
However, this is not the Lord's Prayer, but rather the Disciples' Prayer. In reality, the Lord's
Prayer is found here in John 17. In this prayer, our great High Priest prays for himself, for his
apostles, and for his Church.*

A. His prayer for himself (17:1-5)
 1. The reminder—"Father, the hour is come" (John 17:1).

†*During his prayer, Jesus refers to God as "Father" on six occasions (17:1, 5, 11, 21, 24, and 25). This awesome title is extremely rare in the Old Testament. Our Lord is the first to use it in the New Testament. In fact, he employs two titles found only in this prayer. They are:*
  A. Holy Father (17:11)
  B. Righteous Father (17:25)

2. The report
  a. I have given eternal life to those you gave to me (17:2).
  b. I have glorified you on earth (17:4).
  c. I have finished the work you gave me to do (17:4).
3. The request
  a. "And now, O Father, glorify thou me with thine own self with the glory which I had with thee before the world was" (17:5).

†*The request of Jesus here to receive glory is absolute proof of his deity, when compared with Isaiah's statement: "I am the Lord: that is my name: and my glory will I not give to another, neither my praise to graven images" (Isa. 42:8). Did the Father hear and answer this request? Note Jesus' previous testimony along this line: "Then they took away the stone from the place where the dead was laid. And Jesus lifted up his eyes, and said, Father, I thank thee that thou hast heard me. And I knew that thou hearest me always: but because of the people which stand by I said it, that they may believe that thou hast sent me" (John 11:41-42).*

  b. Allow me to glorify you (17:1).
B. His prayer for his disciples (17:6-19)—"I pray for them: I pray not for the world, but for them which thou hast given me for they are thine" (John 17:9).

†*Our Lord prayed (and prays) constantly for his own.*
  A. He prayed before he chose them. "And it came to pass in those days, that he went out into a mountain to pray, and continued all night in prayer to God. And when it was day, he called unto him his disciples: and of them he chose twelve, whom also he named apostles" (Luke 6:12-13).
  B. He prayed for them during his ministry. "And when he had sent the multitudes away, he went up into a mountain apart to pray: and when the evening was come, he was there alone. And in the fourth watch of the night Jesus went unto them, walking on the sea" (Matt. 14:23, 25).
  C. He prayed for them at the end of his ministry (John 17:9).
  D. He now prays for them (and all believers) in heaven. "Who is he that condemneth? It is Christ that died, yea rather, that is risen again, who is even at the right hand of God, who also maketh intercession for us" (Rom. 8:34). "Wherefore he is able also to save them to the uttermost that come unto God by him, seeing he ever liveth to make intercession for them" (Heb. 7:25).

1. What the Son had already done
  a. He had declared the Father's name to them (17:6).

     b. He had declared the Father's word to them (17:8, 14).

     c. He had kept them—"While I was with them in the world, I kept them in thy name: those that thou gavest me I have kept, and none of them is lost, but the son of perdition; that the scripture might be fulfilled" (John 17:12).

     d. He had sent them into the world (17:18).

     e. He had set himself apart for them (17:14).

    2. What the Father should do

     a. Preserve them (17:11)

     b. Unify them (17:11)

     c. Protect them (17:16)

     d. Sanctify them (17:17)

C. His prayer for the Church (17:20-26)—"Neither pray I for these alone, but for them also which shall believe on me through their word" (John 17:20).

    1. That the Church might be spiritually united (17:21-22)

    2. That the Church might be spiritually mature (17:23)

    3. That the Church might behold his glory (17:24)

THREE: Christ arrives in the Garden of Gethsemane (Matt. 26:36-56; Mark 14:32-52; Luke 22:39-53; John 18:1-12)

✝ *A. This marks the second of two severe periods of mental strain, suffering, and satanic stress in the life of Jesus.*

    1. The first occurred in the wilderness of Judea (Matt. 4:1).

    2. The second now occurs in the Garden of Gethsemane.

B. The book of Hebrews summarizes both periods.

    1. The wilderness of Judea—"For we have not an high priest which cannot be touched with the feeling of our infirmities; but was in all points tempted like as we are, yet without sin" (Heb. 4:15).

    2. The Garden of Gethsemane—"Who in the days of his flesh, when he had offered up prayers and supplications with strong crying and tears unto him that was able to save him from death, and was heard in that he feared" (Heb. 5:7).

    "When Jesus had spoken these words, he went forth with his disciples over the brook Cedron, where was a garden, into the which he entered, and his disciples" (John 18:1).

✝ *C. A number of striking similarities can be seen at this point in the lives of David and Jesus.*

    1. Both crossed the brook Kedron in the hour of personal crisis (2 Sam. 15:23; John 18:1).

    2. Both would leave the city of Jerusalem rejected by its citizens (2 Sam. 15:13: John 1:11).

    3. Both would be betrayed by a close friend (2 Sam. 15:31; Matt. 26:14-16).

    4. Both of their traitors would later hang themselves (2 Sam. 17:23; Matt. 27:3-5).

    5. Both would weep over all of this (2 Sam. 15:23, 30; Luke 19:41).

    6. Both would climb the Mount of Olives and pray (2 Sam. 15:30-32; Matt. 26:30; John 17:1-26).

    7. Both would condemn the use of a sword by a follower to defend them (2 Sam. 16:9-12; Matt. 26:51-53; John 18:10-11).

    8. Both would forgive their tormentors (2 Sam. 16:5-13; 19:18-23; Luke 23:34).

9. Both would be victorious over their enemies (2 Sam. 18:6-8; Rev. 19:11-21).
10. Both would return in triumph to Jerusalem (2 Sam. 19:8-9, 15, 25; Rev. 21:1-4).

A. The agony
  1. First ordeal
    a. He asks Peter, James, and John to watch and pray with him (Matt. 26:36-37).
    b. He is suddenly attacked by the combined forces of hell—"And he taketh with him Peter and James and John, and began to be sore amazed, and to be very heavy; and saith unto them, My soul is exceeding sorrowful unto death: tarry ye here, and watch" (Mark 14:33-34).

† A. *Many artists and songwriters have depicted this prayer for us, and their descriptions usually show a hushed and tranquil scene, with the light from heaven falling upon a kneeling Savior, his hands clasped devoutly in front, his eyes cast heavenward, and his lips moving faintly as he prays his "cup of suffering" prayer. All is silent, subdued, and serene. But this is not the biblical account at all. The careful student can almost hear the shrieks of demons and the crackling flames which filled the gentle Garden of Gethsemane that awful night. Notice our Lord's own description of his feelings during that hour. He says he was:*
  1. *"Sore amazed"—that is, he was suddenly struck with surprised terror (Mark 14:33).*
  2. *"Very heavy"—that is, he experienced the totally unfamiliar, which bore down upon his soul and filled it with uncertainty and acute distress (suggested exegesis here by the late Kenneth S. Wuest, a Greek professor at Moody Bible Institute).*
  3. *"Exceeding sorrowful unto death"—that is, he was so completely surrounded and encircled by grief that it threatened his very life. From all this it becomes evident that the devil made an all-out effort to murder the Savior in the garden in order to prevent his blood being shed a few hours later on the cross. Our Lord realized this and responded accordingly, as we are told in Hebrews 5:7: "Who in the days of his flesh, when he had offered up prayers and supplications with strong crying and tears unto him that was able to save him from death, and was heard in that he feared."*
 B. *The Father heard his cry for aid and sent angels to strengthen him. (See Luke 22:43.) We are told that he wrestled his way through three prayer sessions in the garden, and he referred to the "cup" during each prayer. What was this cup his soul so dreaded to drink from? Some say it was the cup of human suffering, but our Lord was no stranger to suffering and pain, for he had known these things throughout his ministry. Others claim it was the cup of physical death that our Lord abhorred here. But again, it must be realized that he was the Prince of life, and therefore, death would hold no terror for him.*
 C. *What then was the nature of this cursed cup? We are not left groping in the dark here, for the Scriptures plainly inform us that the Gethsemane cup was filled with the sins of all humanity. Our Lord looked deeply into the cesspool of human sin that dark night and groaned as he smelled its foul odor and viewed the rising poisonous fumes. Was there no other way to redeem humanity than by drinking this corrupt cup? There was no other way. In a few short hours he would drain that container of its last bitter drop of human depravity. Hebrews 2:9: "But we see Jesus, who was made a little lower than the angels for the suffering of death, crowned with glory and honour; that he by the grace of God should taste death for every man." (See also Isa. 53; Rom. 4:25; 1 Pet. 2:24; 3:18; 2 Cor. 5:21.)*

      c. He prays his first prayer—"And he went forward a little, and fell on the ground, and prayed that, if it were possible, the hour might pass from him. And he said, Abba, Father, all things are possible unto thee; take away this cup from me: nevertheless not what I will, but what thou wilt" (Mark 14:35-36).

✝ *A. The double title, "Abba, Father," used by Christ here occurs only two other times in the Bible. Abba was the common way young Jewish children addressed their fathers. It conveyed a sense of intimacy and familiarity. Because of the marvelous work of redemption our blessed Lord would accomplish on the cross, the most humble believer could actually refer to the infinite, omnipresent, omniscient, omnipotent, and eternal Creator of the universe as . . ."Abba, Father." The last stanza of Charles Wesley's great hymn, "Arise My Soul, Arise," summarizes this beautiful theological truth: "To God, I'm reconciled./ His pardoning voice I hear;/ He owns me for his child—/ I can no longer fear:/ with confidence I now draw nigh, and 'Father, Abba, Father' cry!"*

  B. This is the first of three "Not my will, but thy will be done" prayers that Jesus would offer up in Gethsemane (see Matt. 26:39, 42, 44). Contrast this submissive will of Christ to that self-centered will of Lucifer. "How art thou fallen from heaven, O Lucifer, son of the morning! how art thou cut down to the ground, which didst weaken the nations! For thou hast said in thine heart, I will ascend into heaven, I will exalt my throne above the stars of God: I will sit also upon the mount of the congregation, in the sides of the north: I will ascend above the heights of the clouds; I will be like the most High" (Isa. 14:12-14). Consider the awesome significance of those four words, "Thy will be done."

    1. If a repentant sinner says them to God, they result in heaven.

    2. If God says them to an unrepentant sinner, they result in hell.

---

      d. He returns to the trio—"And he cometh, and findeth them sleeping, and saith unto Peter, Simon, sleepest thou? couldest not thou watch one hour? Watch ye and pray, lest ye enter into temptation. The spirit truly is ready, but the flesh is weak" (Mark 14:37-38).

    2. Second ordeal

      a. He prays his second prayer—"He went away again the second time, and prayed, saying, O my Father, if this cup may not pass away from me, except I drink it, thy will be done" (Matt. 26:42).

      b. He returns to find the three men asleep again (Mark 14:40).

    3. Third ordeal

      a. He prays his third prayer—"And he came and found them asleep again: for their eyes were heavy. And he left them, and went away again, and prayed the third time, saying the same words" (Matt. 26:43-44).

      b. He returns to awake the slumbering disciples again—"And he cometh the third time, and saith unto them, Sleep on now, and take your rest: it is enough, the hour is come; behold, the Son of man is betrayed into the hands of sinners. Rise up, let us go; lo, he that betrayeth me is at hand" (Mark 14:41-42).

  B. The arrest

    1. The traitor—"And Judas also, which betrayed him, knew the place: for Jesus ofttimes resorted thither with his disciples. Judas then, having received

a band of men and officers from the chief priests and Pharisees, cometh thither with lanterns and torches and weapons" (John 18:2-3). "Now he that betrayed him gave them a sign, saying, Whomsoever I shall kiss, that same is he: hold him fast. And forthwith he came to Jesus, and said, Hail, master; and kissed him. And Jesus said unto him, Friend, wherefore art thou come? Then came they, and laid hands on Jesus, and took him" (Matt. 26:48-50).

†*This is the final of three biblical kisses of deceit.*
    A. *Jacob kissed Isaac (Gen. 27:26-27).*
    B. *Joab kissed Amasa (2 Sam. 20:9).*
    C. *Judas kissed Jesus.*

    2. The mutilator—"Then Simon Peter having a sword drew it, and smote the high priest's servant, and cut off his right ear. The servant's name was Malchus" (John 18:10). "Then said Jesus unto him, Put up again thy sword into his place: for all they that take the sword shall perish with the sword. Thinkest thou that I cannot now pray to my Father, and he shall presently give me more than twelve legions of angels?" (Matt. 26:52-53).
    3. The conciliator—"And Jesus answered and said, Suffer ye thus far. And he touched his ear, and healed him" (Luke 22:51).
  C. The abandonment
    1. Abandoned by the eleven—"But all this was done, that the scriptures of the prophets might be fulfilled. Then all the disciples forsook him, and fled" (Matt. 26:56).
    2. Abandoned by a young man—"And there followed him a certain young man, having a linen cloth cast about his naked body; and the young men laid hold on him: and he left the linen cloth, and fled from them naked" (Mark 14:51-52).

†*Many Bible students believe that this young man was John Mark, who accompanied Paul during his first missionary journey and later wrote the Gospel of Mark.*

  FOUR: Christ suffers his first unfair trial—The appearance before Annas (John 18:12-14, 19-23)
  A. He was scrutinized—"Then the band and the captain and officers of the Jews took Jesus, and bound him, and led him away to Annas first; for he was father in law to Caiaphas, which was the high priest that same year. . . . The high priest then asked Jesus of his disciples, and of his doctrine. Jesus answered him, I spake openly to the world; I ever taught in the synagogue, and in the temple, whither the Jews always resort; and in secret have I said nothing" (John 18:12-13, 19-20).
  B. He was slapped—"And when he had thus spoken, one of the officers which stood by struck Jesus with the palm of his hand, saying, Answerest thou the high priest so?" (John 18:22).
  FIVE: Christ suffers his second unfair trial—The appearance before Caiaphas (Matt. 26:57, 59-68; Mark 14:53-65; Luke 22:54, 63-65; John 18:24).

A. The falsification—"And they that had laid hold on Jesus led him away to Caiaphas the high priest, where the scribes and the elders were assembled" (Matt. 26:57).
  1. The depravity of the leaders—"Now the chief priests, and elders, and all the council, sought false witness against Jesus, to put him to death" (Matt. 26:59).
  2. The distortion of the liars—"But found none: yea, though many false witnesses came, yet found they none. At the last came two false witnesses, and said, This fellow said, I am able to destroy the temple of God, and to build it in three days" (Matt. 26:60-61).

B. The affirmation
  1. "Are you the Christ?"—"But Jesus held his peace. And the high priest answered and said unto him, I adjure thee by the living God, that thou tell us whether thou be the Christ, the Son of God" (Matt. 26:63).
  2. "I am the Christ"—"Jesus saith unto him, Thou hast said: nevertheless I say unto you, Hereafter shall ye see the Son of man sitting on the right hand of power, and coming in the clouds of heaven" (Matt. 26:64).

---

†*Jesus both warned his foes and promised his friends that he would come again. Compare this passage with John 14:1-3.*

C. The condemnation—"Then the high priest rent his clothes, saying, He hath spoken blasphemy; what further need have we of witnesses? behold, now ye have heard his blasphemy. What think ye? They answered and said, He is guilty of death" (Matt. 26:65-66).

---

†*The high priest was forbidden to do this under the Mosaic Law. "And he that is the high priest among his brethren, upon whose head the anointing oil was poured, and that is consecrated to put on the garments, shall not uncover his head, nor rend his clothes" (Lev. 21:10).*

D. The vilification—"And the men that held Jesus mocked him, and smote him" (Luke 22:63). "And when they had blindfolded him, they struck him on the face, and asked him, saying, Prophesy, who is it that smote thee?" (Luke 22:64). "Then did they spit in his face, and buffeted him; and others smote him with the palms of their hands, Saying, Prophesy unto us, thou Christ, Who is he that smote thee?" (Matt. 26:67-68). "And many other things blasphemously spake they against him" (Luke 22:65).

---

† *A. To spit in one's face was considered by the Jews to be an act of total repudiation and gross personal insult.*
  1. A person was considered disgraced for seven days after having his face spit upon (Num. 12:14).
  2. Job's enemies showed their utter contempt for the suffering patriarch by spitting in his face (Job 30:10).

3. *The Savior himself had predicted all this through the prophet Isaiah some seven centuries before it actually happened. "I gave my back to the smiters, and my cheeks to them that plucked off the hair: I hid not my face from shame and spitting" (Isa. 50:6).*
B. *After being blindfolded, they demanded that he tell them who struck him. This reflected a traditional test of messianic status based on a rabbinic interpretation of Isaiah 11:2-4. According to this view the true Messiah could know who was hitting him even though blindfolded.*

SIX: Christ is denied by Simon Peter (Matt. 26:58, 69-75; Mark 14:54, 66-72; Luke 22:54-62; John 18:15-18, 25-27). (Note: An exact chronological arrangement of these denials is impossible. In fact, it has even been suggested that Peter denied his Lord not three times on one occasion, but six times on two occasions, and that Christ predicted both events.)
A. The first warning
  1. Place: The Upper Room
  2. Prophecy: That Peter would deny Christ three times before the cock crowed at all. See John 13:38; Luke 22:34.
B. The second warning
  1. Place: On the way to Gethsemane
  2. Prophecy: That Peter would deny Christ three times before the cock crowed twice. See Mark 14:30.
Whatever the chronology, note the characters, the charges, the concealment, and the contrition in this sordid account.
A. The characters
  1. Peter and John
    a. John went inside—"And Simon Peter followed Jesus, and so did another disciple: that disciple was known unto the high priest, and went in with Jesus into the palace of the high priest" (John 18:15).
    b. Peter waited outside—"But Peter stood at the door without. Then went out that other disciple, which was known unto the high priest, and spake unto her that kept the door, and brought in Peter" (John 18:16).
  2. Several servant maids
  3. Some officers
  4. A kinsman of Malchus
B. The charges
  1. "Then saith the damsel that kept the door unto Peter, Art not thou also one of this man's disciples?" (John 18:17).
  2. "And thou also wast with Jesus of Nazareth" (Mark 14:67b).
  3. "Thou art one of them: for thou art a Galilean, and thy speech agreeth thereto" (Mark 14:70b).
  4. "One of the servants of the high priest, being his kinsman whose ear Peter cut off, saith, Did not I see thee in the garden with him?" (John 18:26).
C. The concealment
  1. "I know not, neither understand I what thou sayest" (Mark 14:68).
  2. "Woman, I know him not" (Luke 22:57).
  3. "Man, I know not what thou sayest" (Luke 22:60).

4. "But he began to curse and to swear, saying, I know not this man of whom ye speak" (Mark 14:71).

D. The contrite

    1. The lie of Peter—"And Peter said, Man, I know not what thou sayest. And immediately, while he yet spake, the cock crew" (Luke 22:60).

    2. The look of Jesus—"And the Lord turned, and looked upon Peter. And Peter remembered the word of the Lord, how he had said unto him, Before the cock crow, thou shalt deny me thrice. And Peter went out, and wept bitterly" (Luke 22:61-62).

---

† *A. The Shakespearean character Juliet once said, "What's in a name?" Here we could rephrase it to read, "What's in a look?" The Lord turned and looked upon Peter. Apparently he had also heard the awful cursing and denials. Peter was stricken in his thoughts and went out, weeping bitterly. It is not our sin that causes us to weep. It is rather seeing the Savior that we have sinned against that causes our tears.*

    B. Note the phrase, "Peter . . . wept bitterly." It is indeed a fact—you can't judge a book by its cover. Imagine yourself in the vicinity of the Garden of Gethsemane on a warm April night some two thousand years ago. As you watch, a man walks up to Jesus and begins kissing him. You would probably conclude, "How this man must love the Master!" Shortly after this you would be shocked to hear another man bitterly cursing Christ. Your conclusions about this would be, "How this man must hate the Master!" But both times you would be wrong. Judas, the man who kissed Christ, really hated him, and Peter, the one who cursed him, really loved him.

SEVEN: Christ suffers his third unfair trial—The appearance before the Sanhedrin (Matt. 27:1; Mark 15:1; Luke 22:66-71). "When the morning was come, all the chief priests and elders of the people took counsel against Jesus to put him to death" (Matt. 27:1). "Then said they all, Art thou then the Son of God? And he said unto them, Ye say that I am. And they said, What need we any further witness? for we ourselves have heard of his own mouth" (Luke 22:70-71).

EIGHT: Christ's betrayer shows remorse and commits suicide (Matt. 27:3-10; Acts 1:18-19).

A. The peddler of blood

    1. His despair—"Then Judas, which had betrayed him, when he saw that he was condemned, repented himself, and brought again the thirty pieces of silver to the chief priests and elders, Saying, I have sinned in that I have betrayed the innocent blood. And they said, What is that to us? see thou to that" (Matt. 27:3-4).

    2. His destruction

        a. The nature of the act—"And he cast down the pieces of silver in the temple, and departed, and went and hanged himself" (Matt. 27:5).

        b. The results of the act—"Now this man purchased a field with the reward of iniquity; and falling headlong, he burst asunder in the midst, and all his bowels gushed out" (Acts 1:18).

B. The parcel of blood

    1. The dilemma of the priests—"And the chief priests took the silver pieces, and said, It is not lawful for to put them into the treasury, because it is the price of blood" (Matt. 27:6).

2. The decision of the priests—"And they took counsel, and bought with them the potter's field, to bury strangers in. Wherefore that field was called, The field of blood, unto this day" (Matt. 27:7-8).

NINE: Christ suffers his fourth unfair trial—The first appearance before Pilate (Matt. 27:2, 11-14; Mark 15:1-5; Luke 23:1-5; John 18:28-38).

A. Round one: Pilate and the Jews (Matt. 27:2; Mark 15:1; Luke 23:1-2; John 18:28-32)
   1. The lawlessness of the Jewish leaders
      a. Their hypocrisy—"Then led they Jesus from Caiaphas unto the hall of judgment: and it was early; and they themselves went not into the judgment hall, lest they should be defiled; but that they might eat the passover" (John 18:28).
      b. Their haughtiness—"Pilate then went out unto them, and said, What accusation bring ye against this man? They answered and said unto him, If he were not a malefactor, we would not have delivered him up unto thee. Then said Pilate unto them, Take ye him, and judge him according to your law. The Jews therefore said unto him, It is not lawful for us to put any man to death" (John 18:29-31).
   2. The lies of the Jewish leaders—"And they began to accuse him, saying, We found this fellow perverting the nation, and forbidding to give tribute to Caesar, saying that he himself is Christ a King" (Luke 23:2).

B. Round two: Pilate and Jesus (Matt. 27:11-14; Mark 15:2-5; Luke 23:3; John 18:33-38a)
   1. Pilate learns about the King—"Then Pilate entered into the judgment hall again, and called Jesus, and said unto him, Art thou the King of the Jews? Jesus answered him, Sayest thou this thing of thyself, or did others tell it thee of me? Pilate answered, Am I a Jew? Thine own nation and the chief priests have delivered thee unto me: what hast thou done?" (John 18:33-35).
   2. Pilate learns about the kingdom—"Jesus answered, My kingdom is not of this world: if my kingdom were of this world, then would my servants fight, that I should not be delivered to the Jews: but now is my kingdom not from hence. Pilate therefore said unto him, Art thou a king then? Jesus answered, Thou sayest that I am a king. To this end was I born, and for this cause came I into the world, that I should bear witness unto the truth. Every one that is of the truth heareth my voice. Pilate saith unto him, What is truth?" (John 18:36-38a)

---

†*This is undoubtedly the second most important and profound question in all the Bible—indeed, in all of history.*
   A. The first was asked by a frightened Philippian jailor: "Sirs, what must I do to be saved?" (Acts 16:30).
   B. The second was asked by a frustrated Roman governor: "What is truth?" The tragedy here is that while the jailor awaited his answer and was saved (Acts 16:31), the governor impatiently walked out and was lost.

C. Round three: Pilate and the Jews (Luke 23:4-5; John 18:38b)—"Then said Pilate to the chief priests and to the people, I find no fault in this man. And they were the more fierce, saying, He stirreth up the people, teaching throughout all Jewry, beginning from Galilee to this place" (Luke 23:4-5).

TEN: Christ suffers his fifth unfair trial—The appearance before Herod Antipas (Luke 23:6-12). "At that time Herod the tetrarch heard of the fame of Jesus" (Matt. 14:1-2).

A. The desire of Herod (Luke 23:6-9)—"When Pilate heard of Galilee, he asked whether the man were a Galilaean. And as soon as he knew that he belonged unto Herod's jurisdiction, he sent him to Herod, who himself also was at Jerusalem at that time. And when Herod saw Jesus, he was exceeding glad: for he was desirous to see him of a long season, because he had heard many things of him; and he hoped to have seen some miracle done by him. Then he questioned with him in many words; but he answered him nothing" (Luke 23:6-9).

B. The derision by Herod (Luke 23:10-12)
 1. The ridicule—"And the chief priests and scribes stood and vehemently accused him. And Herod with his men of war set him at nought, and mocked him, and arrayed him in a gorgeous robe, and sent him again to Pilate" (Luke 23:10-11).
 2. The reconciliation—"And the same day Pilate and Herod were made friends together: for before they were at enmity between themselves" (Luke 23:12).

ELEVEN: Christ suffers his sixth unfair trial—The final appearance before Pilate (Matt. 27:15-26; Mark 15:6-15; Luke 23:13-25; John 18:39–19:16).

A. The selection of a murderer—"Now at that feast he released unto them one prisoner, whomsoever they desired. And there was one named Barabbas, which lay bound with them that had made insurrection with him, who had committed murder in the insurrection" (Mark 15:6-7). "Therefore when they were gathered together, Pilate said unto them, Whom will ye that I release unto you? Barabbas, or Jesus which is called Christ?" (Matt. 27:17). "And they cried out all at once, saying, Away with this man, and release unto us Barabbas: (Who for a certain sedition made in the city, and for murder, was cast into prison)" (Luke 23:18-19).

B. The rejection of the Messiah
 1. The counsel of Pilate
  a. He pointed out he had found no fault with Jesus—"And Pilate, when he had called together the chief priests and the rulers and the people, Said unto them, Ye have brought this man unto me, as one that perverteth the people: and, behold, I, having examined him before you, have found no fault in this man touching those things whereof ye accuse him" (Luke 23:13-14).
  b. He pointed out Herod had found no fault with Jesus—"No, nor yet Herod: for I sent you to him; and, lo, nothing worthy of death is done unto him. I will therefore chastise him, and release him" (Luke 23:15-16).
 2. The concern of the wife of Pilate—"When he was set down on the judgment seat, his wife sent unto him, saying, Have thou nothing to do with that just man: for I have suffered many things this day in a dream because of him" (Matt. 27:19).
 3. The cry of the Jews to Pilate—"And they cried out again, Crucify him" (Mark 15:13). "The Jews answered him, We have a law, and by our law he ought to die, because he made himself the Son of God. . . . And from thenceforth Pilate sought to release him: but the Jews cried out saying, If thou let this man go, thou art not Caesar's friend: whosoever maketh himself a king speaketh

against Caesar. When Pilate therefore heard that saying, he brought Jesus forth, and sat down in the judgment seat in a place that is called the Pavement, but in the Hebrew, Gabbatha. And it was the preparation of the passover, and about the sixth hour: and he saith unto the Jews, Behold your King!" (John 19:7, 12-14). "Then answered all the people, and said, His blood be on us, and on our children" (Matt. 27:25).
4. The cruelty of Pilate—"Then Pilate therefore took Jesus, and scourged him" (John 19:1).
5. The confession of Pilate
   a. His witness to the Jews—"Pilate therefore went forth again, and saith unto them, Behold, I bring him forth to you, that ye may know that I find no fault in him. Then came Jesus forth, wearing the crown of thorns, and the purple robe. And Pilate saith unto them, Behold the man!" (John 19:4-5)
   b. His washing before the Jews—"When Pilate saw that he could prevail nothing, but that rather a tumult was made, he took water, and washed his hands before the multitude, saying, I am innocent of the blood of this just person: see ye to it" (Matt. 27:24).

---

†*The New Scofield Bible aptly summarizes these first six trials. "There were two legal systems that condemned Christ: the Jewish and the Roman, the very two which underlie modern jurisprudence. The arrest and proceedings under Annas, Caiaphas, and the Sanhedrin were under Jewish law; those under Pilate and Herod were under Roman law. The Jewish trial was illegal in several particulars:*
   A. The judge was not impartial and did not protect the accused. There is no evidence that the quorum of twenty-three judges was present; the judges took part in the arrest; and they were hostile (Matt. 26:62-63).
   B. The arrest was unlawful because it was carried out under no formal accusation.
   C. In criminal trials all sessions had to be started and carried on only during the day. Night sessions were illegal.
   D. A verdict of guilty could not be rendered on the same day as the conclusion of the trial. It had to be given on the next day.
   E. The search for hostile testimony was illegal (Matt. 26:59; Mark 14:56; John 11:53).
   F. No accused [person] could be convicted on his own evidence, yet the accusers sought replies and admissions from Christ to condemn him (Matt. 26:63-66; John 18:9).
   G. No valid legal evidence was presented against him." (Oxford University Press, N.Y., 1967, p. 1042.)

TWELVE: Christ suffers his seventh unfair trial—The appearance before the Roman soldiers (Matt. 27:27-30; Mark 15:16-19; John 19:2-3).
A. Christ is belittled—"Then the soldiers of the governor took Jesus into the common hall, and gathered unto him the whole band of soldiers. And they stripped him, and put on him a scarlet robe. And when they had platted a crown of thorns, they put it upon his head, and a reed in his right hand: and they bowed the knee before him, and mocked him, saying, Hail, King of the Jews!" (Matt. 27:27-29)

† A. *According to John's Gospel, both the sixth and seventh trials of Jesus occurred "in a place that is called the Pavement, but in the Hebrew, Gabbatha" (John 19:13b). In New Testament times there was a strong fortress situated on the north side of the temple area known as the Tower of Antonia. That area is now occupied by the Covenant of the Sisters of Zion. Recent excavations beneath this building have revealed a courtyard paved with flagstones called in the Greek* litho-strotos *("paved"), and in the Aramaic* Gabbatha *("raised"). This was the place of which John spoke.*
  B. *Here Pilate had Jesus scourged and condemned to be crucified. After a futile attempt to wash away his guilt, the governor turned Jesus over to the Roman soldiers. Carved in that flagstone pavement can be seen the letter B with a rough, prickly crown at the top and a sword at the bottom. The B represented the word* Basilicus, *which means "the Game of the King," a very popular game among the legion troops. It consisted chiefly in choosing a burlesque king, in loading him down with ludicrous honors, in giving him liberty to satisfy his vices, and then cruelly putting him to death. There is strong evidence in the Gospel accounts that Jesus was the victim of this game.*

  B. Christ is brutalized—"And they spit upon him, and took the reed, and smote him on the head. And after that they had mocked him, they took the robe off from him, and led him away to crucify him" (Matt. 27:30-31).

---

†*On what day of the week was Jesus crucified? There are advocates for both Wednesday and Friday. Harold W. Hoehrer summarizes each position:*
  A. *"The Wednesday crucifixion: Statement of the view—Those who hold the Wednesday crucifixion view believe that Jesus died around sunset on Wednesday, and he arose exactly seventy-two hours later. The most well-known exponent of this view of recent days is W. G. Scroggie. He states that there are two main reasons that support the Wednesday crucifixion date. The primary support for this view is the literal interpretation of Matthew 12:40 where Jesus states: 'For as Jonas was three days and three nights in the belly of the whale; so shall the Son of man be three days and three nights in the heart of the earth.' The proponents of this view feel that although it is recognized that the Jews reckoned any part of a day as a whole day, when nights are mentioned as well as days, then it ceases to be an idiom. Therefore, one must accept it literally as three whole days. There are not three whole days between Friday evening and Sunday morning.*
    "The second support for a Wednesday crucifixion is that in the Friday view there are too many events (Scroggie lists twenty) between Christ's death at 3 P.M. and his burial at 6 P.M. Scroggie proposed that Jesus was buried on Wednesday evening, the body remained in the tomb during Thursday, Nisan 15, the Passover Sabbath, and then on Friday, the day between the Sabbaths, the body was embalmed.
    "In addition to these two main arguments, there is also the argument from typology whereby the lamb was chosen on Nisan 10. In the triumphal entry, Christ, the Lamb of God, appeared in Jerusalem on Saturday, Nisan 10. Thus, with the literal interpretation of Matthew 12:40, a proper amount of time for the many events between the death and embalmment of Christ, and with the corroborative typology, it is felt that the crucifixion of Christ occurring on Wednesday best satisfies the evidence.
    "Critique of the view—This view has not been widely accepted. It is not as strong as it might appear. First, it is based primarily on the verse of Scripture, namely, Matthew 12:40. Admittedly, this is the most difficult verse for those who hold to a Friday crucifixion. However, if one looks at other New Testament passages referring to Christ's resurrection,

it will be immediately obvious that Jesus rose on the third day and not on the fourth (cf. Matt. 16:21; 17:23; 20:19; 27:64; Luke 9:22; 18:33; 24:7, 21, 46; John 2:19-22; Acts 10:40; 1 Cor. 15:4). Also, it is a well-known fact that the Jews reckoned any part of a day as a whole day.

"There are several Old Testament references which show that a part of a day is equivalent to the whole day. In Genesis 42:17 Joseph incarcerated his brothers for three days, and then in verse 18 he spoke to them on the third day, and (from the context) released them on that day. In 1 Kings 20:29 Israel and Syria camped opposite each other for seven days, and on the seventh day they began to battle each other. In 2 Chronicles 10:5 Rehoboam stated that the people of Israel were to return to him in/after three days, and in verse 12 Jeroboam and the people came to Rehoboam on the third day. In Esther 4:16 Esther asks the Jews, 'Neither eat or drink for three days, night or day,' and then she would go in to the king on the third day. Finally, in 1 Samuel 30:12 an abandoned Egyptian servant had not eaten bread or drunk water for three days and three nights, and in verse 13 he states that his master left him behind three days ago. Thus, the Old Testament gives the picture that the expressions 'three days,' 'the third day,' and 'three days and three nights' are used to signify the same period of time. Thus the three days and three nights in Matthew 12:40 is an idiomatic expression of the same time period (viz., the third day) mentioned in the above cited New Testament passages rather than a literal seventy-two-hour period.

"Second, if one takes Matthew 12:40 as referring to a seventy-two-hour period, Christ must have risen no later than 6 P.M. on Saturday evening. Otherwise, he would have risen on the fourth day. But Christians celebrate it on the first day of the week (Acts 20:7; 1 Cor. 16:2) and not on the Sabbath.

"Third, it is true that many events occurred between Christ's death and burial; but the list is not so great when one examines it, for several things could have been done simultaneously by various people. Also, some things could have been done before he actually died.

"Fourth, the corroboration of typology is very weak indeed. This means that Jesus' triumphal entry was on Saturday, the Sabbath. This is unlikely for two reasons: (1) Since Jesus was riding on an animal, he would have been breaking the Mosaic Law which states that even animals were not to work on the Sabbath (Deut. 5:14). (2) Since the people were cutting down branches from the trees (Matt. 21:8; Mark 11:8), they would have also violated the Law (cf. Deut. 5:14; Num. 15:32-36). Certainly if Jesus had violated the Sabbath and caused others to do so, it seems that his enemies would have mentioned something of this during the Passion Week.

B. "The Friday crucifixion: Statement of the view—Jesus predicted that he would die and be raised on the third day (Matt. 16:21; Mark 8:31; Luke 9:22). When one reads these events in the Gospels, one clearly receives the impression that Jesus rose on the third day. Jesus' body was laid in the tomb on the evening of the day of preparation (Friday), the day before the Sabbath (Matt. 27:62; 28:1; Mark 15:42; Luke 23:54, 56; John 19:31, 42).

The women returned home and rested on the Sabbath (Saturday, Luke 23:56). Early on the first day of the week (Sunday), they went to the tomb (Matt. 28:1; Mark 16: 1-2; Luke 24:1; John 20:1) which was empty. Furthermore, on the same day he arose from the grave, Jesus walked with two disciples on the road to Emmaus (Luke 24:21). This, then, points to his crucifixion as having occurred on Friday. With all this evidence, the only plausible conclusion is that Jesus was crucified on Friday and rose on Sunday.

"This view also fits well with Old Testament typology. On Monday, Nisan 10, Jesus presented himself as the Paschal lamb at the triumphal entry. On Nisan 14 he was sacrificed as the Paschal lamb (1 Cor. 5:7), and on Nisan 16 his resurrection was a type of the offering of First Fruits (1 Cor. 15:23). In conclusion, then, with the most natural reading of the New Testament, one would conclude that Jesus was crucified on Friday and was resurrected on Sunday. This is also the common consensus of the Church Fathers and scholars throughout church history, and it is the view generally accepted today." (Chronological Aspects of the Life of Christ, *Zondervan Publishing, Grand Rapids, Mich., 1979, pp. 63, 65, 67, 71-73*)

THIRTEEN: Christ walks the road to Calvary (Matt. 27:31-32; Mark 15:20-21; Luke 23:26-32; John 19:16).
A. The man of Cyrene, bearing up the cross—"And as they led him away, they laid hold upon one Simon, a Cyrenian, coming out of the country, and on him they laid the cross, that he might bear it after Jesus" (Luke 23:26).
B. The maidens of Zion, weeping over the cross
   1. Their mourning—"And there followed him a great company of people, and of women, which also bewailed and lamented him" (Luke 23:27).
   2. His warning—"But Jesus turning unto them said, Daughters of Jerusalem, weep not for me, but weep for yourselves, and for your children. For, behold, the days are coming, in the which they shall say, Blessed are the barren, and the wombs that never bare, and the paps which never gave suck. Then shall they begin to say to the mountains, Fall on us; and to the hills, Cover us. For if they do these things in a green tree, what shall be done in the dry?" (Luke 23:28-31)
FOURTEEN: Christ is crucified on the cross (Matt. 27:33-50; Mark 15:22-37; Luke 23:32-46; John 19:17-30).

†*The following somewhat extended material concerning the overall agony, scourging, and crucifixion of Christ is taken from two magazine articles:* New Wine, *December 1972, Dr. C. Truman Davis; and* JAMA *(Journal of the American Medical Assocation), March 21, 1988, Dr. William D. Edwards:*
   A. *The physical passion of Christ began in Gethsemane. Of the many aspects of this initial suffering, I shall discuss only the one of psychological interest: the bloody sweat. It is interesting that the physician of the group, St. Luke, is the only one to mention this. He says, "And being in agony, he prayed the longer. And his sweat became as drops of blood, trickling down upon the ground" (Luke 22:44). Though very rare, the phenomenon of hematidrosis, or bloody sweat, is well documented. Under great emotional stress, tiny capillaries in the sweat glands can break, thus mixing blood with sweat. This process alone could have marked weakness and possible shock.* (New Wine) *"Then Pilate therefore took Jesus, and scourged him" (John 19:1.)*
   B. *Flogging was a legal preliminary to every Roman execution, and only women and Roman senators or soldiers (except in cases of desertion) were exempt. The usual instrument was a short whip (flagrum or flagellum) with several single or braided leather thongs of variable lengths, in which small iron balls or sharp pieces of sheep bones were tied at intervals. Occasionally, staves also were used. For scourging, the man was stripped of his clothing, and his hands were tied to an upright post. The back, buttocks, and legs were flogged either by two soldiers (lictors) or by one who alternated positions. The severity of the scourging depended on the disposition of the lictors and was intended to weaken the victim to a state just short of collapse or death. After the scourging, the soldiers often taunted their victim. As the Roman soldiers repeatedly struck the victim's back with full force, the iron balls*

would cause deep contusions, and the leather thongs and sheep bones would cut into the skin and subcutaneous tissues. Then, as the flogging continued, the lacerations would tear into the underlying skeletal muscles and produce quivering ribbons of bleeding flesh. Pain and blood loss generally set the stage for circulatory shock. The extent of blood loss may well have determined how long the victim would survive on the cross. At the Praetorium, Jesus was severely whipped. (Although the severity of the scourging is not discussed in the four Gospel accounts, it is implied in one of the epistles—1 Pet. 2:24.) A detailed word study of the ancient Greek text for this verse indicates that the scourging of Jesus was particularly harsh. It is not known whether the number of lashes was limited to 39, in accordance with Jewish law. (JAMA)

C. *When it is determined by the centurion in charge that the prisoner is near death, the beating is finally stopped. The half-fainting Jesus is then untied and allowed to slump to the stone pavement, wet with his own blood. The Roman soldiers see a great joke in this provincial Jew claiming to be a king. They throw a robe across his shoulders and place a stick in his hand for a scepter. They still need a crown to make their travesty complete. A small bundle of flexible branches covered with long thorns (commonly used for firewood) are plaited into a shape of a crown and this is pressed into his scalp. Again there is copious bleeding (the scalp being one of the most vascular areas of the body). After mocking him and striking him across the face, the soldiers take the stick from his hand and strike him across the head, driving the thorns deeper into his scalp. Finally, they tire of their sadistic sport and the robe is torn from his back.*

This had already become adherent to the clots of blood and serum in the wounds, and its removal, just as in the careless removal of a surgical bandage, causes excruciating pain, almost as though he were again being whipped, and the wounds again begin to bleed. In deference to Jewish custom, the Romans return his garments. The heavy horizontal beam of the cross is tied across his shoulders, and the procession of the condemned Christ, two thieves, and the execution party walk along the Via Dolorosa. In spite of his efforts to walk erect, the weight of the heavy wooden beam, together with the shock produced by copious blood loss, is too much. He stumbles and falls. The rough wood of the beam gouges into the lacerated skin and muscles of the shoulders. He tries to rise, but human muscles have been pushed beyond their endurance. The centurion, anxious to get on with the crucifixion, selects a stalwart North African onlooker, Simon of Cyrene, to carry the cross. Jesus follows, still bleeding and sweating the cold, clammy sweat of shock. The 650-yard journey from the fortress Antonia to Golgotha is finally completed. The prisoner is again stripped of his clothes—except for a loincloth which is allowed the Jews. The crucifixion begins. Jesus is offered wine mixed with myrrh, a mild analgesic mixture. He refuses to drink. Simon is ordered to place the cross beam on the ground and Jesus is quickly thrown backward with his shoulders against the wood. The legionnaire feels for the depression at the front of the wrist. He drives a heavy, square, wrought-iron nail through the wrist and deep into the wood. Quickly, he moves to the other side and repeats the action, being careful not to pull the arms too tightly, but to allow some flexion and movement. The beam is then lifted in place at the top of the vertical beam and the title reading "Jesus of Nazareth, King of the Jews" is nailed in place. (New Wine)

"And when they were come to the place, which is called Calvary, there they crucified him, and the malefactors, one on the right hand, and the other on the left" (Luke 23:33).

D. *The Shroud of Turin is considered by many to represent the actual burial cloth of Jesus, and several publications concerning the medical aspects of his death draw conclusions from this assumption. The Shroud of Turin and recent archaeological findings provide valuable information concerning Roman crucifixion practices. Crucifixion probably first began among the Persians. Alexander the Great introduced the practice to Egypt and Carthage, and the Romans appear to have learned of it from the Carthaginians. Although the Romans did not invent crucifixion, they perfected it as a form of torture and capital punishment that was designed to produce a slow death with maximum pain and suffering. It was one of the most disgraceful and cruel methods of execution and usually was reserved only for slaves, foreigners, revolutionaries, and the vilest of criminals. Roman law usually protected Roman citizens from crucifixion, except perhaps in the case of desertion by soldiers. In its earliest form in Persia, the victim was either tied to a tree or was tied to or impaled on an upright post, usually to keep the guilty victim's feet from touching holy ground. Only later was a true cross used; it was characterized by an upright post (stipes) and a horizontal crossbar (patibulum), and it had several variations. Although archaeological and historical evidence strongly indicates that the low Tau cross was preferred by the Romans in Palestine at the time of Christ, crucifixion practices often varied in a given geographic region and in accordance with the imagination of the executioners, and the Latin cross and other forms may have been used.*

It was customary for the condemned man to carry his own cross from the flogging post to the site of crucifixion outside the city walls. He was usually naked, unless this was prohibited by local customs. Since the weight of the entire cross was probably well over 300 pounds, only the crossbar was carried. The patibulum, weighing 75 to 125 pounds, was placed across the nape of the victim's neck and balanced along both shoulders. Usually, the outstretched arms then were tied to the crossbar. The processional to the site of crucifixion was led by a complete Roman military guard, headed by a centurion. One of the soldiers carried a sign (titulus) on which the condemned man's name and crime were displayed. Later, the titulus would be attached to the top of the cross. The Roman guard would not leave the victim until they were sure of his death. Outside the city walls was permanently located the heavy upright wooden stipes, on which the patibulum would be secured. In the case of the Tau cross, this was accomplished by means of a mortise and tenon joint, with or without reinforcement by ropes. To prolong the crucifixion process, a horizontal wooden block or plank, serving as a crude seat (sedile or sedulum), often was attached midway down the stipes. At the site of execution, by law, the victim was given a bitter drink of wine mixed with myrrh (gall) as a mild analgesic. The criminal was then thrown to the ground on his back, with his arms outstretched along the patibulum. The hands could be nailed or tied to the crossbar, but nailing apparently was preferred by the Romans.

The archaeological remains of a crucified body, found in an ossuary near Jerusalem and dating from the time of Christ, indicate that the nails were tapered iron spikes approximately five to seven inches long with a square shaft ⅜ inches across.

Furthermore, ossuary findings and the Shroud of Turin have documented that the nails commonly were driven through the wrists rather than the palms. Although scriptural references are made to nails in the hands, these are not at odds with the archaeological evidence of wrist wounds, since the ancients customarily considered the wrist to be part of the hand. After both arms were fixed to the crossbar, the patibulum and the victim, together, were lifted onto the stipes. On the low cross, four soldiers could accomplish this relatively easily. However, on the tall cross, the soldiers used either wooden forks or ladders. Next, the feet were fixed to the cross, either by nails or ropes. Ossuary findings and the Shroud of Turin suggest that nailing was the preferred Roman practice. Although the feet could be fixed to the sides of the stipes or to a wooden footrest (suppedaneum), they usually were nailed directly to the front of the stipes. To accomplish this, flexion of the knees may have been quite prominent, and the bent legs may have been rotated laterally. When the nailing was completed, the titulus was attached to the cross, by nails or cords, just above the victim's head. (JAMA)

E. *The victim is now crucified. As he slowly sags down with more weight on the nails in the wrists, excruciating, fiery pain shoots along the fingers and up the arms to explode in the brain—the nails in the wrists are putting pressure on the median nerves. As he pushes himself upward to avoid this stretching torment, he places his full weight on the nail through his feet. Again, there is the searing agony of the nail tearing through the nerves between the metatarsal bones of the feet. At this point, another phenomenon occurs. As the arms fatigue, great waves of cramps sweep over the muscles, knotting them in deep, relentless, throbbing pain. With these cramps comes the inability to push himself upward. Hanging by his arms, the pectoral muscles are paralyzed and the intercostal muscles are unable to act. Air can be drawn into the lungs but it cannot be exhaled. Jesus fights to raise himself in order to get even one short breath. Finally, carbon dioxide builds up in the lungs and in the bloodstream and the cramps partially subside. Spasmodically, he is able to push himself upward to exhale and bring in the life-giving oxygen. It was undoubtedly during these periods that he uttered the seven short sentences which are recorded.*

Now begin hours of this limitless pain, cycles of twisting, joint-rending cramps, inter-mittent partial asphyxiation, searing pain as tissue is torn from his lacerated back as he moves up and down against the rough timber. Then another agony begins. A deep, crushing pain in the chest as the pericardium slowly fills with serum and begins to compress the heart. It is now almost over—the loss of tissue fluids has reached a critical level; the compressed heart is struggling to pump heavy, thick, sluggish blood into the tissues; the tortured lungs are making a frantic effort to gasp in small gulps of air. The markedly dehydrated tissues send their flood of stimuli to the brain. His mission of atonement has been completed. Finally he can allow his body to die. With one last surge of strength, he once again presses his torn feet against the nail, straightens his legs, takes a deeper breath, and utters his seventh and last cry, "Father, into thy hands I commend my spirit."

A. The first three hours (9:00 A.M. till noon)—"And when they were come to the place, which is called Calvary, there they crucified him, and the malefactors, one on the right hand, and the other on the left" (Luke 23:33).
  1. The refusal of the wine—"And they gave him to drink wine mingled with myrrh: but he received it not" (Mark 15:23).

---

†*Here is the first of four cups offered to Christ at Calvary.*
  A. *This was the cup of charity. At the site of execution, by law, the victim was given a bitter drink of wine mixed with myrrh (gall) as a mild narcotic or opiate.*
  B. *The second was the cup of mockery. "And the soldiers also mocked him, coming to him, and offering him vinegar" (Luke 23:36).*
  C. *The third was the cup of sympathy. "Now there was set a vessel full of vinegar: and they filled a spunge with vinegar, and put it upon hyssop, and put it to his mouth" (John 19:29). Jesus had refused the first cup at the beginning of his suffering, but now accepted this one at the end of his agony.*
  D. *The fourth was the cup of iniquity. Our Lord himself had spoken of this while in the Garden of Gethsemane. "Then said Jesus unto Peter, Put up thy sword into the sheath: the cup which my Father hath given me, shall I not drink it?" (John 18:11). A verse found in*

*one of the Psalms sung by Christ and his disciples in the Upper Room (Matt. 26:30) in
reality summarized all four cups: "I will take the cup of salvation, and call upon the name of
the Lord" (Psa. 116:13).*

2. The roll of the dice
    a. What the soldiers did—"Then the soldiers, when they had crucified Jesus,
       took his garments, and made four parts, to every soldier a part; and also
       his coat: now the coat was without seam, woven from the top throughout"
       (John 19:23).
    b. Why the soldiers did it—"They said therefore among themselves, Let us
       not rend it, but cast lots for it, whose it shall be: that the scripture might be
       fulfilled, which saith, They parted my raiment among them, and for my
       vesture they did cast lots. These things therefore the soldiers did" (John
       19:23-24).
3. The record of the sign
    a. The words—"JESUS OF NAZARETH THE KING OF THE JEWS" (John 19:19b).
    b. The writer
       (1) The placing of the sign—"And Pilate wrote a title, and put it on the
           cross. And the writing was, JESUS OF NAZARETH THE KING OF
           THE JEWS. This title then read many of the Jews: for the place where
           Jesus was crucified was nigh to the city: and it was written in Hebrew,
           and Greek, and Latin" (John 19:19-20).
       (2) The protesting against the sign—The demand by the priest and the
           denial by the governor. "Then said the chief priests of the Jews to Pilate,
           Write not, The King of the Jews; but that he said, I am King of the Jews"
           (John 19:21). "Pilate answered, What I have written I have written"
           (John 19:22).
4. The ridicule of the crowd
    a. The sarcastic (who they were)
       (1) The people (Luke 23:35)
       (2) The chief priests and scribes (Matt. 27:41)
       (3) The soldiers (Luke 23:36)
       (4) The thieves (Matt. 27:44)
    b. The sarcasm (what they said)
       (1) "And they that passed by railed on him, wagging their heads, and
           saying, Ah, thou that destroyest the temple, and buildest it in three
           days, Save thyself, and come down from the cross" (Mark 15:29-30).

†*To wag or shake one's head was a familiar gesture of derision.*
  *A. God had once warned through Jeremiah that he would cause the pagan Babylonians and
     other heathen nations to look upon the city of Jerusalem because of the sin of its people. "To
     make their land desolate, and a perpetual hissing; every one that passeth thereby shall be
     astonished, and wag his head" (Jer. 18:16). The weeping prophet would later with broken
     heart testify to the terrible accuracy of this prediction. "All that pass by clap their hands at
     thee; they hiss and wag their head at the daughter of Jerusalem, saying, Is this the city that
     men call The perfection of beauty, The joy of the whole earth?" (Lam. 2:15).*
  B. David had predicted this Calvary head-wagging on two occasions (see Psa. 22:7; 109:25).

(2) "Likewise also the chief priests mocking said among themselves with the scribes, He saved others; himself he cannot save. Let Christ the King of Israel descend now from the cross, that we may see and believe. And they that were crucified with him reviled him" (Mark 15:31-32).

†*This crude and cruel statement, "He saved others; himself he cannot save," although uttered with ridicule and hatred, nevertheless voiced a precious and profound truth. Our Lord had already wrestled with this in Gethsemane. The divine decision was made. He could not and would not escape the cup. He must and would indeed die to save others.*

(3) "He trusted in God; let him deliver him now, if he will have him: for he said, I am the Son of God" (Mark 27:43).
(4) "And the soldiers also mocked him, coming to him, and offering him vinegar, and saying, If thou be the king of the Jews, save thyself" (Luke 23:36-37).
(5) "And one of the malefactors which were hanged railed on him, saying, If thou be Christ, save thyself and us" (Luke 23:39).
    5. The request of the Savior—
The first saying of Christ—"Then said Jesus, Father, forgive them; for they know not what they do" (Luke 23:34).

† *A. This prayer has bothered some, as it seems to be a blanket pardon for all involved in Jesus' crucifixion. Of course, we know this is not the case. Forgiveness can come only through faith (Eph. 2:8-9). It has been pointed out by some that the word "forgive" here can also mean "to allow," and is actually translated thereby on at least thirteen other occasions in the New Testament. If this should be the case here, Christ then would pray, "Father, allow them to crucify me." Thus the prayer would be a plea to stay the wrath of a righteous Father as he viewed his beloved Son being murdered by sinful and wicked men. (See Matt. 3:15; 19:14; Mark 1:34.) However, most Bible students would accept the word "forgive" at face value and interpret his prayer as a request for God not to add this horrible crime of regicide (the killing of one's own king) to the personal accounts of those individuals who killed him. Peter and Paul would amplify this point in later sermons (Acts 3:14-15, 17): "But ye denied the Holy One and the Just, and desired a murderer to be granted unto you; and killed the Prince of life, whom God hath raised from the dead; whereof we are witnesses. And now, brethren, I wot that through ignorance ye did it, as did also your rulers."*
    See also 1 Corinthians 2:8: "Which none of the princes of this world knew: for had they known it, they would not have crucified the Lord of glory."
B. The sinlessness of our Savior is again proven here, for he did not pray, "Father, forgive me." He needed no forgiveness, for he knew no sin. In summary, the first cross utterance did not mean that men are excusable, but rather forgivable. (Contrast Rom. 2:1 with 1 Tim. 1:13.)

    6. The repentance of the thief—
The second saying of Christ
        a. The conviction of a dying thief—"And one of the malefactors which were hanged railed on him, saying, If thou be Christ, save thyself and us.

But the other answering rebuked him, saying, Dost not thou fear God, seeing thou art in the same condemnation? And we indeed justly; for we receive the due reward of our deeds: but this man hath done nothing amiss" (Luke 23:39-41).
b. The conversion of a dying thief
(1) Requesting—"And he said unto Jesus, Lord, remember me when thou comest into thy kingdom" (Luke 23:42).
(2) Receiving—"And Jesus said unto him, Verily I say unto thee, To day shalt thou be with me in paradise" (Luke 23:43).

---

†*This statement emphasizes several facts concerning salvation.*
   A. That salvation is offered to anyone, anywhere. Are deathbed conversions valid? They are indeed, for there is one noted here. But we quickly note:
      1. There is one deathbed conversion in the Bible, so no dying man will despair.
      2. There is only one, so no living man will presume. D. L. Moody once said: "Did ever the new birth take place in so strange a cradle?" Observe the contrast here:
         a. In the morning the thief was nailed to a cross. In the evening he was wearing a crown.
         b. In the morning he was an enemy of Caesar. In the evening he was a friend of God.
         c. In the morning he was spurned by men. In the evening he was fellowshiping with angels.
         d. In the morning he died as a criminal on earth. In the evening he lived as a citizen of heaven.
   B. That salvation is by grace through faith alone. This conversion refutes:
      1. The doctrine of sacramentalism. He was saved apart from confirmation, sprinkling, Holy Communion, and church membership.
      2. The doctrine of baptismal regeneration.
      3. The doctrine of purgatory.
      4. The doctrine of universalism. Only one thief was saved.
   C. That salvation will be rejected by some in spite of everything God can do. The other thief died, eternally lost. Here we see three men:
      1. One was dying for sin (the Savior).
      2. One was dying from sin (the repentant thief).
      3. One was dying in sin (the lost thief).
   D. All classes of humanity were represented at the cross. There were the indifferent ("the people stood beholding," Luke 23:35); the religious ("the rulers derided him," Luke 23:35); the materialistic ("the soldiers parted his raiment and cast lots," Luke 23:34); and the earnest seeker ("Lord, remember me" Luke 23:42). The Cross is indeed the judgment of this world. (See John 12:31.)

---

7. The responsibility of John—
The third saying of Christ
   a. His words to Mary—"Now there stood by the cross of Jesus his mother, and his mother's sister, Mary the wife of Cleophas, and Mary Magdalene. When Jesus therefore saw his mother, and the disciple standing by, whom he loved,he saith unto his mother, Woman, behold thy son!" (John 19:25-26).

b. His words to John—"Then saith he to the disciple, Behold thy mother! And from that hour that disciple took her unto his own home" (John 19:27).
B. The second three hours (noon till 3:00 P.M.)—"Now from the sixth hour there was darkness over all the land unto the ninth hour" (Matt. 27:45).
   1. *The fourth saying of Christ*
      a. The cry of the Messiah—"My God, my God, why hast thou forsaken me?" (Mark 15:34b)

---

† *A. This prayer is deeper in its mystery and higher in its meaning than any other single prayer in the Bible. God forsaken by God! Who can understand that? The wisest and most profound believer feels utterly inadequate as he approaches it. It can never be mastered by the mortal mind, even though that mind has experienced new birth. Eternity alone will exegete this. Elizabeth Clephane has so well phrased it:*

    "But none of the ransomed ever knew,
    How deep were the waters crossed;
    Nor how dark was the night,
    That the Lord passed through,
    Ere he found his sheep that was lost."

  B. There are so many unexplained "whys" raised here.
    1. Why did the Father turn his back upon the Son?
    2. Why did not even the Son know the reason?
    3. Why did innocent blood have to be shed for forgiveness of sin?
  C. The first and third of these questions are partially answered in Hebrews 9:22; 1 Peter 2:24; 3:18; and Isaiah 53. But what of the second question? Did not Christ know? According to Philippians 2:5-8, Christ voluntarily abstained from employing some of his divine attributes while upon this earth. Thus:
    1. He abstained from using his omnipresence for a period (John 11:15).
    2. He abstained from using his omnipotence for a period (John 5:19).
    3. He abstained from using his omniscience for a period (Luke 8:45; Mark 13:32). (See also Luke 2:40.)

---

      b. The confusion of the mob—"And some of them that stood by, when they heard it, said, Behold, he calleth Elias. And one ran and filled a spunge full of vinegar, and put it on a reed, and gave him to drink, saying, Let alone; let us see whether Elias will come to take him down" (Mark 15:35-36).
   2. *The fifth saying of Christ*—"After this, Jesus knowing that all things were now accomplished, that the scripture might be fulfilled, saith, I thirst" (John 19:28).

---

†*Thus, he who began his ministry by suffering intense hunger (Matt. 4:2), will now end it by experiencing terrible thirst. And yet, the amazing truth remains:*
  A. The hungry one was and is the eternal Bread of life.
  B. The thirsty one was and is the eternal Water of life.

3. *The sixth saying of Christ*—"When Jesus therefore had received the vinegar, he said, It is finished: and he bowed his head, and gave up the ghost" (John 19:30).

---

† A. *The sixth statement of Jesus is actually one word in the original Greek. It is* tetelestai, *meaning, "It was finished, and as a result it is forever done." This phrase was a farmer's word. When into his herd there was born an animal so beautiful and shapely that it seemed absolutely destitute of faults and defects, the farmer gazed upon the creature with proud, delighted eyes. "Tetelestai!" he said.*

   It was also an artist's word. When the painter or the sculptor had put the last finishing touches to the vivid landscape or the marble bust, he would stand back a few feet to admire his masterpiece, and, seeing in it nothing that called for correction or improvement, would murmur fondly, "Tetelestai! Tetelestai!"

B. *Our Lord cries out, "It is finished!" There are three important places where Scripture employs this word "finish."*

   It is used in Genesis 2:1, referring to the creation of God's works. It is used here in John 19:30, referring to the salvation of his works. (See also John 4:34; 5:36; 17:4.) It is used in Revelation 10:7 and 16:17, referring to the completion of his works.

C. *With gladness we note that he did not say, "I am finished," for he was just beginning. "Lifted up was he to die, 'It is finished,' was his cry; Now in heav'n exalted high; Hallelujah! What a Savior!"*

---

4. *The seventh saying of Christ*—"And when Jesus had cried with a loud voice, he said, Father, into thy hands I commend my spirit: and having said thus, he gave up the ghost" (Luke 23:46).

---

† A. *With this statement Jesus ended his Calvary ordeal as he had begun it, by praying to his Father.*

B. *His death was in and by itself a miracle, for he dismissed his spirit. No mortal man can do this through an act of the will without using a gun, knife, or poison.*

C. *All four Gospel accounts record the death of Christ. But one wonders how such a thing could happen? Was not Christ God incarnate? Indeed he was! How, then, could God have actually died on the cross? To explain this, we must return briefly to the book of Genesis. Here we are told of Adam's creation and of his tragic sin. God had warned him that disobedience would result in death, and so it did. In fact, it brought down upon the head of mankind two kinds of death: physical and spiritual.*

   Both kinds of death here can be defined by one word: separation. *That is the biblical and theological meaning of the word* death. *Physical death is separation, the parting of the soul from the body. Spiritual death is likewise separation, the parting of the unsaved person from God. This is sometimes called the second death (see Rev. 20:6, 14; 21:8).*

   So then, these two hellish enemies, physical and spiritual death, let loose by Adam, continued to curse and terrorize the human race for over forty centuries. Then, in the fullness of time, God sent his beloved Son to our world. The Father referred to his Son as the last Adam (among other names) in 1 Corinthians 15:45. Why this title? Because he had come to undo what the first Adam had previously done; that is, he came to rid mankind of those two evil enemies, physical and spiritual death. This he did while on the cross, where he died spiritually, being separated from God; and he died physically as he accomplished both tasks.

Spiritual death was immediately given the death blow. Paul later assures us that nothing can now separate the believer from the love of God (Rom. 8:35-39). But what about physical death? Paul answers this question in 1 Corinthians 15:51-55: "Behold, I shew you a mystery; We shall not all sleep, but we shall all be changed. In a moment, in the twinkling of an eye, at the last trump: for the trumpet shall sound, and the dead shall be raised incorruptible, and we shall be changed. For this corruptible must put on incorruption, and this mortal must put on immortality. So when this corruptible shall have put on incorruption, and this mortal shall have put on immortality, then shall be brought to pass the saying that is written, Death is swallowed up in victory. O death, where is thy sting? O grave, where is thy victory?"

FIFTEEN: Christ's death introduces some supernatural events (Matt. 27:51-56; Mark 15:38-41; Luke 23:45, 47-49).
A. The heavenly action
   1. The temple—"And the vail of the temple was rent in twain from the top to the bottom" (Mark 15:38a).
   2. The terrain—"And the earth did quake, and the rocks rent" (Matt. 27:51b).

† *"The veil that was torn, or rent, divided the holy place from the holy of holies, into which only the high priest might enter on the Day of Atonement" (see Exod. 26:31, note; Lev. 16:1-39). The tearing of that veil, which was a type of the human body of Christ (Heb. 10:20), signified that a 'new and living way' was opened for all believers into the very presence of God, with no other sacrifice or priesthood except Christ's (cf. Heb. 9:1-8; 10:19-22).* (The Scofield Bible, *Oxford University Press, N.Y., 1967, p. 1044*)

   3. The tombs—"And the graves were opened; and many bodies of the saints which slept arose, and came out of the graves after his resurrection, and went into the holy city, and appeared unto many" (Matt. 27:52-53).

† *John Walvoord writes: "As a careful reading of this account reveals, the raising of the bodies of the saints, although mentioned here, actually occurred after the resurrection of Jesus. This event is nowhere explained in the Scriptures, but seems to be a fulfillment of the feast of the first fruits of harvest mentioned in Leviticus 23:10-14. On that occasion, as a token of the coming harvest, the people would bring a handful of grain to the priest. The resurrection of these saints, occurring after Jesus himself was raised, is a token of the coming harvest when all the saints will be raised"* (Matthew, *Moody Press, Chicago, 1974, p. 236*). *There are two theories concerning the exact nature of their resurrection:*
   A. These "saints" (probably well-known citizens of Jerusalem) were raised from the dead, as was Lazarus (though he eventually died again).
   B. These saints actually received glorified bodies, never again to die.

B. The human reaction—"Now when the centurion, and they that were with him, watching Jesus, saw the earthquake, and those things that were done, they feared greatly, saying, Truly this was the Son of God. And many women were there beholding afar off, which followed Jesus from Galilee, ministering unto him: among which was Mary Magdalene, and Mary the mother of James and Joses, and the mother of Zebedee's children" (Matt. 27:54-56).

---

† *A. The Roman centurion at Calvary affirmed both the royalty and righteousness of Jesus.*
    1. His testimony as recorded by Matthew: "Truly, this was the Son of God."
    2. His testimony as recorded by Luke: "Certainly, this was a righteous man" (Luke 23:47).
  B. He thus became the final of five individuals who attested to the sinlessness of Jesus during
    those horrible hours before and at the time of the crucifixion. The first four were:
    1. Pilate (John 19:4)
    2. Pilate's wife (Matt. 27:19)
    3. Judas (Matt. 27:4)
    4. The dying thief (Luke 23:41)

SIXTEEN: Christ's body is removed from the cross and placed in a tomb (Matt. 27:57-61; Mark 15:42-47; Luke 23:50-56; John 19:31-42).
  A. Piercing of his body
    1. The broken legs of the two—"The Jews therefore, because it was the preparation, that the bodies should not remain upon the cross on the sabbath day, (for that sabbath day was an high day,) besought Pilate that their legs might be broken, and that they might be taken away. Then came the soldiers, and brake the legs of the first, and of the other which was crucified with him" (John 19:31-32).
    2. The broken heart of the one—"But when they came to Jesus, and saw that he was dead already, they brake not his legs: But one of the soldiers with a spear pierced his side, and forthwith came there out blood and water" (John 19:33-34).
  B. Preparing of his body
    1. Obtained by Joseph of Arimathaea—"When the even was come, there came a rich man of Arimathaea, named Joseph, who also himself was Jesus' disciple: He went to Pilate, and begged the body of Jesus. Then Pilate commanded the body to be delivered" (Matt. 27:57-58).
    2. Anointed by Nicodemus—"And there came also Nicodemus, which at the first came to Jesus by night, and brought a mixture of myrrh and aloes, about an hundred pound weight. Then took they the body of Jesus, and wound it in linen clothes with the spices, as the manner of the Jews is to bury" (John 19:39-40).

---

†*A "hundred pound weight" would equal approximately 75 pounds, a very large amount, such as was used in royal burials. He and Nicodemus wrapped Jesus' body in the clean linen cloths with the spices. The custom was to use about half as many pounds of spices as the weight of the body being prepared. The body would be prepared by rubbing it with myrrh and aloes, and then wrapping it with linen strips.*

  C. Placing of his body—"Now in the place where he was crucified there was a garden; and in the garden a new sepulchre, wherein was never man yet laid"

(John 19:41). "And when Joseph had taken the body, he wrapped it in a clean linen cloth, and laid it in his own new tomb, which he had hewn out in the rock: and he rolled a great stone to the door of the sepulchre, and departed" (Matt. 27:59-60).

Day Eight: Saturday

Christ's tomb is officially sealed (Matt. 27:62-66).

ONE: The petition

A. Remembering—"Now the next day, that followed the day of the preparation, the chief priests and Pharisees came together unto Pilate, Saying, Sir, we remember that that deceiver said, while he was yet alive, After three days I will rise again" (Matt. 27:62-63).

---

†*How tragic to realize that the only group to remember the oft-repeated prophecies of Jesus concerning his resurrection consisted of his enemies and not his friends. They simply forgot (See Luke 24:5-8; John 20:9).*

B. Requesting—"Command therefore that the sepulchre be made sure until the third day, lest his disciples come by night, and steal him away, and say unto the people, He is risen from the dead: so the last error shall be worse than the first" (Matt.27:64).

TWO: The permission—"Pilate said unto them, Ye have a watch: go your way, make it as sure as ye can. So they went, and made the sepulchre sure, sealing the stone, and setting a watch" (Matt. 27:65-66).

The Forty-day Period

ONE: Christ risen from the dead (Matt. 28; Mark 16; Luke 24; John 20–21)

---

†*Foster writes: "A French philosopher decided to create a new religion for France following the wild excesses of the French Revolution which severed most of the nation from Christianity. He approached the great French statesman Tallyrand for advice on how to proceed. Tallyrand replied sarcastically that it should be a very simple task for the philosopher to create a substitute for Christianity: all he needed to do would be to have himself crucified and then raised from the dead!"* (Studies in the Life of Christ, R. C. Foster, Baker Books, Grand Rapids, Mich., 1979)

Indications of the resurrection (an empty grave).

A. The trip to the tomb—"In the end of the sabbath, as it began to dawn toward the first day of the week, came Mary Magdalene and the other Mary to see the sepulchre" (Matt. 28:1). "And when the sabbath was past, Mary Magdalene, and Mary the mother of James, and Salome, had bought sweet spices, that they might come and anoint him" (Mark 16:1).

B. The terror at the tomb—"And, behold, there was a great earthquake: for the angel of the Lord descended from heaven, and came and rolled back the stone from the door, and sat upon it. His countenance was like lightning, and his raiment white as snow: and for fear of him the keepers did shake, and became as dead men" (Matt. 28:2-4).

†*The splendor and glory of angels is almost inconceivable. Note two other references to their brightness: "And I saw another mighty angel come down from heaven, clothed with a cloud: and a rainbow was upon his head, and his face was as it were the sun, and his feet as pillars of fire" (Rev. 10:1). "And after these things I saw another angel come down from heaven, having great power; and the earth was lightened with his glory" (Rev. 18:1).*

C. The transaction in the tomb
   1. The frustrated women—"And very early in the morning the first day of the week, they came unto the sepulchre at the rising of the sun. And they said among themselves, Who shall roll us away the stone from the door of the sepulchre?" (Mark 16:2-3).
   2. The frightened women—"And when they looked, they saw that the stone was rolled away: for it was very great. And entering into the sepulchre, they saw a young man sitting on the right side, clothed in a long white garment; and they were affrighted" (Mark 16:4-5).
   3. The favored women—An angel tells them of Christ's resurrection. "And he saith unto them, Be not affrighted: Ye seek Jesus of Nazareth, which was crucified: he is risen; he is not here: behold the place where they laid him. But go your way, tell his disciples and Peter that he goeth before you into Galilee: there shall ye see him, as he said unto you" (Mark 16:6-7).
D. The testimony from the tomb—"And they departed quickly from the sepulchre with fear and great joy; and did run to bring his disciples word" (Matt. 28:8).
E. The talk about the tomb
   1. What was said—"It was Mary Magdalene, and Joanna, and Mary the mother of James, and other women that were with them, which told these things unto the apostles. And their words seemed to them as idle tales, and they believed them not" (Luke 24:10-11).
   2. What was seen—"Then arose Peter, and ran unto the sepulchre; and stooping down he beheld the linen clothes laid by themselves, and departed, wondering in himself at that which was come to pass" (Luke 24:12).

Validations of the Resurrection (a risen Lord)
A. *The first appearance:* To Mary Magdalene (Mark 16:9-11; John 20:11-18)—"Now when Jesus was risen early the first day of the week, he appeared first to Mary Magdalene, out of whom he had cast seven devils" (Mark 16:9).
   1. The preliminaries
      a. The report—"The first day of the week cometh Mary Magdalene early, when it was yet dark, unto the sepulchre, and seeth the stone taken away from the sepulchre. Then she runneth, and cometh to Simon Peter, and to the other disciple, whom Jesus loved, and saith unto them, They have taken away the Lord out of the sepulchre, and we know not where they have laid him" (John 20:1-2).
      b. The race—"Peter therefore went forth, and that other disciple, and came to the sepulchre. So they ran both together: and the other disciple did outrun Peter, and came first to the sepulchre. And he stooping down, and looking in, saw the linen clothes lying; yet went he not in" (John 20:3-5).
      c. The response—"Then cometh Simon Peter following him, and went into the sepulchre, and seeth the linen clothes lie, and the napkin, that was about his head, not lying with the linen clothes, but wrapped together in

a place by itself. Then went in also that other disciple, which came first to the sepulchre, and he saw, and believed. For as yet they knew not the scripture, that he must rise again from the dead. Then the disciples went away again unto their own home" (John 20:6-10).

2. The particulars

   a. The sorrowful one—"But Mary stood without at the sepulchre weeping: and as she wept, she stooped down, and looked into the sepulchre" (John 20:11).

   b. The shining ones—"And seeth two angels in white sitting, the one at the head, and the other at the feet, where the body of Jesus had lain. And they say unto her, Woman, why weepest thou? She saith unto them, Because they have taken away my Lord, and I know not where they have laid him" (John 20:12-13).

   c. The sovereign one

     (1) Mary's error—"And when she had thus said, she turned herself back, and saw Jesus standing, and knew not that it was Jesus. Jesus saith unto her, Woman, why weepest thou? whom seekest thou? She, supposing him to be the gardener, saith unto him, Sir, if thou have borne him hence, tell me where thou hast laid him, and I will take him away" (John 20:14-15).

---

†*Why did Mary fail to recognize Jesus? Probably for several reasons:*
   A. Her eyes were blinded with tears.
   B. The early morning light was still too dim.
   C. She was not expecting to see him.

---

     (2) Mary's ecstasy

       (a) Recognizing—"Jesus saith unto her, Mary. She turned herself, and saith unto him, Rabboni; which is to say, Master" (John 20:16).

---

† *A. This was undoubtedly one of the two most dramatic "recognition meetings" in all the Bible. The first involved Joseph revealing himself to his brothers in Egypt (see Gen. 45:1-3).*
   B. It was a Samaritan woman to whom Christ first revealed his messiahship (see John 4:25-26). It is now to another woman, Mary Magdalene, that Christ first appears in his resurrection body. Both were formerly women of questionable moral background (see Mark 16:9).

       (b) Rejoicing—"Jesus saith unto her, Touch me not; for I am not yet ascended to my Father: but go to my brethren, and say unto them, I ascend unto my Father, and your Father; and to my God, and your God" (John 20:17).

       (c) Reporting—"Mary Magdalene came and told the disciples that she had seen the Lord, and that he had spoken these things unto her" (John 20:18).

  B. *The second appearance:* To the group of women (Matt. 28:9-15)

   1. The devotion of the women—"And as they went to tell his disciples, behold,

Jesus met them, saying, All hail. And they came and held him by the feet, and worshipped him. Then said Jesus unto them, Be not afraid: go tell my brethren that they go into Galilee, and there shall they see me" (Matt. 28:9-10).

---

† *A. Note his phrase, "Go to my brethren." There is a progressive intimacy between Jesus and his disciples. He calls them servants (John 13:13), friends (John 15:15), and here, brethren.*
B. Note also the phrase, "I ascend unto my Father." Some hold that Christ ascended that very first Easter Sunday to sprinkle his blood as the ultimate sacrifice within the heavenly sanctuary.

---

   2. The deception of the soldiers (Matt. 28:11-15)
       a. They told the truth—"Now when they were going, behold, some of the watch came into the city, and shewed unto the chief priests all the things that were done. And when they were assembled with the elders, and had taken counsel, they gave large money unto the soldiers, Saying, Say ye, his disciples came by night, and stole him away while we slept. And if this come to the governor's ears, we will persuade him, and secure you" (Matt 28:11-14).

---

†*There are at least two glaring flaws in this "official explanation concerning the empty tomb."*
   A. In the first place the soldiers were to say they had fallen asleep. But if so, how could they have known that "his disciples came . . . and stole him away"?
   B. In the second place, if it were true, why were they not put to death for sleeping on duty? (See Acts 12:19.)

---

       b. They sold the truth—"So they took the money, and did as they were taught: and this saying is commonly reported among the Jews until this day" (Matt. 28:15).
   C. *The third appearance:* To Simon Peter (Luke 24:34; 1 Cor. 15:5)—"Saying, The Lord is risen indeed, and hath appeared to Simon" (Luke 24:34). "And that he was seen of Cephas, then of the twelve" (1 Cor. 15:5).

---

†*What a meeting this must have been. The last time these two saw each other, the one was bitterly cursing and denying the other.*

   D. *The fourth appearance:* To two disciples en route to Emmaus (Mark 16:12-13; Luke 24:13-35)—"And, behold, two of them, went that same day to a village called Emmaus, which was from Jerusalem about threescore furlongs. And they talked together of all these things which had happened" (Luke 24:13-14).
       1. The reunion with Jesus—"And it came to pass, that, while they communed together and reasoned, Jesus himself drew near, and went with them. But their eyes were holden that they should not know him" (Luke 24:15-16).
       2. The request from Jesus—"And he said unto them, What manner of communications are these that ye have one to another, as ye walk, and are sad?" (Luke 24:17).

3. The reply to Jesus
   a. The facts—"And the one of them, whose name was Cleopas, answering
      said unto him, Art thou only a stranger in Jerusalem, and hast not
      known the things which are come to pass there in these days? And
      he said unto them, What things? And they said unto him, Concerning
      Jesus of Nazareth, which was a prophet mighty in deed and word
      before God and all the people: and how the chief priests and our rulers
      delivered him to be condemned to death, and have crucified him" (Luke
      24:18-20).
   b. The frustration—"But we trusted that it had been he which should have
      redeemed Israel: and beside all this, to day is the third day since these
      things were done. Yea, and certain women also of our company made us
      astonished, which were early at the sepulchre; and when they found not
      his body, they came, saying, that they had also seen a vision of angels,
      which said that he was alive. And certain of them which were with us
      went to the sepulchre, and found it even so as the women had said: but
      him they saw not" (Luke 24:21-24).

†*The phrase "today is the third day since these things were done" may have been a reference to the
Jewish belief that after the third day the soul left the body for good. In other words, the situation
was now hopeless.*

4. The rebuke by Jesus
   a. Chiding—"Then he said unto them, O fools, and slow of heart to believe
      all that the prophets have spoken: Ought not Christ to have suffered these
      things, and to enter into his glory?" (Luke 24:25-26)
   b. Correcting—"And beginning at Moses and all the prophets, he expounded
      unto them in all the scriptures the things concerning himself" (Luke 24:27).
5. The recognition of Jesus
   a. The meal—"And they drew nigh unto the village, whither they went: and
      he made as though he would have gone further. But they constrained him,
      saying, Abide with us: for it is toward evening, and the day is far spent.
      And he went in to tarry with them. And it came to pass, as he sat at meat
      with them, he took bread, and blessed it, and brake, and gave to them"
      (Luke 24:28- 30).

†*The two disciples reminded their unrecognized friend that "the day is far spent." Spiritually
speaking, however, it was just the opposite. The terrible night of Calvary was far spent. The
glorious morning of the resurrection was now at hand. "The night is far spent, the day is
at hand: let us therefore cast off the works of darkness, and let us put on the armour of light"
(Rom. 13:12).*

   b. The miracle—"And their eyes were opened, and they knew him; and he
      vanished out of their sight" (Luke 24:31).

    c. The meditation—"And they said one to another, Did not our heart burn within us, while he talked with us by the way, and while he opened to us the scriptures?" (Luke 24:32).

  6. The report concerning Jesus—"And they rose up the same hour, and returned to Jerusalem, and found the eleven gathered together, and them that were with them, Saying, The Lord is risen indeed, and hath appeared to Simon. And they told what things were done in the way, and how he was known of them in breaking of bread" (Luke 24:33-35).

E. *The fifth appearance:* To the apostles in the Upper Room (Mark 16:14; Luke 24:36-48; John 20:19-23)

  1. Appearing to his disciples

    a. Their thoughts of fear—"And as they thus spake, Jesus himself stood in the midst of them, and saith unto them, Peace be unto you. But they were terrified and affrighted, and supposed that they had seen a spirit" (Luke 24:36-37).

    b. His words of cheer—"And he said unto them, Why are ye troubled? and why do thoughts arise in your hearts? Behold my hands and my feet, that it is I myself: handle me, and see; for a spirit hath not flesh and bones, as ye see me have. And when he had thus spoken, he shewed them his hands and his feet" (Luke 24:38-40).

  2. Eating with his disciples—"And while they yet believed not for joy, and wondered, he said unto them, Have ye here any meat? And they gave him a piece of a broiled fish, and of an honeycomb. And he took it, and did eat before them" (Luke 24:41-43).

---

†*Following his resurrection our Lord was eventually recognized when he performed the simplest of tasks:*

  A. After pronouncing a name (John 20:16)

  B. After a simple greeting (Matt. 28:9)

  C. After the breaking of bread (Luke 24:30-31)

---

  3. Breathing on his disciples—"Then said Jesus to them again, Peace be unto you: as my Father hath sent me, even so send I you. And when he had said this, he breathed on them, and saith unto them, Receive ye the Holy Ghost: Whose soever sins ye remit, they are remitted unto them; and whose soever sins ye retain, they are retained" (John 20:21-23).

  4. Reasoning with his disciples—"Then opened he their understanding, that they might understand the scriptures" (Luke 24:45).

F. *The sixth appearance:* To Thomas and the apostles (John 20:24-31)—"But Thomas, one of the twelve, called Didymus, was not with them when Jesus came" (John 20:24).

  1. The report to Thomas—"The other disciples therefore said unto him, We have seen the Lord" (John 20:25a).

  2. The reluctance of Thomas—"But he said unto them, Except I shall see in his hands the print of the nails, and put my finger into the print of the nails, and thrust my hand into his side, I will not believe" (John 20:25b).

3. The recognition by Thomas
   a. The manifestation—"And after eight days again his disciples were within, and Thomas with them: then came Jesus, the doors being shut, and stood in the midst, and said, Peace be unto you" (John 20:26).
   b. The invitation—"Then saith he to Thomas, Reach hither thy finger, and behold my hands; and reach hither thy hand, and thrust it into my side: and be not faithless, but believing" (John 20:27).
   c. The adoration—"And Thomas answered and said unto him, My Lord and my God" (John 20:28).
   d. The observation—"Jesus saith unto him, Thomas, because thou hast seen me, thou hast believed: blessed are they that have not seen, and yet have believed" (John 20:29).
   e. The evaluation—"And many other signs truly did Jesus in the presence of his disciples, which are not written in this book: But these are written, that ye might believe that Jesus is the Christ, the Son of God; and that believing ye might have life through his name" (John 20:30-31).

---

†*What kind of body did Jesus have after his resurrection? This is of great importance to the Christian, for he or she will someday have a similar body, as testified by both Paul and John (see Phil. 3:21; 1 John 3:1-3).*
   A. *His new body had flesh and bone (Luke 24:39-40).*
   B. *He ate food in the new body (Luke 24:41-43; John 21:12-13; Acts 10:41).*
   C. *His new body still bore the marks of his crucifixion (John 20:25-27; Luke 24:40; Rev. 5:6).*
   D. *His new body was not subjected to material laws (John 20:19; Luke 24:31, 36).*

G. *The seventh appearance:* To seven apostles by the Sea of Galilee (John 21)—"There were together Simon Peter, and Thomas called Didymus, and Nathanael of Cana in Galilee, and the sons of Zebedee, and two other of his disciples" (John 21:2).
   1. The chagrin—"Simon Peter saith unto them, I go a fishing. They say unto him, We also go with thee. They went forth, and entered into a ship immediately; and that night they caught nothing" (John 21:3).
   2. The command—"But when the morning was now come, Jesus stood on the shore: but the disciples knew not that it was Jesus. Then Jesus saith unto them, Children, have ye any meat? They answered him, No. And he said unto them, Cast the net on the right side of the ship, and ye shall find. They cast therefore, and now they were not able to draw it for the multitude of fishes" (John 21:4-6).
   3. The coals—"As soon then as they were come to land, they saw a fire of coals there, and fish laid thereon, and bread. Jesus saith unto them, Bring of the fish which ye have now caught. Simon Peter went up, and drew the net to land full of great fishes, an hundred and fifty and three: and for all there were so many, yet was not the net broken. Jesus then cometh, and taketh bread, and giveth them, and fish likewise" (John 21:9-11, 13).
   4. The confession—"So when they had dined, Jesus saith to Simon Peter, Simon, son of Jonas, lovest thou me more than these? He saith unto him, Yea, Lord; thou knowest that I love thee. He saith unto him, Feed my lambs. He saith to

him again the second time, Simon, son of Jonas, lovest thou me? He saith unto him, Yea, Lord; thou knowest that I love thee. He saith unto him, Feed my sheep. He saith unto him the third time, Simon, son of Jonas, lovest thou me? Peter was grieved because he said unto him the third time, Lovest thou me? And he said unto him, Lord, thou knowest all things; thou knowest that I love thee. Jesus saith unto him, Feed my sheep" (John 21:15-17).

5. The cross—"Verily, verily, I say unto thee, When thou wast young, thou girdedst thyself, and walkedst whither thou wouldest: but when thou shalt be old, thou shalt stretch forth thy hands, and another shall gird thee, and carry thee whither thou wouldest not. This spake he, signifying by what death he should glorify God. And when he had spoken this, he saith unto him, Follow me" (John 21:18-19).

6. The confusion—"Then Peter, turning about, seeth the disciple whom Jesus loved following; which also leaned on his breast at supper, and said, Lord, which is he that betrayeth thee? Peter seeing him saith to Jesus, Lord, and what shall this man do? Jesus saith unto him, If I will that he tarry till I come, what is that to thee? follow thou me. Then went this saying abroad among the brethren, that that disciple should not die: yet Jesus said not unto him, He shall not die; but, If I will that he tarry till I come, what is that to thee?" (John 21:20-23).

H. *The eighth appearance:* To the apostles and 500 disciples (Matt. 28:16-20; Mark 16:15-18; 1 Cor. 15:6)

1. The great crowd—"After that, he was seen of above five hundred brethren at once; of whom the greater part remain unto this present, but some are fallen asleep" (1 Cor. 15:6).

   a. The twofold reaction—"And when they saw him, they worshipped him: but some doubted" (Matt. 28:17).

   b. The fourfold reassurance—"And these signs shall follow them that believe; In my name shall they cast out devils; they shall speak with new tongues; They shall take up serpents; and if they drink any deadly thing, it shall not hurt them; they shall lay hands on the sick, and they shall recover" (Mark 16:17-18).

2. The Great Commission—"And Jesus came and spake unto them, saying, All power is given unto me in heaven and in earth. Go ye therefore, and teach all nations, baptizing them in the name of the Father, and of the Son, and of the Holy Ghost: Teaching them to observe all things whatsoever I have commanded you: and, lo, I am with you alway, even unto the end of the world. Amen" (Matt. 28:18-20).

I. *The ninth appearance:* To James, the half brother of Christ (1 Cor. 15:7). "After that, he was seen of James; then of all the apostles" (1 Cor. 15:7).

J. *The tenth appearance:* To the eleven on the Mount of Olives (Luke 24:49-50; Acts 1:3-8)

1. The final command—"And, being assembled together with them, commanded them that they should not depart from Jerusalem, but wait for the promise of the Father, which, saith he, ye have heard of me" (Acts 1:4).

2. The final question—"When they therefore were come together, they asked of him, saying, Lord, wilt thou at this time restore again the kingdom to Israel? And he said unto them, It is not for you to know the times or the seasons, which the Father hath put in his own power" (Acts 1:6- 7).

    3. The final promise—"But ye shall receive power, after that the Holy Ghost is come upon you: and ye shall be witnesses unto me both in Jerusalem, and in all Judaea, and in Samaria, and unto the uttermost part of the earth" (Acts 1:8).

    4. The final blessing—"And he led them out as far as to Bethany, and he lifted up his hands, and blessed them" (Luke 24:50).

TWO: Christ is ascended into heaven (Mark 16:19-20; Luke 24:51-53; Acts 1:9-11) "And while they looked stedfastly toward heaven as he went up, behold, two men stood by them in white apparel; which also said, Ye men of Galilee, why stand ye gazing up into heaven? this same Jesus, which is taken up from you into heaven, shall so come in like manner as ye have seen him go into heaven" (Acts 1:10-11).

A. Where he ascended—"So then after the Lord had spoken unto them, he was received up into heaven, and sat on the right hand of God" (Mark 16:19).

B. How he ascended—"And when he had spoken these things, while they beheld, he was taken up; and a cloud received him out of their sight" (Acts 1:9).

C. Why he ascended—"In my Father's house are many mansions: if it were not so, I would have told you. I go to prepare a place for you. And if I go and prepare a place for you, I will come again, and receive you unto myself; that where I am, there ye may be also" (John 14:2-3).

PART TWO: TOPICAL OVERVIEW

PART TWO: TOPICAL OVERVIEW

THE MIRACLES OF CHRIST

ONE: Changing water into wine
TWO: Healing a nobleman's son
THREE: Healing a Capernaum demoniac
FOUR: Healing Peter's mother-in-law
FIVE: The first great catch of fish
SIX: Healing a leper
SEVEN: Healing a paralytic
EIGHT: Healing a withered hand
NINE: Healing a centurion's servant
TEN: Raising a widow's son
ELEVEN: Calming the stormy sea
TWELVE: Healing the maniac of Gadara
THIRTEEN: Healing the woman of a bloody flux
FOURTEEN: Raising Jairus' daughter
FIFTEEN: Healing two blind men
SIXTEEN: Healing a dumb demoniac
SEVENTEEN: Healing a cripple of thirty-eight years
EIGHTEEN: The feeding of the 5,000
NINETEEN: Walking on water
TWENTY: Healing a demoniac girl
TWENTY-ONE: Healing a deaf man with a speech impediment
TWENTY-TWO: The feeding of the 4,000
TWENTY-THREE: Healing a blind man in Bethsaida
TWENTY-FOUR: Healing in Jerusalem of a man born blind
TWENTY-FIVE: Healing of a demoniac boy
TWENTY-SIX: The miracle of the tribute money
TWENTY-SEVEN: Healing of a blind and mute demonic
TWENTY-EIGHT: Healing of a crippled woman of eighteen years
TWENTY-NINE: Healing of the man with dropsy
THIRTY: Healing of ten lepers
THIRTY-ONE: Raising of Lazarus
THIRTY-TWO: Healing of blind Bartimaeus
THIRTY-THREE: Destroying a fig tree
THIRTY-FOUR: Restoring a severed ear
THIRTY-FIVE: The second great catch of fish

THE MIRACLES OF CHRIST
ONE: Changing water into wine (John 2:1-11)
    A. The occasion
        1. The ceremony—"And the third day there was a marriage in Cana of Galilee; and the mother of Jesus was there: and both Jesus was called, and his disciples, to the marriage" (John 2:1-2).

---

†*It is significant that our Lord chose a wedding at which to perform his first recorded miracle. The oldest and greatest of three grand institutions given by God to man is that of marriage. God himself performed the first wedding in Eden (see Gen. 2:20-25). The Father would later choose that relationship between a man and wife to illustrate the love of Christ for his Church (see Eph. 5:22-33). Finally, the great event of the ages, yet to come, is a wedding—the marriage of God's Son to his chosen Bride (see Rev. 19:6-9).*

---

        2. The crisis—"And when they wanted wine, the mother of Jesus saith unto him, They have no wine" (John 2:3).

---

† *A. The wedding feast probably lasted a week, as in the cases of Jacob (Gen. 29:27) and Samson (Judg. 14:17). On the third day they ran out of wine. This presented a serious problem and might have led to a lawsuit. The responsible party was apparently Mary.*
  B. She quietly told him the problem. This marked the second of four public encounters Mary had with Jesus. The other three are:
    1. In the Jerusalem temple (Luke 2:41-52)
    2. In Capernaum (Mark 3:31-35)
    3. At Calvary (John 19:26-27)

    B. The observation—"Jesus saith unto her, Woman, what have I to do with thee? mine hour is not yet come" (John 2:4).

---

†*This was not a crude or uncaring statement. It might be paraphrased: "Dear lady, the work I came to do is yet in the future!" His usage of the word "hour" here is significant. It refers to Calvary. Note its later occurrences:*

A. *At the feast of tabernacles*—"Then they sought to take him: but no man laid hands on him, because his hour was not yet come" (John 7:30).
B. *In the temple treasury*—"These words spake Jesus in the treasury, as he taught in the temple: and no man laid hands on him; for his hour was not yet come" (John 8:20).
C. *In the Upper Room*—"Now before the feast of the passover, when Jesus knew that his hour was come that he should depart out of this world unto the Father, having loved his own which were in the world, he loved them unto the end" (John 13:1).
D. *On the Mount of Olives*—"These words spake Jesus, and lifted up his eyes to heaven, and said, Father, the hour is come; glorify thy Son, that thy Son also may glorify thee" (John 17:1).

C. The order
   1. From the mother—"His mother saith unto the servants, Whatsoever he saith unto you, do it" (John 2:5).

+*While no Christian should pray to Mary, all believers would profit greatly from heeding her advice here.*

   2. From the Messiah—"And there were set there six waterpots of stone, after the manner of the purifying of the Jews, containing two or three firkins apiece. Jesus saith unto them, Fill the water pots with water" (John 2:6-7a).

+*These six vessels would hold approximately 120 gallons total.*

D. The obedience—"And they filled them up to the brim. And he saith unto them, Draw out now, and bear unto the governor of the feast. And they bare it" (John 2:7-8).

+*Jesus used waterpots to accomplish his first miracle. He desires to do the same today, but now he uses living, earthly vessels. If we allow him, he fills us with the water of God's Word; and when we pour it out (give it out) it becomes the wine of the Spirit.*

E. The opinion—"When the ruler of the feast had tasted the water that was made wine, and knew not whence it was: (but the servants which drew the water knew;) the governor of the feast called the bridegroom, and saith unto him, Every man at the beginning doth set forth good wine; and when men have well drunk, then that which is worse: but thou hast kept the good wine until now" (John 2:9-10).

+ *A. Was this real wine? The Greek word used here,* oinos, *can refer to either grape juice or wine.*
   1. Examples in which it means juice:
      a. "Neither do men put new wine [unfermented grape juice] into old bottles, else the bottles break, and the wine runneth out" (Matt. 9:17).
      b. "He treadeth the winepress of the fierceness and wrath of Almighty God" (Rev. 19:15).
   2. Examples in which it means wine:

     a. *"Be not drunk with wine" (Eph. 5:18).*

     b. *"Drink no longer water, but use a little wine for thy stomach's sake and thine often infirmities" (1 Tim. 5:23).*

B. *If it was real wine Jesus created, it bore little if any resemblance to the modern product.*

   1. *In New Testament times wine was first boiled before storage, then diluted with three to ten parts water before serving.*

   2. *The Old Testament distinguishes between this wine and the strong, coarse, undiluted wine prepared solely to make one intoxicated.*

     a. *Both Noah and Lot became drunk on this wine (Gen. 9:21; 19:32-34).*

     b. *Drinking this kind of wine may have caused the death of Aaron's two priestly sons, both killed by God (Lev. 10:1-9).*

     c. *It was for the sin of national drunkenness that God would destroy Israel (Isa. 28:1-8).*

     d. *Daniel refused to defile himself by drinking this kind of wine (Dan. 1:8).*

     e. *The book of Proverbs warns against this kind of wine. "Wine is a mocker, strong drink is raging: and whosoever is deceived thereby is not wise" (Prov. 20:1). "Look not thou upon the wine when it is red, when it giveth his colour in the cup, when it moveth itself aright. At the last it biteth like a serpent, and stingeth like an adder" (Prov. 23:31-32).*

     f. *Habakkuk forbids the giving of this wine to one's neighbor (Hab. 2:14).*

     g. *Even the pagan Greeks felt only barbarians drank undiluted wine.*

     h. *The rabbis held that undiluted wine could not be blessed.*

C. *Whatever the meaning of the word wine here in John 2, the sincere believer must carefully consider other Scripture passages even in the practice of social drinking. "Abstain from all appearance of evil" (1 Thess. 5:22). "Whether therefore ye eat, or drink, or whatsoever ye do, do all to the glory of God. Give none offence, neither to the Jews, nor to the Gentiles, nor to the church of God" (1 Cor. 10:31-32).*

   F. The omnipotence—"This beginning of miracles did Jesus in Cana of Galilee, and manifested forth his glory; and his disciples believed on him" (John 2:11).

TWO: Healing a nobleman's son (John 4:43-54)

   A. Supplication—"The nobleman saith unto him, Sir, come down ere my child die" (John 4:49).

   B. Affirmation—"Jesus saith unto him, Go thy way; thy son liveth. And the man believed the word that Jesus had spoken unto him, and he went his way" (John 4:50).

   C. Investigation—"And as he was now going down, his servants met him, and told him, saying, Thy son liveth. Then enquired he of them the hour when he began to amend. And they said unto him, Yesterday at the seventh hour the fever left him" (John 4:51-52).

   D. Regeneration—"So the father knew that it was at the same hour, in the which Jesus said unto him, Thy son liveth: and himself believed, and his whole house" (John 4:53).

✝ A. *This is the first of five miracles performed by Jesus in which a non-Jewish individual was involved. The other four are:*

   1. *A centurion's servant (Matt 8:13)*

   2. *The maniac of Gadara (Mark 5:8)*

   3. *A Canaanite girl (Matt. 15:28)*

   4. *One of the ten lepers (Luke 17:11)*

  B. *This is also the first of three miracles performed while the recipient was miles away. The other two are:*

1. The centurion's servant (Matt. 8:13)
2. The Canaanite girl (Matt. 15:28; Mark 7:30)
C. This is the only recorded miracle which resulted in the spiritual salvation of an entire home (John 4:53).

THREE: Healing a Capernaum demoniac (Mark 1:21-28; Luke 4:31-37)
   A. The predicament of the man—"And there was in their synagogue a man with an unclean spirit; and he cried out" (Mark 1:23).
   B. The acknowledgment of the demon—"Saying, Let us alone; what have we to do with thee, thou Jesus of Nazareth? art thou come to destroy us? I know thee who thou art, the Holy One of God" (Mark 1:24).
   C. The commandment of the Lord—"And Jesus rebuked him, saying, Hold thy peace, and come out of him" (Mark 1:25).
   D. The amazement of the crowd—"And when the unclean spirit had torn him, and cried with a loud voice, he came out of him. And they were all amazed, insomuch that they questioned among themselves, saying, What thing is this? what new doctrine is this? for with authority commandeth he even the unclean spirits, and they do obey him" (Mark 1:26-27).

---

† *A. Who were these unclean spirits? In short, they were known as demons. This is the first instance of Christ exorcising a demon from a human being. There would be many other occasions. (See Matt. 8:32; 9:33; 12:22; 15:28; 17:18; Luke 8:2; 13:10-17.) Demons are fallen angels who sided with Lucifer (who became the devil) during the rebellion in heaven before the creation of man. (See Isa. 14:12-15; Ezek. 28:15-17; Rev. 12:4; Eph. 6:12.) Their activities are manifold and filled with malice.*
   1. They oppose God's purpose (Dan. 9:11-14).
   2. They execute Satan's program (1 Tim. 4:1; Rev. 16:12-14).
   3. They afflict earth's people. Some cause:
      a. Insanity (Matt. 8:28; 17:15)
      b. Muteness of speech (Matt. 9:33)
      c. Blindness (Matt. 12:22)
      d. The person to harm himself (Mark 5:5)
      e. Paralysis (Luke 13:11)
      f. Deafness (Mark 9:25)
   4. The number of demons is apparently very high. Jesus cast out seven from Mary Magdalene (Mark 16:9; Luke 8:2), and possibly as many as 6,000 from the maniac at Gadara (Mark 5:9).
   B. What did they know about Jesus?
      1. They knew he was the Holy One of God (Mark 1:24; Luke 8:28).
      2. They knew he was the Messiah and the very Son of God (Luke 4:41). "Thou believest that there is one God; thou doest well: the devils also believe, and tremble" (James 2:19).

FOUR: Healing Peter's mother-in-law (Matt. 8:14-17; Mark 1:29-34; Luke 4:38-41)
   A. The scope of this event
      1. He healed the mother.
         a. The suffering mother—"And when Jesus was come into Peter's house, he saw his wife's mother laid, and sick of a fever" (Matt. 8:14).

    b. The serving mother—"And he touched her hand, and the fever left her: and she arose, and ministered unto them" (Matt. 8:15).

---

†*This marks the first of seven miracles Jesus performed on the Sabbath. These are:*
  A. *Peter's mother-in-law (see Mark 1:29-31)*
  B. *The man with a withered hand (Matt. 12:9-14)*
  C. *A woman bowed down for eighteen years (Luke 13:10-17)*
  D. *The man with dropsy (Luke 14:1-4)*
  E. *The demon-possessed man in Capernaum (Mark 1:21-28)*
  F. *The paralytic man at Bethesda (John 5:2-10)*
  G. *The man born blind (John 9:1-14)*

---

  2. He healed the many.
    a. Those plagued by diseases—"Now when the sun was setting, all they that had any sick with divers diseases brought them unto him; and he laid his hands on every one of them, and healed them" (Luke 4:40).

---

†*Note that he healed "every one of them," regardless of their sicknesses, totally unlike those individuals who attempt to heal today.*

---

    b. Those plagued by demons—"And devils also came out of many, crying out, and saying, Thou art Christ the Son of God. And he rebuking them suffered them not to speak: for they knew that he was Christ" (Luke 4:41).
  B. The Scripture for this event—"That it might be fulfilled which was spoken by Esaias the prophet, saying, Himself took our infirmities, and bare our sicknesses" (Matt. 8:17).

---

† *A. Is there physical healing in the atonement? Here Matthew paraphrases from Isaiah 53:4-5. To answer this, several facts must be kept in mind:*
  1. *Matthew's statement (8:17) is written in the past tense, indicating that Isaiah's prophecy had already been fulfilled (probably a reference to 8:16ff). "When the even was come, they brought unto him many that were possessed with devils: and he cast out the spirits with his word, and healed all that were sick" (Matt. 8:16).*
  2. *While God did give certain men the gift of healing, there is strong evidence that it was being phased out at the completion of the New Testament. Consider, for example, the ministry of Paul, who had the gift of healing:*
    a. *He was not able to heal himself of his thorn in the flesh. In fact, God told Paul it was not the divine will for the apostle to be healed. (See 2 Cor. 12:7-10.) Note Paul's reaction to this: "For this thing I besought the Lord thrice, that it might depart from me. And he said unto me, My grace is sufficient for thee: for my strength is made perfect in weakness.*
      Most gladly therefore will I rather glory in my infirmities, that the power of Christ may rest upon me. Therefore I take pleasure in infirmities, in reproaches, in necessities, in persecutions, in distresses for Christ's sake: for when I am weak, then am I strong" (2 Cor. 12:8-10).
    b. *He was not able to heal his close friend Timothy. "Drink no longer water, but use a little wine for thy stomach's sake and thine often infirmities" (1 Tim. 5:23).*

     c. He was not able to heal Trophimus. "Erastus abode at Corinth: but Trophimus have I left at Miletum sick" (2 Tim. 4:20).

B. *Two extended quotes are helpful at this point.*

  1. *As taken from the New Scofield Bible (concerning Isa. 53:4): "Because Matthew quotes this passage and applies it to physical disease (cf. Matt. 8:17 with context) it has been conjectured by some that disease as well as sin was included in the atoning death of Christ. But Matthew asserts that the Lord fulfilled the first part of Isaiah 53:4 during the healing ministry of His service on earth. Matthew 8:17 makes no reference to Christ's atoning death for sin. The Lord took away the diseases of men by healing them. He died for our sins, not for our diseases. For physical disease in itself is not sin; it is merely one of the results of sin. Thus Isaiah 53:5-6 prophesies that Christ would bear our sins on the cross (cf. 1 Pet. 2:24-25). His death was substitutionary and atoning." (Oxford University Press, New York, 1967, p. 759)*

  2. *As taken from the writings of William L. Pettingill: "Much confusion has resulted from a failure just here to 'rightly divide the Word of Truth.' Many who emphasize the so-called doctrine of Divine Healing base their teaching upon such scenes as we are now considering in the eighth chapter of Matthew. And we are told that because Jesus Himself took our infirmities and bore our diseases, therefore it is contrary to His will that His disciples should now have any infirmities or diseases. It is all very plausible and attractive, especially in this day when even the Lord's people are so unwilling to enter into the fellowship of His sufferings, or to be made conformable unto His death. Without entering into the subject more fully here, it is worthwhile to point out that bodily healing is a characteristic feature of the Kingdom, and is usually associated in the Scriptures with the Gospel of the Kingdom. In the Church of God it is not characteristic but exceptional. The reason is that the Church is appointed to a ministry of suffering. The glory is yet to be revealed, for it belongs to the Kingdom and will not come to the Church until the Kingdom is manifested. It must be remembered that the infirmities that He took included death itself as well as disease. And we cannot rightly claim to be delivered from disease until death has been abolished in fact as well as by promise. Potentially, all this has been accomplished on the Cross, but the Lord's people are still dying, and will continue to die until the Day of Adoption, to wit, the redemption of the body.*

    "All confusion in this matter would be cleared up if God's people would stop reading Church truth into the Gospel of the Kingdom and remember that the manifestation of the Kingdom is deferred until the Church is completed. As for the sufferings of this present time, we reckon that they are 'not worthy to be compared with the glory which shall be revealed to usward. For the earnest expectation of the Creation waiteth for the revealing of the sons of God,' and 'the Creation itself also shall be delivered from the bondage of corruption into the liberty of the glory of the children of God. For we know that the whole Creation groaneth and travaileth in pain together until now. And not only so, but ourselves also, who have the firstfruits of the Spirit, even we ourselves groan within ourselves, waiting for our adoption, to wit, the redemption of our body. For in hope were we saved: but hope that is seen is not hope; for who hopeth for that which he seeth? But if we hope for that which we see not, then do we with patience wait for it' (Rom. 8:18-25). This Scripture ought surely to make it clear that though we are already children of God, the revelation of that fact is yet to come; that though our bodies have been bought with the redemption blood, we have not yet entered into the full benefit of it, nor can we until the great Day of Adoption, to wit, the redemption of our body—at our Lord's coming. It is of that Day that Paul writes to the Philippians, saying, 'Our citizenship is in Heaven: whence also we wait for a Saviour, the Lord Jesus Christ; who shall fashion anew the body of our humiliation, that it may be conformed to the body of his glory, according to the

working whereby he is able even to subject all things unto himself' (Phil. 3:20-21). Or, as it is written again, 'We shall all be changed in a moment, in the twinkling of an eye. The dead shall be raised incorruptible and we shall be changed.' And again, 'We shall be like him, for we shall see him as he is.' And yet again, 'When he shall be manifested, then shall ye also with him be manifested in glory'—that is, in a glorified state or condition (1 Cor. 15:51-52; 2 John 3:2; Col. 3:3). That will be divine healing, indeed. Meanwhile, let it be remembered that He is perfectly able to heal even now, when healing is according to His will, whether it be with the use of means or without. And if He deliver us from sickness, we shall be thankful; if he choose for us to suffer bodily affliction, we shall also thank Him, for He knoweth best, and He doeth it. Blessed be His holy name!" (The Gospel of the Kingdom, *Fundamental Truth Publishers, Findlay, Ohio, pp. 99-102*)

FIVE: The first great catch of fish (Luke 5:1-11)
   A. The request—"And he entered into one of the ships, which was Simon's, and prayed him that he would thrust out a little from the land. And he sat down, and taught the people out of the ship. Now when he had left speaking, he said unto Simon, Launch out into the deep, and let down your nets for a draught" (Luke 5:3-4).
   B. The reluctance—"And Simon answering said unto him, Master, we have toiled all the night, and have taken nothing: nevertheless at thy word I will let down the net" (Luke 5:5).

---

†*In essence, this was an act of faith. Jesus was asking Peter, the experienced professional, to do two things contrary to good fishing practice:*
   A. To launch out into the deep part of the lake
   B. To do this in the bright daylight hours

   C. The results—"And when they had this done, they inclosed a great multitude of fishes: and their net brake. And they beckoned unto their partners, which were in the other ship, that they should come and help them. And they came, and filled both the ships, so that they began to sink" (Luke 5:6-7).
   D. The remorse—"When Simon Peter saw it, he fell down at Jesus' knees, saying, Depart from me; for I am a sinful man, O Lord. For he was astonished, and all that were with him, at the draught of the fishes which they had taken" (Luke 5:8-9).
   E. The reassurance—"And Jesus said unto Simon, Fear not; from henceforth thou shalt catch men" (Luke 5:10b).

---

† *A. Peter, like Isaiah the prophet, upon seeing the person of God, fell to his knees, both men being reminded of their own personal sinfulness. (See Gen. 6:5.) Each man was subsequently reassured, cleansed, and called to the Lord's ministry. (See Isa. 6: 6-9.)*
   B. J. Vernon McGee writes: "Simon Peter did catch men. Remember how well he did on the day of Pentecost. The Lord's answer to Peter is certainly significant; 3,000 souls came to Christ after his first sermon! Peter was fishing according to God's instruction. There is another lesson here. Do you know there is another fisherman? Do you know that Satan also is a fisherman? (See 2 Tim. 2:26.) Satan has his hook out in the water too. God is fishing for your soul, and Satan also is fishing for your soul with a hook baited with the things of the world. You might say God's hook is a cross." (Luke, pp. 69, 72)

SIX: Healing a leper (Matt. 8:2-4; Mark 1:40-45; Luke 5:12 -16)
  A. The worship by the leper
     1. The tears of the leper—"And there came a leper to him, beseeching him, and
        kneeling down to him, and saying unto him, If thou wilt, thou canst make me
        clean" (Mark 1:40).
     2. The transformation of the leper
        a. The compassion involved—"And Jesus, moved with compassion, put forth his
           hand, and touched him, and saith unto him, I will; be thou clean" (Mark 1:41).

---

†*This is the first of at least six occasions on which Jesus was moved with compassion as he
performed his miracles:*
   A. Raising the widow's dead son at Nain (Luke 7:13)
   B. Healing the maniac of Gadara (Mark 5:19)
   C. Healing two blind men (Matt. 20:34)
   D. Feeding the 5,000 (Matt. 14:14; Mark 6:34)
   E. Feeding the 4,000 (Matt. 15:32)

---

        b. The cleansing involved—"And as soon as he had spoken, immediately the
           leprosy departed from him, and he was cleansed" (Mark 1:42).
     3. The testimony of the leper—"And he straitly charged him, and forthwith sent
        him away; and saith unto him, See thou say nothing to any man: but go thy
        way, shew thyself to the priest, and offer for thy cleansing those things which
        Moses commanded, for a testimony unto them" (Mark 1:43-44).
  B. The witness of the leper—"But he went out, and began to publish it much, and to blaze
     abroad the matter, insomuch that Jesus could no more openly enter into the city, but
     was without in desert places: and they came to him from every quarter" (Mark 1:45).

---

† *A. This is the first of five miracles performed by Jesus when he told the recipient not to broadcast
   what had been done.*
   1. The raising of Jairus's daughter (Luke 8:56)
   2. The healing of two blind men (Matt. 9:31)
   3. The healing of a deaf man with a speech impediment (Mark 7:36-37)
   4. The healing of a blind man in Bethsaida (Mark 8:26)
   B. It is ironic to note:
   1. Back then, Jesus commanded these individuals not to spread abroad his fame, but they did.
   2. Today he commands us to do this, but we don't (See Matt. 28:19-20).
   *C. He ordered the cured man to present himself to the priest for the Mosaic cleansing. (See Lev.
   14:3-4, 10, 22.) This excited request from a healed leper doubtless caused much confusion and
   amazement in the temple among the priests. Up until this point there was no need for the
   cleansing ceremony, for no Israelite had ever been healed of leprosy until Jesus came (with
   the single exception of Miriam—see Num. 12:13-15; Naaman, of course, was a Syrian—see
   2 Kings 5:1, 14).*

SEVEN: Healing a paralytic (Matt. 9:1-8; Mark 2:1-12; Luke 5:17-26)
  A. Some faithful friends

1. The helplessness of the paralytic
   a. The intervening by his friends—"And they come unto him, bringing one sick of the palsy, which was borne of four" (Mark 2:3).
   b. The ingenuity of his friends—"And when they could not come nigh unto him for the press, they uncovered the roof where he was: and when they had broken it up, they let down the bed wherein the sick of the palsy lay" (Mark 2:4).
2. The healing of the paralytic
   a. Spiritual healing—"When Jesus saw their faith, he said unto the sick of the palsy, Son, thy sins be forgiven thee" (Mark 2:5).
   b. Physical healing—"I say unto thee, Arise, and take up thy bed, and go thy way into thine house. And immediately he arose, took up the bed, and went forth before them all; insomuch that they were all amazed, and glorified God, saying, We never saw it on this fashion" (Mark 2:11-12).

---

†*J. Vernon McGee writes: "There are many people who are not going to receive the message of salvation unless you lift a corner of their stretcher and carry them to the place where they can hear the word of the Lord. They are paralyzed—immobilized by sin and by many other things the world holds for them. Some are paralyzed by prejudice and others by indifference. They are never going to hear Jesus say to them, 'Son, thy sins be forgiven thee,' unless you take the corner of their stretcher and bring them to Him." (Luke, p. 74)*

B. Some faithless foes (Mark 2:6-12)
   1. The denouncing by the scribes—"But there were certain of the scribes sitting there, and reasoning in their hearts, Why doth this man thus speak blasphemies? who can forgive sins but God only?" (Mark 2:6-7).
   2. The defense by the Savior—"And immediately when Jesus perceived in his spirit that they so reasoned within themselves, he said unto them, Why reason ye these things in your hearts? Whether is it easier to say to the sick of the palsy, Thy sins be forgiven thee; or to say, Arise, and take up thy bed, and walk? But that ye may know that the Son of man hath power on earth to forgive sins, (he saith to the sick of the palsy,) I say unto thee, Arise, and take up thy bed, and go thy way into thine house" (Mark 2:8-11).
EIGHT: Healing a withered hand (Matt. 12:9-14; Mark 3:1-6; Luke 6:6-11)
   A. The occasion for this miracle—"And it came to pass also on another sabbath, that he entered into the synagogue and taught: and there was a man whose right hand was withered" (Luke 6:6).
   B. The objection to this miracle
      1. The legalists of the Sabbath—"And the scribes and Pharisees watched him, whether he would heal on the sabbath day; that they might find an accusation against him" (Luke 6:7).
      2. The Lord of the Sabbath
         a. Defending his miracle—"And he saith unto them, Is it lawful to do good on the sabbath days, or to do evil? to save life, or to kill? But they held their peace" (Mark 3:4). "And he said unto them, What man shall there be among you, that shall have one sheep, and if it fall into a pit on the

sabbath day, will he not lay hold on it, and lift it out? How much then is a man better than a sheep? Wherefore it is lawful to do well on the sabbath days" (Matt. 12:11-12).

    b. Decreeing his miracle—"And when he had looked round about on them with anger, being grieved for the hardness of their hearts, he saith unto the man, Stretch forth thine hand. And he stretched it out: and his hand was restored whole as the other" (Mark 3:5).

†This is the only explicit reference to the anger of Jesus in the New Testament.

  C. The outcome of this miracle—"And they were filled with madness; and communed one with another what they might do to Jesus" (Luke 6:11). "And the Pharisees went forth, and straightway took counsel with the Herodians against him, how they might destroy him" (Mark 3:6).

NINE: Healing a centurion's servant (Matt. 8:5-13; Luke 7:1-10)

  A. The centurion's concern for an individual

    1. The problem—"And a certain centurion's servant, who was dear unto him, was sick, and ready to die" (Luke 7:2).

    2. The plea—"And when he heard of Jesus, he sent unto him the elders of the Jews, beseeching him that he would come and heal his servant" (Luke 7:3).

  B. The centurion's love for Israel—"And when they came to Jesus, they besought him instantly, saying, That he was worthy for whom he should do this: For he loveth our nation, and he hath built us a synagogue" (Luke 7:4-5).

  C. The centurion's faith in Immanuel

    1. His reliance upon Christ

      a. The confidence involved—"Then Jesus went with them. And when he was now not far from the house, the centurion sent friends to him, saying unto him, Lord, trouble not thyself: for I am not worthy that thou shouldest enter under my roof: Wherefore neither thought I myself worthy to come unto thee: but say in a word, and my servant shall be healed. For I also am a man set under authority, having under me soldiers, and I say unto one, Go, and he goeth; and to another, Come, and he cometh; and to my servant, Do this, and he doeth it" (Luke 7:6-8).

      b. The commendation involved—"When Jesus heard these things, he marvelled at him, and turned him about, and said unto the people that followed him, I say unto you, I have not found so great faith, no, not in Israel" (Luke 7:9).

† A. This is the first of two cases involving miracles in which Jesus was amazed at the great amount of faith he found in the one requesting the miracle. Both individuals were Gentiles. The other was the Syro-phoenician mother (Matt. 15:28).

* B. How sad to note that he marveled over the unbelief and lack of faith in his own countrymen. "But Jesus said unto them, A prophet is not without honour, but in his own country, and among his own kin, and in his own house. . . . And he marvelled because of their unbelief. And he went round about the villages, teaching" (Mark 6:4, 6).*

2. His reward from Christ
    a. The physical healing of his servant—"And they that were sent, returning to the house, found the servant whole that had been sick" (Luke 7:10).
    b. The spiritual healing of his soul—"And I say unto you, That many shall come from the east and west, and shall sit down with Abraham, and Isaac, and Jacob, in the kingdom of heaven. But the children of the kingdom shall be cast out into outer darkness: there shall be weeping and gnashing of teeth" (Matt. 8:11-12).

TEN: Raising a widow's son (Luke 7:11-17)
    A. The widow's sorrow—"Now when he came nigh to the gate of the city, behold, there was a dead man carried out, the only son of his mother, and she was a widow: and much people of the city was with her" (Luke 7:12).
    B. The widow's Savior—"And when the Lord saw her, he had compassion on her, and said unto her, Weep not" (Luke 7:13).
    C. The widow's son
        1. Resurrected by the Messiah—"And he came and touched the bier: and they that bare him stood still. And he said, Young man, I say unto thee, Arise" (Luke 7:14).
        2. Reunited to the mother—"And he that was dead sat up, and began to speak. And he delivered him to his mother" (Luke 7:15).
            a. The people affirm the glory of God—"And there came a fear on all: and they glorified God" (Luke 7:16).
            b. The people acknowledge the prophet of God—"A great prophet is risen up among us . . . God hath visited his people" (Luke 7:16).

---

† A. *This marks the first of three persons raised from the dead by Christ. The other two are Jairus's daughter (Luke 8:54-56) and Lazarus (John 11:43). The last resurrection had occurred some seven centuries previous to this when the bones of Elisha had restored to life a young man (2 Kings 13:20-22).*

B. *This is the first recorded instance in which Jesus was recognized by the Jewish crowds as a prophet, although the earliest acknowledgment came from a non-Jewish Samaritan woman (see John 4:19).*
    1. *Jesus called himself a prophet (Matt. 13:57; John 4:44).*
    2. *Herod Antipas suspected it (Matt. 14:5).*
    3. *The crowds on two future occasions would acknowledge it.*
        a. *During the Feast of Tabernacles (John 7:40)*
        b. *During the triumphal entry (Matt. 21:11)*
    4. *The 5,000 men Christ fed believed it (John 6:14).*
    5. *A former blind man testified to it (John 9:17).*
    6. *The two disciples en route to Emmaus spoke of it (Luke 24:19).*

ELEVEN: Calming the stormy sea (Matt. 8:18, 23-27; Mark 4:35-41; Luke 8:22-25)

---

†*One of the most famous Old Testament miracles had to do with a sleeping Hebrew prophet in a boat during a storm. One of the most famous New Testament miracles also had to do with a sleeping Hebrew prophet in a boat during a storm. The Old Testament prophet was Jonah. The*

New Testament prophet was Jesus. The second would later use the experience of the first as a sign to an unbelieving generation: "For as Jonas was three days and three nights in the whale's belly; so shall the Son of man be three days and three nights in the heart of the earth" (Matt. 12:40).

A. The stormy sea—"And the same day, when the even was come, he saith unto them, Let us pass over unto the other side. And when they had sent away the multitude, they took him even as he was in the ship. And there were also with him other little ships. And there arose a great storm of wind, and the waves beat into the ship, so that it was now full" (Mark 4:35-37).

† *A. Note the phrase, "they took him even as he was." Our Lord was a real man, with dirt under his fingernails, sweat on his brow, and, on this occasion, weariness in his bones.*
B. The Greek word here refers to a violent storm, a furious squall of hurricane proportion. The Sea of Galilee, situated in a basin surrounded by mountains, is particularly susceptible to sudden, violent storms. Cool air from the Mediterranean is drawn down through the narrow mountain passes connecting the two bodies of water, and clashes with the hot, humid air lying over the lake. Thus, in a matter of seconds, the quiet Galilean waters can be turned into a howling, life-threatening watery nightmare for all those sailing upon it.

B. The desperate plea—"And he was in the hinder part of the ship, asleep on a pillow: and they awake him, and say unto him, Master, carest thou not that we perish?" (Mark 4:38).

†*He was asleep. Here was true humanity and undiminished Deity. This is the only reference to Jesus being asleep in the Gospel accounts.*

1. The miracle—"And he arose, and rebuked the wind, and said unto the sea, Peace, be still. And the wind ceased, and there was a great calm" (Mark 4:39).

†*The language of this verse strongly suggests that the vicious storm may have been caused by satanic activity, perhaps in an attempt to drown Jesus.*
A. The Greek word for rebuke is epitimao, *a word Jesus used in denouncing both Satan and his demons.*
1. The rebuking of demons (Luke 9:42; Matt. 17:18)
2. The rebuking of Satan (Mark 8:33; Jude 1:9)
B. The Greek word for peace, phimoo, *used only here and in Mark 1:25 (where Jesus denounced a demon), means literally, "be muzzled, be gagged." This action often referred to the muzzling of a wild dog.*

2. The marvel—"But the men marvelled, saying, What manner of man is this, that even the winds and the sea obey him!" (Matt. 8:27).

†*There are many lessons to be learned today from this miracle. Three questions should be asked when the storms of life beset the Christian.*
- A. *Is this storm one of punishment or purification? That is, am I being chastened for my sin (as was true in the case of Jonah), or is this simply a trial allowed by God to purify me (as was true here with the disciples)?*
- B. *Have I made room for him on board? Am I aware of his presence?*
- C. *What does he want me to do in the time of the storm? In a nutshell, three things:*
  - 1. *He wants me to thank him for the storm. "In every thing give thanks: for this is the will of God in Christ Jesus concerning you" (1 Thess. 5:18).*
  - 2. *He wants me to fellowship with him in the storm. "Pray without ceasing" (1 Thess. 5:17).*
  - 3. *He wants me to trust him through the storm. "Trust in the Lord with all thine heart; and lean not unto thine own understanding. In all thy ways acknowledge him, and he shall direct thy paths" (Prov. 3:5-6).*

TWELVE: Healing the maniac of Gadara (Matt. 8:28-34; Mark 5:1-20; Luke 8:26-39)

---

†*This episode might rightly be entitled, "How a madman became a missionary." It involves the fullest and most frightening description of demon possession in all the Bible. As the story opens, Jesus and his disciples cross the Sea of Galilee from west to east and have landed in the Gentile region of Gadara. There they are immediately confronted by a wild, bleeding, shrieking maniac.*

- A. The madman of Gadara
  - 1. The Gerasene maniac, controlled by demons
    - a. His home—"Who had his dwelling among the tombs" (Mark 5:3).
    - b. His helplessness
      - (1) He was naked (Luke 8:27).
      - (2) He was "exceeding fierce" (Matt. 8:28).
      - (3) He was totally unmanageable (Mark 5:3-4).
      - (4) He was constantly crying and cutting himself with stones (Mark 5:5).
      - (5) He was seized upon and driven about by a legion of demons (Luke 8:29; Mark 5:9).
  - 2. The Galilean Messiah, controller of demons
    - a. They knew him—"And behold, they cried out, saying, What have we to do with thee, Jesus, thou Son of God?" (Matt. 8:29)
    - b. They feared him—"Art thou come hither to torment us before the time?" (Matt. 8:29) "I adjure thee by God, that thou torment me not" (Mark 5:7b).

---

†*They apparently knew about future judgment. Various New Testament writers attest to this judgment of fallen angels.*
- A. *Paul: "Know ye not that we shall judge angels? how much more things that pertain to this life?" (1 Cor. 6:3).*
- B. *Peter: "For if God spared not the angels that sinned, but cast them down to hell, and delivered them into chains of darkness, to be reserved unto judgment" (2 Pet. 2:4).*

C. Jude: *"And the angels which kept not their first estate, but left their own habitation, he hath reserved in everlasting chains under darkness unto the judgment of the great day" (Jude 6).*
In fact, Jesus said that hell itself was originally created for the devil and his angels, all of which will eventually spend eternity there. "Then shall he say also unto them on the left hand, Depart from me, ye cursed, into everlasting fire, prepared for the devil and his angels" (Matt. 25:41). "And the devil that deceived them was cast into the lake of fire and brimstone, where the beast and the false prophet are, and shall be tormented day and night for ever and ever" (Rev. 20:10).

c. They obeyed him.
  (1) The rebuke—"For he said unto him, Come out of the man, thou unclean spirit" (Mark 5:8).
  (2) The ringleader—"And he asked him, What is thy name? And he answered, saying, My name is Legion: for we are many" (Mark 5:9).

†*A legion in the Roman army consisted of 6,000 soldiers. This may be an indication of the number of demons in the man.*

  (3) The request—"And he besought him much that he would not send them away out of the country. Now there was there nigh unto the mountains a great herd of swine feeding. And all the devils besought him, saying, Send us into the swine, that we may enter into them" (Mark 5:10-12).

†*Why did the demons desire the bodies of pigs? Several reasons have been suggested:*
  A. To kill Jesus and his disciples. Few animals are more dangerous than angry wild pigs.
  B. To turn the community against Jesus by drowning the pigs. If this was the plan, they succeeded.

  (4) The release—"And forthwith Jesus gave them leave. And the unclean spirits went out, and entered into the swine: and the herd ran violently down a steep place into the sea, (they were about two thousand;) and were choked in the sea" (Mark 5:13).

†*This is the first of two occasions on which Jesus performed a miracle in a way which had destructive results. The other miracle was the withering of the fig tree (Matt. 21:19).*

B. The missionary from Gadara
  1. His deliverance by Christ—"Then they went out to see what was done; and came to Jesus, and found the man, out of whom the devils were departed, sitting at the feet of Jesus, clothed, and in his right mind: and they were afraid" (Luke 8:35). "And they began to pray him to depart out of their coasts" (Mark 5:17).

†*These people were more interested in money than in men. They preferred gold to God. They wanted their pigs more than they desired what Christ had to offer. John Oxenham has vividly captured their tragic philosophy in his poem:*

"Rabbi, begone!
Thy powers bring loss to us and ours; Our ways are not as Thine—
Thou lovest men—we swine.

O get Thee gone, O Holy One,
And take these fools of Thine;
Their souls? What care we for their souls? Since we have lost our swine."

Then Christ went sadly,
He had wrought for them a sign
Of love and tenderness divine—
They wanted swine.

Christ stands without your door and gently knocks,
But if your gold or swine the entrance blocks
He forces no man's hold, He will depart,
And leave you to the treasures of your heart.
—from "Gadara, A.D. 31"

---

2. His desire—As expressed to Christ
    a. The request—"And when he was come into the ship, he that had been possessed with the devil prayed him that he might be with him" (Mark 5:18).
    b. The response—"Howbeit Jesus suffered him not, but saith unto him, Go home to thy friends, and tell them how great things the Lord hath done for thee, and hath had compassion on thee" (Mark 5:19).

---

†*This is in great contrast to Jesus' usual command to the one experiencing the miracle, in which he tells the person not to make it known.*

---

3. His declaration for Christ—"And he departed, and began to publish in Decapolis how great things Jesus had done for him: and all men did marvel" (Mark 5:20).

---

†*Decapolis (literally, "ten cities") was a league of ten cities characterized by high Greek culture, allied together for purposes of trading. All but one city (Scythopolis) were east of the Galilean Sea and Jordan River. This convert thus became the greatest missionary to Gentiles since the preacher to Nineveh, Jonah the prophet.*

THIRTEEN: Healing the woman of a bloody flux (Matt. 9:20-22; Mark 5:25-34; Luke 8:43-48)
  A. The hurting patient
    1. Her years of frustration—"And a certain woman, which had an issue of blood twelve years, and had suffered many things of many physicians, and had

spent all that she had, and was nothing bettered, but rather grew worse, when she had heard of Jesus, came in the press behind, and touched his garment" (Mark 5:25-27).

†*This poor woman's condition carried with it religious and social consequences as well as physical consequences. According to Leviticus 15:19-30, she would have been considered unclean for twelve long years. Note also she had spent all her resources on her problem. Thus, she was pain-wracked, penniless, and prohibited from social gatherings. But then, we read, "she . . . heard of Jesus."*

    2. Her hour of expectation—"For she said, If I may touch but his clothes, I shall be whole" (Mark 5:28).
    3. Her moment of realization—"And straightway the fountain of her blood was dried up; and she felt in her body that she was healed of that plague" (Mark 5:29).
  B. The healing physician
    1. The announcement—"And Jesus said, Who touched me? When all denied, Peter and they that were with him said, Master, the multitude throng thee and press thee, and sayest thou, Who touched me? And Jesus said, Somebody hath touched me: for I perceive that virtue is gone out of me" (Luke 8:45-46).

†*The two statements of Jesus here point out two profound insights concerning his earthly ministry.*
  A. His total dependence upon the Holy Spirit—Note his question, "Who touched me?" Even though Christ retained his divine attributes (his omnipresence, his omnipotence, his omniscience) upon coming to earth, he chose not to use them in an independent way, but depended upon the Holy Spirit to lead, advise, and empower him. In other words, Jesus may not have known at that moment who touched him. A similar example can be seen later when he was asked concerning the date of the second coming. His answer was: "But of that day and that hour knoweth no man, no, not the angels which are in heaven, neither the Son, but the Father" (Mark 13:32). (See also Matt. 4:1; John 5:19; Phil. 2: 5-8.)
  B. The awful demands upon his physical body—Note his statement: "Virtue is gone out of me." The Greek word for virtue here is dunamis, *and refers to power or strength. How taxing it must have been upon his body to perform his mighty miracles.*

    2. The acknowledgment—"And when the woman saw that she was not hid, she came trembling, and falling down before him, she declared unto him before all the people for what cause she had touched him, and how she was healed immediately" (Luke 8:47).
    3. The assurance—"And he said unto her, Daughter, thy faith hath made thee whole; go in peace, and be whole of thy plague" (Mark 5:34).

†*This is the only time Jesus uses the title "Daughter."*
On a previous occasion he had referred to a paralytic who had been healed as "Son" (Matt. 9:2).

FOURTEEN: Raising Jairus's daughter from the dead (Matt. 9:18-19, 23-26; Mark 5:22-24, 35-43; Luke 8:41-42, 49-56).

A. The agony of Jairus (Mark 5:22-24, 35-43; Luke 8:41-42, 49-56)

   1. His dying daughter

      a. Jairus's report to Jesus—"And, behold, there cometh one of the rulers of the synagogue, Jairus by name; and when he saw him, he fell at his feet. And besought him greatly, saying, My little daughter lieth at the point of death" (Mark 5:22-23a). "For he had one only daughter, about twelve years of age" (Luke 8:42a).

      b. Jairus's request to Jesus—"I pray thee, Come and lay thy hands on her, that she may be healed: and she shall live" (Mark 5:23b).

   2. His dead daughter

      a. The terrible message—"While he yet spake, there came from the ruler of the synagogue's house certain which said, Thy daughter is dead: why troublest thou the Master any further?" (Mark 5:35).

---

†*Wrong. This is precisely the time for a believer to "trouble . . . the Master." As the song admonishes:*

> *"Got any rivers you think are uncrossable?*
> *Got any mountains you can't tunnel through?*
> *God specializes in things thought impossible.*
> *What He's done for others, He'll do for you!"*

---

      b. The tender message—"As soon as Jesus heard the word that was spoken, he saith unto the ruler of the synagogue, Be not afraid, only believe" (Mark 5:36). "And all wept, and bewailed her: but he said, Weep not; she is not dead, but sleepeth. And they laughed him to scorn, knowing that she was dead" (Luke 8:52-53).

B. The amazement of Jairus—Upon reaching Jairus's home, Jesus went into the room where the dead girl lay. "And he put them all out, and took her by the hand, and called, saying, Maid, arise. And her spirit came again, and she arose straightway: and he commanded to give her meat. And her parents were astonished: but he charged them that they should tell no man what was done" (Luke 8:54-56).

---

†*There are three "firsts" associated with this miracle:*

   A. It is the first time in human history that a female was raised from the dead.

   B. It is the first mention of that special apostolic trio, Peter, James, and John. They would be singled out again:

      1. On the Mount of Transfiguration (Matt. 17:1)

      2. In the Garden of Gethsemane (Mark 14:33)

   C. It is the first time the word "sleep" is used to describe the death of a believer. After this, its employment will become very familiar:

      1. Concerning the death of Lazarus—"These things said he: and after that he saith unto them, Our friend Lazarus sleepeth; but I go, that I may awake him out of sleep" (John 11:11).

2. *Concerning an event after the death of Christ—"And the graves were opened; and many bodies of the saints which slept arose" (Matt. 27:52).*

3. *Concerning the martyrdom of Stephen—"And he kneeled down, and cried with a loud voice, Lord, lay not this sin to their charge. And when he had said this, he fell asleep" (Acts 7:60).*

4. *Concerning the bodies of departed believers at the present time—"For God hath not appointed us to wrath, but to obtain salvation by our Lord Jesus Christ, who died for us, that, whether we wake or sleep, we should live together with him" (1 Thess. 5:9-10).*

5. *Concerning the rapture—"For if we believe that Jesus died and rose again, even so them also which sleep in Jesus will God bring with him" (1 Thess. 4:14).*

FIFTEEN: Healing two blind men (Matt. 9:27-31)

A. The request of the sightless—"And when Jesus departed thence, two blind men followed him, crying, and saying, Thou Son of David, have mercy on us" (Matt 9:27).

†*It has been said that God will hush every harp in heaven to hear and answer this kind of prayer. This is the first of at least five miracles performed by Christ to answer such a prayer request.*

A. The Syro-phoenician mother (Matt. 15:22)

B. The father of a demon-possessed son (Matt. 17:15)

C. Ten lepers (Luke 17:13)

D. Blind Bartimaeus (Luke 18:38)

B. The response of the sinless

1. The test of Jesus—"And when he was come into the house, the blind men came to him: and Jesus saith unto them, Believe ye that I am able to do this? They said unto him, Yea, Lord" (Matt. 9:28).

2. The touch of Jesus—"Then touched he their eyes, saying, according to your faith be it unto you" (Matt. 9:29).

3. The testimony for Jesus—"And their eyes were opened; and Jesus straitly charged them, saying, See that no man know it. But they, when they were departed, spread abroad his fame in all that country" (Matt. 9:30-31).

SIXTEEN: Healing a dumb demoniac (Matt. 9:32-34)—"As they went out, behold, they brought to him a dumb man possessed with a devil" (Matt. 9:32).

A. The miracle—"And when the devil was cast out, the dumb spake" (Matt. 9:33).

B. The marvel—"The multitudes marveled, saying, It was never so seen in Israel" (Matt. 9:33b).

C. The malice—"But the Pharisees said, He casteth out devils through the prince of the devils" (Matt. 9:34).

†*This is the first of many occasions on which wicked Pharisees viciously accused Jesus of being demon-possessed. Note some of these occasions:*

A. After he had healed a blind, mute, and demonic man: "But when the Pharisees heard it, they said, This fellow doth not cast out devils, but by Beelzebub the prince of the devils" (Matt. 12:24).

B. During the Feast of Tabernacles: "The people answered and said, Thou hast a devil: who goeth about to kill thee?" (John 7:20).

C. After he claimed to be greater than Abraham: "Then answered the Jews, and said unto him, Say we not well that thou art a Samaritan, and hast a devil? Then said the Jews unto him, Now we know that thou hast a devil. Abraham is dead, and the prophets; and thou sayest, If a man keep my saying, he shall never taste of death" (John 8:48, 52).

D. After his sermon on the Good Shepherd: "And many of them said, He hath a devil, and is mad; why hear ye him?" (John 10:20).

SEVENTEEN: The healing of a man crippled for thirty-eight years (John 5:1-16)
   A. The cripple and the Christ (first meeting)
      1. Wallowing on his bed of affliction
         a. The misery by the Bethesda waters—"Now there is at Jerusalem by the sheep market a pool, which is called in the Hebrew tongue Bethesda, having five porches" (John 5:2).
            (1) A great crowd was there—"In these lay a great multitude of impotent folk, of blind, halt, withered" (John 5:3a).
            (2) A certain man was there—"And a certain man was there, which had an infirmity thirty and eight years" (John 5:5).

---

†*The earliest manuscripts omit these words, which appear to be a late insertion to explain why the pool water was "stirred" (v. 7). People believed that an angel came and stirred it. According to local tradition, the first one in the water would be healed. But the Bible nowhere teaches this kind of superstition, a situation which would be a most cruel contest for many ill people. No extant Greek manuscript before A.D. 400 contains these words.* (The Bible Knowledge Commentary, Victor Books, Wheaton, Ill., 1983, p. 289)

---

         b. The moving of the Bethesda waters—"Waiting for the moving of the water" (John 5:3b). "For an angel went down at a certain season into the pool, and troubled the water: whosoever then first after the troubling of the water stepped in was made whole of whatsoever disease he had" (John 5:4).
         c. The miracle at the Bethesda waters
            (1) The Savior's invitation—"When Jesus saw him lie, and knew that he had been now a long time in that case, he saith unto him, Wilt thou be made whole?" (John 5:6).
            (2) The sick man's ignorance—He did not realize to whom he was speaking. "The impotent man answered him, Sir, I have no man, when the water is troubled, to put me into the pool: but while I am coming, another steppeth down before me" (John 5:7).

---

†*The statement, "Sir, I have no man," is profound in its spiritual implications. Both Luke and Paul later write concerning its importance:*
   A. *Luke's testimony—"And Philip ran thither to him, and heard him read the prophet Esaias, and said, Understandest thou what thou readest? And he said, How can I, except some man should guide me? And he desired Philip that he would come up and sit with him"* (Acts 8:30-31).

B. *Paul's testimony*—"*How then shall they call on him in whom they have not believed? and how shall they believe in him of whom they have not heard? and how shall they hear without a preacher? and how shall they preach, except they be sent? as it is written, How beautiful are the feet of them that preach the gospel of peace, and bring glad tidings of good things!*" *(Rom. 10:14-15).*

2. Walking with his bed of affliction—"Jesus saith unto him, Rise, take up thy bed, and walk. And immediately the man was made whole, and took up his bed, and walked: and on the same day was the sabbath" (John 5:8-9).
B. The cripple and the critics
  1. First round—"The Jews therefore said unto him that was cured, It is the sabbath day: it is not lawful for thee to carry thy bed. He answered them, He that made me whole, the same said unto me, Take up thy bed, and walk" (John 5:10-11).
  2. Second round—"Then asked they him, What man is that which said unto thee, Take up thy bed, and walk? And he that was healed wist not who it was: for Jesus had conveyed himself away, a multitude being in that place" (John 5:12-13).
C. The cripple and the Christ (final meeting)
  1. His warning from Jesus—"Afterward Jesus findeth him in the temple, and said unto him, Behold, thou art made whole: sin no more, lest a worse thing come unto thee" (John 5:14).

†*While Scripture is clear that personal suffering is* not *always a punishment caused by individual sin (John 9:1-3), this case seems to be the exception.*

2. His witness for Jesus—"The man departed, and told the Jews that it was Jesus, which had made him whole. And therefore did the Jews persecute Jesus, and sought to slay him, because he had done these things on the sabbath day" (John 5:15-16).
EIGHTEEN: The feeding of the 5,000 (Matt. 14:14-21; Mark 6:31-44; Luke 9:10-17; John 6:1-13)

† A. *This is the only recorded miracle of Christ mentioned by all four Gospel writers. It may have been the greatest. It was certainly the most involved, for it touched the lives of perhaps as many as 20,000 people (5,000 men plus their wives and children).*
  B. *At this time, Jesus fulfilled the prophecies of Ezekiel concerning the ministry of the promised Good Shepherd. "For thus saith the Lord God; Behold, I, even I, will both search my sheep, and seek them out. As a shepherd seeketh out his flock in the day that he is among his sheep that are scattered; so will I seek out my sheep, and will deliver them out of all places where they have been scattered in the cloudy and dark day. . . . I will feed them in a good pasture, and upon the high mountains of Israel shall their fold be: there shall they lie in a good fold, and in a fat pasture shall they feed upon the mountains of Israel" (Ezek. 34:11-12, 14).*

A. The sensitive Shepherd
  1. He knew the needs of the twelve—"And the apostles gathered themselves together unto Jesus, and told him all things, both what they had done, and

what they had taught. And he said unto them, Come ye yourselves apart into a desert place, and rest a while: for there were many coming and going, and they had no leisure so much as to eat. And they departed into a desert place by ship privately" (Mark 6:30-32).

†*The disciples needed this rest, for they had just learned of John the Baptist's martyrdom. In addition, they were approaching the danger of burnout.*

    2. He knew the needs of the crowd—"And Jesus, when he came out, saw much people, and was moved with compassion toward them, because they were as sheep not having a shepherd" (Mark 6:34).
        a. They needed to be taught—"And he began to teach them many things" (Mark 6:34). "And he received them, and spake unto them of the Kingdom of God" (Luke 9:11b).

†*Hosea the prophet had once cried out: "My people are destroyed for lack of knowledge" (Hos. 4:6). To counteract this, our Lord invested a great amount of time during his earthly ministry in teaching the Word of God. "And they were astonished at his doctrine: for he taught them as one that had authority, and not as the scribes" (Mark 1:22). (See also Matt. 4:23; 5:2; 7:29; 9:35; 11:1; 13:54; John 6:59; 7:14, 28; 8:2, 20; 18:20.)*

        b. They needed to be healed—"And healed them that had need of healing" (Luke 9:11c).
        c. They needed to be fed.
           (1) The observation of the two: Philip's calculation—"When Jesus then lifted up his eyes, and saw a great company come unto him, he saith unto Philip, Whence shall we buy bread, that these may eat? And this he said to prove him: for he himself knew what he would do. Philip answered him, Two hundred pennyworth of bread is not sufficient for them, that every one of them may take a little" (John 6:5-7). Andrew's confirmation—"One of his disciples, Andrew, Simon Peter's brother, saith unto him, There is a lad here, which hath five barley loaves, and two small fishes: but what are they among so many?" (John 6:8-9)
           (2) The opinion of the twelve—"And when it was evening, his disciples came to him, saying, This is a desert place, and the time is now past; send the multitude away, that they may go into the villages, and buy themselves victuals" (Matt. 14:15).
    B. The systematic Shepherd—"And he commanded them to make all sit down by companies upon the green grass. And they sat down in ranks, by hundreds, and by fifties" (Mark 6:39-40). "And Jesus said, Make the men sit down. Now there was much grass in the place. So the men sat down, in number about five thousand" (John 6:10).

†*"The Greek word translated* ranks *means fundamentally 'garden beds' and can only be translated ranks or divisions by a metaphor. This term is a particularly vivid and poetic touch in*

Mark. The lanes of green grass and the solid groups of people dressed in gay colors of the East looked just like a flower garden. 'And they sat down in garden beds, by hundreds and by fifties.' The whole mountainside must have been alive with the beautiful wild flowers that abound in Palestine in early spring. This must have made the scene even more attractive. 'Law and order' was always the first principle in Jesus' handling the vast multitudes that thronged his ministry. All would now be able to hear and see. All could be readily served with aisles for the apostles to use in going from one group to another. It would be easily ascertained whether all had been served and whether anyone desired more food. An estimate of the number in the crowd was more readily made by reason of this orderly arrangement. The people probably were permitted to follow their own inclinations as families and friends grouped together or people who happened to be near together now changed to orderly formation. There seems to have been no effort at mathematical exactness in the arrangement." (Studies in the Life of Christ, R. C. Foster, Baker Books, Grand Rapids, Mich., p. 635)

C. The sovereign Shepherd—"And when he had taken the five loaves and the two fishes, he looked up to heaven, and blessed, and brake the loaves, and gave them to his disciples to set before them; and the two fishes divided he among them all. And they did all eat, and were filled" (Mark 6:41-42).

---

†*It is estimated that it would have required some fifteen tons of food to feed this great multitude.*

D. The sufficient Shepherd—"When they were filled, he said unto his disciples, Gather up the fragments that remain, that nothing be lost. Therefore they gathered them together, and filled twelve baskets with the fragments of the five barley loaves, which remained over and above unto them that had eaten" (John 6:12-13).
E. The saddened Shepherd—"Then those men, when they had seen the miracle that Jesus did, said, This is of a truth that prophet that should come into the world. When Jesus therefore perceived that they would come and take him by force, to make him a king, he departed again into a mountain himself alone" (John 6:14-15).

---

† *A. There is a note of sorrow at the end of this otherwise fantastic miracle. Rightfully recognizing him as a prophet, the 5,000 men wrongly attempted to make him their king. But both their motive and their method were wrong.*
  1. Their motive was wrong. Jesus himself would point this out during his sermon on the following day. "Jesus answered them and said, Verily, verily, I say unto you, Ye seek me, not because ye saw the miracles, but because ye did eat of the loaves, and were filled. Labour not for the meat which perisheth, but for that meat which endureth unto everlasting life, which the Son of man shall give unto you: for him hath God the Father sealed" (John 6:26-27). In a previous incident, another group of men had made the same mistake. "Now when he was in Jerusalem at the passover, in the feast day, many believed in his name, when they saw the miracles which he did. But Jesus did not commit himself unto them, because he knew all men, and needed not that any should testify of man: for he knew what was in man" (John 2:23-25).

2. *Their method was wrong. Jesus did not come to be crowned by sinful people, but rather to be crucified for sinful people. The Father alone will someday give the Son his rightful kingdom. "And the seventh angel sounded; and there were great voices in heaven, saying, The kingdoms of this world are become the kingdoms of our Lord, and of his Christ; and he shall reign for ever and ever" (Rev. 11:15). (See also Psa. 2:7-12; Dan. 7:13-14; Isa. 6:9-11.)*

B. *At least five reasons have been suggested concerning why this miracle was performed.*

1. *To demonstrate Christ's compassion upon people—He was concerned not only with their souls, but also with their bodies.*

2. *To test his disciples—This undoubtedly strengthened their faith. They would remember it all their lives.*

3. *To prove his messianic claims—The Jews had a tradition that when the Messiah came, he would feed them with bread as Moses had once done. Note the following dialogue which took place on the next day between the crowd and Jesus: "Our fathers did eat manna in the desert; as it is written, He gave them bread from heaven to eat. Then Jesus said unto them, Verily, verily, I say unto you, Moses gave you not that bread from heaven; but my Father giveth you the true bread from heaven. . . . And Jesus said unto them, I am the bread of life: he that cometh to me shall never hunger; and he that believeth on me shall never thirst" (John 6:31-32, 35).*

4. *To show the value of small things when given over to Christ—Especially is this seen by the giving of the loaves, not only in matters of quantity (five loaves), but also in quality (they were barley loaves). Wheat loaves were the normal diet back then. Barley loaves were eaten only by the very poor.*

5. *To illustrate God's faithfulness—In fact, this miracle was simply an unforgettable illustration of a profound principle Jesus had previously taught during his Sermon on the Mount. "Therefore take no thought, saying, What shall we eat? or, What shall we drink? or, Wherewithal shall we be clothed? But seek ye first the kingdom of God, and his righteousness; and all these things shall be added unto you" (Matt. 6:31, 33).*

NINETEEN: Walking on water (Matt. 14:24-33; Mark 6:47-52; John 6:16-21)—"And straightway he constrained his disciples to get into the ship, and to go to the other side before unto Bethsaida, while he sent away the people. And when he had sent them away, he departed into a mountain to pray" (Mark 6:45-46). "And when even was now come, his disciples went down unto the sea, and entered into a ship, and went over the sea toward Capernaum. And it was now dark, and Jesus was not come to them" (John 6:16-17).

A. The frustration in the ship—"But the ship was now in the midst of the sea, tossed with waves: for the wind was contrary" (Matt. 14:24). "And the sea arose" (John 6:18). "And he saw them toiling in rowing" (Mark 6:48).

B. The apparition on the sea—"And in the fourth watch of the night Jesus went unto them, walking on the sea. And when the disciples saw him walking on the sea, they were troubled, saying, It is a spirit; and they cried out for fear" (Matt. 14:25-26).

C. The consolation from the Savior—"But straightway Jesus spake unto them, saying, Be of good cheer; it is I; be not afraid" (Matt. 14:7).

---

†*A similar event would later occur on the first Easter Sunday night in Jerusalem, when Christ would reassure his frightened disciples who once again had mistaken him for a ghost. "And as they thus spake, Jesus himself stood in the midst of them, and saith unto them, Peace be unto*

you. But they were terrified and affrighted, and supposed that they had seen a spirit. And he said unto them, Why are ye troubled? and why do thoughts arise in your hearts? Behold my hands and my feet, that it is I myself: handle me, and see; for a spirit hath not flesh and bones, as ye see me have" (Luke 24:36-39).

D. The desperation of the sailor
1. His try—"And Peter answered him and said, Lord, if it be thou, bid me come unto thee on the water. And he said, Come. And when Peter was come down out of the ship, he walked on the water, to go to Jesus" (Matt. 14:28-29).
2. His cry—"But when he saw the wind boisterous, he was afraid; and beginning to sink, he cried, saying, Lord, save me. And immediately Jesus stretched forth his hand, and caught him, and said unto him, O thou of little faith, wherefore didst thou doubt?" (Matt. 14:30-31)

† *A. This is the shortest prayer in the Bible, consisting of only three words. The longest prayer is found in 1 Kings 8:23-53, as offered up by Solomon at the dedication of the temple. It contains over 1,000 words.*
B. It has been suggested that this miracle serves as a remarkable review of that relationship between Christ and his Church. Note the following comparisons:
1. In Matthew 14, Christ sent his followers away in a boat on the sea and then ascended a hill to pray. The disciples then ran into a great storm on the Sea of Galilee.
2. In Acts 1, Christ sends all his followers away and then ascends into heaven to pray. "But ye shall receive power, after that the Holy Ghost is come upon you: and ye shall be witnesses unto me both in Jerusalem, and in all Judaea, and in Samaria, and unto the uttermost part of the earth. And when he had spoken these things, while they beheld, he was taken up; and a cloud received him out of their sight" (Acts 1:8-9). As his disciples we often run into great storms on the sea of life.
3. In Matthew 14, Christ remained on the hill for awhile to pray for his own. In Romans 8, we are told he will remain in heaven for awhile to pray for us. "Who is he that condemneth? It is Christ that died, yea rather, that is risen again, who is even at the right hand of God, who also maketh intercession for us" (Rom. 8:34).
4. In Matthew 14, Christ eventually came for his own. In 1 Thessalonians 4, Christ will eventually come for us. "For the Lord himself shall descend from heaven with a shout, with the voice of the archangel, and with the trump of God: and the dead in Christ shall rise first: Then we which are alive and remain shall be caught up together with them in the clouds, to meet the Lord in the air: and so shall we ever be with the Lord" (1 Thess. 4:16-17).
5. In Matthew 14, he spoke peace to the troubled waters. In Isaiah 2 he will speak peace to the troubled nations. "And he shall judge among the nations, and shall rebuke many people: and they shall beat their swords into plowshares, and their spears into pruninghooks: nation shall not lift up sword against nation, neither shall they learn war any more" (Isa. 2:4).
C. In light of all this, there are six all-important facts the Christian must realize in the hour of his or her storm:
1. Christ allowed me to be here, therefore he knows about the storm.
2. He is watching over me and praying for me during the storm.
3. He will come to me at the proper time in the storm.

    4. He will help my faith to grow by the storm.

    5. He will see me safely through the storm.

    6. He will enable me to help others going through a similar *storm. "Blessed be God, even the Father of our Lord Jesus Christ, the Father of mercies, and the God of all comfort; who comforteth us in all our tribulation, that we may be able to comfort them which are in any trouble, by the comfort wherewith we ourselves are comforted of God. For as the sufferings of Christ abound in us, so our consolation also aboundeth by Christ" (2 Cor. 1:3-5).*

TWENTY: Healing a demoniac girl (Matt. 15:21-28; Mark 7:24-30)

  A. The brokenhearted mother

    1. The place involved—"Then Jesus went thence, and departed into the coasts of Tyre and Sidon" (Matt. 15:21).

    2. The problem involved—"For a certain woman, whose young daughter had an unclean spirit, heard of him, and came and fell at his feet" (Mark 7:25).

    3. The plea involved—"And, behold, a woman of Canaan came out of the same coasts, and cried unto him, saying, Have mercy on me, O Lord, thou Son of David; my daughter is grievously vexed with a devil" (Matt. 15:22).

  B. The hard-hearted ministers—"But he answered her not a word. And his disciples came and besought him, saying, Send her away; for she crieth after us" (Matt. 15:23).

†*W. L. Pettingill writes: "It will not be forgotten that this woman was a Gentile, and not only a Gentile, but a Canaanite, a representative of that race which was under God's peculiar curse. 'Thou shalt drive out the Canaanites'—this was the word to Israel upon their entering the land of Canaan; and the promise of Zechariah 14:21, looking forward to the restored land and restored Temple worship, says, 'In that day there shall be no more the Canaanite in the house of Jehovah of hosts.' But grace is without any limit and overleaps all obstacles. Through Israel's failure, this despised outcast receives the blessing of the Lord that maketh rich. It is at first a most astonishing thing to see the Lord Jesus refusing to respond to this woman's cry of need. It is so unlike him, whose ears are always open to the slightest call upon his name. But he cannot answer her. She is calling upon him as the Son of David; and so he is, but as such—as Son of David— he has nothing to do with a Canaanite."* (The Gospel of the Kingdom, *Fundamental Truth Publishers, Findlay, Ohio, p. 183)*

  C. The kindhearted Messiah

    1. His gentle reminder—"But he answered and said, I am not sent but unto the lost sheep of the house of Israel. . . . But he answered and said, It is not meet to take the children's bread, and to cast it to dogs" (Matt. 15:24, 26).

    2. Her graceful reaction

      a. Her worship of Jesus—"Then came she and worshipped him" (Matt. 15:25a).

      b. Her words to Jesus

        (1) The reasoning involved—"And she answered and said unto him, Yes, Lord: yet the dogs under the table eat of the children's crumbs" (Mark 7:28).

†*She had now dropped the Jewish title, "Son of David"—this was his name as Israel's King. "Lord, help me!" was her cry, and it is not in his heart to resist that call. The Bread of life belonged first to the children of the household, that is, to the Jews.*

(2) The reward involved—"Then Jesus answered and said unto her, O woman, great is thy faith: be it unto thee even as thou wilt. And her daughter was made whole from that very hour" (Matt. 15:28).

TWENTY-ONE: Healing a deaf man with a speech impediment (Mark 7:31-37)

A. The request to Jesus—"And they bring unto him one that was deaf, and had an impediment in his speech; and they beseech him to put his hand upon him" (Mark 7:32).

B. The reaction by Jesus

1. He touched and held the man—"And he took him aside from the multitude, and put his fingers into his ears, and he spit, and touched his tongue" (Mark 7:33).

---

†*This is the first of three occasions on which Jesus spat when accomplishing a miracle. The other two are:*

A. Upon healing a blind man in Bethsaida (Mark 8:23)

B. Upon healing a blind man in Jerusalem (John 9:6)

It should be noted that all three cases involved blind individuals.

---

2. He transformed and healed the man—"And looking up to heaven, he sighed, and saith unto him, Ephphatha, that is, Be opened. And straightway his ears were opened, and the string of his tongue was loosed, and he spake plain" (Mark 7:34-35).

C. The report concerning Jesus—"And he charged them that they should tell no man: but the more he charged them, so much the more a great deal they published it; and were beyond measure astonished, saying, He hath done all things well: he maketh both the deaf to hear, and the dumb to speak" (Mark 7:36-37).

---

†*This short but sublime statement, "He hath done all things well" perfectly summarizes the earthly ministry of Jesus perhaps more than any other in the entire New Testament.*

TWENTY-TWO: The feeding of the 4,000 men and their families (Matt. 15:32-38; Mark 8:1-9)

---

†*Some have attempted to show the feeding of the 5,000 and that of the 4,000 were actually the same event, suggesting that the Gospel writers got their details mixed up. But Jesus himself told us that they were two separate and distinct events. "When I brake the five loaves among five thousand, how many baskets full of fragments took ye up? They say unto him, Twelve. And when the seven among four thousand, how many baskets full of fragments took ye up? And they said, Seven" (Mark 8:19-20).*

A. Compared with the feeding of the 5,000: There are several similarities between these two miracles.

1. Christ showed compassion toward both groups.

2. He asked his disciples what should be done.

3. He had the people sit down in orderly groups.

4. He supernaturally fed them by multiplying a few fish and loaves.

B. Contrasted with the feeding of the 5,000: There are a number of differences between these two miracles.

1. The size of the crowd: One had 5,000 men; the other 4,000.

2. The duration involved: The 5,000 men had been with him for one day; the 4,000 for three days.

3. The original food: Christ used five loaves and two fishes to feed the 5,000, while using seven loaves and an unspecified number of fish in caring for the 4,000.

4. The remains: Twelve baskets were left over at the feeding of 5,000, and seven after the 4,000.

5. The Gospel record: All four Gospel writers record the feeding of the 5,000, while only Matthew and Mark speak of the 4,000.

TWENTY-THREE: Healing a blind man in Bethsaida (Mark 8:22-26)

A. The first touch by the Savior

1. The request—"And he cometh to Bethsaida; and they bring a blind man unto him, and besought him to touch him" (Mark 8:22).

2. The reaction—"And he took the blind man by the hand, and led him out of the town; and when he had spit on his eyes, and put his hands upon him, he asked him if he saw ought" (Mark 8:23).

3. The results—"And he looked up, and said, I see men as trees, walking" (Mark 8:24).

B. The final touch by the Savior

1. Restoring—"After that he put his hands again upon his eyes, and made him look up: and he was restored, and saw every man clearly" (Mark 8:25).

---

† *A. This is the only recorded miracle which took place in two stages.*

B. The spiritual application here is crystal clear and sorely needed today. We need that second touch by Jesus, allowing us to see "every man clearly" as God does.

---

2. Requesting—"And he sent him away to his house, saying, Neither go into the town, nor tell it to any in the town" (Mark 8:26).

TWENTY-FOUR: Healing in Jerusalem a man born blind (John 9:1-41)

---

†*With the exception of the raising of Lazarus (John 11), more space is given over to this miracle than to any other in the entire New Testament.*

A. Lack of consideration—The disciples and the blind man: "And as Jesus passed by, he saw a man which was blind from his birth. And his disciples asked him, saying, Master, who did sin, this man, or his parents, that he was born blind?" (John 9:1-2).

---

†*At first reading, this seems to be a very silly question, for how could this poor, sightless man be suffering for his sin if he was born blind? However, some rabbis felt a baby could sin in its mother's womb, or that its soul might have sinned in a preexistent state. They also held that terrible punishments from God came upon certain people because of the sin of their parents.*

This grievous error, of course, is totally refuted by both Moses and Ezekiel. "The fathers shall not be put to death for the children, neither shall the children be put to death for the fathers: every man shall be put to death for his own sin" (Deut. 24:16). "The soul that sinneth, it shall die. The son shall not bear the iniquity of the father, neither shall the father bear the iniquity of the son: the righteousness of the righteous shall be upon him, and the wickedness of the wicked shall be upon him" (Ezek. 18:20).

B. Evangelization—The Savior and the blind man (their first meeting)
　　1. Jesus viewed the man as a subject of God's plan. "Jesus answered, Neither hath this man sinned, nor his parents: but that the works of God should be made manifest in him" (John 9:3).

†*Here Jesus corrects that terrible teaching that says that all suffering is a direct result of personal sin. The disciples at this point had made the same false assumption that Job's three "friends" had once made (see Job 4:7-8; 8:20; 20:4-5), and that many modern "faith healers" today still make. However, God himself had severely rebuked the companions of Job for their wicked judgment: "And it was so, that after the Lord had spoken these words unto Job, the Lord said to Eliphaz the Temanite, My wrath is kindled against thee, and against thy two friends: for ye have not spoken of me the thing that is right, as my servant Job hath" (Job 42:7).*

　　2. Jesus viewed himself as a servant in God's plan.
　　　　a. The mission—"I must work the works of him that sent me, while it is day: the night cometh, when no man can work. As long as I am in the world, I am the light of the world" (John 9:4-5).
　　　　b. The miracle—"When he had thus spoken, he spat on the ground, and made clay of the spittle, and he anointed the eyes of the blind man with the clay, and said unto him, Go, wash in the pool of Siloam, (which is by interpretation, Sent.) He went his way therefore, and washed, and came seeing" (John 9:6-7).

†*This is the only occasion on which Jesus commanded the healed person to do something in order to bring about the miracle.*

C. Speculation—The neighbors and the blind man
　　1. Their confusion—"The neighbours therefore, and they which before had seen him that he was blind, said, Is not this he that sat and begged? Some said, This is he: others said, He is like him: but he said, I am he" (John 9:8-9).
　　2. His clarification—"Therefore said they unto him, How were thine eyes opened? He answered and said, A man that is called Jesus made clay, and anointed mine eyes, and said unto me, Go to the pool of Siloam, and wash: and I went and washed, and I received sight" (John 9:10-11).
D. Interrogation—The parents and the blind man
　　1. The demands—"But the Jews did not believe concerning him, that he had

been blind, and received his sight, until they called the parents of him that had received his sight. And they asked them, saying, Is this your son, who ye say was born blind? how then doth he now see?" (John 9:18-19).
2. The denials—"His parents answered them and said, We know that this is our son, and that he was born blind: But by what means he now seeth, we know not; or who hath opened his eyes, we know not: he is of age; ask him: he shall speak for himself. These words spake his parents, because they feared the Jews: for the Jews had agreed already, that if any man did confess that he was Christ, he should be put out of the synagogue. Therefore said his parents, He is of age; ask him" (John 9:20-23).

---

†*How tragic to contemplate the strong possibility that these seeing parents of a sightless son refused the light offered by Christ and probably died still blinded by their sins. Why did this happen? Solomon gives us the sad answer: "The fear of man bringeth a snare: but whoso putteth his trust in the Lord shall be safe" (Prov. 29:25). This sad truth is reconfirmed on two additional occasions apart from John 9:*
A. *"Nevertheless among the chief rulers also many believed on him; but because of the Pharisees they did not confess him, lest they should be put out of the synagogue: For they loved the praise of men more than the praise of God" (John 12:42-43).*
B. *"But the fearful, and unbelieving, and the abominable, and murderers, and whoremongers, and sorcerers, and idolaters, and all liars, shall have their part in the lake which burneth with fire and brimstone: which is the second death" (Rev. 21:8).*

E. Castigation—The Pharisees and the blind man
1. Round one
a. The denunciation of Christ by the critics—"Therefore said some of the Pharisees, This man is not of God, because he keepeth not the sabbath day. Others said, How can a man that is a sinner do such miracles? And there was a division among them" (John 9:16).

---

†*Whenever Jesus enters the scene a division automatically develops. A person might accept his claims or deny them, but he or she cannot ignore them.*

"What will you do with Jesus?
Neutral you cannot be!
Someday your heart will be asking,
What will he do with me?"

---

b. The defense of Christ by the convert—"They say unto the blind man again, What sayest thou of him, that he hath opened thine eyes? He said, He is a prophet" (John 9:17).
2. Round two
a. The denunciation of Christ by the critics
(1) They said he was ungodly—"Then again called they the man that was blind, and said unto him, Give God the praise: we know that this man is a sinner" (John 9:24).

(2) They said he was unknown—"Then they reviled him, and said, Thou art his disciple; but we are Moses' disciples. We know that God spake unto Moses: as for this fellow, we know not from whence he is" (John 9:28-29).

b. The defense of Christ by the convert
   (1) He offers a personal argument—"He answered and said, Whether he be a sinner or no, I know not: one thing I know that, whereas I was blind, now I see" (John 9:25).
   (2) He offers a philosophical argument—"The man answered and said unto them, Why herein is a marvelous thing, that ye know not from whence he is, and yet he hath opened mine eyes. Now we know that God heareth not sinners: but if any man be a worshipper of God, and doeth his will, him he heareth. Since the world began was it not heard that any man opened the eyes of one that was born blind. If this man were not of God, he could do nothing" (John 9:30-33).

---

†*The man was probably right in his claim here, for there is no record either in sacred or secular history of a person born blind later recovering his sight.*

---

3. Round three—Unable to destroy his testimony, the frustrated Pharisees excommunicate the cured man from the synagogue. "They answered and said unto him, Thou wast altogether born in sins, and dost thou teach us? And they cast him out" (John 9:34).

---

† *A. By their statement here, the Pharisees also held to the false doctrine that suffering was due to personal sin.*
  B. To be excommunicated (cast out) from the synagogue was a horrible experience. Immediately one became a social and religious leper, to be shunned by all. Practically speaking, the victim was reduced to the status of a nonperson.

F. Summation—The Savior and the blind man (their final meeting): "And Jesus said, For judgment I am come into this world" (John 9:39a).
   1. "That they which see not might see" (John 9:39b). All converts to Christ belong to this group.
      a. Jesus' words to the former blind man—"Jesus heard that they had cast him out; and when he had found him, he said unto him, Dost thou believe on the Son of God? He answered and said, Who is he, Lord, that I might believe on him? And Jesus said unto him, Thou hast both seen him, and it is he that talketh with thee" (John 9:35-37).
      b. Jesus' worship by the former blind man—"And he said, Lord, I believe. And he worshipped him" (John 9:38).

---

†*Note the progressive revelation given to this man by the Holy Spirit concerning the person of Christ:*

A. *In 9:11 he calls him a man.*
B. *In 9:17 he calls him a prophet.*
C. *In 9:32 he calls him a miracle worker.*
D. *In 9:33 he calls him a messenger from God.*
E. *In 9:35-38 he worships him as the Son of God.*

---

2. "That they which see might be made blind" (John 9:39c). All critics of Christ belong to this group. "And some of the Pharisees which were with him heard these words, and said unto him, Are we blind also? Jesus said unto them, If ye were blind, ye should have no sin: but now ye say, We see; therefore your sin remaineth" (John 9:40-41).

TWENTY-FIVE: Healing a demoniac boy (Matt. 17:14-21; Mark 9:14-29; Luke 9:37-43)

---

†*Leaving the mount of transfiguration, our Lord enters the valley of disfiguration. On the mountain, the friends of heaven (Moses and Elijah) had comforted him. In the valley the foes of hell would challenge him.*

A. The victims
1. The helpless father—"And, behold, a man of the company cried out, saying, Master, I beseech thee, look upon my son: for he is mine only child" (Luke 9:38).

---

†*This is the final of three instances in which Jesus would supernaturally minister to an only child.*
   A. He raised from the dead the only son of a widow (Luke 7:12).
   B. He raised from the dead the only daughter of Jairus (Luke 8:42).

---

2. The hopeless son
   a. The source of his problem—The boy was controlled by a demon (Mark 9:17; Luke 9:39).
   b. The symptoms of his problem
      (1) The evil spirit would dash him upon the ground (Mark 9:18).
      (2) It would throw him into the fire and water (Mark 9:22).
      (3) It caused him to foam at the mouth and grind his teeth (Mark 9:18).
      (4) It tore at him (Luke 9:39).
      (5) It bruised him (Luke 9:39).
      (6) It was slowly killing him (Mark 9:18).
   c. The span of his problem—"And he asked his father, How long is it ago since this came unto him? And he said, Of a child. And ofttimes it hath cast him into the fire, and into the waters, to destroy him: but if thou canst do any thing, have compassion on us, and help us" (Mark 9:21-22).
   3. The hapless disciples—"And I brought him to thy disciples, and they could not cure him" (Matt. 17:16).

---

† *A. On two previous occasions, however, they had been able to cast out demons. "And they cast out many devils, and anointed with oil many that were sick, and healed them" (Mark 6:13).*

"And the seventy returned again with joy, saying, Lord, even the devils are subject unto us through thy name" (Luke 10:17).

B. Why then could they not help this heartbroken father? There were at least four reasons.
 1. They had too little faith (Matt. 17:20).
 2. They had too little self-denial (Mark 9:29).
 3. They had too little prayer (Mark 9:29).
 4. They had too much bickering (Mark 9:14).
C. It is so easy to become an Ichabod Christian (meaning "the glory of the Lord hath departed," see 1 Sam. 4:21-22) without even being aware of it until the crisis comes.

 B. The victor
  1. Jesus encouraged the father.
   a. The strength of faith—"Jesus said unto him, If thou canst believe, all things are possible to him that believeth" (Mark 9:23).

---

†*Contrast the two statements here:*
 A. That of the father—"If thou canst do anything" (Mark 9:22).
 B. That of the Savior—"If thou canst believe, all things" (Mark 9:23).

---

   b. The struggle for faith—"And straightway the father of the child cried out, and said with tears, Lord, I believe; help thou mine unbelief" (Mark 9:24).

---

† *A. This kind of struggling, desperate faith, even though plagued with doubt, will reach the heart of God immediately. The psalmist spoke of this: "Like as a father pitieth his children, so the Lord pitieth them that fear him. For he knoweth our frame; he remembereth that we are dust" (Psa. 103:13-14).*
 B. Question: How much faith does it take to please God?
 C. Response: How much faith do you have?
 D. Illustration: Let us suppose you face a million-dollar need but only have a 10-dollar bill. God's plan in solving this is both gracious and simple: Give him your 10 dollars and he will add the remaining $999,990. However small our faith, he wants it all. Our problem, however, is that all too often we shortchange him on the 10 dollars.

---

  2. Jesus excoriated the demon
   a. The rebuke—"When Jesus saw that the people came running together, he rebuked the foul spirit, saying unto him, Thou dumb and deaf spirit, I charge thee, come out of him, and enter no more into him" (Mark 9:25).
   b. The results—"And the spirit cried, and rent him sore, and came out of him: and he was as one dead; insomuch that many said, He is dead" (Mark 9:26).
  3. Jesus emancipated the son—"But Jesus took him by the hand, and lifted him up; and he arose" (Mark 9:27).
  4. Jesus enlightened the disciples
   a. Their confusion—"And when he was come into the house, his disciples asked him privately, Why could not we cast him out?" (Mark 9:28).

      b. His clarification—"And he said unto them, This kind can come forth by nothing, but by prayer and fasting" (Mark 9:29).

TWENTY-SIX: The miracle of the tribute money (Matt. 17:24-27)

    A. The tax involved—"And when they were come to Capernaum, they that received tribute money came to Peter, and said, Doth not your master pay tribute?" (Matt. 17:24).

---

†*This temple tax, owed by all Jews from age twenty upward, was two drachma, approximately two days' wages. It was to be used for the temple upkeep and repair. There were three specific occasions recorded in the Old Testament when this tax was collected.*

    A. During the time of Moses (Exod. 30:13; 38:26)

    B. During the time of Joash—This Judean king actually had a special chest built and placed outside by the temple gate to receive the tax (2 Chron. 24:9-14).

    C. During the time of Nehemiah (Neh. 10:32)

    B. The truth involved—"He saith, Yes. And when he was come into the house, Jesus prevented him, saying, What thinkest thou, Simon? of whom do the kings of the earth take custom or tribute? of their own children, or of strangers? Peter saith unto him, Of strangers. Jesus saith unto him, Then are the children free" (Matt. 17:25-26).

---

† *A. Here Peter committed a serious blunder. He committed Jesus to do something without first asking him. Nathan the prophet once did the same thing when advising King David. It also had to do with the temple. Upon hearing David's desire to construct a temple, Nathan responded: "Then Nathan said unto David, Do all that is in thine heart; for God is with thee" (1 Chron. 17:2). But then God stepped in: "And it came to pass the same night, that the word of God came to Nathan, saying, Go and tell David my servant, Thus saith the Lord, Thou shalt not build me an house to dwell in" (1 Chron. 17:3-4). The conclusion of the matter was that God had already determined that Solomon (David's son) would build the temple.*

    B. Jesus told Peter why he should not *have to pay the tax:*

       1. He owned the temple (Mal. 3:1).

       2. He had previously cleansed the temple (John 2:16).

       3. He was the eternal Son of God (Matt. 16:16).

    C. He then told Peter why he should *pay the tax:*

       1. To maintain a good testimony—"Notwithstanding, lest we should offend them." Here the Savior gave a beautiful example of properly using our Christian liberty, as later echoed by the Apostle Paul in 1 Corinthians 8–10. "But take heed lest by any means this liberty of yours become a stumblingblock to them that are weak. But when ye sin so against the brethren, and wound their weak conscience, ye sin against Christ. To the weak became I as weak, that I might gain the weak: I am made all things to all men, that I might by all means save some" (1 Cor. 8:9, 12; 9:22).

       2. To increase Peter's faith

       3. To illustrate his work as the second Adam—When correctly understood, this amazing miracle serves to illustrate not only the deity of Christ, but even more, his perfect humanity. What was he doing here? In essence, Jesus was fulfilling the very first

*command in the Bible given to Adam concerning the world of nature: "And God . . .
said . . . subdue it; and have dominion over the fish of the sea, and over the fowl of the air,
and over every living thing that moveth upon the earth" (Gen. 1:28). Our Lord thus, in
some mysterious manner (lost to us after Adam's sin), was able to communicate and
exercise control over a fish swimming in the waters of Galilee.*

C. The testimony involved—"Notwithstanding, lest we should offend them, go
thou to the sea, and cast an hook, and take up the fish that first cometh up; and
when thou hast opened his mouth, thou shalt find a piece of money: that take,
and give unto them for me and thee" (Matt. 17:27).
TWENTY-SEVEN: Healing of a blind and mute demoniac (Matt. 12:22; Luke 11:14)—"Then
was brought unto him one possessed with a devil, blind, and dumb: and he healed him,
insomuch that the blind and dumb both spake and saw" (Matt 12:22).

†*This miracle is noteworthy for two reasons:*
A. *It is Jesus' shortest recorded miracle. Less space is given to it than to any other miracle.*
B. *In spite of this, Jesus probably did more for the person involved than can be found in any
other miracle. It would be difficult to imagine being in a more desperate situation than
the one that is described at this point. Here was a blind, deaf, mute, and demon-possessed
man. But then Jesus passed by. And the results?*
1. *The man could see.*
2. *The man could hear.*
3. *The man could speak.*
4. *The man could worship.*
Thus, in a split second he received sight, sound, speech, and (probably) salvation.

TWENTY-EIGHT: Healing a woman crippled for eighteen years (Luke 13:10-17)
A. The helpless one—"And, behold, there was a woman which had a spirit of
infirmity eighteen years, and was bowed together, and could in no wise lift up
herself" (Luke 13:11).
1. Her call—"And when Jesus saw her, he called her to him, and said unto her,
Woman, thou art loosed from thine infirmity" (Luke 13:12).
2. Her cure—"And he laid his hands on her: and immediately she was made
straight, and glorified God" (Luke 13:13).
B. The heartless one
1. His hostility—"And the ruler of the synagogue answered with indignation, because that Jesus had healed on the sabbath day, and said
unto the people, There are six days in which men ought to work: in
them therefore come and be healed, and not on the sabbath day" (Luke
13:14).
2. His hypocrisy—"The Lord then answered him, and said, Thou hypocrite,
doth not each one of you on the sabbath loose his ox or his ass from the
stall, and lead him away to watering? And ought not this woman, being a
daughter of Abraham, whom Satan hath bound, lo, these eighteen years, be
loosed from this bond on the sabbath day?" (Luke 13:15-16).

† A. *This woman was probably a believer. Jesus refers to her as "a daughter of Abraham." In addition, the text indicates that she was a faithful member of the synagogue (Luke 13:10-11).*
  B. *In spite of this, she had been bound by Satan for nearly two decades. Here it should be said that although Satan (or his fallen angels) cannot possess a believer, he can oppress and physically afflict a child of God. There are two classic examples of this satanic physical affliction in the Scriptures.*
    1. *The example of Job (Job 1–2)—"So went Satan forth from the presence of the Lord, and smote Job with sore boils from the sole of his foot unto his crown" (Job 2:7).*
    2. *The example of Paul—"And lest I should be exalted above measure through the abundance of the revelations, there was given to me a thorn in the flesh, the messenger of Satan to buffet me, lest I should be exalted above measure" (2 Cor. 12:7).*
  C. *Jesus used his sharpest rebuke yet in performing a miracle. He said to the synagogue ruler, "Thou hypocrite!"*

TWENTY-NINE: Healing of the man with dropsy (Luke 14:1-6)
  A. The *what* of the miracle—"And, behold, there was a certain man before him which had the dropsy. And they held their peace. And he took him, and healed him, and let him go" (Luke 14:2, 4).
  B. The *where* of the miracle—"He went into the house of one of the chief Pharisees to eat bread" (Luke 14:1).
  C. The *when* of the miracle—"On the sabbath day" (Luke 14:1).
  D. The *why* of the miracle—"And they held their peace. And he took him, and healed him, and let him go; and answered them, saying, Which of you shall have an ass or an ox fallen into a pit, and will not straightway pull him out on the sabbath day? And they could not answer him again to these things" (Luke 14:4-6).

---

† A. *This was the only recorded miracle done during a meal in the home of a Pharisee.*
  B. *It was probably a setup arranged by the wicked Jewish leaders to trap Jesus, hoping he would do something unlawful.*
    1. *It was on the Sabbath.*
    2. *A very sick man was there who suffered from dropsy. Dropsy was an abnormal accumulation of watery fluid in the body, which caused hideous swelling in the abdomen, legs, and feet. It was symptomatic of cardiac disease. In light of this, it is highly unlikely that this poor, suffering creature would be invited to the home of a Pharisee, especially on the Sabbath. To the contrary, he would have been utterly refused entrance.*

THIRTY: Healing of ten lepers (Luke 17:11-19)
  A. The request of the ten
    1. Their cry—"And as he entered into a certain village, there met him ten men that were lepers, which stood afar off: and they lifted up their voices, and said, Jesus, Master, have mercy on us" (Luke 17:12-13).
    2. Their command—"And when he saw them, he said unto them, Go show yourselves unto the priests" (Luke 17:14).
    3. Their cleansing—"And it came to pass, that, as they went, they were cleansed" (Luke 17:14).

B. The return of the one
    1. Who he was—"And he was a Samaritan" (Luke 17:16).
    2. Why he came
        a. To offer testimony to God the Father—"And one of them, when he saw
           that he was healed, turned back, and with a loud voice glorified God"
           (Luke 17:15).
        b. To offer thanksgiving to God the Son—"And fell down on his face at his
           feet, giving him thanks: and he was a Samaritan" (Luke 17:16).
    3. What he experienced
        a. The sadness of Jesus—"And Jesus answering said, Were there not ten
           cleansed? but where are the nine? There are not found that returned to give
           glory to God, save this stranger" (Luke 17:17-18).
        b. The salvation from Jesus—"And he said unto him, Arise, go thy way: thy
           faith hath made thee whole" (Luke 17:19).

---

† *A. This is the second of three miracles demonstrating the tragic fact that the one (or ones)
experiencing physical salvation did not apparently experience spiritual salvation. These three
cases are:*
    *1. The cripple by the pool of Bethesda (John 5:1-16)—"Jesus saith unto him, Rise, take up thy
    bed, and walk. And immediately the man was made whole, and took up his bed, and
    walked: and on the same day was the sabbath. Afterward Jesus findeth him in the temple,
    and said unto him, Behold, thou art made whole: sin no more, lest a worse thing come unto
    thee" (John 5:8-9, 14).*
    2. The nine lepers here in Luke 17
    *3. The servant of the high priest whose name was Malchus (John 18:10)—There is no
    evidence that he accepted Christ after having his severed ear restored.*
  *B. The great sin of the nine lepers was that of thanklessness. In some ways this is the ultimate
  sin, and goes along with pride and self-will, the root of all other sins. Paul says that this
  transgression in the ancient world caused all mankind to turn from God. "Because that,
  when they knew God, they glorified him not as God, neither were thankful; but became vain
  in their imaginations, and their foolish heart was darkened. Professing themselves to be wise,
  they became fools, and changed the glory of the uncorruptible God into an image made like
  to corruptible man, and to birds, and fourfooted beasts, and creeping things" (Rom. 1:21-23).*

THIRTY-ONE: The raising of Lazarus (John 11:1-46)

---

†*More space is given over to this miracle than to any other of the thirty-five performed by Jesus.
More individuals are mentioned by name here than can be found in any other miracle (Lazarus,
Mary, Martha, and Thomas).*

A. The sickness of Lazarus
    1. The background—"Now a certain man was sick, named Lazarus, of Bethany,
       the town of Mary and her sister Martha. (It was that Mary which anointed the
       Lord with ointment, and wiped his feet with her hair, whose brother Lazarus
       was sick)" (John 11:1-2).

†*Note the frequency of their names in this chapter:*
A. Lazarus in mentioned six times (11:1, 2, 5, 11, 14, 43).
B. Mary is mentioned seven times (11:1, 2, 19, 20, 28, 31, 32).
C. Martha is mentioned eight times (11:1, 5, 19, 20, 21, 24, 30, 39).
The reason for this can be seen by a statement made during Christ's Good Shepherd sermon, preached just prior to this: "He calleth his own sheep by name, and leadeth them out" (John 10:3).

2. The beckoning—"Therefore his sisters sent unto him, saying, Lord, behold, he whom thou lovest is sick" (John 11:3).
B. The sermon on Lazarus
   1. The declaration involved—"When Jesus heard that, he said, This sickness is not unto death, but for the glory of God, that the Son of God might be glorified thereby" (John 11:4).
   2. The devotion involved—"Now Jesus loved Martha, and her sister, and Lazarus" (John 11:5).
   3. The delay involved—"When he had heard therefore that he was sick, he abode two days still in the same place where he was" (John 11:6).
   4. The decision involved—"Then after that saith he to his disciples, Let us go into Judaea again" (John 11:7).
   5. The dialogue involved
      a. The concern—"His disciples say unto him, Master, the Jews of late sought to stone thee; and goest thou thither again?" (John 11:8).
      b. The commitment—"Jesus answered, Are there not twelve hours in the day? If any man walk in the day, he stumbleth not, because he seeth the light of this world. But if a man walk in the night, he stumbleth, because there is no light in him. These things said he: and after that he saith unto them, Our friend Lazarus sleepeth; but I go, that I may awake him out of sleep" (John 11:9-11).
      c. The confusion—"Then said his disciples, Lord, if he sleep, he shall do well. Howbeit Jesus spake of his death: but they thought that he had spoken of taking of rest in sleep" (John 11:12-13).
      d. The clarification—"Then said Jesus unto them plainly, Lazarus is dead. And I am glad for your sakes that I was not there, to the intent ye may believe; nevertheless let us go unto him" (John 11:14-15).
      e. The conclusion—"Then said Thomas, which is called Didymus, unto his fellow disciples, Let us also go, that we may die with him" (John 11:16).

†*The New Testament relates three incidents between Thomas and Christ. The Gospel of John records all three. In each of them he lives up to his reputation as Doubting Thomas.*
A. Here he doubts the power of Christ.
B. In the Upper Room he doubts the promise of Christ. "Thomas saith unto him, Lord, we know not whither thou goest; and how can we know the way?" (John 14:5).
C. After the resurrection he at first doubted the very person of Christ (John 20:24-29). "But Thomas, one of the twelve, called Didymus, was not with them when Jesus came. The other disciples therefore said unto him, We have seen the Lord. But he said unto

*them, Except I shall see in his hands the print of the nails, and put my finger into
the print of the nails, and thrust my hand into his side, I will not believe" (John 20:24-25).*

C. The sorrow over Lazarus—"Then when Jesus came, he found that he had lain in
the grave four days already. Now Bethany was nigh unto Jerusalem, about fifteen
furlongs off: and many of the Jews came to Martha and Mary, to comfort them
concerning their brother" (John 11:17-19).

✝*We note that he waited until Lazarus had been dead for four days. He may have done this because of
the superstition among the Jews that after death the spirit hovered over the body for three days, and a
resurrection up to that time was at least remotely possible. But after this period, all hope was gone.*

1. Martha's sorrow
   a. The meeting with Jesus—"Then Martha, as soon as she heard that Jesus was
   coming, went and met him: but Mary sat still in the house" (John 11:20).
   (1) Her frustration—"Then said Martha unto Jesus, Lord, if thou hadst
   been here, my brother had not died" (John 11:21).
   (2) Her faith
   (a) In the promise of Christ—"But I know, that even now, whatsoever
   thou wilt ask of God, God will give it thee. Jesus saith unto her, Thy
   brother shall rise again. Martha saith unto him, I know that he shall
   rise again in the resurrection at the last day" (John 11:22-24).
   (b) In the person of Christ—"Jesus said unto her, I am the resurrection,
   and the life: he that believeth in me, though he were dead, yet shall
   he live: and whosoever liveth and believeth in me shall never die.
   Believest thou this? She saith unto him, Yea, Lord: I believe that thou
   art the Christ, the Son of God, which should come into the world"
   (John 11:25-27).
   b. The ministry for Jesus—"And when she had so said, she went her way,
   and called Mary her sister secretly, saying, The Master is come, and calleth
   for thee" (John 11:28).

✝ A. *Martha, and not Mary, is the heroine of this story. (See Luke 10:38-42 where the opposite was
   true.)*
   1. *It was Martha who went to meet Jesus while Mary remained in the house (John 11:20).*
   2. *Martha's great testimony here ranks equally as important as that given by Simon Peter on
   another occasion. (Compare 11:27 with Mark 16:16.)*
   B. *Martha's words to Mary here are the most beneficial and blessed ones a believer can give to
   another believer in the hour of greatest need.*

2. Mary's sorrow—"As soon as she heard that, she arose quickly, and came unto
   him. . . . Then when Mary was come where Jesus was, and saw him, she fell
   down at his feet, saying unto him, Lord, if thou hadst been here, my brother
   had not died" (John 11:29, 32).

†*Upon meeting Jesus, Mary said the exact same thing Martha had just said. To rephrase the poem: "The most useless words of tongue or pen, are these four words, 'It might have been.'"*

---

3. Jesus' sorrow
   a. The tears of the Christ— "When Jesus therefore saw her weeping, and the Jews also weeping which came with her, he groaned in the spirit, and was troubled, And said, Where have ye laid him? They said unto him, Lord, come and see. Jesus wept" (John 11:33-35).

---

† *A. This is the shortest verse in the English Bible, but in some ways it is the longest. This is the first of at least three occasions on which our Lord wept.*
   1. He wept over the city of Jerusalem (Luke 19:41).
   2. He wept in Gethsemane—"Who in the days of his flesh, when he had offered up prayers and supplications with strong crying and tears unto him that was able to save him from death, and was heard in that he feared" (Heb. 5:7).
B. What caused his tears?
   1. He wept because of his true humanity (see Heb. 4:14-16).
   2. He wept because of the wicked men he saw around him (see John 11:37, 46).

---

   b. The taunts of the crowd—"And some of them said, Could not this man, which opened the eyes of the blind, have caused that even this man should not have died?" (John 11:37).
D. The summons to Lazarus
   1. The preparation—"Jesus therefore again groaning in himself cometh to the grave. It was a cave, and a stone lay upon it" (John 11:38).

---

†*Twice we read of Jesus groaning (John 11:33, 38). The Greek word here is* embrim, *suggesting anger. It is translated "indignation" in Mark 14:5. Thus, the groanings of Christ may have indicated his grief and anger over death itself, a tragic (and unnecessary) result of Adam's sin. (See Rom. 5:12.)*

---

   a. The request—"Jesus said, Take ye away the stone" (John 11:39a).
   b. The reluctance—"Martha . . . saith unto him, Lord, by this time he stinketh: for he hath been dead four days" (John 11:39b).
   c. The reminder—"Jesus saith unto her, Said I not unto thee, that, if thou wouldest believe, thou shouldest see the glory of God?" (John 11:40)."Then they took away the stone from the place where the dead was laid" (John 11:41a).
   2. The prayer—"And Jesus lifted up his eyes, and said, Father, I thank thee that thou hast heard me" (John 11:41b). "And I knew that thou hearest me always: but because of the people which stand by I said it, that they may believe that thou hast sent me" (John 11:42).
   3. The proclamation—"And when he thus had spoken, he cried with a loud voice, Lazarus, come forth" (John 11:43).

† A. *This is the first of three great cries from the lips of the Savior. All three have to do with the glorious subject of resurrection.*
  1. *The cry from the cemetery: "Lazarus, come forth!"*
  2. *The cry from the cross: "Jesus when he had cried again with a loud voice, yielded up the ghost. And, behold, the vail of the temple was rent in twain from the top to the bottom; and the earth did quake, and the rocks rent; and the graves were opened; and many bodies of the saints which slept arose" (Matt. 27:50-52).*
  3. *The cry from the clouds: "For the Lord himself shall descend from heaven with a shout, with the voice of the archangel, and with the trump of God: and the dead in Christ shall rise first" (1 Thess. 4:16).*
  B. *Lazarus becomes the final of three individuals raised from the dead by Jesus.*
  1. *He raised the widow's son (Luke 7:11-17).*
  2. *He raised Jairus's daughter (Mark 5:22-24, 35-43).*

4. The presentation—"And he that was dead came forth, bound hand and foot with graveclothes: and his face was bound about with a napkin. Jesus saith unto them, Loose him, and let him go" (John 11:44).

†*Here we see an example of that desired cooperation God seeks between the Savior and the soul winner in raising dead sinners to newness of life. Jesus issued three commands in accomplishing this miracle. The first and third were directed toward the friends of the corpse, while the second was given to the corpse itself. Note:*
  A. *"Take ye away the stone" (John 11:39). The job of the soul winner is to first remove all human barriers so that Christ can come in direct contact with a lost person.*
  B. *"Lazarus, come forth" (John 11:43). Only Christ, of course, can do this.*
  C. *"Loose him, and let him go" (John 11:44). In a word, this speaks of discipleship, that is, ministering to the new convert.*

THIRTY-TWO: The healing of blind Bartimaeus and his companion (Matt. 20:29-34; Mark 10:46-52; Luke 18:35-43)
  A. Bartimaeus the beggar
    1. His cry
      a. The place involved—"And they came to Jericho: and as he went out of Jericho with his disciples and a great number of people, blind Bartimaeus, the son of Timaeus, sat by the highway side begging" (Mark 10:46).
      b. The plea involved—"And when he heard that it was Jesus of Nazareth, he began to cry out, and say, Jesus, thou Son of David, have mercy on me" (Mark 10:47).
    2. His critics
      a. Their rebuke—"And many charged him that he should hold his peace" (Mark 10:48a).
      b. His response—"But he cried the more a great deal, Thou son of David, have mercy on me" (Mark 10:48b).

3. His call—"And Jesus stood still, and commanded him to be called. And they call the blind man, saying unto him, Be of good comfort, rise; he calleth thee" (Mark 10:49).
B. Bartimaeus the believer
   1. Running to Jesus—"And he, casting away his garment, rose, and came to Jesus" (Mark 10:50).
   2. Requesting from Jesus—"And Jesus answered and said unto him, What wilt thou that I should do unto thee? The blind man said unto him, Lord, that I might receive my sight" (Mark 10:51).
   3. Receiving from Jesus—"And Jesus said unto him, Go thy way; thy faith hath made thee whole. And immediately he received his sight, and followed Jesus in the way" (Mark 10:52).

---

† *A. This marks Jesus' final visit to Jericho. He will now leave for Jerusalem. (See Matt. 20:29.) Before this, he had told the story of a man who left Jerusalem for Jericho (the parable of the Good Samaritan—Luke 10:25-37). But now the original Good Samaritan would reverse the trip, leaving Jericho for Jerusalem, where he would soon "fall among thieves."*
B. This is also the only New Testament miracle associated with the city of Jericho.
   1. The most famous Old Testament miracle concerning Jericho occurred in Joshua 6:20 (the shouting down of Jericho's walls).
   2. The final Old Testament miracle concerning Jericho is recorded in 2 Kings 2:18-22 (the purifying of some poisoned water).
C. Of the fifteen miracle healing events, involving twenty-six people, only one person is named: Bartimaeus.
D. Note the spiritual insight of the blind beggar:
   1. He asked the right person—"Jesus, thou Son of David."
   2. He asked in the right way—"Have mercy on me."
   3. He asked at the right time—When the blind man first inquired concerning the noise, the crowd told him, "Jesus of Nazareth passeth by" (Luke 18:37).

THIRTY-THREE: Destroying a fig tree (Matt. 21:17-20, 43; Mark 11:12-14, 20-21)

---

†*This is the only one of Christ's thirty-five recorded miracles that would cause him great pain and sorrow. It was so important that years later the Apostle Paul took three entire chapters (Rom. 9–11) to expand upon its theological implications.*

A. What he found—"And on the morrow, when they were come from Bethany, he was hungry: and seeing a fig tree afar off having leaves, he came, if haply he might find any thing thereon: and when he came to it, he found nothing but leaves; for the time of figs was not yet" (Mark 11:12-13).

---

†*This particular kind of fig tree found in Israel is different from all other fruit trees in that it bears its fruit before its leaves. This is not the case with apple, pear, cherry, or any other fruit-bearing trees. Even though the tree was apparently blooming earlier than usual, Jesus had the right to see fruit, for the leaves were there.*

B. What he did—"He . . . said unto it, Let no fruit grow on thee henceforward for ever. And presently the fig tree withered away" (Matt. 21:19).

C. Why he did it—This tree was a symbol of Israel, that divinely favored but fruitless fig tree. Christ was therefore setting Israel aside because of this absence of fruit. Later that same day he made this clear to the Pharisees. "Jesus saith unto them, Did ye never read in the scriptures, The stone which the builders rejected, the same is become the head of the corner: this is the Lord's doing, and it is marvellous in our eyes? Therefore say I unto you, The kingdom of God shall be taken from you, and given to a nation bringing forth the fruits thereof" (Matt. 21:42-43).

---

† A. *As has been previously noted, Jesus had every right to find fruit upon the tree of Israel. Its green and massive foliage was impressive indeed, for to it was given the tabernacle, the temple, the Old Testament Scriptures, plus the ministries of godly prophets, priests, and kings. But upon close inspection, it bore no fruit.*

B. *The overriding lesson from this miracle is painfully obvious —God desires fruit.*

    1. *His chosen nation failed to bear fruit. "Israel is an empty vine, he bringeth forth fruit unto himself: according to the multitude of his fruit he hath increased the altars; according to the goodness of his land they have made goodly images" (Hos. 10:1).*

    2. *His present plan is for believers to bear fruit. "Herein is my Father glorified, that ye bear much fruit; so shall ye be my disciples" (John 15:8).*

THIRTY-FOUR: Restoring a severed ear (Matt. 26:51-54; Mark 14:46-47; Luke 22:49-51; John 18:10-11)

A. The ill-advised action of Peter

    1. The violence of his act—"Then Simon Peter having a sword drew it, and smote the high priest's servant, and cut off his right ear" (John 18:10).

    2. The victim of his act—"The servant's name was Malchus" (John 18:10).

B. The all-wise reaction of Christ

    1. Rebuking the apostle—"Then said Jesus unto him, Put up again thy sword into his place: for all they that take the sword shall perish with the sword" (Matt. 26:52).

    2. Reviewing the options

        a. What he could do—"Thinkest thou that I cannot now pray to my Father, and he shall presently give me more than twelve legions of angels?" (Matt. 26: 53).

---

†*A legion in the Roman army consisted of 6,000 soldiers. Thus Christ had at his immediate disposal at least 72,000 angels. But he chose to die for sinners.*

---

        b. What he would do—"Then said Jesus unto Peter, Put up thy sword into the sheath: the cup which my Father hath given me, shall I not drink it?" (John 18:11).

    3. Restoring the ear—"And Jesus answered and said, Suffer ye thus far. And he touched his ear, and healed him" (Luke 22:51).

✝ *A. This is the only miracle of Christ performed on an enemy.*
B. It is also the last miracle before the crucifixion.

THIRTY-FIVE: The second great catch of fish (John 21:1-14)

✝*This is the final of Christ's thirty-five recorded miracles, and the only one performed after his resurrection.*

A. The fishermen on the sea
1. The place—"After these things Jesus shewed himself again to the disciples at the sea of Tiberias; and on this wise shewed he himself" (John 21:1).

✝*This is the seventh of the ten resurrection appearances made by Christ. It marks the only appearance at which a miracle was involved. Even before his crucifixion, Jesus had promised to meet his disciples at this place (see Matt. 26:32).*

---

2. The personalities—"There were together Simon Peter, and Thomas called Didymus, and Nathanael of Cana in Galilee, and the sons of Zebedee, and two other of his disciples" (John 21:2).
3. The particulars—"Simon Peter saith unto them, I go a fishing. They say unto him, We also go with thee. They went forth, and entered into a ship immediately; and that night they caught nothing" (John 21:3).
B. The fisher of men on the shore
1. The call—"Then Jesus saith unto them, Children, have ye any meat? They answered him, No" (John 21:5).
2. The command—"And he said unto them, cast the net on the right side of the ship, and ye shall find" (John 21:6a).
3. The catch—"They cast therefore, and now they were not able to draw it for the multitudes of fishes" (John 21:6b). "Simon Peter went up, and drew the net to land full of great fishes, an hundred and fifty and three: and for all there were so many, yet was not the net broken" (John 21:11).

✝*John's Gospel alone records both the first and the final miracle of Christ. His first (John 2) occurred at a wedding. His final miracle (John 21) was on a seashore. Both involved food and fellowship. At the wedding there was wine to drink, and at the seashore fish to eat. Both acts were accomplished to increase the faith of his followers. "This beginning of miracles did Jesus in Cana of Galilee, and manifested forth his glory; and his disciples believed on him" (John 2:11). "And many other signs truly did Jesus in the presence of his disciples, which are not written in this book: But these are written, that ye might believe that Jesus is the Christ, the Son of God; and that believing ye might have life through his name" (John 20:30-31).*

---

4. The commitment—"Therefore that disciple whom Jesus loved saith unto Peter, It is the Lord. Now when Simon Peter heard that it was the Lord,

he girt his fisher's coat unto him, (for he was naked,) and did cast himself into the sea" (John 21:7).

5. The coals of fire—"As soon then as they were come to land, they saw a fire of coals there, and fish laid thereon, and bread" (John 21:9).

---

†*There may have been a double miracle involved here, for Jesus already had fish and bread available even before the disciples had brought in their catch.*

---

6. The communion—"Jesus saith unto them, Come and dine. And none of the disciples durst ask him, Who art thou? knowing that it was the Lord. Jesus then cometh, and taketh bread, and giveth them, and fish likewise" (John 21:12-13).

7. The confession
   a. Round one—"So when they had dined, Jesus saith to Simon Peter, Simon, son of Jonas, lovest thou me more than these? He saith unto him, Yea, Lord; thou knowest that I love thee. He saith unto him, Feed my lambs" (John 21:15).

---

† *A. Jesus' question, "Lovest thou me more than these?" may have referred to at least one of three things. He could have meant:*
   1. *"Do you love me more than you love these men?"*
   2. *"Do you love me more than fishing?"*
   3. *"Do you love me more than these men love me?" It would seem that Jesus had the third meaning in mind, based on Matthew 26:33. "Peter answered and said unto him, Though all men shall be offended because of thee, yet will I never be offended" (Matt. 26:33).*

   B. Three times he is asked if he really loves the Savior. Three times he answers in the affirmative. In the Greek New Testament, there are two different kinds of love. One is phileo *love, which refers to warm affection between human beings. The other kind of love is* agapao *love, which is a divine love—God's love for sinful mankind. This love is never found in the heart of anyone prior to the ascension of Christ. In fact, Jesus asks Peter three times (John 21:15-19) if he really loves him. The first two times Jesus uses the second kind of love and asks the following question: "Peter, do you* agapao *me?" On both occasions Peter answers by choosing the first word. He says, "Lord, you know I* phileo *you." Finally, our Lord uses the first word also. The reason for all this (as Peter would later find out) is explained in Romans 5:5 by Paul: "The love* [agapao] *of God is shed abroad in our hearts by the Holy Ghost which is given unto us." Thus, the reason Peter answered the way he did was because the Holy Spirit had not yet come at Pentecost and it was therefore impossible for him to love Christ with this divine* agapao *love. Also to be noted here is Jesus' request that Peter feed his lambs (John 21:15) and his sheep (21:16-17). Again there is a play on the Greek here, for Christ uses two different words for "feed." He says, "Be grazing my baby lambs, but discipline my older sheep." Today we have this truth in reverse. We discipline the young and feed the old.*

   C. Peter had once denied Christ three times in the presence of the Savior's enemies. Jesus was now giving him the opportunity to affirm his love three times. God is the God of the second chance.

1. *As seen in the life of Jonah—"And the word of the Lord came unto Jonah the second time, saying, Arise, go unto Nineveh, that great city, and preach unto it the preaching that I bid thee" (Jonah 3:1-2).*
2. *As seen in the life of John Mark. This young man had once failed God by abandoning Paul and Barnabas during their first missionary journey (see Acts 13:13; 15:36-39). But Mark, like Jonah and Peter, served the God of the second chance. Years later, just prior to his martyrdom in Rome, the Apostle Paul testified of this: "Only Luke is with me. Take Mark, and bring him with thee: for he is profitable to me for the ministry" (2 Tim. 4:11).*

D. *In essence, Christ's words here constituted the final part of a twofold commission given to Peter. Both parts were issued by Jesus on the shores of Galilee. Each occurred following a supernatural catch of fish. One part was spoken at the beginning of Jesus' ministry, before his crucifixion; the other was at the end of his ministry, after his resurrection. Here is that twofold commission:*
   1. *First part—"Catch fish." "When Simon Peter saw it, he fell down at Jesus' knees, saying, Depart from me; for I am a sinful man, O Lord. For he was astonished, and all that were with him, at the draught of fishes which they had taken: And so was also James, and John, the sons of Zebedee, which were partners with Simon. And Jesus said unto Simon, Fear not; from henceforth thou shalt catch men" (Luke 5:8-10).*
   2. *Second part—"Feed sheep."*

E. *Thus, in Luke 5, Jesus stressed soul winning; but here in John 21, he emphasizes sheep-tending. To his credit, Peter would faithfully carry out both parts of Christ's commission.*
   1. *He fulfilled the first section at Pentecost through the spoken word when he let down his net and caught fish—some 3,000 of them (see Acts 2:41).*
   2. *He fulfilled the second section at Babylon through the written Word, by writing 1 and 2 Peter, in order to feed the sheep. "As newborn babes, desire the sincere milk of the word, that ye may grow thereby" (1 Pet. 2:2). "Feed the flock of God which is among you, taking the oversight thereof, not by constraint, but willingly; not for filthy lucre, but of a ready mind; neither as being lords over God's heritage, but being ensamples to the flock" (1 Pet. 5:2-3).*

---

   b. Round two—"He saith to him again the second time, Simon, son of Jonas, lovest thou me? He saith unto him, Yea, Lord; thou knowest that I love thee. He saith unto him, Feed my sheep" (John 21:16).
   c. Round three—"He saith unto him the third time, Simon, son of Jonas, lovest thou me? Peter was grieved because he said unto him the third time, Lovest thou me? And he said unto him, Lord, thou knowest all things; thou knowest that I love thee. Jesus saith unto him, Feed my sheep" (John 21:17).
8. The cross—"Verily, verily, I say unto thee, When thou wast young, thou girdedst thyself, and walkedst whither thou wouldest: but when thou shalt be old, thou shalt stretch forth thy hands, and another shall gird thee, and carry thee whither thou wouldest not. This spake he, signifying by what death he should glorify God. And when he had spoken this, he saith unto him, Follow me" (John 21:18-19).
9. The concern—"Then Peter, turning about, seeth the disciple whom Jesus loved following; which also leaned on his breast at supper, and said, Lord, which is he that betrayeth thee? Peter seeing him saith to Jesus, Lord, and what shall this man do?" (John 21:20-21).

10. The chastisement—"Jesus saith unto him, If I will that he tarry till I come, what is that to thee? follow thou me" (John 21:22).
11. The confusion—"Then went this saying abroad among the brethren, that that disciple should not die: yet Jesus said not unto him, He shall not die; but, If I will that he tarry till I come, what is that to thee?" (John 21: 23).
12. The confirmation—"This is the disciple which testifieth of these things, and wrote these things: and we know that his testimony is true. And there are also many other things which Jesus did, the which, if they should be written every one, I suppose that even the world itself could not contain the books that should be written. Amen" (John 21:24-25).

A BRIEF SUMMARY OF CHRIST'S MIRACLES

A. The number of his miracles—There are thirty-five recorded miracles of Jesus found in the Gospel accounts. We know, however, that this number is not a fixed one. This fact is attested to by both John and Matthew.

    1. The testimony of John—"And many other signs truly did Jesus in the presence of his disciples, which are not written in this book" (John 20:30). "And there are also many other things which Jesus did, the which, if they should be written every one, I suppose that even the world itself could not contain the books that should be written. Amen" (John 21:25).

    2. The testimony of Matthew—"And Jesus went about all Galilee, teaching in their synagogues, and preaching the gospel of the kingdom, and healing all manner of sickness and all manner of disease among the people. And his fame went throughout all Syria: and they brought unto him all sick people that were taken with divers diseases and torments, and those which were possessed with devils, and those which were lunatick, and those that had the palsy; and he healed them" (Matt. 4:23-24). (Note: Matthew describes no less than eight additional occasions when Jesus performed similar mass healings. See 8:16; 9:35; 12:15; 14:14; 35; 15:30-31; 19:2.)

B. The classification of his miracles—The thirty-five recorded miracles can be place under seven basic categories.

    1. Healing (sixteen miracles)—Our Lord healed:
        a. The lepers (see miracles 6, 30)
        b. The blind (see 15, 23, 24, 32)
        c. The deaf (see 21)
        d. The crippled (see 17)
        e. The fever-ridden (see 2, 4, 9)
        f. One with an internal ailment (see 13)
        g. The deformed (see 8)
        h. One with palsy (see 7)
        i. One with dropsy (see 29)
        j. The maimed (see 34)

    2. Financing (one miracle; see 26)

    3. Feeding (five miracles)
        a. Providing drink (see 1)
        b. Providing meat (see 5, 18, 22, 35)

    4. Protecting (two miracles)—On two occasions Jesus saves his disciples from drowning (see 11, 19).

5. Casting out demons (seven miracles)
   a. From a boy (see 25)
   b. From a girl (see 20)
   c. From a woman (see 28)
   d. From four men (see 3, 12, 16, 27)
6. Resurrecting (three miracles)—Jesus restored from the dead:
   a. A little daughter (see 14)
   b. A young son (see 10)
   c. An older brother (see 31)
7. Judging (one miracle; see 33)
C. Interesting facts about his miracles
   1. They were performed anywhere and everywhere.
      a. At a wedding (see 1)
      b. At funerals (see 10, 14, 31)
      c. In graveyards (see 12, 31)
      d. In synagogues (see 3, 8, 28)
      e. In homes (see 4, 7, 14, 20, 29)
      f. On the seashore (see 5, 35)
      g. On the sea (see 11, 19)
      h. In a garden (see 34)
      i. On a mountain (see 18, 22)
      j. By a pool (see 17)
   2. Our Lord touched the person during eleven of his miracles. (See 4, 6, 14, 15, 19, 21, 23, 25, 28, 32, 34.)
   3. On one occasion he was touched. (See 13.)
   4. On three occasions he spat while accomplishing the miracles. (See 21, 22, 24.)
   5. Five of his miracles were performed on the Sabbath. (See 8, 17, 24, 28, 29.)
   6. Jesus was filled with compassion as he performed on the Sabbath. (See 8, 17, 24, 28-29.)
   7. He was filled with amazement during two of his miracles. (See 9, 20.)
   8. He groaned during two of his miracles. (See 21, 31.)
   9. He wept during one miracle. (See 31.)
   10. At least four of his miracles had far-reaching results:
       a. One resulted in the full-time call of Peter, Andrew, James, and John. (See 5.)
       b. Another sealed his doom with the Pharisees. (See 31.)
       c. The third signified the divine rejection of Israel. (See 33.)
       d. The fourth doubtless saved Peter from instant death. (See 34.)
   11. Sometimes he would ask a question as he performed the miracle.
       a. "Woman, what are you doing to me?" (See 1.)
       b. "Which is easier to say, Your sins be forgiven you, or, Take up your bed and walk?" (See 7.)
       c. "Is it lawful to do good on the Sabbath?" (See 8.)
       d. "Where is your faith?" (See 11.)
       e. "What is your name?" (See 12.)
       f. "Who touched my clothing?" (See 13.)
       g. "Do you believe that I can do this?" (See 15.)
       h. "Do you wish to get well?" (See 17.)

    i. "Where shall we buy loaves of bread?" (See 18.)
    j. "What made you doubt?" (See 19.)
    k. "How many loaves do you have?" (See 22.)
    l. "Do you see anything?" (See 23.)
    m. "From whom do the kings of the earth collect tribute?" (See 26.)
    n. "If Satan is casting out Satan . . . how then shall his kingdom stand?" (See 27.)
    o. "Where have you laid him?" (See 31.)
    p. "What do you wish for me to do for you?" (See 32.)
    q. "Children, have you anything to eat?" (See 35.)

12. Sometimes he issued a command as he performed the miracle.
    a. "Fill up the water jars with water." (See 1.)
    b. "Launch out where it is deep and let down your nets for a catch." (See 5.)
    c. "Stretch out your hand." (See 8.)
    d. "Rise, take up your pallet and walk." (See 7, 17.)
    e. "Have the men recline for eating in groups of fifty." (See 18.)
    f. "Come." (See 19.)
    g. "Go and wash in the Pool of Siloam." (See 24.)
    h. "Go to the sea and cast in a hook and take the first fish that comes up." (See 26.)
    i. "Lazarus, come forth." (See 31.)
    j. "Cast out the net on the right side of the boat and you will find some." (See 35.)

13. One miracle was accomplished in two phases. (See 23.)
14. Only one miracle is recorded by all four Gospel writers. (See 18.)
15. The first and final miracles are recorded by John's Gospel alone. (See 1, 35.)
16. The shortest miracle (See 27)
17. The longest miracle (See 31)
18. The saddest miracle (See 33)

THE PARABLES OF CHRIST
ONE: Two houses in a hurricane
TWO: Forgiving the fifty and the five hundred
THREE: Subduing the strong man
FOUR: The sovereign sower
FIVE: The secret of the seed
SIX: Satan's tares in the Savior's field
SEVEN: The mighty mustard seed
EIGHT: The cook's leaven and the kingdom of heaven
NINE: Finding a fortune in a field
TEN: The price of the pearl
ELEVEN: Sorting out a sea catch
TWELVE: A trained man and his treasure
THIRTEEN: Feasting friends of the bridegroom
FOURTEEN: A new cloth on an old cloth
FIFTEEN: Fresh fruit and broken bottles
SIXTEEN: A generation of gripers
SEVENTEEN: The forgiven who wouldn't forgive
EIGHTEEN: How to know your neighbor
NINETEEN: The spirits and the swept house
TWENTY: A fool in a fix
TWENTY-ONE: Readiness as opposed to carelessness
TWENTY-TWO: The fruitless fig tree
TWENTY-THREE: On being a winner at the banquet dinner
TWENTY-FOUR: The fools and a henpecked husband
TWENTY-FIVE: The missing sheep, the misplaced silver, and the miserable son
TWENTY-SIX: The stewing of a steward
TWENTY-SEVEN: When Hades petitioned Paradise
TWENTY-EIGHT: When our best is but the least
TWENTY-NINE: A widow and a weary judge
THIRTY: A haughty Pharisee and a humble publican
THIRTY-ONE: A diagnosis of defilement
THIRTY-TWO: Hourly workers and daily wages
THIRTY-THREE: The sons who reversed their roles
THIRTY-FOUR: The vicious vine keepers
THIRTY-FIVE: A wedding guest with no wedding garment
THIRTY-SIX: The fig tree and the future

THE PARABLES OF CHRIST
ONE: Two houses in a hurricane (Matt. 7:24-27; Luke 6:43-49)

---

†*Jesus ended his all-important Sermon on the Mount by relating this, his first recorded parable. Just prior to its telling he had issued a vivid description of and strong denunciation against false religious teachers. (See Matt. 7:15-23.) Thus, this parable serves as a warning concerning profession without possession, of reputation without regeneration.*

A. The unshakable house of the farsighted man—"Therefore whosoever heareth these sayings of mine, and doeth them, I will liken him unto a wise man, which built his house upon a rock: and the rain descended, and the floods came, and the winds blew, and beat upon that house; and it fell not: for it was founded upon a rock" (Matt. 7:24-25).
B. The unstable house of the foolish man—"And every one that heareth these sayings of mine, and doeth them not, shall be likened unto a foolish man, which built his house upon the sand: and the rain descended, and the floods came, and the winds blew, and beat upon that house; and it fell: and great was the fall of it" (Matt. 7:26-27).

---

†*In essence, the first parable is but an extension of the first Psalm. Both describe two men. One was wise, the other foolish. In Psalm 1 we see:*
A. The wise man described (Psa. 1:1-3)
B. The foolish man described (Psa. 1:4-6)

TWO: Forgiving the fifty and the five hundred (Luke 7:36-50)
A. The background of the parable—Christ's feet had been anointed by a broken hearted sinful woman as he sat at dinner with Simon the Pharisee, who secretly condemned the Savior for allowing this action.
B. The reason for the parable
1. To show the corruption of the Pharisee's heart.
2. To show the correctness of the sinful woman's heart.
C. The nature of the parable—"There was a certain creditor which had two debtors: the one owed five hundred pence, and the other fifty. And when they had nothing to pay, he frankly forgave them both. Tell me therefore, which of them will love him most?" (Luke 7:41-42)

D. The answer to the parable—"Simon answered and said, I suppose that he, to whom he forgave most. And he said unto him, Thou hast rightly judged" (Luke 7:43).
E. The application of the parable—"And he turned to the woman, and said unto Simon, Seest thou this woman? I entered into thine house, thou gavest me no water for my feet: but she hath washed my feet with tears, and wiped them with the hairs of her head. Thou gavest me no kiss: but this woman since the time I came in hath not ceased to kiss my feet. My head with oil thou didst not anoint: but this woman hath anointed my feet with ointment" (Luke 7:44-46).
F. The results of the parable
  1. The sinful woman was cleansed—"And he said unto her, Thy sins are forgiven" (Luke 7:48).
  2. The Pharisees were confused—"And they that sat at meat with him began to say within themselves, Who is this that forgiveth sins also?" (Luke 7:49).

†*Three key concepts make up this parable: Repentance, forgiveness, and affection.*
  A. Repentance (from sin) leads to forgiveness (from God), resulting in affection (for Christ).
  B. No repentance (from sin) leads to no forgiveness (from God), resulting in no affection (for Christ).

THREE: Subduing the strong man (Matt. 12:22-37; Mark 3:22-30)
A. The unreasonable charge—"Then was brought unto him one possessed with a devil, blind, and dumb: and he healed him, insomuch that the blind and dumb both spake and saw. But when the Pharisees heard it, they said, This fellow doth not cast out devils, but by Beelzebub the prince of the devils" (Matt. 12:22, 24).

†*The wicked Pharisees could not deny the power of Christ, so they attempted to degrade it. Beelzebub was looked upon as a filthy deity, the god of the flies of the dung pile.*

B. The unanswerable defense—"And Jesus knew their thoughts, and said unto them, Every kingdom divided against itself is brought to desolation; and every city or house divided against itself shall not stand: And if Satan cast out Satan, he is divided against himself; how shall then his kingdom stand? Or else how can one enter into a strong man's house, and spoil his goods, except he first bind the strong man? and then he will spoil his house" (Matt. 12:25-26, 29).
C. The unpardonable sin—"Wherefore I say unto you, All manner of sin and blasphemy shall be forgiven unto men: but the blasphemy against the Holy Ghost shall not be forgiven unto men. And whosoever speaketh a word against the Son of man, it shall be forgiven him: but whosoever speaketh against the Holy Ghost, it shall not be forgiven him, neither in this world, neither in the world to come" (Matt. 12:31-32).

† *A. What is the nature of the unpardonable sin? Taken in its proper context it involves crediting to the devil the works of Christ performed through the Holy Spirit during his earthly ministry. Here the wicked Pharisees had actually seen the Savior's mighty works with their own eyes*

*and had heard his marvelous words with their own ears. After experiencing this dazzling
display of deity, what was their reaction? They claimed both he and his ministry were from
hell. To sin against such light was unpardonable. What more could God himself do to convince
them? Can the unpardonable sin be committed today? Taking into consideration what has
already been said, it cannot. Christ is no longer walking this earth in his physical body
performing miracles and preaching sermons.*

B. In the ultimate sense, of course, the unpardonable sin is still committed today by the masses
who die in their sins, refusing to accept Christ as Savior.

FOUR: The sovereign sower
  A. The information in this parable—A sower (Christ) casts seed (the Word of God)
     upon four kinds of soil.
     1. Roadside soil (Matt. 13:4; Mark 4:4; Luke 8:5)—"And when he sowed, some seeds
        fell by the way side, and the fowls came and devoured them up" (Matt. 13:4).
     2. Shallow rocky soil (Matt. 13:5-6; Mark 4:5-6; Luke 8:6)—"Some fell upon stony
        places, where they had not much earth: and forthwith they sprung up,
        because they had no deepness of earth: and when the sun was up, they were
        scorched; and because they had no root, they withered away" (Matt. 13:5-6).
     3. Thorn-infested soil (Matt. 13:7; Mark 4:7; Luke 8:7)—"And some fell among
        thorns; and the thorns sprung up, and choked them" (Matt. 13:7).
     4. Fertile soil (Matt. 13:8; Mark 4:8; Luke 8:8)—"But other fell into good ground,
        and brought forth fruit, some an hundredfold, some sixtyfold, some
        thirtyfold" (Matt. 4:8).
  B. The interpretation of this parable
     1. The roadside soil (Matt. 13:19; Mark 4:15; Luke 8:12) "When any one heareth
        the word of the kingdom, and understandeth it not, then cometh the wicked
        one, and catcheth away that which was sown in his heart. This is he which
        received seed by the way side" (Matt. 13:19).

---

†*"In this illustration, the fault did not lie with the seed, the problem was with the soil. It was
too hard. But can a hard heart be changed? Yes, it can be plowed up and prepared for the seed.
The prophet Hosea advised: 'Break up your fallow ground, for it is time to seek the Lord' (Hos.
10:12)."* (Meet Yourself in the Parables, *Warren Wiersbe, Victor Books, 1983, p. 23.)

---

     2. The shallow rocky soil (Matt. 13:20-21; Mark 4:16-17; Luke 8:13) "But he that
        received the seed into stony places, the same is he that heareth the word, and
        anon with joy receiveth it; yet hath he not root in himself, but dureth for a
        while: for when tribulation or persecution ariseth because of the word, by and
        by he is offended" (Matt. 13:20-21).

---

†*"This represents an emotional hearer who hears the Word but does not really receive it so that it
is rooted in his heart. His response is purely emotional, shallow, and temporary. Jesus was not
saying that the man (or woman) was saved and then lost his or her salvation. He was saying that
the person never had salvation to begin with. It was a shallow, emotional experience that was
only on the surface. Sun is good for a plant, but in this case the sun destroyed the plant. In the
parable, the sun represents persecution. Persecution is good for God's child. It tests a person's*

faith, proves the reality of his profession, and helps him grow. But all of this is true if a person is truly born again and has spiritual roots. Just as the sun helps the plant to draw up water and nourishment from the soil, so suffering and persecution help the true believer trust the Lord and draw on his great resources. But there must be roots. The problem with a hard heart was lack of understanding, and the problem with the shallow heart was lack of depth." (Meet Yourself in the Parables, *Warren Wiersbe, Victor Books, 1983, p. 25*).

---

3. The thorn-infested soil (Matt. 13:22; Mark 4:18-19; Luke 8:14) "And these are they which are sown among thorns; such as hear the word, and the cares of this world, and the deceitfulness of riches, and the lusts of other things entering in, choke the word, and it becometh unfruitful" (Mark 4:18-19).

---

†*"The weeds represent those influences from the world that choke the seed and keep it from bearing fruit. Jesus identified these weeds as 'the care of the world, and the deceitfulness of riches' (v. 22). In theological terms, the person with this heart never really repented and turned from his sins. He received the Word, but the soil was infested with other seeds, and when they germinated the weeds crowded out the good plants. The earth did not produce thorns until sin entered the world (see Gen. 3:17-19). The thorns in this section of the parable represent that which is sinful. It is important to note that none of these first three hearts underwent salvation. The proof of salvation is not listening to the Word, or having a quick emotional response to the Word, or even cultivating the Word so that it grows in a life. The proof of salvation is fruit, for as Christ said, 'Ye shall know them by their fruits' (Matt. 7:16)."* (Meet Yourself in the Parables, *Warren Wiersbe, Victor Books, 1983, pp. 26-27*)

---

4. The fertile soil (Matt. 13:23; Mark 4:20; Luke 8:15) "But he that received seed into the good ground is he that heareth the word, and understandeth it; which also beareth fruit, and bringeth forth, some an hundredfold, some sixty, some thirty" (Matt. 13:23).

---

†*"The fact that Jesus called this heart 'good ground' does not mean he was saying people basically have good hearts. The heart of man is basically sinful, and, apart from the working of God's grace, it could never receive God's Word and produce fruit for God's glory. This heart is good in contrast to the other three hearts. It receives the Word (unlike the shallow heart), understands the Word (unlike the hard heart), and holds fast what it receives (unlike the crowded heart). If you combine the descriptions in Matthew 13:23, Mark 4:20, and Luke 8:15, you discover all these characteristics, and they lead to fruitfulness."* (Meet Yourself in the Parables, *Warren Wiersbe, Victor Books, 1983, p. 27.*)

FIVE: The secret of the seed (Mark 4:26-29)—"And he said, So is the kingdom of God, as if a man should cast seed into the ground; and should sleep, and rise night and day, and the seed should spring and grow up, he knoweth not how. For the earth bringeth forth fruit of herself; first the blade, then the ear, after that the full corn in the ear. But when the fruit is brought forth, immediately he putteth in the sickle, because the harvest is come" (Mark 4:26-29).

†*This parable describes the development of the kingdom of God, that is to say, God's dealings with this world in both the physical and spiritual realms. It is a progressive thing. An analogy here can be seen in the divine progressive revelation of our Bible. God did not reveal all of its truths in the book of Genesis, or even in the Old Testament. Centuries were involved in its writing. But by the time one reaches the book of Revelation, the seed sprout in Genesis has become the fully developed plant.*

SIX: Satan's tares in the Savior's field
    A. The information in this parable (Matt. 13:24-30)
        1. The diligence of the sower—"Another parable put he forth unto them, saying, The kingdom of heaven is likened unto a man which sowed good seed in his field" (Matt. 13:24).
        2. The discovery of the sower
          a. The revenge by his adversary—"But while men slept, his enemy came and sowed tares among the wheat, and went his way. But when the blade was sprung up, and brought forth fruit, then appeared the tares also" (Matt. 13:25-26).
          b. The report by his assistants—"So the servants of the householder came and said unto him, Sir, didst not thou sow good seed in thy field? from whence then hath it tares?" (Matt. 13:27).
        3. The discernment of the sower—"He said unto them, An enemy hath done this. The servants said unto him, Wilt thou then that we go and gather them up?" (Matt. 13:28).
        4. The dilemma of the sower—"But he said, Nay; lest while ye gather up the tares, ye root up also the wheat with them" (Matt. 13:29).
        5. The decision of the sower—"Let both grow together until the harvest: and in the time of harvest I will say to the reapers, Gather ye together first the tares, and bind them in bundles to burn them: but gather the wheat into my barn" (Matt. 13:30).

†*Three questions may be asked concerning the tares in this parable:*
    A. *What are the tares? The Palestinian farmer called them "bearded darnel." In fact, they are a poisonous rye-grass plant, giving every appearance at the beginning to be regular wheat, until both plants reach maturity. Then the tares are easily recognized.*
    B. *Who (humanly speaking) are the real tares today? It can be said that they are not the ultra-liberals or scoffing agnostics, but rather those religious individuals who know the vocabulary and concepts of salvation, but who have in their hearts totally rejected the Christ of salvation.*
    C. *Where (humanly speaking) are the real tares today? For the most part they would not be found in the congregations of the cults, or among liberal assemblies. Rather these people have often succeeded in infiltrating the membership of Bible-believing churches.*

    B. The interpretation of this parable (Matt. 13:36-43)
        1. The man is Christ.
        2. The enemy is the devil.
        3. The field is the world.
        4. The wheat is believers.
        5. The tares are unbelievers.
        6. The harvest is the end of the age.

7. The reapers are angels.
8. The granary is heaven.
9. The furnace is hell.

SEVEN: The mighty mustard seed (Matt. 13:31-32; Mark 4:30-32; Luke 13:18-19) "Another parable put he forth unto them, saying, The kingdom of heaven is like to a grain of mustard seed, which a man took, and sowed in his field: which indeed is the least of all seeds: but when it is grown, it is the greatest among herbs, and becometh a tree, so that the birds of the air come and lodge in the branches thereof" (Matt. 13:31-32).

---

† A. *The mustard seed was indeed the smallest of all seeds sown in the field. It took 750 seeds to weigh a gram. As there are 28 grams in one ounce, and 16 ounces in a pound, it would take 336,000 of these seeds to equal a pound. And yet this tiny seed can, in a very few weeks, grow into a mustard plant 15 feet high.*

B. *Jesus compares all of this with the kingdom of God.*

1. *Christ's first coming and the kingdom—At that time, it was but a tiny seed. The Roman rulers had ridiculed it, and the Jewish leaders had rejected it. In fact, the last question asked of Christ by his disciples just prior to his ascension had to do with the kingdom. "When they therefore were come together, they asked of him, saying, Lord, wilt thou at this time restore again the kingdom to Israel?" (Acts 1:6).*

2. *Christ's second coming and the kingdom. At that time, it will become as the mighty mustard plant. "And the seventh angel sounded; and there were great voices in heaven, saying, The kingdoms of this world are become the kingdoms of our Lord, and of his Christ; and he shall reign for ever and ever" (Rev. 11:15).*

EIGHT: The cook's leaven and kingdom of heaven (Matt. 13:33)—"Another parable spake he unto them; The kingdom of heaven is like unto leaven, which a woman took, and hid in three measures of meal, till the whole was leavened" (Matt. 13:33).

---

† A. *The key to interpreting this parable is one's understanding of the word "leaven." What does it stand for? There are two main views:*

1. *It represents the gospel. This is the position of the postmillennialist. He is the one who believes the preaching of the gospel in and by itself will be able to usher in the thousand-year era of peace, at the end of which Christ will return.*

2. *It represents the presence of evil. This is the position of the premillennialist. He is one who believes that in spite of gospel preaching, the world will become worse and that only the second coming of the King himself at the beginning of the millennium can usher in that golden era of peace. This seems to be the correct view. In fact, there are three symbols for evil in the Bible. These are:*

   a. *Leprosy (Lev. 13–14; Num. 5:2)*

   b. *The serpent (Gen. 3:1-2, 4, 13-14; Num. 21:8-9; Psa. 58:4; Isa. 27:1; Matt. 23:33; Rev. 12:9; 20:2)*

   c. *Leaven—The New Scofield Bible says the following: "Leaven, as a symbolic or typical substance, is always mentioned in the Old Testament in an evil sense. The usage of the word in the New Testament explains its symbolic meaning. It is malice and wickedness as contrasted with sincerity and truth (1 Cor. 5:6-8). It is evil doctrine (Matt. 16:12) in its threefold form of Pharisaism, Sadduceeism, and Herodianism*

(Matt. 16:6; Mark 8:15). The leaven of the Pharisees was externalism in religion (Matt. 23:14-16, 23-28); of the Sadducees, skepticism as to the supernatural and as to the Scriptures (Matt. 22:23, 29); of the Herodians, worldliness (Matt. 22:16-21; Mark 3:6)." (Oxford University Press, New York, 1967, p. 1015.)

  B. *Thus, this parable predicts the growth of satanic evil until the whole world is affected. It also answers the question of why Christ has not yet come.*
    1. *The postmillennialist says he has not returned because things are not yet good enough.*
    2. *The premillennialist says he has not returned because things are not yet bad enough.*
    (See 1 Tim. 4:1-3; 2 Tim. 3:1-9; 4:1-4; 2 Pet. 3.)

NINE: Finding a fortune in a field (Matt. 13:44)—"Again, the kingdom of heaven is like unto treasure hid in a field; the which when a man hath found, he hideth, and for joy thereof goeth and selleth all that he hath, and buyeth that field" (Matt. 13:44).

†*The treasure here probably represents Israel, and the man is Christ. Often in the Old Testament, God describes that nation as his special treasure. Note: "Now therefore, if ye will obey my voice indeed, and keep my covenant, then ye shall be a peculiar treasure unto me above all people: for all the earth is mine" (Exod. 19:5). "For thou art an holy people unto the Lord thy God, and the Lord hath chosen thee to be a peculiar people unto himself, above all the nations that are upon the earth" (Deut. 14:2). "For the Lord hath chosen Jacob unto himself, and Israel for his peculiar treasure" (Psa. 135:4). "And they shall be mine, saith the LORD of hosts, in that day when I make up my jewels; and I will spare them, as a man spareth his own son that serveth him" (Mal. 3:17).*

TEN: The price of a pearl (Matt. 13:45-46)—"Again, the kingdom of heaven is like unto a merchant man, seeking goodly pearls: who, when he had found one pearl of great price, went and sold all that he had, and bought it" (Matt. 13:45-46).

† A. *Many believe that the pearl here represents the Church. If so, this marks the first hint of it. Christ would officially announce his plans to build it in Matthew 16:18.*
  B. *Thus, we have described in parables 9 and 10 God's two most precious possessions, the hidden treasure (Israel) and the costly pearl (the Church).*
  C. *Both prized possessions are highlighted in the construction of the Holy City, New Jerusalem (Rev. 21:1-2).*
    1. *The twelve gates in the wall surrounding the city consist of twelve pearls (Rev. 21:21).*
      a. *Each gate was supervised by a special angel (Rev. 21:12).*
      b. *Each gate was named after one of the twelve tribes of Israel (Rev. 21:12).*
    2. *The twelve foundations of the city are named after the twelve apostles of Christ (Rev. 21:14).*

ELEVEN: Sorting out a sea catch (Matt. 13:47-50)—"Again, the kingdom of heaven is like unto a net, that was cast into the sea, and gathered of every kind: which, when it was full, they drew to shore, and sat down, and gathered the good into vessels, but cast the bad away. So shall it be at the end of the world: the angels shall come forth, and sever the wicked from among the just, and shall cast them into the furnace of fire: there shall be wailing and gnashing of teeth" (Matt. 13:47-50).

†*God has assigned angels a very important role in the future gathering, punishing, and rewarding of human beings (Matt. 13:39, 41, 49; 24:31; 25:31-32).*

TWELVE: A trained man and his treasure (Matt. 13:52)—"Then said he unto them, Therefore every scribe which is instructed unto the kingdom of heaven is like unto a man that is an householder, which bringeth forth out of his treasure things new and old" (Matt. 13:52).

† *A. A scribe was one who copied, contemplated, and communicated the Word of God in regard to the people of Israel.*
  B. Ezra was the most famous of the biblical scribes. "This Ezra went up from Babylon; and he was a ready scribe in the law of Moses, which the LORD God of Israel had given; and the king granted him all his request, according to the hand of the LORD his God upon him. For Ezra had prepared his heart to seek the law of the LORD, and to do it, and to teach in Israel statutes and judgments" (Ezra 7:6, 10).
  C. What marvelous truths modern-day scribes (diligent Bible students) can still bring from the ultimate treasure, God's Word. "O the depth of the riches both of the wisdom and knowledge of God! how unsearchable are his judgments, and his ways past finding out!" (Rom. 11:33).

THIRTEEN: Feasting friends of the bridegroom (Matt. 9:14-15; Mark 2:18-20; Luke 5:33-35)—"Then came to him the disciples of John, saying, Why do we and the Pharisees fast oft, but thy disciples fast not? And Jesus said unto them, Can the children of the bridechamber mourn, as long as the bridegroom is with them? but the days will come, when the bridegroom shall be taken from them, and then shall they fast" (Matt. 9:14-15).

† *A. Jesus was not at this point discouraging fasting.*
    1. He himself once fasted for forty days (Matt. 4:2).
    2. He laid down rules for fasting (Matt. 6:16-18).
    3. He indicated that fasting on certain occasions was necessary to experience the power of God (Matt. 17:21).
    4. Following his ascension, his followers would fast (Acts 14:23; 1 Cor. 7:5; 2 Cor. 6:5).
  B. However, as long as he was with the disciples (right up to the very hour of Calvary), the main priority of the Savior was to teach and train them.

FOURTEEN: A new cloth on an old coat (Matt. 9:16; Mark 2:21; Luke 5:36)—"And he spake also a parable unto them; No man putteth a piece of a new garment upon an old; if otherwise, then both the new maketh a rent, and the piece that was taken out of the new agreeth not with the old" (Luke 5:36).
FIFTEEN: Fresh fruit and broken bottles (Matt. 9:17; Mark 2:22; Luke 5:37-39)—"And no man putteth new wine into old bottles; else the new wine will burst the bottles, and be spilled, and the bottles shall perish. But new wine must be put into new bottles; and both are preserved" (Luke 5:37-38).

†*Warren Wiersbe writes: "In these days of sanforized fabrics, and glass and plastic bottles, the illustration about cloth and wineskins may confuse some. The Jews did not have preshrunk cloth*

for their clothing, and they frequently kept their liquids in skins. If a woman sewed a patch on a garment that had already been washed, the next time it was washed the patch would shrink and ruin both the patch and the garment. If new wine was poured into dry, brittle skins, the pressure of the gas from the fermentation would break the skin and the wine would be lost. Jesus was neither a conformer (like the Pharisees) nor a reformer (like John the Baptist). He was (and is) a Transformer. He does not reject either the old or the new: He transforms the old so that it is fulfilled in the new. 'Think not that I am come to destroy the law, or the prophets; I am not come to destroy, but to fulfill' (Matt. 5:17). If I have an acorn, I can destroy it in one of two ways. I can put it on the sidewalk and beat it to a pulp with a hammer. Or, I can plant it in the ground where it will die and produce an oak tree. The acorn would be destroyed by being fulfilled. Jesus did not come to patch up the old, worn-out Jewish religion. He came to fulfill it in His life, teaching, and death and resurrection. He transformed the old by fulfilling it in the new. To put new cloth on an old garment would destroy both. To put new wine in brittle wineskins would destroy both. To try to mix Law and Grace, Moses and Christ, would destroy both. But to permit the Law to be fulfilled in Grace, and Moses to be fulfilled in Christ, is what God accomplished."
(Meet Yourself in the Parables, *Victor Books, Wheaton, Ill., 1979, pp. 38-39*)

SIXTEEN: A generation of gripers (Matt. 11:16-19; Luke 7:29-35)
   A. The complainers—"But the Pharisees and lawyers rejected the counsel of God against themselves, being not baptized of him. And the Lord said, Whereunto then shall I liken the men of this generation? and to what are they like?" (Luke 7:30-31).
   B. The complaint—"They are like unto children sitting in the marketplace, and calling one to another, and saying, We have piped unto you, and ye have not danced; we have mourned to you, and ye have not wept. For John the Baptist came neither eating bread nor drinking wine; and ye say, He hath a devil. The Son of man is come eating and drinking; and ye say, Behold a gluttonous man, and a winebibber, a friend of publicans and sinners!" (Luke 7:32-34)
      1. Griping because John fasted
      2. Griping because Jesus feasted

---

† A. *Perhaps the Holy Spirit had Jesus' generation in mind when he inspired the writing of the following words: "There is a generation that curseth their father, and doth not bless their mother. There is a generation that are pure in their own eyes, and yet is not washed from their filthiness. There is a generation, O how lofty are their eyes! and their eyelids are lifted up. There is a generation, whose teeth are as swords, and their jaw teeth as knives, to devour the poor from off the earth, and the needy from among men" (Prov. 30:11-14).*
   B. *The ultimate tragedy here was that this generation which began by criticizing the Savior would end by crucifying him. The gripers would become vipers.*

SEVENTEEN: The forgiven who wouldn't forgive (Matt. 18:21-35)
   A. Scene One: The servant and his master (first meeting)
      1. The debt he owed—"Therefore is the kingdom of heaven likened unto a certain king, which would take account of his servants. And when he had begun to reckon, one was brought unto him, which owed him ten thousand talents" (Matt. 18:23-24).

2. The disaster he faced—"But forasmuch as he had not to pay, his lord commanded him to be sold, and his wife, and children, and all that he had, and payment to be made" (Matt. 18:25).

3. The desperation he displayed—"The servant therefore fell down, and worshipped him, saying, Lord, have patience with me, and I will pay thee all" (Matt. 18:26).

4. The deliverance he gained—"Then the lord of that servant was moved with compassion, and loosed him, and forgave him the debt" (Matt. 18:27).

B. Scene Two: The servant and his servant—"But the same servant went out, and found one of his fellowservants, which owed him an hundred pence: and he laid hands on him, and took him by the throat, saying, Pay me that thou owest" (Matt. 18:28).

1. The pitiful request of the lesser servant—"And his fellowservant fell down at his feet, and besought him, saying, Have patience with me, and I will pay thee all" (Matt. 18:29).

2. The pitiless response of the greater servant—"And he would not: but went and cast him into prison, till he should pay the debt" (Matt. 18:30).

---

† A. *Consider the staggering contrasts concerning both the amounts owed and the attitudes displayed in this parable.*

1. *The amount owed to the king—It amounted to 10,000 talents. The servant here was no doubt a tax-collecting governor of sorts, entrusted by the king to rule over a city or province. He had apparently either embezzled or misappropriated vast sums of money collected for the king.*

   a. *One talent would purchase a slave.*

   b. *One talent represented 20 years' wages for the average workman.*

   c. *The total annual tax bill for all of Palestine was less than 1,000 talents. Yet the gracious king forgave all this.*

2. *The amount owed to the servant—It was only 100 pence, which amounted to approximately four months' wages (1/60 of a talent). Yet the greedy servant refused to forgive.*

B. *This great principle of the importance for the forgiven to forgive is brought out time and again in the New Testament. "And lead us not into temptation, but deliver us from evil: For thine is the kingdom, and the power, and the glory, for ever. Amen. For if ye forgive men their trespasses, your heavenly Father will also forgive you" (Matt. 6:13-14). "And be ye kind one to another, tenderhearted, forgiving one another, even as God for Christ's sake hath forgiven you" (Eph. 4:32).*

C. Scene Three: The servant and his master (final meeting) "So when his fellowservants saw what was done, they were very sorry, and came and told unto their lord all that was done" (Matt. 18:31).

1. The outrage over this injustice

   a. Reminding the wicked servant—"Then his lord, after that he had called him, said unto him, O thou wicked servant, I forgave thee all that debt, because thou desiredst me" (Matt. 18:32).

   b. Rebuking the wicked servant—"Shouldest not thou also have had compassion on thy fellowservant, even as I had pity on thee?" (Matt. 18:33).

    2. The outcome of this injustice—"and his lord was wroth, and delivered him to the tormentors, till he should pay all that was due unto him" (Matt. 18:34).

EIGHTEEN: How to know your neighbor (Luke 10:30-35)

    A. The actors involved—A traveler, some robbers, a priest, a Levite, and a Samaritan

    B. The action involved

        1. The trip—"A certain man went down from Jerusalem to Jericho" (Luke 10:30).

        2. The trouble—"And fell among thieves, which stripped him of his raiment, and wounded him, and departed, leaving him half dead" (Luke 10:30).

        3. The test

            a. Failed by the priest—"And by chance there came down a certain priest that way: and when he saw him, he passed by on the other side" (Luke 10:31).

            b. Failed by the Levite—"And likewise a Levite, when he was at the place, came and looked on him, and passed by on the other side" (Luke 10:32).

            c. Passed by the Samaritan

                (1) His compassion upon the traveler—"And went to him, and bound up his wounds, pouring in oil and wine" (Luke 10:34a).

                (2) His care for the traveler—"And set him on his own beast, and brought him to an inn, and took care of him" (Luke 10:34b).

                (3) His commitment to the traveler—"And on the morrow when he departed, he took out two pence, and gave them to the host, and said unto him, Take care of him; and whatsoever thou spendest more, when I come again, I will repay thee" (Luke 10:35).

    C. The attitudes involved

        1. That of the robbers—"What is thine is mine."

        2. That of the priest and Levite—"What is mine is mine."

        3. That of the Samaritan—"What is mine is thine."

---

  † *A. There is a twofold irony and surprise in this parable:*

     1. Concerning the two who should have helped the victim but did not.

       a. The priest—He might have just come from the temple after presenting the sacrifices to God.

       b. The Levite—He might have just come from the temple after proclaiming the Scriptures. But neither would lift a finger to help a fellow human being.

     2. Concerning the one who should not have helped the victim, but did. He was a Samaritan and a member of a race hated by the Jews (Luke 10:33).

   B. Jesus related this parable to answer a question posed by a lawyer. The question was, "Who is my neighbor?" The answer, of course, is that my neighbor is anyone I can help.

NINETEEN: The spirits and the swept house (Matt. 12:43-45; Luke 11:24-26)

    A. The case of reformation without regeneration—"When the unclean spirit is gone out of a man, he walketh through dry places, seeking rest; and finding none, he saith, I will return unto my house whence I came out. And when he cometh, he findeth it swept and garnished" (Luke 11:24-25).

    B. The consequences of reformation without regeneration—"Then goeth he, and taketh to him seven other spirits more wicked than himself; and they enter in, and dwell there: and the last state of that man is worse than the first" (Luke 11:26).

† A. *Here is a case of* reformation *without* regeneration *. The man in the parable turned over a new leaf, but not a new life. This can prove to be a very dangerous situation. To illustrate:*
   1. *An unbelieving drunk through sheer human willpower is able to dry out and become a respectable member of society.*
   2. *He then is filled with pride and ridicules the saving grace of God, boasting that human determination is sufficient for all things.*
   3. *In this state he becomes far more valuable to Satan than when he was a poor derelict.*
  B. *In this parable Jesus strongly suggests that there are degrees of evil in the hierarchy of the demonic world. Various Scripture verses seem to support this. Note the diverse actions caused by various demons.*
   1. *Seducing and false spirits—They are associated with false doctrine (2 Cor. 11:4; 1 Tim. 4:1; 1 John 4:1-6).*
   2. *Unclean and evil spirits—They seem to cause physical suffering (Matt. 10:1; Luke 7:21; Acts 5:16; 8:7).*
   3. *Miracle-working spirits—These may attempt to imitate the work of God (Rev. 16:13-14).*
   4. *Foul spirits—These are linked to sexual immorality (Rev. 18:2-3).*
   5. *Violent spirits (Acts 19:12-16; 1 Sam. 18:10-11)*
   6. *Lying spirits (1 Kings 22:22-23)*

TWENTY: A fool in a fix (Luke 12:13-21)

---

†*Jesus related this parable to warn a listener concerning the sin of covetousness (Luke 12:13-15). Warren Wiersbe writes:*
"Covetousness is a desire for things and it can be the beginning of all kinds of sin. Eve coveted being like God and took the forbidden fruit. Lot's wife coveted Sodom and was killed on the spot. Achan coveted some spoils of war and destroyed himself and his family. David coveted his neighbor's wife and plunged himself, his family, and his nation into trouble. The last of the Ten Commandments is, 'Thou shalt not covet.' By coveting, we can break all the other nine commandments." (Meet Yourself in the Parables, *Victor Books, Wheaton, Ill., 1979, p. 115.) In the New Testament, Paul confessed that this command, more than any other, caused him to realize his own wretched, sinful condition (Rom. 7:7-9).*

  A. His dilemma—"And he spake a parable unto them, saying, The ground of a certain rich man brought forth plentifully: and he thought within himself, saying, What shall I do, because I have no room where to bestow my fruits?" (Luke 12:16-17).
  B. His decision—"And he said, This will I do: I will pull down my barns, and build greater; and there will I bestow all my fruits and my goods" (Luke 12:18).
  C. His delusion—"And I will say to my soul, Soul, thou hast much goods laid up for many years; take thine ease, eat, drink, and be merry" (Luke 12:19).
  D. His destruction—"But God said unto him, Thou fool, this night thy soul shall be required of thee: then whose shall those things be, which thou hast provided?" (Luke 12:20)

---

†*This marks the only occasion in the Bible in which God himself personally calls an individual a fool. The man was a fool:*

A. *Because he thought he could satisfy his eternal soul with materialistic goods—Note this statement, "And I will say to my soul, Soul, thou hast much goods laid up" (12:19). See Jesus' statement in Matthew 4:4; 16:26. The only real soul food is the Word of God. Our Lord had warned concerning this on two previous occasions: "But he answered and said, It is written, Man shall not live by bread alone, but by every word that proceedeth out of the mouth of God" (Matt. 4:4). "For what is a man profited, if he shall gain the whole world, and lose his own soul? or what shall a man give in exchange for his soul?" (Matt. 16:26)*

B. *Because he smugly assumed he would naturally live to a ripe old age—Again, observe his misplaced confidence: "Thou hast much goods laid up for many years." (See Prov. 27:1; 29:1; Psa. 9:12; James 4:13-15.)*

C. *Because he was totally self-centered—The personal pronouns "me, mine, and I" are to be found twelve times in this short account.*

TWENTY-ONE: Readiness as opposed to carelessness (Matt. 24:42-51; Luke 12:35-48)

A. The merits of readiness

1. The rules for readiness—"Let your loins be girded about, and your lights burning; and ye yourselves like unto men that wait for their lord, when he will return from the wedding; that when he cometh and knocketh, they may open unto him immediately" (Luke 12:35-36).

2. The reason for readiness—"Be ye therefore ready also: for the Son of man cometh at an hour when ye think not" (Luke 12:40).

3. The results of readiness—"Blessed are those servants, whom the lord when he cometh shall find watching: verily I say unto you, that he shall gird himself, and make them to sit down to meat, and will come forth and serve them. . . . Blessed is that servant, whom his lord when he cometh shall find so doing. Of a truth I say unto you, that he will make him ruler over all that he hath" (Luke 12:37, 43-44).

B. The misery of carelessness

1. How it begins—"But and if that servant say in his heart, My lord delayeth his coming; and shall begin to beat the menservants and maidens, and to eat and drink, and to be drunken" (Luke 12:45).

2. How it ends

a. The surprise involved—"The lord of that servant will come in a day when he looketh not for him, and at an hour when he is not aware, and will cut him in sunder, and will appoint him his portion with the unbelievers" (Luke 12:46).

b. The stripes involved—"And that servant, which knew his lord's will, and prepared not himself, neither did according to his will, shall be beaten with many stripes. But he that knew not, and did commit things worthy of stripes, shall be beaten with few stripes. For unto whomsoever much is given, of him shall be much required: and to whom men have committed much, of him they will ask the more" (Luke 12:47-48).

---

† A. *Both Paul and Peter may have had this parable in mind when they wrote the following: "For yourselves know perfectly that the day of the Lord so cometh as a thief in the night. For when they shall say, Peace and safety; then sudden destruction cometh upon them, as travail upon a woman with child; and they shall not escape" (1 Thess. 5:2-3). "But the day of the Lord will*

come as a thief in the night; in the which the heavens shall pass away with a great noise, and the elements shall melt with fervent heat, the earth also and the works that are therein shall be burned up" (1 Pet. 3:10).

B. *The Bible is clear that there will be degrees of rewards in heaven (1 Cor. 3:11-15). But will there be degrees of punishment in hell? This parable seems to suggest so. Note also the words of Paul concerning this concept: "But we are sure that the judgment of God is according to truth against them which commit such things. Who will render to every man according to his deeds: For as many as have sinned without law shall also perish without law: and as many as have sinned in the law shall be judged by the law" (Rom. 2:2, 6, 12).*

TWENTY-TWO: The fruitless fig tree (Luke 13:6-9)
  A. The abandonment by the vineyard owner
      1. The problem—"He spake also this parable; A certain man had a fig tree planted in his vineyard; and he came and sought fruit thereon, and found none" (Luke 13:6).
      2. The plan—"Then said he unto the dresser of his vineyard, Behold, these three years I come seeking fruit on this fig tree, and find none: cut it down; why cumbereth it the ground?" (Luke 13:7).
  B. The advice to the vineyard owner—"And he answering said unto him, Lord, let it alone this year also, till I shall dig about it, and dung it: and if it bear fruit, well: and if not then after that thou shalt cut it down" (Luke 13:8-9).
TWENTY-THREE: On being a winner at the banquet dinner (Luke 14:7-14)

---

† A. *This parable is very similar to a song recorded by Isaiah the prophet concerning the nation Israel (see Isa. 5:1-7).*
  B. *The unique aspect of the parable is seen in the fact that it is the only unfinished one related to Christ. Did the owner listen to his assistant?*
  C. *A controversy has risen concerning the identity of the vineyard dresser. Who is this assistant who begs the owner to spare the fig tree? Some would suggest that he is Christ, who champions Israel (the fig tree) before the Father.*

  A. How to be honored as a guest
      1. Negative—"And he put forth a parable to those which were bidden, when he marked how they chose out the chief rooms; saying unto them, When thou art bidden of any man to a wedding, sit not down in the highest room; lest a more honourable man than thou be bidden of him; and he that bade thee and him come and say to thee, Give this man place; and thou begin with shame to take the lowest room" (Luke 14:7-9).
      2. Positive
          a. Your response—"But when thou art bidden, go and sit down in the lowest room; that when he that bade thee cometh, he may say unto thee, Friend, go up higher: then shalt thou have worship in the presence of them that sit at meat with thee" (Luke 14:10).
          b. Your reward—"For whosoever exalteth himself shall be abased; and he that humbleth himself shall be exalted" (Luke 14:11).

† A. Warren Wiersbe writes: *"Jesus had watched the guests assemble and fight for the best seats. The Pharisees always wanted the best seats at the feasts (Matt. 23:6), and their guests followed their bad example. We laugh at this, but the same mad scramble goes on today. There are more status seekers and pyramid climbers in churches and other Christian organizations than we care to admit. The competition can be strong as Christians argue over who has the greatest church, the biggest Sunday School, or the most sacrificial missionary program. This mad scramble for the top seats only shows how false is our view of success. As if where a man sits can change the man! Paul sat in a prison while Nero sat on the throne of the Roman Empire, yet no one doubts who was the better man."* (Meet Yourself in the Parables, *Victor Books, Wheaton, Ill., 1979, pp. 93-94)*

B. *Both James and Peter would write concerning this very thing: "But he giveth more grace. Wherefore he saith, God resisteth the proud, but giveth grace unto the humble. . . . Humble yourselves in the sight of the Lord, and he shall lift you up" (James 4:6, 10). "Likewise, ye younger, submit yourselves unto the elder. Yea, all of you be subject one to another, and be clothed with humility: for God resisteth the proud, and giveth grace to the humble. Humble yourselves therefore under the mighty hand of God, that he may exalt you in due time" (1 Pet. 5:5-6).*

B. How to be honored as a host
1. Negative—"Then said he also to him that bade him, When thou makest a dinner or a supper, call not thy friends, nor thy brethren, neither thy kinsmen, nor thy rich neighbours; lest they also bid thee again, and a recompence be made thee" (Luke 14:12).
2. Positive
   a. Your response—"But when thou makest a feast, call the poor, the maimed, the lame, the blind" (Luke 14:13).
   b. Your reward—"And thou shalt be blessed; for they cannot recompense thee: for thou shalt be recompensed at the resurrection of the just" (Luke 14:14).

---

†*Jesus amplified this during one of his final parables: "Then shall the King say unto them on his right hand, Come, ye blessed of my Father, inherit the kingdom prepared for you from the foundation of the world: For I was an hungred, and ye gave me meat: I was thirsty, and ye gave me drink: I was a stranger, and ye took me in: naked, and ye clothed me: I was sick, and ye visited me: I was in prison, and ye came unto me. Then shall the righteous answer him, saying, Lord, when saw we thee an hungred, and fed thee? or thirsty, and gave thee drink? When saw we thee a stranger, and took thee in? or naked, and clothed thee? Or when saw we thee sick, or in prison, and came unto thee? And the King shall answer and say unto them, Verily I say unto you, Inasmuch as ye have done it unto one of the least of these my brethren, ye have done it unto me" (Matt. 25:34-40).*

TWENTY-FOUR: Two fools and a henpecked husband (Luke 14:15-24)
A. The invitation (first listing)—"Then said he unto him, A certain man made a great supper, and bade many: and sent his servant at supper time to say to them that were bidden, Come; for all things are now ready" (Luke 14:16-17).

†*Note the features of this gracious invitation:*
    A. Its urgency—"Come!"
    B. Its sufficiency—"All things."
    C. Its availability—"Are now ready."

    B. The invited—"And they all with one consent began to make excuse" (Luke 14:18a).
        1. First excuse—"The first said unto him. I have bought a piece of ground, and I must needs go and see it: I pray thee have me excused" (Luke 14:18b).
        2. Second excuse—"And another said, I have bought five yoke of oxen, and I go to prove them: I pray thee have me excused" (Luke 14:19).
        3. Third excuse—"And another said, I have married a wife, and therefore I cannot come" (Luke 14:20).

†*Someone has aptly described these three unresponsive individuals as two fools and a henpecked husband. Note each of their pitiful excuses:*
    A. First: Only a fool would buy a field without seeing it.
    B. Second: Only a fool would purchase oxen without trying them.
    C. Third: No comment necessary.

    C. The invitation (final listing)
        1. The revised guest list
            a. Consisting of suffering people—"So that servant came, and shewed his lord these things. Then the master of the house being angry said to his servant, Go out quickly into the streets and lanes of the city, and bring in hither the poor, and the maimed, and the halt, and the blind. And the servant said, Lord, it is done as thou hast commanded, and yet there is room" (Luke 14:21-22).
            b. Consisting of scattered people—"And the lord said unto the servant, Go out into the highways and hedges, and compel them to come in, that my house may be filled" (Luke 14:23).
        2. The rejected guest list—"For I say unto you, That none of those men which were bidden shall taste of my supper" (Luke 14:24).

†*While the general thrust of this parable speaks of Israel's rejection of God's kingdom banquet and the subsequent call of the Gentiles, it can also be applied to every human being on earth.*
    A. To refuse God's gracious salvation invitation is to experience his hell.
    B. To receive God's gracious salvation invitation is to experience his heaven. "Behold, I stand at the door, and knock: if any man hear my voice, and open the door, I will come in to him, and will sup with him, and he with me" (Rev. 3:20).

TWENTY-FIVE: The missing sheep, the misplaced silver, and the miserable son (Luke 15:1-32)

†*Jesus related this threefold parable to answer a charge leveled against him by his enemies: "And the Pharisees and scribes murmured, saying, this man receiveth sinners, and eateth with them" (Luke 15:2).*

A. The missing sheep
   1. The actors
      a. A lost sheep (percentage involved—one out of 100)
      b. A seeking shepherd (a type of the Son)
      c. Some joyful neighbors
   2. The action
      a. The search—"What man of you, having an hundred sheep, if he lose one of them, doth not leave the ninety and nine in the wilderness, and go after that which is lost, until he find it?" (Luke 15:4)
      b. The sighting—"And when he hath found it, he layeth it on his shoulders, rejoicing" (Luke 15:5).
      c. The singing
         (1) On earth—"And when he cometh home, he calleth together his friends and neighbours, saying unto them, Rejoice with me; for I have found my sheep which was lost" (Luke 15:6).
         (2) In heaven—"I say unto you, that likewise joy shall be in heaven over one sinner that repenteth, more than over ninety and nine just persons, which need no repentance" (Luke 15:7).
B. The misplaced silver
   1. The actors (objects)
      a. A misplaced coin (percentage involved—one out of ten)
      b. A diligent woman (possible type of the Holy Spirit)
      c. Some joyful neighbors
   2. The action
      a. The search—"Either what woman having ten pieces of silver, if she lose one piece, doth not light a candle, and sweep the house, and seek diligently till she find it?" (Luke 5:8)
      b. The sighting—"And when she hath found it, she calleth her friends and her neighbours together, saying, Rejoice with me; for I have found the piece which I had lost" (Luke 15:9).
      c. The singing
         (1) On earth (Luke 15:9b)
         (2) In heaven (Luke 15:10)
C. The younger misguided son
   1. Actors
      a. A younger son (percentage involved—one of two)
      b. A wise and wonderful Father (a type of the heavenly Father)
      c. An older son
      d. A pig farmer
   2. Action
      The rebellion of the younger son
      a. The foolishness he exhibited
         (1) In seeking his inheritance—"And he said, A certain man had two sons: And the younger of them said to his father, Father, give me the portion

of goods that falleth to me. And he divided unto them his living"
(Luke 15:11-12).
(2) In squandering his inheritance—"And not many days after the younger
son gathered all together, and took his journey into a far country, and
there wasted his substance with riotous living" (Luke 15:13).
b. The famine he endured—"And when he had spent all, there arose a
mighty famine in that land; and he began to be in want. And he went and
joined himself to a citizen of that country; and he sent him into his fields to
feed swine. And he would fain have filled his belly with the husks that the
swine did eat: and no man gave unto him" (Luke 15:14-16).
3. Recall
The realization of the younger son: "And when he came to himself, he said, How
many hired servants of my father's have bread enough and to spare, and I
perish with hunger!" (Luke 5:17)
4. Reaction
The repentance of the younger son: "I will arise and go to my father, and will say unto
him, Father, I have sinned against heaven, and before thee, and am no more
worthy to be called thy son: make me as one of thy hired servants" (Luke 15:18-19).

---

† A. *This boy is one of at least eight individuals in the Bible to utter those three difficult words,*
"I have sinned." The others were:
1. *Pharaoh (Exod. 9:27; 10:16)*
2. *Balaam (Num. 22:34)*
3. *Achan (Josh. 7:20)*
4. *Saul (1 Sam. 26:21)*
5. *David (2 Sam. 12:13; 24:10)*
6. *Job (Job 7:20)*
7. *Judas (Matt. 27:4)*
B. *As the context indicates, however, only three of these were genuinely sorrowful for their sin.*
These were: David, Job, and the prodigal son.

---

5. Response
The reunion with the younger son
a. The father's compassion—"And he arose, and came to his father. But when
he was yet a great way off, his father saw him, and had compassion, and
ran, and fell on his neck, and kissed him" (Luke 15:20).
b. The son's confession—"And the son said unto him, Father, I have sinned
against heaven, and in thy sight, and am no more worthy to be called thy
son" (Luke 15:21).
6. Result—The restoration of the younger son
a. The father's proposal (what he did) "But the father said to his servants,
Bring forth the best robe, and put it on him; and put a ring on his hand,
and shoes on his feet: and bring hither the fatted calf, and kill it; and let us
eat, and be merry" (Luke 15:22-23).
b. The father's purpose (why he did it) "For this my son was dead, and is alive
again; he was lost, and is found. And they began to be merry" (Luke 15:24).

D. The older misguided son
   1. His resentment
      a. The basis—"Now his elder son was in the field: and as he came and drew nigh to the house, he heard musick and dancing. And he called one of the servants, and asked what these things meant. And he said unto him, Thy brother is come; and thy father hath killed the fatted calf, because he hath received him safe and sound" (Luke 15:25-27).
      b. The boycott—"And he was angry, and would not go in: therefore came his father out, and intreated him" (Luke 15:28).
      c. The bitterness—He complained to his father.
         (1) "My service to you has never been rewarded." "And he answering said to his father, Lo, these many years do I serve thee, neither transgressed I at any time thy commandment: and yet thou never gavest me a kid, that I might make merry with my friends" (Luke 15:29).
         (2) "His sin against you is now being rewarded." "But as soon as this thy son was come, which hath devoured thy living with harlots, thou hast killed for him the fatted calf" (Luke 15:30).
   2. His reassurance—"And he said unto him, Son, thou art ever with me, and all that I have is thine. It was meet that we should make merry, and be glad: for this thy brother was dead, and is alive again; and was lost, and is found" (Luke 15:31-32).

---

†*At least four questions may be asked concerning this threefold parable:*
   A. What is its intended lesson? Here three positions may be seen.
      1. It speaks of the redemption of a lost sinner.
      2. It speaks of the restoration of a backslidden believer.
      3. It speaks of both.
   B. What is the key word found in this threefold parable? It is the word "rejoice," appearing in various forms some seven times. (Luke 15:6, 7, 8, 10, 24, 29, 32).
   C. What is the reason for this rejoicing? In all cases it results from the recovery of something that was lost.
   D. Who does the rejoicing which Jesus said occurs in heaven when the lost is found? There are three suggestions:
      1. The angels are the ones rejoicing.
         a. Because they are said to be present at the creation and redemption of this world (see Job 38:4-7; Luke 2:8-14)
         b. Because they are interested in knowing as much as possible about the subject of salvation (1 Pet. 1:12)
         c. Because they are said to be ministers to the heirs of salvation (Heb. 1:13-14)
      2. The Savior himself is the one who rejoices. Note: "Looking unto Jesus the author and finisher of our faith; who for the joy that was set before him endured the cross, despising the shame, and is set down at the right hand of the throne of God" (Heb. 12:2). "Now unto him that is able to keep you from falling, and to present you faultless before the presence of his glory with exceeding joy" (Jude 1:24).
      3. The redeemed saints in heaven are the ones rejoicing. "Wherefore seeing we also are compassed about with so great a cloud of witnesses, let us lay aside every weight, and the sin which doth so easily beset us, and let us run with patience the race that is set before us" (Heb. 12:1).

TWENTY-SIX: The stewings of a steward (Luke 16:1-13)

---

†*Warren Wiersbe writes: "A modern businessman can certainly identify with the elements in this parable! Dishonest employees, kickbacks, price fixing—they have always been a part of business and probably always will be. The amazing thing is that Christ used these things to teach important spiritual lessons."* (Meet Yourself in the Parables, *Victor Books, Wheaton, Ill., 1979, p. 79*)

A. The crisis
   1. The dishonesty of this steward—"And he said also unto his disciples, There was a certain rich man, which had a steward; and the same was accused unto him that he had wasted his goods" (Luke 16:1).
   2. The dismissal of this steward—"And he called him, and said unto him, How is it that I hear this of thee? give an account of thy stewardship; for thou mayest be no longer steward" (Luke 16:2).
B. The concern—"Then the steward said within himself, What shall I do? for my lord taketh away from me the stewardship: I cannot dig; to beg I am ashamed" (Luke 16:3).
C. The craftiness
   1. His plan—"I am resolved what to do, that, when I am put out of the stewardship, they may receive me into their houses" (Luke 16:4).
   2. His performance—"So he called every one of his lord's debtors unto him, and said unto the first, How much owest thou unto my lord? And he said, An hundred measures of oil. And he said unto him, Take thy bill, and sit down quickly, and write fifty. Then said he to another, And how much owest thou? And he said, An hundred measures of wheat. And he said unto him, Take thy bill, and write fourscore" (Luke 16:5-7).

---

† *A. One hundred measures of oil would be approximately 800 gallons, the yield of 450 olive trees.*
  B. One hundred measures of wheat would amount to 1,000 bushels, the yield of 100 acres.

D. The commendation—"And the lord commended the unjust steward, because he had done wisely: for the children of this world are in their generation wiser than the children of light" (Luke 16:8).

---

†*The "Lord" here is a reference to the steward's master, who gives grudging recognition to the shrewdness he demonstrated. It is not the Lord Jesus offering this approval.*

E. The conclusion
   1. The *what* of the matter—"And I say unto you, Make to yourselves friends of the mammon of unrighteousness; that, when ye fail, they may receive you into everlasting habitations. He that is faithful in that which is least is faithful also in much: and he that is unjust in the least is unjust also in much" (Luke 16:9-10).

2. The *why* of the matter—"If therefore ye have not been faithful in the unrighteous mammon, who will commit to your trust the true riches? And if ye have not been faithful in that which is another man's, who shall give you that which is your own? No servant can serve two masters: for either he will hate the one, and love the other; or else he will hold to the one, and despise the other. Ye cannot serve God and mammon" (Luke 16:11-13).

---

†*The thrust of this parable seems to be threefold:*
    A. Realize that we are but stewards, controlling things (our time, talents, treasure), but owning nothing.
    B. Realize that someday our Master will check our bookkeeping.
    C. In light of this, we are to plan ahead, make friends, but be honest in all of our dealings.

    F. The convicted—"And the Pharisees also, who were covetous, heard all these things: and they derided him" (Luke 16:14).
TWENTY-SEVEN: When Hades petitioned Paradise (Luke 16:19-31)
    A. The two persons in the parable
        1. The rich man—"There was a certain rich man, which was clothed in purple and fine linen, and fared sumptuously every day" (Luke 16:19).
        2. The beggar
            a. His pain—"And there was a certain beggar named Lazarus, which was laid at his gate, full of sores" (Luke 16:20).
            b. His poverty—"And desiring to be fed with the crumbs which fell from the rich man's table: moreover the dogs came and licked his sores" (Luke 16:21).
    B. The two places in the parable
        1. Paradise—"And it came to pass, that the beggar died, and was carried by the angels into Abraham's bosom" (Luke 16:22).
        2. Perdition—"The rich man also died, and was buried; and in hell he lift up his eyes, being in torments, and seeth Abraham afar off, and Lazarus in his bosom" (Luke 16:22-23).

---

† *A. Wealth itself is never presented as a vice in the Bible, nor is poverty looked upon as a virtue. God evaluates people by their attitudes and actions, not by their financial assets. The rich man went to hell because he was lost, and not because he was wealthy. The beggar went to heaven because he was saved, and not because he was poor.*
    B. Observe that Lazarus was assisted by angels. This is in keeping with their assigned duties as seen in Hebrews: "Are they not all ministering spirits, sent forth to minister for them who shall be heirs of salvation?" (Heb. 1:14)
    C. Observe also the phrase, "Abraham's bosom."
        1. It is held by a number of Bible students that before Jesus died, the souls of all men descended into an abode located somewhere in the earth, known as Hades *in the New Testament, and* Sheol *in the Old Testament.*
        2. Originally, there were two sections of Hades, one for the saved and one for the lost. The saved section is sometimes called "paradise" (see Luke 23:43), and the other times referred to as "Abraham's bosom" (see Luke 16:22). There is no name given for the unsaved section apart from the general designation of Hades.

3. *In Luke 16:19-31 the Savior relates the account of a poor believer who died and went to the saved part of Hades, and of a rich believer who died and went to the unsaved section. However, many believe that all this changed after Christ had made full payment for the believer's sins on Calvary. The Scofield Bible suggests that during the time of his death and resurrection, our Lord descended into Hades, depopulated Paradise, and led a spiritual triumphal entry into the heavenlies with all the saved up to that time. Ephesians 4:8-10 is offered as proof of this.*

4. *In his book* Revelation, *the late Dr. Donald Grey Barnhouse wrote: "When he ascended on High (Eph. 4:8) he emptied Hell of Paradise and took it straight to the presence of God. Captivity was taken captive . . . from that moment onward there was to be no separation whatsoever for those who believe in Christ. The gates of hell would never more prevail against any believer (Matt. 16:18). But what of the lost? The state of the unsaved dead remained (and remains) unchanged after the cross. They remain in Hades awaiting the final Great White Judgment Throne (Rev. 20:11-15). But a glorious change has occurred concerning the state of those who fall asleep in Jesus." Note the following Scripture verses: "For to me to live is Christ and to die is gain. For I am in a strait betwixt two, having a desire to depart, and to be with Christ; which is far better" (Phil. 1:21, 23). "To be absent from the body [is to be] present with the Lord" (2 Cor. 5:8).*

C. The two prayers in the parable
   1. The rich man's prayer concerning relief for his body
      a. The request—"And he cried and said, Father Abraham, have mercy on me, and send Lazarus, that he may dip the tip of his finger in water, and cool my tongue; for I am tormented in this flame" (Luke 16:24).

---

†*At least three facts may be concluded from this statement concerning the state of the dead:*
   A. *They are not annihilated. God does* not *destroy the wicked.*
   B. *They are not unconscious. The doctrine of soul sleep is unscriptural.*
   C. *They* may *be given temporary bodies, awaiting their final ones. If this is the case, it applies to both the saved and the lost (see Matt. 17:1-3; 2 Cor. 5:1; Rev. 6:9-11).*

---

      b. The refusal—"But Abraham said, Son, remember that thou in thy lifetime receivedst thy good things, and likewise Lazarus evil things: but now he is comforted, and thou art tormented" (Luke 16:25).
      c. The reason—"And beside all this, between us and you there is a great gulf fixed: so that they which would pass from hence to you cannot; neither can they pass to us, that would come from thence" (Luke 16:26).
   2. The rich man's prayer concerning redemption for his brothers
      a. The request—"Then he said, I pray thee therefore, father, that thou wouldest send him to my father's house: for I have five brethren; that he may testify unto them, lest they also come into this place of torment" (Luke 16:27-28).
      b. The refusal—"Abraham saith unto him, They have Moses and the prophets; let them hear them" (Luke 16:29).

c. The reason—"And he said, Nay, father Abraham: but if one went unto them from the dead, they will repent. And he said unto him, If they hear not Moses and the prophets, neither will they be persuaded, though one rose from the dead" (Luke 16:30-31).

---

† A. *Concerning the words of the rich man—This statement has a prophetic ring to it, for a few months later Jesus would perform his greatest single miracle, the resurrection of a decaying corpse—the body of Lazarus (John 11:43-44). But what was the result of this mighty miracle? Did it result in hundreds of conversions? To the contrary—the foes of Christ became even more vicious in their hatred and opposition.*
  1. *They determined to kill Christ (John 11:53).*
  2. *They debated the possibility of killing Lazarus (John 12:10). This is the reason why God does not do mighty miracles today. God's will is accomplished through faith and not through signs. After the rapture many miracles and signs will occur during the tribulation, but sinful people will not believe. (See Rev. 9:20-21.)*
  B. *Concerning the words of Abraham—This verse (Luke 16:31) indirectly answers a question asked by many, and that is, "Do the departed saints in glory know what is happening back on earth?" Apparently, up to a point, they do, for here Abraham speaks of a man (Moses) who would not even be born until some six centuries after the "father of the faithful" had departed this earth.*

TWENTY-EIGHT: When our best is but the least (Luke 17:7-10)
  A. The required actions of a faithful servant—"But which of you, having a servant plowing or feeding cattle, will say unto him by and by, when he is come from the field, Go and sit down to meat? And will not rather say unto him, Make ready wherewith I may sup, and gird thyself, and serve me, till I have eaten and drunken; and afterward thou shalt eat and drink? Doth he thank that servant because he did the things that were commanded him? I trow not" (Luke 17:7-9).
  B. The required attitude of a faithful servant—"So likewise ye, when ye shall have done all those things which are commanded you, say, We are unprofitable servants: we have done that which was our duty to do" (Luke 17:10).

---

† A. *John the Baptist had once rebuked some proud Pharisees as follows: "Bring forth therefore fruits meet for repentance: And think not to say within yourselves, We have Abraham to our Father: for I say unto you, that God is able of these stones to raise up children unto Abraham" (Matt. 3:8-9). The unvarnished (and unsettling) truth as gleaned from this parable and John's statement is sobering indeed—God simply does not need us.*
  B. *However, while Jesus indeed rightfully expects us to serve him, he condescends to serve us also. Note the following Scripture verses: "After that he poureth water into a bason, and began to wash the disciples' feet, and to wipe them with the towel wherewith he was girded" (John 13:5). "Henceforth I call you not servants: for the servant knoweth not what his lord doeth: but I have called you friends; for all things that I have heard of my Father I have made known unto you" (John 15:15). "Blessed are those servants, whom the lord when he cometh shall find watching: verily I say unto you, that he shall gird himself, and make them to sit down to meat, and will come forth and serve them" (Luke 12:37).*

TWENTY-NINE: A widow and a weary judge (Luke 18:1-8)
  A. How persistence was rewarded by a sinful judge—"And he spake a parable
     unto them to this end, that men ought always to pray, and not to faint; saying,
     There was in a city a judge, which feared not God, neither regarded man: And
     there was a widow in that city; and she came unto him, saying, Avenge me of
     mine adversary. And he would not for a while: but afterward he said within
     himself, Though I fear not God, nor regard man; yet because this widow
     troubleth me, I will avenge her, lest by her continual coming she weary me"
     (Luke 18:1-5).
  B. How persistence is rewarded by the sovereign judge—"And the Lord said, Hear
     what the unjust judge saith. And shall not God avenge his own elect, which cry
     day and night unto him, though he bear long with them? I tell you that he will
     avenge them speedily. Nevertheless when the Son of man cometh, shall he find
     faith on the earth?" (Luke 18:6-8).

---

†*In this parable Jesus both contrasts and compares two judges—an earthly, uncaring, finite judge
with the heavenly, all-caring, infinite Judge.*
  A. *The contrast:*
    1. *The earthly Judge responded to a request that he might rid himself of a bothersome
       woman.*
    2. *The heavenly Judge responds to our requests so that he might receive us and
       bless us.*
  B. *The comparison: Both judges respond to persistence.*

THIRTY: A haughty Pharisee and a humble publican (Luke 18:9-14)
  A. Two men enter the temple—"And he spake this parable unto certain which
     trusted in themselves that they were righteous, and despised others: Two men
     went up into the temple to pray; the one a Pharisee, and the other a publican"
     (Luke 18:9-10).

---

† A. *The temple in Jerusalem served as a place where one could offer up both animal sacrifices and
     personal prayers to God. Both were of equal importance. Jesus himself had emphasized the
     prayer aspect: "And said unto them, It is written, My house shall be called the house of prayer;
     but ye have made it a den of thieves" (Matt. 21:13). Here our Lord quotes from both the Old
     Testament prophets Isaiah (56:7) and Jeremiah (7:11).*
  B. *There are various instances of temple prayers in the New Testament.*
    1. *As offered up by Simeon (Luke 2:25-32)*
    2. *As offered up by Anna (Luke 2:36-38)*
    3. *As offered up by Peter and John (Acts 3:1)*

---

    1. The Pharisee—His prayer of arrogance. "The Pharisee stood and prayed thus
       with himself, God, I thank thee, that I am not as other men are, extortioners,
       unjust, adulterers, or even as this publican. I fast twice in the week, I give
       tithes of all that I possess" (Luke 18:11-12).

† A. *The Mosaic Law ordered a fast on one day out of the year—the Day of Atonement (Lev. 23:26-32). Later, to commemorate various national calamities, other fasts were observed (Zech. 8:19). The Pharisees, however, had gone beyond the Law by fasting twice a week on Monday and Thursday. These days were established by tradition because Moses was supposed to have ascended Mount Sinai on a Thursday and descended on a Monday.*

B. *Note that the Pharisee compared himself with the worst kind of people, the extortioners, the unjust, the sexually impure, and the hated tax collectors, "this publican." Paul later warned about this: "For we dare not make ourselves of the number, or compare ourselves with some that commend themselves: but they measuring themselves by themselves, and comparing themselves among themselves, are not wise" (2 Cor. 10:12). In a real sense, the Pharisee was not even praying. He was rather talking to himself about himself. The true and only standard for the believer is not another saint, or a sinner, but the Savior. (See Heb. 12:2-3; 1 Pet. 2:21.)*

2. The publican—His prayer of abasement—"And the publican, standing afar off, would not lift up so much as his eyes unto heaven, but smote upon his breast, saying, God be merciful to me a sinner" (Luke 18:13).

† A. *The publicans (greedy tax collectors) usually come across badly in the New Testament. (See Matt. 5:46; 11:19; 18:17; 21:31.) But there were at least two notable exceptions: Matthew (Matt. 10:3), and Zacchaeus (Luke 19:2). In fact, on occasion, publicans responded favorably to Jesus: "And all the people that heard him, and the publicans, justified God, being baptized with the baptism of John" (Luke 7:29). (See also Luke 15:1-2.)*

B. *The publican correctly responded concerning his own unworthiness before God, as once did Isaiah and Simon Peter. "Then said I, Woe is me! for I am undone; because I am a man of unclean lips, and I dwell in the midst of a people of unclean lips: for mine eyes have seen the King, the LORD of hosts" (Isa. 6:5). "When Simon Peter saw it, he fell down at Jesus' knees, saying, Depart from me; for I am a sinful man, O Lord." This is surely a prayer that God hears and responds to in love.*

B. Two men exit the temple.
1. The Pharisee—Rejected and excluded by God

†*His prayer was rejected on the basis of James 4:3. "Ye ask, and receive not, because ye ask amiss, that ye may consume it upon your lusts" (James 4:3).*

2. The publican—Received and exalted by God

†*His prayer was received on the basis of Psalm 32:5. "I acknowledged my sin unto thee, and mine iniquity have I not hid. I said, I will confess my transgressions unto the LORD; and thou forgavest the iniquity of my sin. Selah" (Psa. 32:5).*

THIRTY-ONE: A diagnosis of defilement (Matt. 15:10-20; Mark 7:14-23)
A. Defilement explained

1. What it isn't—"There is nothing from without a man, that entering into him can defile him: but the things which come out of him, those are they that defile the man" (Mark 7:15).
2. What it is—"And when he was entered into the house from the people, his disciples asked him concerning the parable. And he saith unto them, Are ye so without understanding also? Do ye not perceive, that whatsoever thing from without entereth into the man, it cannot defile him; because it entereth not into his heart, but into the belly, and goeth out into the draught, purging all meats? And he said, That which cometh out of the man, that defileth the man" (Mark 7:17-20).

B. Defilement epitomized—"Then came his disciples, and said unto him, Knowest thou that the Pharisees were offended, after they heard this saying? But he answered and said, Every plant, which my heavenly Father hath not planted, shall be rooted up. Let them alone: they be blind leaders of the blind. And if the blind lead the blind, both shall fall into the ditch" (Matt. 15:12-14).

C. Defilement exhibited—"For from within, out of the heart of men, proceed evil thoughts, adulteries, fornications, murders, thefts, covetousness, wickedness, deceit, lasciviousness, an evil eye, blasphemy, pride, foolishness: all these evil things come from within, and defile the man" (Mark 7:21-23).

---

†*Jesus related this parable after a confrontation with the Pharisees.*
  A. *Their accusation: "Why do thy disciples transgress the tradition of the elders? for they wash not their hands when they eat bread" (Matt. 15:2).*
  B. *His answer: "But he answered and said unto them, Why do ye also transgress the commandment of God by your tradition? . . . Ye hypocrites, well did Esaias prophesy of you, saying, This people draweth nigh unto me with their mouth, and honoureth me with their lips; but their heart is far from me. But in vain they do worship me, teaching for doctrines the commandments of men" (Matt. 15:3, 7-9).*

THIRTY-TWO: Hourly workers and daily wages (Matt. 20:1-16)
  A. The agreement
    1. The workers—"For the kingdom of heaven is like unto a man that is an householder, which went out early in the morning to hire labourers into his vineyard" (Matt. 20:1).
    2. The wages—"And when he had agreed with the labourers for a penny a day, he sent them into his vineyard" (Matt. 20:2).
    3. The work schedule
      a. Some worked from 6:00 A.M. to 6:00 P.M. (Matt. 20:1-2).
      b. Some worked from 9:00 A.M. to 6:00 P.M. (Matt. 20:3-4).
      c. Some worked from noon to 6:00 P.M. (Matt. 20:5).
      d. Some worked from 3:00 P.M. to 6:00 P.M. (Matt. 20:5).
      e. Some worked from 5:00 P.M. to 6:00 P.M. (Matt. 20:6-7).
  B. The argument
    1. The payoff—"So when even was come, the lord of the vineyard saith unto his steward, Call the labourers, and give them their hire, beginning from the last unto the first. And when they came that were hired about the eleventh hour, they received every man a penny" (Matt. 20:8-9).

2. The protest
   a. Their resentment—"But when the first came, they supposed that they should have received more; and they likewise received every man a penny. And when they had received it, they murmured against the goodman of the house, Saying, These last have wrought but one hour, and thou hast made them equal unto us, which have borne the burden and heat of the day" (Matt. 20:10-12).
   b. His reminder—"But he answered one of them, and said, Friend, I do thee no wrong: didst not thou agree with me for a penny? Take that thine is, and go thy way: I will give unto this last, even as unto thee. Is it not lawful for me to do what I will with mine own? Is thine eye evil, because I am good?" (Matt. 20:13-15).

---

† A. *The interpretation of this parable*
   1. *Negative considerations:*
      a. *It has nothing to do with the subjects of salvation or rewards.*
      b. *It was not related to describe the ideal working arrangements between management and labor.*
   2. *Positive considerations: It may have served as an object lesson to illustrate both the sovereignty and the fairness of God. If so, Jesus was referring to that divine plan for Jews and Gentiles.*
      a. *The first workers hired would represent Israel. They began "working" in God's vineyard as early as 2000 B.C. in the time of Abraham.*
      b. *The last workers to be hired would represent the Gentiles. As a group, they did not "clock in" until the advent of the Apostle Paul, some twenty centuries later. And yet, in the fullest sense, both groups will share equally in the glorious millennium, God's ultimate payday.*
   B. *The applications of this parable*
   1. *We are not to question or criticize God's dealings, either with us or with other believers. To do so leads to either pride or envy.*
      a. *Pride, when we feel we are God's special child*
      b. *Envy, when we feel someone else is his special child*
   2. *Both Jesus and Paul warned of this.*
      a. *Jesus rebuked the Apostle Peter. Our Lord had just predicted the eventual martyrdom of Peter. We read: "Then Peter, turning about, seeth the disciple whom Jesus loved following; which also leaned on his breast at supper, and said, Lord, which is he that betrayeth thee? Peter seeing him saith to Jesus, Lord, and what shall this man do? Jesus saith unto him, If I will that he tarry till I come, what is that to thee? follow thou me" (John 21:20-22).*
      b. *Paul rebuked the Roman church. "Who art thou that judgest another man's servant? to his own master he standeth or falleth. Yea, he shall be holden up: for God is able to make him stand. . . . But why dost thou judge thy brother? or why dost thou set at nought thy brother? for we shall all stand before the judgment seat of Christ" (Rom. 14:4, 10).*

THIRTY-THREE: Two sons who reversed their roles (Matt. 21:28-32)—"But what think ye? A certain man had two sons" (Matt. 21:28).

A. The individuals in the parable
1. A rebellious son—"I won't go!" (But he did.) "But what think ye? A certain man had two sons; and he came to the first, and said, Son, go work to day in my vineyard. He answered and said, I will not: but afterward he repented, and went" (Matt. 21:28-29).
2. A religious son—"I will go!" (But he didn't.) "And he came to the second, and said likewise. And he answered and said, I go, sir: and went not" (Matt. 21:30).
B. The application of the parable—"Whether of them twain did the will of his father? They say unto him, The first. Jesus saith unto them, Verily I say unto you, That the publicans and the harlots go into the kingdom of God before you. For John came unto you in the way of righteousness, and ye believed him not: but the publicans and the harlots believed him: and ye, when ye had seen it, repented not afterward, that ye might believe him" (Matt. 21:31-32).

---

† A. *Who are the true believers? Will the real sons of God please stand? The ultimate test of ownership is obedience. One's sonship is demonstrated by one's submission. Both Old Testament and New Testament Israel failed this test. Their words were correct, but their works were corrupt. They said, "I go, sir"; and went not.*
1. *Old Testament Israel*
a. *Their words—"And all the people answered together, and said, All that the Lord hath spoken we will do. And Moses returned the words of the people unto the Lord" (Exod. 19:8).*
b. *Their works—"Wherefore the Lord said, forasmuch as this people draw near me with their mouth, and with their lips do honour me, but have removed their heart far from me, and their fear toward me is taught by the precept of men" (Isa. 29:13).*
2. *New Testament Israel*
a. *Their words—"We are Abraham's seed" (John 8:33). "Abraham is our father" (John 8:39a).*
b. *Their works—"Jesus saith unto them, If ye were Abraham's children, ye would do the works of Abraham" (John 8:39b). Later, when advising the disciples concerning the Pharisees, our Lord concluded sadly: "All therefore whatsoever they bid you observe, that observe and do; but do not ye after their works: for they say, and do not" (Matt. 23:3).*
B. *Who then are the true believers? Upon being told that his mother and brothers were waiting to speak to him, Jesus once replied: "But he answered and said unto him that told him, Who is my mother? and who are my brethren? And he stretched forth his hand toward his disciples, and said, Behold my mother and my brethren! For whosoever shall do the will of my Father which is in heaven, the same is my brother, and sister, and mother" (Matt. 12:48-50).*

THIRTY-FOUR: The vicious vine keepers (Matt. 21:33- 46; Mark 12:1-12; Luke 20:9-19)
A. The industry—"And he began to speak unto them by parables. A certain man planted a vineyard, and set an hedge about it, and digged a place for the winefat, and built a tower, and let it out to husbandmen, and went into a far country" (Mark 12:1).
B. The accountability—"And when the time of the fruit drew near, he sent his servants to the husbandmen, that they might receive the fruits of it" (Matt. 21:34).

C. The treachery
   1. One servant was beaten and sent away empty-handed (Mark 12:3).
   2. The second servant was wounded in the head and shamefully treated (Mark 12:4).
   3. The third servant was stoned (Matt. 21:35).
   4. The final servant was killed (Mark 12:5).
D. The strategy—"Then said the lord of the vineyard, What shall I do? I will send my beloved son: it may be they will reverence him when they see him" (Luke 20:13).
E. The conspiracy—"But when the husbandmen saw him, they reasoned among themselves, saying, This is the heir: come, let us kill him, that the inheritance may be ours. So they cast him out of the vineyard, and killed him. What therefore shall the lord of the vineyard do unto them?" (Luke 20:14-15).
F. The ferocity—"When the lord therefore of the vineyard cometh, what will he do unto those husbandmen? They say unto him, He will miserably destroy those wicked men, and will let out his vineyard unto other husbandmen, which shall render him the fruits in their seasons" (Matt. 21:40-41).

---

†*As the context indicates, Jesus deals with the nation Israel in this parable. It contains a historical, prophetical, and spiritual element.*
   A. The historical element
      1. The divine Householder did plant a special vineyard—Israel (Isa. 5:1-7).
      2. In the fullness of time he did send forth his servants to obtain fruit, but they were badly treated (see Acts 7:51-52).
         a. Zechariah the high priest was stoned to death (2 Chron. 24:20-21).
         b. Isaiah the prophet was (probably) sawn asunder (Heb. 11:37).
         c. Elijah and Elisha were mocked.
         d. Jeremiah was beaten and imprisoned.
         e. Amos was rejected by the religious leaders (Amos 7).
      3. Finally, the divine Householder did send his beloved Son (Gal. 4:4).
   B. The prophetical element
      1. The Son would be killed by crucifixion.
      2. The city of the wicked workers would be destroyed (Titus the Roman general burned Jerusalem in A.D. 70).
   C. The spiritual element—The Father did not *do what the crowd suggested in the parable, namely, to "miserably destroy those wicked men." To the contrary, the divine plan called not for destruction resulting from wrath, but rather for redemption resulting from grace.*

THIRTY-FIVE: A wedding guest with no wedding garment (Matt. 22:1-14)
   A. The invitations to the wedding—"The kingdom of heaven is like unto a certain king, which made a marriage for his son" (Matt. 22:2).
      1. The exclusive guest list
         a. First invitation
            (1) The request—"And sent forth his servants to call them that were bidden to the wedding" (Matt. 22:3a).
            (2) The refusal—"And they would not come" (Matt. 22:3b).

b. Final invitation
  (1) The request—"Again, he sent forth other servants, saying, Tell them
      which are bidden, Behold, I have prepared my dinner: my oxen and my
      fatlings are killed, and all things are ready: come unto the marriage"
      (Matt. 22:4).
  (2) The ridicule—"But they made light of it, and went their ways, one to
      his farm, another to his merchandise" (Matt. 22:5).
  (3) The ruthlessness—"And the remnant took his servants, and entreated
      them spitefully, and slew them" (Matt. 22:6).
  (4) The reprisal—"But when the king heard thereof, he was wroth: and he
      sent forth his armies, and destroyed those murderers, and burned up
      their city" (Matt. 22:7).
2. The expanded guest list—"Then saith he to his servants, The wedding is
   ready, but they which were bidden were not worthy" (Matt. 22:8).
  a. The invitation—"Go ye therefore into the highways, and as many as ye
     shall find, bid to the marriage" (Matt. 22:9).
  b. The ingathering—"So those servants went out into the highways, and
     gathered together all as many as they found, both bad and good: and the
     wedding was furnished with guests" (Matt. 22:10).
B. The incident at the wedding
  1. The problem
    a. The guest without a robe—"And when the king came in to see the guests,
       he saw there a man which had not on a wedding garment" (Matt. 22:11).
    b. The guest without a reply—"And he saith unto him, Friend, how camest
       thou in hither not having a wedding garment? And he was speechless"
       (Matt. 22:12).
  2. The punishment—"Then said the king to the servants, Bind him hand and
     foot, and take him away, and cast him into outer darkness; there shall be
     weeping and gnashing of teeth" (Matt. 22:13).

---

† *A. In this parable, the millennial kingdom of heaven is likened to a royal wedding prepared by the
   king for his son. The entire kingdom is invited to attend. As we have already seen, many
   refused to come.*
B. There were three separate stages in a mideastern wedding:
  *1. The betrothal stage—This consisted of the selection of the bride and the payment of the
     dowry. This step often occurred when both bride and groom were still children. They were
     then considered engaged.*
  *2. The presentation stage—When the couple was old enough, the bride was brought to the
     house of the groom's father, where the wedding service took place.*
  *3. The celebration stage—Following the private marriage ceremony, the public marriage
     supper would begin.*
*C. It was during this joyous stage when the king saw an invited wedding guest not wearing a
   wedding garment.*
  *1. The anger of the king—Often at royal weddings each guest would be provided with his
     or her own wedding garment which bore the imprint of both the king and his son. To
     refuse to wear this garment was looked upon as a terrible insult directed toward the groom
     himself.*

2. *The silence of the guest—We are told, "And he was speechless." In reality, what could he have said?*
   a. *He could not have pled ignorance, for he knew exactly what was expected of him.*
   b. *He could not have pled poverty, for the garments were given out at no charge.*

THIRTY-SIX: The fig tree and the future (Matt. 24:32-35; Mark 13:28-31; Luke 21:19-33)
   A. The information in the parable—"And he spake to them a parable; Behold the fig tree, and all trees; When they now shoot forth, ye see and know of your own selves that the summer is nigh at hand" (Luke 21:29-30). "So ye in like manner, when ye shall see these things come to pass, know that [he] is nigh, even at the doors. Verily I say unto you, that this generation shall not pass away, till all these things be done" (Mark 13:29-30).
   B. The suggested interpretation of the parable
      1. The fig tree is Israel.
      2. The other trees represent those Gentile nations, such as Russia, which play a vital role in the final days.
      3. The leaf-bearing event may refer to Israel's modern return to the land.
      4. The generation that would not pass away may speak of that generation born in 1948.
      5. The "things to be accomplished" phrase could speak of Christ's second coming.
THIRTY-SEVEN: Virgins, vessels, and vigilance (Matt. 25:1-13)—"Then shall the kingdom of heaven be likened unto ten virgins, which took their lamps, and went forth to meet the bridegroom. And five of them were wise, and five were foolish. . . . While the bridegroom tarried, they all slumbered and slept" (Matt. 25:1-2, 5).
   A. The wait of the guests
      1. The complacent: An absence of oil—"They that were foolish took their lamps, and took no oil with them" (Matt. 25:3).
      2. The consistent: An abundance of oil—"But the wise took oil in their vessels with their lamps" (Matt. 25:4).
   B. The fate of the guests
      1. The coming of the groom—"And at midnight there was a cry made, Behold, the bridegroom cometh; go ye out to meet him. Then all those virgins arose, and trimmed their lamps" (Matt. 26:6-7).
         a. The request of the foolish—"And the foolish said unto the wise, Give us of your oil; for our lamps are gone out" (Matt. 25:8).
         b. The refusal of the wise—"But the wise answered, saying, Not so; lest there be not enough for us and you: but go ye rather to them that sell, and buy for yourselves" (Matt. 25:9).
      2. The closing of the room—"And while they went to buy, the bridegroom came; and they that were ready went in with him to the marriage: and the door was shut. Afterward came also the other virgins, saying, Lord, Lord, open to us. But he answered and said, Verily I say unto you, I know you not. Watch therefore, for ye know neither the day nor the hour wherein the Son of man cometh" (Matt. 25:10-13).

---

†*The following interpretation is suggested for this parable:*
   A. *The chronology of the parable—When does the action in the parable take place? It occurs during the coming great tribulation, perhaps at the very end.*

B. *The characters in the parable*
1. *The bridegroom is Christ.*
2. *The bride is the Church.*
3. *The ten virgins represent Israel, awaiting the coming of their Messiah.*
   a *The five foolish ones had not experienced the new birth.*
   b. *The five wise ones* had *experienced the new birth.*

THIRTY-EIGHT: A nobleman, ten servants, and ten pounds (Luke 19:11-27)

†*Jesus related this parable to explain both the* what *and the* when *of the kingdom of heaven.*
"And as they heard these things, he added and spake a parable, because he was nigh to Jerusalem, and because they thought that the kingdom of God should immediately appear" (Luke 19:11).

A. The assignment to the servants—"He said therefore, A certain nobleman went into a far country to receive for himself a kingdom, and to return. And he called his ten servants, and delivered them ten pounds, and said unto them, Occupy till I come" (Luke 19:12-13).
B. The accounting from the servants—"And it came to pass, that when he was returned, having received the kingdom, then he commanded these servants to be called unto him, to whom he had given the money, that he might know how much every man had gained by trading" (Luke 19:15).
   1. First servant
      a. His report—"Then came the first, saying, Lord, thy pound hath gained ten pounds" (Luke 19:16).
      b. His reward—"And he said unto him, Well, thou good servant: because thou hast been faithful in a very little, have thou authority over ten cities" (Luke 19:17).
   2. Second servant
      a. His report—"And the second came, saying, Lord, thy pound hath gained five pounds" (Luke 19:18).
      b. His reward—"And he said likewise to him, Be thou also over five cities" (Luke 19:19).

† A. *Warren Wiersbe writes: "Please note that not all the servants had the same success. One man multiplied his pound ten times, while another multiplied his five times. We must not expect everyone to produce the same results. In the parable of the sower (Matt. 13:23), some people produced fruit thirty fold, some sixty fold, and some a hundred fold. God gives each of us different abilities and opportunities. He does not ask us to produce the same results, but He does ask all of us to be faithful and do our best. How do these 'cities' apply to Christians today? First, here in this life we have a greater capacity for ministry and greater opportunities for service. The pound was taken from the unfaithful servant and given to the man with ten pounds (vv. 24-26). What we do not use, we may lose, and what we use faithfully proves that we can be trusted with more. David was faithful to take care of his father's sheep, so God was able to entrust the nation to his care. Joshua was faithful as Moses' servant and God made him Moses' successor. Young Timothy assisted Paul in his ministry and in a few years was called to take Paul's*

place in the churches. Faithfulness in service indicates we are trustworthy to become rulers with God." (Meet Yourself in the Parables, *Victor Books, Wheaton, Ill., 1979, pp. 154-55)*

B. *What is the difference between the pound parable here in Luke 19 and the talent parable related shortly after this in Matthew 25? It has been suggested that the difference is as follows:*

  1. *The pounds represent the opportunities of life.*

  2. *The talents speak of the different gifts God imparts to us.*

C. *Whatever the case, both the pound and the talent parables stress three all-important themes:*

  1. *My abilities and opportunities from God in the past*

  2. *My dependability for God at the present*

  3. *My accountability to God in the future*

---

  3. Third servant

    a. His report—"And another came, saying, Lord, behold, here is thy pound, which I have kept laid up in a napkin: For I feared thee, because thou art an austere man: thou takest up that thou layedst not down, and reapest that thou didst not sow" (Luke 19:20-21).

    b. His rejection

      (1) The man is rebuked—"And he saith unto him, Out of thine own mouth will I judge thee, thou wicked servant. Thou knewest that I was an austere man, taking up that I laid not down, and reaping that I did not sow: Wherefore then gavest not thou my money into the bank, that at my coming I might have required mine own with usury?" (Luke 19:22-23)

      (2) The money is repossessed—"And he said unto them that stood by, Take from him the pound, and give it to him that hath ten pounds" (Luke 19:24).

THIRTY-NINE: A traveler, three stewards, and eight talents (Matt. 25:14-30)

A. Similarities between the talent parable and the pound parable

  1. Both parables describe the stewardship arrangements between a departing master and his servants.

  2. Both relate the accounting episode upon the master's return.

  3. Both record faithfulness on the part of at least two servants who are subsequently rewarded.

  4. Both record the unfaithfulness on the part of one servant who is subsequently punished.

B. Contrasts between the talent and pound parable

  1. The master of the servants—He is a nobleman in Luke 19 and a traveler in Matthew 25.

  2. The number of servants—There are ten in the pound parable and three in the talent parable.

  3. The responsibility of the servants—In Luke 19 each servant receives the same, approximately $5000, the value of a pound. In Matthew 25 the first servant is entrusted with five talents ($1.5 million), the second servant two talents ($600,000), and the third servant one talent ($300,000).

  4. The accomplishments of the faithful servants—In Luke 19 the first servant increased his pound 1,000 percent. In Matthew 25 the first two servants doubled their original sum.

  5. The punishment of the unfaithful servants—In Luke 19 the man lost the original pound, but in Matthew 25 the man not only had the talent taken from him, but was then cast into outer darkness.

FORTY: Separating the sheep from the goats (Matt. 25:31-46)
  A. The separator—"When the Son of man shall come in his glory, and all the holy
     angels with him, then shall he sit upon the throne of his glory" (Matt. 25:31).
  B. The separation—"And before him shall be gathered all nations: and he shall
     separate them one from another, as a shepherd divideth his sheep from the
     goats" (Matt. 25:32).
  C. The separated—"And he shall set the sheep on his right hand, but the goats on
     the left" (Matt. 25:33).
     1. The sheep—"Ye blessed" (Matt. 25:34).
        a. The nature of their reward—"Then shall the King say unto them on his
           right hand, Come, ye blessed of my Father, inherit the kingdom prepared
           for you from the foundation of the world" (Matt. 25:34).
        b. The basis of their reward—"For I was an hungred, and ye gave me meat:
           I was thirsty, and ye gave me drink: I was a stranger, and ye took me in:
           naked, and ye clothed me: I was sick, and ye visited me: I was in prison,
           and ye came unto me" (Matt. 25:35-36).
        c. The explanation of their reward
           (1) Their question—"Then shall the righteous answer him, saying, Lord,
               when saw we thee an hungred, and fed thee? or thirsty, and gave thee
               drink? When saw we thee a stranger, and took thee in? or naked, and
               clothed thee? Or when saw we thee sick, or in prison, and came unto
               thee?" (Matt. 25:37-39).
           (2) His answer—"And the King shall answer and say unto them, Verily I
               say unto you, Inasmuch as ye have done it unto one of the least of these
               my brethren, ye have done it unto me" (Matt. 25:40).
     2. The goats—"Ye cursed" (Matt. 25:41)
        a. The nature of their punishment—"Then shall he say also unto them on
           the left hand, Depart from me, ye cursed, into everlasting fire, prepared
           for the devil and his angels. . . . And these shall go away into everlasting
           punishment: but the righteous into life eternal" (Matt. 25:41, 46).
        b. The basis of their punishment—"For I was an hungred, and ye gave me no
           meat: I was thirsty, and ye gave me no drink: I was a stranger, and ye took
           me not in: naked, and ye clothed me not: sick, and in prison, and ye visited
           me not" (Matt. 25:42-43).
        c. The explanation of their punishment
           (1) Their question—"Then shall they also answer him, saying, Lord, when
               saw we thee an hungred, or athirst, or a stranger, or naked, or sick, or in
               prison, and did not minister unto thee?" (Matt. 25:44).
           (2) His answer—"Then shall he answer them, saying, Verily I say unto you,
               Inasmuch as ye did it not to one of the least of these, ye did it not to
               me" (Matt. 25:45).

---

†*At first reading this parable seems to teach that salvation can be earned by good works, which of
course is totally refuted by a host of Scripture verses (Eph. 2:8-9; Titus 3:5, etc.). At least five
questions need to be answered in rightly interpreting this parable.*
  A. *When does this judgment take place? The context clearly indicates that it occurs at the end
     of the tribulation.*

B. Who is being judged here? *According to 25:32 it will be the Gentiles.*

C. What is the basis of this judgment? *It is based on how they have treated or mistreated a certain group during the tribulation.*

D. Who is this group? *Christ calls them "my brethren" (25:40); thus they are Jewish people.*

E. Why would some Gentiles risk their lives during the reign of the antichrist to help persecuted and suffering Jews? *The new birth experience would offer the only logical explanation for such behavior. Thus, the good works spoken of here are not the basis for salvation, but rather the proof of salvation.*

A BRIEF SUMMARY OF CHRIST'S PARABLES
  A. The purpose for his parables—Jesus used the parabolic method for two reasons:
    1. As a method of revealing great spiritual truths to those who possessed sincere hearts.
    2. As a method of concealing great spiritual truths from those who possessed insincere hearts. The following verses clearly bring this out: "And the disciples came, and said unto him, Why speakest thou unto them in parables? He answered and said unto them, Because it is given unto you to know the mysteries of the kingdom of heaven, but to them it is not given" (Matt. 13:10-11).
  B. Areas of life represented by his parables
    1. Farming
    2. Fishing
    3. Weddings
    4. Shepherding
    5. Baking
    6. Praying
    7. Banquet dining
    8. The building world
    9. The business world
    10. The legal profession
    11. Father and son relationships
    12. Employee and employer relationships
    13. Master and servant relationships
  C. Subjects referred to in his parables
    1. Right foundations
    2. Godly virtues (forgiveness, obedience, compassion, etc.)
    3. Ungodly vices (greed, cruelty, disobedience, etc.)
    4. The Word of God
    5. The Son of God
    6. The sovereignty of God
    7. Satan and evil
    8. The human heart
    9. Redemption and restoration
    10. Stewardship
    11. Prayer
    12. Heaven and hell

13. Millennium
14. Final judgment
15. The kingdom of heaven—Of all the subjects illustrated by Jesus' parables, the kingdom of heaven was the most frequently referred to by far.
   a. Definition of the kingdom of heaven
      (1) First meaning—That general rule of the Father from heaven over the affairs of men from creation to the Millennium. Both saved and unsaved belong to this kingdom. (See Dan. 4:17, 32; Matt. 8:12; 22:2; 25:1.)
      (2) Second meaning—That specific rule of the Son from Jerusalem over the affairs of men during the Millennium. Only saved people will enter this kingdom. (See Matt. 6:10, 13; 25:34; 26:29.)
   b. Distinguished from the kingdom of God
      (1) On rare occasions the kingdom of God is used interchangeably for the kingdom of heaven (Millennial meaning). Compare Mark 1:14-15 with Matthew 3:1-2. See also Acts 1:3, 6.
      (2) The most common meaning, however, is a reference to the new birth. See John 3:3, 5; Acts 8:12; 19:8; 20:25; 28:23, 31; 1 Corinthians 15:50.

THE SERMONS OF CHRIST
ONE: The Scroll of Isaiah Sermon in Nazareth
TWO: The Sermon on the Mount
THREE: The Source of Life Sermon
FOUR: The Bread of Life Sermon
FIVE: The Feast of Tabernacles Sermon
SIX: The Temple Treasury Sermon
SEVEN: The Good Shepherd Sermon
EIGHT: The Mount Olivet Discourse Sermon
NINE: The Thursday Night Passover Sermon.

THE SERMONS OF CHRIST
ONE: The Scroll of Isaiah Sermon in Nazareth (Luke 4:16-30)
    A. The occasion for the sermon—"And he came to Nazareth, where he had been brought up: and, as his custom was, he went into the synagogue on the sabbath day, and stood up for to read" (Luke 4:16).

---

†*Note the phrase, "as his custom was." Our Lord had faithfully attended the synagogue services each Sabbath day while growing up in Nazareth. He had already fulfilled that admonition later written in the book of Hebrews: "Not forsaking the assembling of ourselves together, as the manner of some is; but exhorting one another: and so much the more, as ye see the day approaching" (Heb. 10:25).*

    B. The text of the sermon (taken from Isa. 61:1-3)—"And there was delivered unto him the book of the prophet Esaias. And when he had opened the book, he found the place where it was written, The Spirit of the Lord is upon me, because he hath anointed me to preach the gospel to the poor; he hath sent me to heal the broken-hearted, to preach deliverance to the captives, and recovering of sight to the blind, to set at liberty them that are bruised, to preach the acceptable year of the Lord" (Luke 4:17-19).

---

†*In an amazing demonstration of "rightly dividing the word of truth" (2 Tim. 2:15), Jesus stopped his reading with the words, "the acceptable year of the Lord," and did not finish the last half of the sentence in Isaiah 61:2 which declares: "and the day of vengeance of our God." He did this because:*
    A. The "acceptable year" belonged to his first coming.
    B. The "day of vengeance" spoke of his second coming.

    C. The interest in the sermon—"And he closed the book, and he gave it again to the minister, and sat down. And the eyes of all them that were in the synagogue were fastened on him" (Luke 4:20).
    D. The announcement in the sermon—"And he began to say unto them, This day is this scripture fulfilled in your ears" (Luke 4:21).
    E. The power of the sermon—"And all bare him witness, and wondered at the gracious words which proceeded out of his mouth. And they said, Is not this Joseph's son?" (Luke 4:22).

F. The application of the sermon—"And he said unto them, Ye will surely say unto me this proverb, physician, heal thyself: whatsoever we have heard done in Capernaum, do also here in thy country. And he said, Verily I say unto you, No prophet is accepted in his own country" (Luke 4:23-24).

    1. As illustrated by Elijah and a starving widow—"But I tell you of a truth, many widows were in Israel in the days of Elias, when the heaven was shut up three years and six months, when great famine was throughout all the land; but unto none of them was Elias sent, save unto Sarepta, a city of Sidon, unto a woman that was a widow" (Luke 4:25-26).

    2. As illustrated by Elisha and a suffering warrior—"And many lepers were in Israel in the time of Eliseus the prophet; and none of them was cleansed, saving Naaman the Syrian" (Luke 4:27).

---

†He refers to a widow and a soldier in an attempt to convict his hometown people of their unbelief.

    A. Both were Gentiles.

        1. The widow was a Phoenician.

        2. The soldier was a Syrian.

    B. Each was ministered to by one of the two most famous Old Testament prophets.

        1. Elijah ministered to the widow.

        2. Elisha ministered to the soldier.

    C. Both the widow and the soldier experienced a unique miracle.

        1. The widow saw her dead son raised. This had never before happened in human history (1 Kings 17:9-16).

        2.The soldier was healed of leprosy. He was the only man in the Old Testament to be delivered from this terrible disease (2 Kings 5:1-14).

G. The reaction to the sermon

    1. The anger against him—"And all they in the synagogue, when they heard these things, were filled with wrath" (Luke 4:28).

    2. The attempt against him—"And rose up, and thrust him out of the city, and led him unto the brow of the hill whereon their city was built, that they might cast him down headlong. But he passing through the midst of them went his way" (Luke 4:28-30).

---

†This marks the first of at least seven attempts to kill Jesus by the Jewish religious leaders prior to his death at Calvary. These incidents occurred:

    A. In Jerusalem after he had healed a cripple on the Sabbath (John 5:15-18)

    B. In Jerusalem during the Feast of Tabernacles (John 7:30)

    C. In Jerusalem after he claimed to be greater than Abraham (John 8:59)

    D. In Jerusalem after he claimed to be equal with the Father (John 10:31-33). (Note: Humanly speaking, the Jewish leaders did not crucify Christ because he claimed to be the Messiah. In truth, following the feeding of the 5,000, a number of them had recognized him as the Christ and attempted to crown him king on the spot—see John 6:14-15. The fact is, they turned against him because he said he was the Son of God himself.)

E. In Jerusalem after the resurrection of Lazarus (John 11:53)
F. In Jerusalem following his Mount Olivet Discourse (Matt. 26:3-4)

TWO: The Sermon on the Mount (Matt. 5:1-7:29; Luke 6:17-49)

---

† *A. Probably no other sermon in all of history has been more misunderstood and misinterpreted*
  than the Sermon on the Mount.
   1. Liberal theologians, although blatantly denying the deity of Christ and the inerrancy of
    Scripture, have for centuries used and misused Christ's words here, twisting them to fit
    their own humanistic and unbiblical social gospel. One false claim along this line is that a
    person can be saved by keeping the concepts of the Sermon on the Mount (as if this were
    possible for a non-Christian).
   2. Others, however, who do accept the Bible as God's Word, have also erred, concluding that
    Jesus' lofty message here does not in the least apply to us today, but refers to a totally
    different dispensation. Thus, while the first group misuses it, this group ignores it.
  B. Both views are soundly refuted by the Apostle Paul: "All scripture is given by inspiration of
   God, and is profitable for doctrine, for reproof, for correction, for instruction in righteousness:
   That the man of God may be perfect, throughly furnished unto all good works" (2 Tim. 3:16-17).
  C. The following outline is based on the interpretation that in the Sermon on the Mount Jesus
   was instructing and encouraging born-again believers in their day (in spite of opposition) to
   live by those kingdom principles which will become universal during the millennium.
  D. A number of people believe that the sermon may have been delivered on one of the twin peaks
   on the Horns of Hattin, located about four miles west of the Sea of Galilee and some eight miles
   southwest of Capernaum. It was in this exact area on July 15, A.D. 1187, that a very famous
   battle was fought. At that time the brilliant Moslem military leader Saladin met and utterly
   crushed an army of European Crusaders. Saladin would later that same year, on October 12,
   capture the city of Jerusalem.

A. The believer and the kingdom (Matt. 5:1-16; Luke 6:24-26)
  1. Positive characteristics—Things which should be achieved
    a. The roles of believers
      (1) The poor in spirit (Matt. 5:3)

---

† *A. The word "blessed" is a translation of the Greek word* makarios, *found some fifty times in the*
  Greek New Testament. Jesus uses it no less than nine times during his opening remarks in this
  sermon. Makarios *would be better rendered by the English word "happy."*
  B. Dr. J. Dwight Pentecost writes: "The word happy, *as used among the Greeks, originally*
   described the condition of the Greek gods who were deemed to be satisfied, or content, because
   they had everything they desired and were free to enjoy everything they possessed without
   restriction. To the Greek mind, happiness had to do with material possessions and the freedom
   to enjoy them. Their happiness had to do with unrestrained, unlimited gratification of physical
   desires. Since no limits were ever put upon their deities, the Greeks deemed the gods to be
   happy. When they lived with the same liberty they ascribed to their gods, they deemed them-
   selves a happy people. Happiness for the Greeks was related to the physical and material world.
   But when our Lord spoke of happiness, he related it to holiness. Such is the biblical concept, for

in the New Testament, happiness is identified with purity of character. The Word sees sin as the fountainhead of misery, and holiness as the source of peace, satisfaction, and contentment—all that we include in our word happy. So, when the Lord said, 'Blessed are the poor in spirit,' he gave the first characteristic of holiness that produces happiness, so as to lay the foundation of a godly, happy life. The Lord showed what must characterize a man who says he is holy, and the blessing that comes from God upon one who has received His gift of righteousness by faith in Christ. How significant that the very characteristic the world despises, discounts, and calls a sign of weakness, our Lord exalted. The world can never provide the foundation for a happy life, for the world cannot produce holiness—and there is no happiness apart from holiness." (The Sermon on the Mount, *Multnomah Press, Portland, Ore., 1980, p. 21*)

C. Why are the "poor in spirit" happy? Because they recognize their own spiritual poverty and are qualified to be filled by the riches of his grace. There are two local churches described in the book of Revelation which vividly illustrate this concept. One recognized its true condition; the other did not.

   1. Smyrna, the happy church—"I know thy works, and tribulation, and poverty, (but thou art rich) and I know the blasphemy of them which say they are Jews, and are not, but are the synagogue of Satan" (Rev. 2:9).

   2. Laodicea, the wretched church—"I know thy works, that thou art neither cold nor hot: I would thou wert cold or hot. So then because thou art lukewarm, and neither cold nor hot, I will spue thee out of my mouth. Because thou sayest, I am rich, and increased with goods, and have need of nothing; and knowest not that thou art wretched, and miserable, and poor, and blind, and naked" (Rev. 3:15-17).

---

(2) The mournful (Matt. 5:4)

---

† A. J. Dwight Pentecost wrote: "Our Lord did not promise, 'Blessed are they that moan, for they shall be comforted,' but, 'Blessed are they that mourn.' When we carry some burden that brings tears, our natural response is to complain, to moan, to question God's wisdom and benevolence, God's right to do this to us. He did not say, 'Those who moan will be comforted,' but, 'those who mourn.' The biblical concept of mourning is recognizing a need, and then presenting that need to the God of all comfort. When one, in desperation, oppression, loneliness, bereavement, discouragement, anxiety, earnestness, desire, devotion, presents his need to God, God commissions the angels of heaven to dry tears from his eyes. God sent Isaiah to Israel to proclaim a message: 'Comfort ye, comfort ye my people' (Isa. 40:1). Comfort for that beleaguered nation was found in a Person who would come to dry their tears. The Lord Jesus Christ came to the nation Israel in the fullness of God's time. He said, in Matthew 11:28-29, 'Come unto me, all ye that labour and are heavy laden, and I will give you rest.'" (The Sermon on the Mount, *Multnomah Press, Portland, Ore., 1980, pp. 31-32*)

B. There are four classic examples in the Old Testament where men of God mourned over their own sins and the sins of Israel:

   1. Daniel (9:3-19)

   2. Isaiah (6:5)

   3. Ezra (9:5-15)

   4. Nehemiah (1:4-11)

---

(3) The meek (Matt. 5:5)

† A. *It should be immediately understood that meekness is not weakness. To the contrary, one of the most fearless and courageous individuals in the entire Word of God was Moses. Consider his amazing life: At age eighty he confronted the mightiest monarch of his day, the Egyptian pharaoh. Ignoring the king's threats, Moses thundered down ten terrible plagues upon the land. He then led his people across the surging waters of the Red Sea, through a burning desert up to the very borders of the promised land. He was hardly a coward. And how did God describe this champion of courage? "(Now the man Moses was very meek, above all the men which were upon the face of the earth)" (Num. 12:3).*

B. *In light of all this, biblical meekness may be defined as subdued strength. Moses never used this divine strength for his own selfish interests. Although he was constantly slandered by his own people, he refused to retaliate. Like the Savior, who could have instantly marshalled twelve legions of angels to protect him in Gethsemane, Moses chose instead to pray for, rather than destroy his enemies.*

C. *J. Dwight Pentecost writes: "The sign of a meek man is that he recognizes divinely constituted authority and submits himself to every manifestation of it. He is subject to the authority of government; he is subject to the authority of the employer; he is subject to authority in the home; and he is subject to authority in the assembly of believers. Lawlessness or rebellion against any divinely constituted authority is lawlessness against God. One who is lawless is not meek, because meekness means submission to God and confidence in God."* (The Sermon on the Mount, *Multnomah Press, Portland, Ore., 1980, p. 39*)

---

(4) Those who hunger and thirst after righteousness (Matt. 5:6)

---

† A. *Jesus is saying here that the secret of spiritual growth is a spiritual appetite. In other words, those who eat little will grow a little; those who eat much will grow much.*

B. *One of the greatest books ever written on the person of God is entitled,* The Pursuit of God, *by the late A. W. Tozer. In this book, Dr. Tozer wrote: "In this hour of all but universal darkness, one cheering gleam appears. Within the fold of conservative Christianity, there are to be found increasing numbers of persons whose religious lives are marked by a growing hunger after God himself. They are eager for spiritual realities, and will not be put off with words, nor will they be content with correct 'interpretations' of truth. They are athirst for God, and they will not be satisfied until they have drunk deep at the fountain of living water."* (Christian Publications, Inc., Harrisburg, Penn., p. 7)

---

(5) The merciful (Matt. 5:7)

---

†*The Romans spoke of four cardinal virtues—wisdom, justice, temperance, and courage. But mercy was not among them. Both divine mercy and grace can be thought of as opposite sides of the same coin.*

A. *God's mercy is not receiving what we deserve; that is, hell.*

B. *God's grace is receiving what we do not deserve; that is, heaven.*

Thus the merciful person is one who both sees and serves another human being in Jesus' stead.

---

(6) The pure in heart (Matt. 5:8)

†*The word "pure" here is the Greek word* **katharos**, *which can also be translated by the English words, "clean and clear." Katharos is an important word in the book of Revelation, referring to:*
    A. The garb worn by angels (Rev. 15:6)
    B. The heavenly city (Rev. 21:18)
    C. The river of life—"And he shewed me a pure river of life, clear as crystal, proceeding out of the throne of God and of the Lamb" (Rev. 22:1).

(7) The peacemakers (Matt. 5:9)

†*The role of the peacemakers is later described by Paul:*
    A. Their leader is the God of peace (1 Cor. 14:33).
    B. They aspire after peace with all people (Rom. 12:18).
    C. They proclaim the gospel of peace (Eph. 6:15).

(8) Those persecuted for righteousness' sake (Matt. 5:10-12)

†*What is to be the reaction of those who are persecuted for righteousness' sake? In a word, they are to rejoice. Two reasons are given for this:*
    A. Because of the relationship down here—To suffer in this manner is a great privilege, for it associates one with the godly prophets of the past who were also persecuted.
    B. Because of the rewards up there—"For great is your reward in heaven" (Matt. 5:12).

    b. The rewards of believers
        (1) To possess the kingdom of heaven (Matt. 5:3)
        (2) To be comforted (Matt. 5:4)
        (3) To inherit the earth (Matt. 5:5)
        (4) To be filled (Matt. 5:6)
        (5) To obtain mercy (Matt. 5:7)
        (6) To see God (Matt. 5:8)
        (7) To be called the sons of God (Matt. 5:9)
        (8) To possess the kingdom of heaven (Matt. 5:10)
    c. The relationship of believers
        (1) They are to function as the salt of the earth (Matt. 5:13).

†*In the ancient world, on occasion, salt was considered to be more valuable than gold. It was certainly more practical. Roman soldiers were paid in salt. If one were derelict in his duty, he was said to be "not worth his salt." Salt prevents, provides, and promotes.*
    A. It prevents:
        1. Corruption
        2. Dehydration
    B. It provides flavor.
    C. It promotes thirst.
In a spiritual sense, the salt of the believer's testimony can accomplish all three functions.

(2) They are to function as the light of the world (Matt. 5:14).

†*The believer receives this divine light from Christ (John 1:9) so that he might reflect it for Christ. "Do all things without murmurings and disputings: That ye may be blameless and harmless, the sons of God, wi thout rebuke, in the midst of a crooked and perverse nation, among whom ye shine as lights in the world" (Phil. 2:14-15).*

   2. Negative characteristics—Things that should be avoided
      a. Money seeking—"No man can serve two masters: for either he will hate
         the one, and love the other; or else he will hold to the one, and despise the
         other. Ye cannot serve God and mammon. Therefore I say unto you, Take
         no thought for your life, what ye shall eat, or what ye shall drink; nor yet
         for your body, what ye shall put on. Is not the life more than meat, and the
         body than raiment?" (Matt. 6:24-25)

† *A. The word "mammon" is an Aramaic word, pointing to wealth or riches. The word "despise"
     here refers to the act of placing a low value on something or someone. Jesus is not saying here
     that one must hate money in order to serve God. He is saying that possessions must be placed
     on the lowest rung of our priority ladder.*
  *B. An Islamic proverb says: "He that seeks after this world is like one that drinks sea water. The
     more he drinks the thirstier he becomes, until it slays him."*

      b. Men pleasing—"Behold the fowls of the air: for they sow not, neither do
         they reap, nor gather into barns; yet your heavenly Father feedeth them.
         Are ye not much better than they?" (Matt. 6:26)
   B. The Law and the kingdom (Matt. 5:17-20; 7:12)
      1. The divine fulfiller of the Law—"Think not that I am come to destroy the law,
         or the prophets: I am not come to destroy, but to fulfil. For verily I say unto
         you, Till heaven and earth pass, one jot or one tittle shall in no wise pass from
         the law, till all be fulfilled" (Matt. 5:17-18).
      2. The divine fulfilling of the Law—"Therefore all things whatsoever ye would
         that men should do to you, do ye even so to them: for this is the law and the
         prophets" (Matt. 7:12).

† *A. This famous command, known by millions as the Golden Rule, is in reality the Gracious Rule,
     for one must experience the saving grace of God to fully practice its teaching.*
  *B. Some have accused Christ of plagiarism here, claiming that he simply repeated what the
     Chinese philosopher Confucius and others had already said centuries before. Note, though, the
     words attributed to them: "Do not do unto others that which you would not have them do unto
     you." A quick comparison shows that there is a tremendous difference between these two
     statements. One is negative, the other positive. An example of the usage of both concepts can be
     seen in the parable of the Good Samaritan.*
     *1. The negative usage, as demonstrated by the priest and Levite. They did not in the slightest
        either harm or harass the poor bleeding and half-dead victim. In essence, they simply did*

not *do to him that which they would not desire for him to do to them in the same situation. But they left him to die.*

2. *The positive usage was demonstrated by the Good Samaritan. He "bound up his wounds, pouring in oil and wine, and set him on his own beast, and brought him to an inn, and took care of him" (Luke 10:34). Why did he do this? Because the Good Samaritan would have desired the same treatment if the situation had been reversed. The difference between Confucius' words and those of Jesus is the difference between death and life.*

C. The Old Testament and the kingdom (Matt. 5:21-48)
  1. In relationship to murder (Matt. 5:21-26)
    a. The basic concept—"Ye have heard that it was said by them of old time, Thou shalt not kill; and whosoever shall kill shall be in danger of the judgment" (Matt. 5:21).

---

† *A. Jesus here refers to the Sixth Commandment, "Thou shalt not kill" (Exod. 20:13). The word "kill" literally means "murder," that is, the unlawful taking of a human life.*
  B. The judgment mentioned here has in view the common local courts, arranged according to Deuteronomy 16:18, consisting of seven judges and two assistant Levites.

---

    b. The broadened concept—"But I say unto you, That whosoever is angry with his brother without a cause shall be in danger of the judgment: and whosoever shall say to his brother, Raca, shall be in danger of the council: but whosoever shall say, Thou fool, shall be in danger of hell fire" (Matt. 5:22).

---

†*Jesus equates anger and hatred with murder. He is saying that a devilish attitude is as serious as a devilish act. Finally, he warns that to hate and harass one's brother may result (unless, of course, repented of) in both human and divine retribution. John the apostle later amplified upon this: "Whosoever hateth his brother is a murderer: and ye know that no murderer hath eternal life abiding in him" (1 John 3:15).*

---

  2. In relationship to adultery (5:27-30)
    a. The basic concept—"Ye have heard that it was said by them of old time, Thou shalt not commit adultery" (Matt. 5:27).
    b. The broadened concept—"But I say unto you, That whosoever looketh on a woman to lust after her hath committed adultery with her already in his heart" (Matt. 5:28).

---

†*Our Lord treats the Seventh Commandment, "Thou shalt not commit adultery" (Exod. 20:14), as he did the Sixth Commandment. Evil acts are the result of evil attitudes. As Solomon once observed: "For as [a man] thinketh in his heart, so is he" (Prov. 23:7). The Apostle Paul was attempting to drive home this concept when he addressed his peers, the Jewish leaders, in the following manner: "Thou that sayest a man should not commit adultery, dost thou commit adultery?" (Rom. 2:22).*

3. In relationship to divorce (Matt 5:31-32)
    a. The basic concept—"It hath been said, Whosoever shall put away his wife, let him give her a writing of divorcement" (Matt. 5:31).
    b. The broadened concept—"But I say unto you, That whosoever shall put away his wife, saving for the cause of fornication, causeth her to commit adultery: and whosoever shall marry her that is divorced committeth adultery" (Matt. 5:32).

4. In relationship to oath taking (Matt. 5:33-37)
    a. The basic concept—"Again, ye have heard that it hath been said by them of old time, Thou shalt not forswear thyself, but shalt perform unto the Lord thine oaths" (Matt. 5:33).
    b. The broadened concept
      (1) Negative—"But I say unto you, Swear not at all; neither by heaven; for it is God's throne: Nor by the earth; for it is his footstool: neither by Jerusalem; for it is the city of the great King. Neither shalt thou swear by thy head, because thou canst not make one hair white or black" (Matt. 5:34-36).
      (2) Positive—"But let your communication be, Yea, yea; Nay, nay: for whatsoever is more than these cometh of evil" (Matt. 5:37).

---

†*The Pharisees knew that they would be held accountable if they swore by God's name and broke their oath (see Lev. 19:12; Num. 30:2; Deut. 23:21). In light of this, they had invented four lesser oaths. Thus, one might swear by heaven, earth, Jerusalem, or his own head. But Jesus here points out that these oaths were just as binding. He then concluded:*
    A. Don't swear by heaven, for it is God's throne.
    B. Don't swear by the earth, for it is God's footstool.
    C. Don't swear by your own head, for it is God's creation.

---

5. In relationship to retaliation (Matt 5:38-42)
    a. The basic concept—"Ye have heard that it hath been said, An eye for an eye, and a tooth for a tooth" (Matt. 5:38).

---

†*Stanley Toussaint writes: "The Lord first alludes to the Old Testament phrases, 'eye for an eye,' and 'tooth for a tooth' (Exod. 21:22-25; Lev. 24:20; Deut. 19:18-21). It cannot be doubted that the law made complete provision for absolute vengeance by its law of retaliation* (lex talionis). *However, this provision was modified in two ways. First, the retaliation generally was not to be performed without the authority of a legal court (Exod. 21:22; Num. 35:9-34). Second, while the letter of the law made provision for absolute retaliation, the spirit of the law and the Old Testament show a more excellent way. Such passages as Leviticus 19:17-18; Deuteronomy 32:35; Psalm 94:1; Proverbs 20:22; and Proverbs 24:29 show that a person was to leave the matter of vengeance to the Lord. It is in the light of the spirit of the law that the Lord presents his interpretation; it is not a new meaning, but it is a higher meaning. There is evidence that the more discerning Jews had already seen this meaning in relationship to the law's provision for retaliation. Jesus said that no retaliation was to be made. Rather, the injured party is to be gracious and beneficent to the one who has done the wrong. Four illustrations are given of this principle. It must be remembered that personal wrongs are in view and not social and governmental crimes"* (Behold, the King, *Multnomah Press, Portland, Ore., 1980, p. 104)*

  b. The broadened concept—"But I say unto you, That ye resist not evil: but
     whosoever shall smite thee on thy right cheek, turn to him the other also.
     And if any man will sue thee at the law, and take away thy coat, let him
     have thy cloak also. And whosoever shall compel thee to go a mile, go
     with him twain. Give to him that asketh thee, and from him that would
     borrow of thee turn not thou away" (Matt. 5:39-42).
6. In relationship to love (Matt. 5:43-48)
  a. The basic concept—"Ye have heard that it hath been said, Thou shalt love
     thy neighbour, and hate thine enemy" (Matt. 5:43).

---

†*This statement cannot be found in the Old Testament. It was no doubt one of the common (but
incorrect) teachings of the rabbis. In fact, to the contrary, the Old Testament teaches just the
opposite. Note: "If thou meet thine enemy's ox or his ass going astray, thou shalt surely bring
it back to him again. If thou see the ass of him that hateth thee lying under his burden, and
wouldest forbear to help him, thou shalt surely help with him" (Exod. 23:4-5). "If thine enemy
be hungry, give him bread to eat; and if he be thirsty, give him water to drink" (Prov. 25:21).*

---

  b. The broadened concept—"But I say unto you, Love your enemies, bless
     them that curse you, do good to them that hate you, and pray for them
     which despitefully use you, and persecute you" (Matt. 5:44).
D. Worship and the kingdom (Matt. 6:1–7:11)
  1. Giving (Matt. 6:1-4; Luke 6:38)
    a. The rules
      (1) Fruitless giving—"Take heed that ye do not your alms before men, to be
          seen of them: otherwise ye have no reward of your Father which is in
          heaven. Therefore when thou doest thine alms, do not sound a trumpet
          before thee, as the hypocrites do in the synagogues and in the streets,
          that they may have glory of men. Verily I say unto you, They have their
          reward" (Matt. 6:1-2).
      (2) Fruitful giving—"But when thou doest alms, let not thy left hand know
          what thy right hand doeth" (Matt. 6:3).
    b. The rewards—"That thine alms may be in secret: and thy Father which
       seeth in secret himself shall reward thee openly" (Matt. 6:4). "Give, and it
       shall be given unto you; good measure, pressed down, and shaken
       together, and running over, shall men give into your bosom. For with the
       same measure that ye mete withal it shall be measured to you again" (Luke
       6:38).
  2. Praying (Matt. 6:5-15; 6:7-11)
    a. Essentials in prayer
      (1) Those prayers God rejects—"And when thou prayest, thou shalt not be
          as the hypocrites are: for they love to pray standing in the synagogues
          and in the corners of the streets, that they may be seen of men. Verily I
          say unto you, They have their reward. . . . But when ye pray, use not
          vain repetitions, as the heathen do: for they think that they shall be
          heard for their much speaking" (Matt. 6:5, 7).
      (2) Those prayers God receives—"But thou, when thou prayest, enter into

thy closet, and when thou hast shut thy door, pray to thy Father which is in secret; and thy Father which seeth in secret shall reward thee openly" (Matt. 6:6). "For your Father knoweth what things ye have need of, before ye ask him" (6:8b).
    b. Elements in prayer (Matt. 6:9-13)

---

† A. *This prayer, the most well known and oft quoted in the entire Bible, has been greatly misunderstood concerning both its name and nature.*
    1. *Its name—It is not the Lord's Prayer, but the Disciples' Prayer. The Lord's Prayer is found in John 17.*
    2. *Its nature*
        a. *Some have overused it, memorizing and reciting it, feeling there is a magical blessing attached to it.*
        b. *Others have underused it, concluding that it belongs to another dispensational age.*
  B. *These positions are, of course, in error. In essence, what is referred to as the Lord's Prayer is a model prayer, given by the Savior to his own, serving as a guideline to help them pray more fruitfully.*
  C. *Luke provides the background which led to this prayer: "And it came to pass, that, as he was praying in a certain place, when he ceased, one of his disciples said unto him, Lord, teach us to pray, as John also taught his disciples" (Luke 11:1). It is extremely significant to observe that on no occasion is it ever recorded that the disciples ask: "Lord, teach us to preach," or, "Lord, teach us to work miracles." But they did ask him to instruct them in prayer. The implications are staggering, for this indicates that the prayer life of Christ had more influence on them than the sermons he preached or the miracles he performed.*
  D. *Note the various elements listed in this prayer.*

---

(1) Faith—"Our Father, who art in heaven" (Matt. 6:9)

---

†*The first two words here serve as a reminder concerning my* horizontal *responsibility ("our") and my* vertical *responsibility ("Father").*

---

(2) Worship—"Hallowed be thy name" (Matt. 6:9).

---

†*David felt this part of prayer to be so important that he appointed a select group of men who did nothing else in the temple but praise and worship God. (See 1 Chron. 23:5; 25:1, 7.) In the book of Revelation John sees four special angels who exist solely to worship God and who "rest not day and night, saying Holy, holy, holy, Lord God Almighty, which was, and is, and is to come" (Rev. 4:8). See also Christ's statement to the Samaritan woman (John 4:23-24).*

---

(3) Expectation—"Thy kingdom come" (Matt. 6:10).

---

†*This kingdom is that blessed millennial kingdom spoken of so much in the Old Testament (see Isa. 2:2-4; 25:8; 35:1, 8, 10; 65:20, 25) and later previewed by John in the New Testament (Rev. 20:1-6).*

(4) Submission—"Thy will be done in earth, as it is in heaven" (Matt. 6:10).

†*Jesus would later give the finest example of this element in Gethsemane (see Matt. 26:39).*

(5) Petition—"Give us this day our daily bread" (Matt. 6:11).

†*This suggests that our praying should be as regular and as often as our eating—namely, daily.*

(6) Confession—"And forgive us our debts" (Matt. 6:12).

†*The blood of Christ will forgive us of every sin, but not of one excuse. Only confessed sin can be forgiven (see 1 John 1:9).*

(7) Compassion—"As we forgive our debtors" (Matt. 6:12).
(8) Dependence—"And lead us not into temptation but deliver us from evil" (Matt. 6:13).

†*It should be understood that while God has never promised to keep us from temptation, he has promised to preserve us in and through temptation. (See 1 Cor. 10:13.)*

(9) Acknowledgment—"For thine is the kingdom, and the power, and the glory, forever, Amen" (Matt. 6:13).

† *A. Some ten centuries prior to this, one of Israel's earliest kings had prayed in a similar fashion: "Wherefore David blessed the Lord before all the congregation: and David said, Blessed be thou, Lord God of Israel our father, for ever and ever. Thine, O Lord, is the greatness, and the power, and the glory, and the victory, and the majesty: for all that is in the heaven and in the earth is thine; thine is the kingdom, O Lord, and thou art exalted as head above all" (1 Chron. 29:10-11). Now, 1,000 years later, Israel's ultimate King, the son of David, appears upon the scene, "exalted as head above all."*
B. Someone has pointed out the extraordinary collection of relationships which emerge in this prayer:
  1. That of father and child (Our Father)
  2. That of God and worshiper (Hallowed be thy name)
  3. That of king and subject (Thy kingdom come)
  4. That of master and servant (Thy will be done)
  5. That of benefactor and suppliant (Give us this day our daily bread)
  6. That of creditor and debtor (Forgive us our debts)
  7. That of guide and pilgrim (Lead us not into temptation)
  8. That of Redeemer and redeemed (Deliver us from the evil one)

c. Encouragements in prayer (Matt. 7:7-11)
   (1) The rewards involved—"Ask, and it shall be given you; seek, and ye shall find; knock, and it shall be opened unto you: For every one that asketh receiveth; and he that seeketh findeth; and to him that knocketh it shall be opened. Or what man is there of you, whom if his son ask bread, will he give him a stone? Or if he ask a fish, will he give him a serpent?" (Matt. 7:7-10).
   (2) The rationale involved—"If ye then, being evil, know how to give good gifts unto your children, how much more shall your Father which is in heaven give good things to them that ask him?" (Matt. 7:11).
3. Fasting (Matt. 6:16-18)
   a. As practiced by the hypocrites—"Moreover when ye fast, be not, as the hypocrites, of a sad countenance: for they disfigure their faces, that they may appear unto men to fast. Verily I say unto you, They have their reward" (Matt. 6:16).
   b. As practiced by the humble—"But thou, when thou fastest, anoint thine head, and wash thy face; that thou appear not unto men to fast, but unto thy Father which is in secret: and thy Father, which seeth in secret, shall reward thee openly" (Matt. 6:17-18).
4. Earning (Matt. 6:19-23)
   a. Earthly treasure is insecure and corruptible—"Lay not up for yourselves treasures upon earth, where moth and rust doth corrupt, and where thieves break through and steal" (Matt. 6:19).
   b. Eternal treasure is secure and incorruptible—"But lay up for yourselves treasures in heaven, where neither moth nor rust doth corrupt, and where thieves do not break through nor steal: for where your treasure is, there will your heart be also" (Matt. 6:20-21).
5. Serving (Matt. 6:24)—"No man can serve two masters: for either he will hate the one, and love the other; or else he will hold to the one, and despise the other. Ye cannot serve God and mammon" (Matt. 6:24).
6. Trusting (Matt. 6:25-34)
   a. The illustrations
      (1) The fowls of the air—"Behold the fowls of the air: for they sow not, neither do they reap, nor gather into barns; yet your heavenly Father feedeth them. Are ye not much better than they?" (Matt. 6:26).
      (2) The lilies of the field—"And why take ye thought for raiment? Consider the lilies of the field, how they grow; they toil not, neither do they spin: and yet I say unto you, That even Solomon in all his glory was not arrayed like one of these. Wherefore, if God so clothe the grass of the field, which to day is, and to morrow is cast into the oven, shall he not much more clothe you, O ye of little faith?" (Matt. 6:28-30)

---

†*Warren Wiersbe wrote: "Consider what Jesus taught about worry.*
 A. *"Worry is unreasonable. Life is more than food and clothing. To worry about things is to neglect what is most important—life itself. What good is an expensive wardrobe if the person wearing it is cheap and infantile? What good is a sumptuous feast if the persons eating it are starved morally and spiritually? It is unreasonable to worry about externals that cannot contribute to eternal things.*

B. "*Worry is unnatural. The ravens and the lilies do not worry. Why? Because all of nature knows that the Father will meet their needs. 'He giveth to the beast his food, and to the young ravens which cry' (Psa. 147:9). And, 'Thou openest thine hand, and satisfiest the desire of every living thing' (Psa. 145:16). Even if a sparrow falls to the ground dead, it does not fall alone, for the Father never forgets even a sparrow (Luke 12:6; Matt. 10:29).*

C. "*Worry is unavailing. Worry cannot make us taller or help us live longer. In fact, it does just the opposite—it shortens our lives! Since worry does not accomplish anything good, why worry?*

D. "*Worry is unnecessary. The fact that the Father takes care of us does not mean we should be careless or complacent, or that we should expect the Father to do for us what we must do for ourselves. But it does mean that He cares for us because we are valuable to Him. He cares for the grass, the flowers, and the birds, and surely He will care for His children.*

E. "*Worry is unspiritual. The unbelievers of the world have a right to worry, but Christians are different from them. Christians have a heavenly Father who cares for them, so any worrying is an evidence of unbelief and a poor witness to the world.*" (Meet Yourself in the Parables, *Victor Books, Wheaton, Ill., 1983, pp. 120-21)*

---

b. The invitation—"Therefore take no thought, saying, What shall we eat? or, What shall we drink? or, Wherewithal shall we be clothed? (For after all these things do the Gentiles seek:) for your heavenly Father knoweth that ye have need of all these things. But seek ye first the kingdom of God, and his righteousness; and all these things shall be added unto you. Take therefore no thought for the morrow: for the morrow shall take thought for the things of itself. Sufficient unto the day is the evil thereof" (Matt. 6:31-34).

---

†*Wiersbe wrote: "To begin with, our Father in heaven never slumbers or sleeps. He is always alert to our needs. We do not have to pound at His door or wake Him up. He knows our needs even before we know them. Furthermore, the Father is not irritated when we come to ask for help. He never refuses, He never offers excuses, He never argues. He loves us and is anxious to meet our every need. He is generous to us. You can be sure that the begging neighbor would have to pay back whatever he borrowed, but God does not require this of His children. He gives graciously and generously to us, and He keeps on giving.*" (Meet Yourself in the Parables, *Victor Books, Wheaton, Ill., 1983, p. 73)*

---

7. Judging (Matt. 7:1-5)—"Judge not, that ye be not judged. For with what judgment ye judge, ye shall be judged: and with what measure ye mete, it shall be measured to you again. And why beholdest thou the mote that is in thy brother's eye, but considerest not the beam that is in thine own eye? Or how wilt thou say to thy brother, Let me pull out the mote out of thine eye; and, behold, a beam is in thine own eye? Thou hypocrite, first cast out the beam out of thine own eye; and then shalt thou see clearly to cast out the mote out of thy brother's eye" (Matt. 7:1-5).

---

† A. *Jesus here lists three reasons against passing judgment upon another:*
   1. *The one judging will himself be judged.*
   2. *The one judging will be judged by the same measuring stick he uses to measure others.*

3. *The one judging is often more corrupted by the same sin he condemns others for. Consider the utter hypocrisy as desribed by Jesus:*
  a. *Here is a man blinded by a huge "wooden" sin the size of a building beam.*
  b. *Here is another man bothered by a small "wooden" sin the size of a mote. And the result? The first tries to condemn the second!*
B. *Honest and critical evaluation on the part of one believer toward another is sometimes necessary. This should only be done, however, if the person evaluating is not guilty of the same sin and if three rules are carefully observed:*
  1. *Is my criticism unkind? (Prov. 18:8)*
  2. *Is my criticism untrue? (Exod. 23:1)*
  3. *Is my criticism unnecessary? (Prov. 11:13)*

---

8. Witnessing (Matt. 7:6)—"Give not that which is holy unto the dogs, neither cast ye your pearls before swine, lest they trample them under their feet, and turn again and rend you" (Matt. 7:6).

---

†*The hogs and dogs probably refer to apostate religious teachers (see 2 Pet. 2:22).*

E. The entrance to the kingdom (Matt. 7:13-27)
  1. The way (Matt. 7:13-14)
    a. The gate to hell—"Enter ye in at the strait gate: for wide is the gate, and broad is the way, that leadeth to destruction, and many there be which go in thereat" (Matt. 7:13).
    b. The gate to heaven—"Because strait is the gate, and narrow is the way, which leadeth unto life, and few there be that find it" (Matt. 7:14).
  2. The warning (Matt. 7:15-23)
    a. Concerning false prophets
      (1) Their deceit—"Beware of false prophets, which come to you in sheep's clothing, but inwardly they are ravening wolves" (Matt. 7:15).

---

†*Various Old Testament prophets had warned Israel concerning the danger of false shepherds. "Son of man, prophesy against the shepherds of Israel, prophesy, and say unto them, Thus saith the Lord God unto the shepherds; Woe be to the shepherds of Israel that do feed themselves! should not the shepherds feed the flocks? Ye eat the fat, and ye clothe you with the wool, ye kill them that are fed: but ye feed not the flock. The diseased have ye not strengthened, neither have ye healed that which was sick, neither have ye bound up that which was broken, neither have ye brought again that which was driven away, neither have ye sought that which was lost; but with force and with cruelty have ye ruled them" (Ezek. 34:2-4). "For, lo, I will raise up a shepherd in the land, which shall not visit those that be cut off, neither shall seek the young one, nor heal that that is broken, nor feed that that standeth still: but he shall eat the flesh of the fat, and tear their claws in pieces. Woe to the idle shepherd that leaveth the flock! the sword shall be upon his arm, and upon his right eye: his arm shall be clean dried up, and his right eye shall be utterly darkened" (Zech. 11:16-17).*

---

(2) Their description—"Ye shall know them by their fruits. Do men gather

grapes of thorns, or figs of thistles? Even so every good tree bringeth
forth good fruit; but a corrupt tree bringeth forth evil fruit. A good
tree cannot bring forth evil fruit, neither can a corrupt tree bring forth
good fruit" (Matt. 7:16-18).
(3) Their destruction—"Every tree that bringeth not forth good fruit is
hewn down, and cast into the fire" (Matt. 7:19).
b. Concerning false profession
(1) The caution—"Not every one that saith unto me, Lord, Lord, shall
enter into the kingdom of heaven; but he that doeth the will of my
Father which is in heaven" (Matt. 7:21).
(2) The claim—"Many will say to me in that day, Lord, Lord, have we not
prophesied in thy name? and in thy name have cast out devils? and in
thy name done many wonderful works?" (Matt. 7:22).
(3) The condemnation—"And then will I profess unto them, I never knew
you: depart from me, ye that work iniquity" (Matt. 7:23).

---

† *A. Note the terrible twofold deception described here.*
    1. Religious deceivers deceive others.
    2. Religious deceivers deceive themselves.
  *B. It is tragically possible to mouth the words of God, to imitate the works, of God, but never
personally to know the true witness from God, that is, Jesus Christ.*

---

3. The wisdom (Matt. 7:24-27)
a. Its abundance as seen by the first builder—"Therefore whosoever heareth
these sayings of mine, and doeth them, I will liken him unto a wise man,
which built his house upon a rock: and the rain descended, and the floods
came, and the winds blew, and beat upon that house; and it fell not: for it
was founded upon a rock" (Matt. 7:24-25).
b. Its absence as seen by the second builder—"And every one that heareth
these sayings of mine, and doeth them not, shall be likened unto a foolish
man, which built his house upon the sand: and the rain descended, and
the floods came, and the winds blew, and beat upon that house; and it fell:
and great was the fall of it" (Matt. 7:26-27).
THREE: The Source of Life Sermon (John 5:17-47)—"For as the Father hath life in himself;
so hath he given to the Son to have life in himself" (John 5:26).
A. The oneness with the Father
1. His equality with the Father—"Therefore the Jews sought the more to kill
him, because he not only had broken the sabbath, but said also that God was
his Father, making himself equal with God" (John 5:18).

---

†*Humanly speaking, the reason the Jewish religious leaders attempted to kill Christ was not
because he claimed to be the Messiah, but because he made himself equal with God. This same
incident occurred at a later date: "The Jews answered him, saying, For a good work we stone
thee not; but for blasphemy; and because that thou, being a man, makest thyself God" (John
10:33).*

2. His dependence upon the Father—"Then answered Jesus and said unto them, Verily, verily, I say unto you, The Son can do nothing of himself, but what he seeth the Father do: for what things soever he doeth, these also doeth the Son likewise" (John 5:19).

†*This verse is associated closely with one found in the epistles in which Paul writes concerning Christ: "But made himself of no reputation, and took upon him the form of a servant, and was made in the likeness of men" (Phil. 2:7). The "made himself of no reputation" is a translation of the Greek word* kenos, *which means "to make empty."*
Question: Of what did Christ empty himself?
Answer: He did not give up (empty) his divine attributes (his omnipotence, omniscience, etc.) when coming to earth; but he did agree not to use them, depending totally upon the Father and the Holy Spirit.

3. His responsibilities from the Father
   a. Concerning future resurrection—"For as the Father raiseth up the dead, and quickeneth them; even so the Son quickeneth whom he will" (John 5:21).
   b. Concerning future judgment—"For the Father judgeth no man, but hath committed all judgment unto the Son" (John 5:22).

†*Jesus later referred again to this profound truth, as does the Apostle Paul: "When the Son of man shall come in his glory, and all the holy angels with him, then shall he sit upon the throne of his glory: and before him shall be gathered all nations: and he shall separate them one from another, as a shepherd divideth his sheep from the goats" (Matt. 25:31-32). "And the times of this ignorance God winked at; but now commandeth all men every where to repent: because he hath appointed a day, in the which he will judge the world in righteousness by that man whom he hath ordained; whereof he hath given assurance unto all men, in that he hath raised him from the dead" (Acts 17:30-31).*

4. His esteem by the Father
   a. He is loved—"For the Father loveth the Son, and sheweth him all things that himself doeth: and he will shew him greater works than these, that ye may marvel" (John 5:20).
   b. He is honored—"That all men should honour the Son, even as they honour the Father. He that honoureth not the Son honoureth not the Father which hath sent him" (John 5:23).
5. His submission to the Father—"I can of mine own self do nothing: as I hear, I judge: and my judgment is just; because I seek not mine own will, but the will of the Father which hath sent me" (John 5:30).
6. His authority from the Father—"I am come in my Father's name, and ye receive me not: if another shall come in his own name, him ye will receive" (John 5:43).

†*They will, indeed, and the one they receive will be the antichrist. "And all that dwell upon the earth shall worship him, whose names are not written in the book of life of the Lamb slain from the foundation of the world" (Rev. 13:8).*

B. The twofold resurrection accomplished by Christ
  1. The resurrection of the saved
      a. Present-day spiritual resurrection—"Verily, verily, I say unto you, He that heareth my word, and believeth on him that sent me, hath everlasting life, and shall not come into condemnation; but is passed from death unto life" (John 5:24).
      b. Future-day physical resurrection—"Verily, verily, I say unto you, The hour is coming, and now is, when the dead shall hear the voice of the Son of God: and they that hear shall live. . . . Marvel not at this: for the hour is coming, in the which all that are in the graves shall hear his voice" (John 5:25, 28). "And shall come forth; they that have done good, unto the resurrection of life" (John 5:29a).
  2. The resurrection of the unsaved—"And hath given him authority to execute judgment also, because he is the Son of man" (John 5:27). "And they that have done evil, unto the resurrection of damnation" (John 5:29b).

---

†*This twofold resurrection seems to refer to those occurring just prior to and following the Millennium, as described by both Daniel the prophet and John the apostle. "And many of them that sleep in the dust of the earth shall awake, some to everlasting life, and some to shame and everlasting contempt" (Dan. 12:2). "And I saw thrones, and they sat upon them, and judgment was given unto them: and I saw the souls of them that were beheaded for the witness of Jesus, and for the word of God, and which had not worshipped the beast, neither his image, neither had received his mark upon their foreheads, or in their hands; and they lived and reigned with Christ a thousand years. But the rest of the dead lived not again until the thousand years were finished. This is the first resurrection" (Rev. 20:4-5).*

C. The fourfold witness concerning Christ
  1. Witnessed to by John the Baptist (John 5:33-35) "Ye sent unto John, and he bare witness unto the truth" (John 5:33).
  2. Witnessed to by his own works—"But I have greater witness than that of John: for the works which the Father hath given me to finish, the same works that I do, bear witness of me, that the Father hath sent me" (John 5:36).
  3. Witnessed to by the Father—"And the Father himself, which hath sent me, hath borne witness of me. Ye have neither heard his voice at any time, nor seen his shape. And ye have not his word abiding in you: for whom he hath sent, him ye believe not" (John 5:37-38).
  4. Witnessed to by the Scriptures (John 5:39-47)—"Search the scriptures; for in them ye think ye have eternal life: and they are they which testify of me. . . . Do not think that I will accuse you to the Father: there is one that accuseth you, even Moses, in whom ye trust. For had ye believed Moses, ye would have believed me: for he wrote of me. But if ye believe not his writings, how shall ye believe my words?" (John 5:39, 45-47).

---

†*Where and when did Moses (author of the first five Old Testament books) refer to Christ? He wrote of him as follows:*

A. *The Seed of the woman (Gen. 3:15)*
B. *The giver of peace (Gen. 49:10)*
C. *The Passover Lamb (Exod. 12:3-13)*
D. *The slaughtered goat and the scapegoat (Lev. 16:7-10)*
E. *The red heifer (Num. 19:2)*
F. *The brazen serpent (Num. 21:8-9)*
G. *The great Prophet of God (Deut. 18:15)*
H. *The Angel of the Lord—as appearing to:*
   1. *Hagar (Gen. 16:7)*
   2. *Abraham (Gen. 22:11-18)*
   3. *Jacob (Gen. 48:16)*
   4. *Moses (Exod. 3:2)*

FOUR: The Bread of Life Sermon (John 6:22-71)—"And Jesus said unto them, I am the bread of life: he that cometh to me shall never hunger; and he that believeth on me shall never thirst. . . . I am that bread of life" (John 6:35, 48).

---

†*This is the first of at least seven great "I am" statements uttered by Christ, as recorded in the Gospel of John:*
   A. *I am the Bread of life (6:35).*
   B. *I am the Light of the world (8:12; 9:5).*
   C. *I am the Door (10:9).*
   D. *I am the Good Shepherd (10:11).*
   E. *I am the Resurrection and the Life (11:25).*
   F. *I am the Way and the Truth (14:6).*
   G. *I am the true Vine (15:1)*

A. Christ and the crowd (John 6:22-40)
   1. He speaks about God's salvation
      a. Their confusion
         (1) They sought him only for physical bread (John 6:26).
         (2) They were ignorant about pleasing God—"Then said they unto him, What shall we do, that we might work the works of God?" (John 6:28).
         (3) They assumed the Old Testament manna came from Moses—"Our fathers did eat manna in the desert; as it is written, He gave them bread from heaven to eat" (John 6:31).
      b. His correction
         (1) They were to seek him for that living bread—"And Jesus said unto them, I am the bread of life: he that cometh to me shall never hunger; and he that believeth on me shall never thirst" (John 6:35).
         (2) They would please God by believing on his Son—"Jesus answered and said unto them, This is the work of God, that ye believe on him whom he hath sent" (John 6:29).
         (3) The Old Testament manna came from God and was a type of himself—"Then Jesus said unto them, Verily, verily, I say unto you, Moses gave

you not that bread from heaven; but my Father giveth you the true bread from heaven. For the bread of God is he which cometh down from heaven, and giveth life unto the world" (John 6:32-33).

2. He speaks about God's sovereignty
   a. This guarantees that all the elect would come to Christ—"All that the Father giveth me shall come to me; and him that cometh to me I will in no wise cast out" (John 6:37).
   b. This guarantees that all the elect would continue in Christ—"And this is the Father's will which hath sent me, that of all which he hath given me I should lose nothing, but should raise it up again at the last day. And this is the will of him that sent me, that every one which seeth the Son, and believeth on him, may have everlasting life: and I will raise him up at the last day" (John 6:39-40).

---

†*This great truth, "that all which he hath given me I should lose nothing," is amplified by the Apostle Jude: "Now unto him that is able to keep you from falling, and to present you faultless before the presence of his glory with exceeding joy, to the only wise God our Saviour, be glory and majesty, dominion and power, both now and ever. Amen" (Jude 1:24-25).*

B. Christ and the clergy (John 6:41-59)
   1. They were ignorant concerning his origin—"And they said, Is not this Jesus, the son of Joseph, whose father and mother we know? how is it then that he saith, I came down from heaven?" (John 6:42)
   2. They were ignorant concerning his offer—"I am the living bread which came down from heaven: if any man eat of this bread, he shall live for ever: and the bread that I will give is my flesh, which I will give for the life of the world. The Jews therefore strove among themselves, saying, How can this man give us his flesh to eat?" (John 6:51-52).

---

†*Our Lord continued here by saying that one must "eat" of his flesh and "drink" of his blood to be saved. (See John 6:53-55.) Much controversy has surrounded these verses.*
   A. The fiction involved
      1. In the past, the political world of Rome associated these words with cannibalism. In fact, the early church was falsely accused of this very thing.
      2. At the present, the religious world of Rome associates them with the doctrine of transubstantiation. This is the belief that at Communion the wafer and wine actually become the body and blood of Christ.
   B. The facts involved
      1. Both of the above positions are refuted by Jesus in John 6:63. "It is the spirit that quickeneth; the flesh profiteth nothing: the words that I speak unto you, they are spirit, and they are life" (John 6:63).
      2. Thus, to "eat his body and drink his blood" is simply to accept his sacrifice on the cross. To refuse his body and blood is to reject his sacrifice on the cross.

C. Christ and the carnal (John 6:59-66)

1. Many now decide against Christ—"These things said he in the synagogue, as he taught in Capernaum. Many therefore of his disciples, when they had heard this, said, This is an hard saying; who can hear it?" (John 6:59-60)
2. Many now depart from Christ—"From that time many of his disciples went back, and walked no more with him" (John 6:66).

---

†*It should be noted that there is a difference between an apostle and a disciple.*
    A. A disciple literally means "a learner." There were many such disciples who joined Christ for a while, but would leave when the going became difficult.
    B. An apostle literally means "one sent forth." There were only twelve apostles during the earthly ministry of Jesus.

D. Christ and the chosen (John 6:67-71)
    1. Jesus and the eleven apostles—"Then said Jesus unto the twelve, Will ye also go away? Then Simon Peter answered him, Lord, to whom shall we go? thou hast the words of eternal life. And we believe and are sure that thou art that Christ, the Son of the living God" (John 6:67-69).
    2. Jesus and the evil apostle
        a. The nature of this apostle—"Jesus answered them, Have not I chosen you twelve, and one of you is a devil?" (John 6:70).

---

†*Note: Some believe that Judas will be the future antichrist because of this passage and others which refer to him.*
    A. In Luke 22:3 and John 13:27, it is recorded that Satan entered Judas. This is never said of any other individual in the Bible.
    B. There are two instances in the New Testament where the title "Son of Perdition" is used. In the first instance, Jesus used it to refer to Judas (John 17:12); and on the second occasion, Paul referred to the antichrist (2 Thess. 2:3).

---

        b. The name of this apostle—"He spake of Judas Iscariot the son of Simon: for he it was that should betray him, being one of the twelve" (John 6:71).

---

†*Iscariot means "a man from Kerioth." This was a Judean city. Thus, Judas was the only non-Galilean apostle, and, on the surface, the least probable to betray Christ.*

FIVE: The Feast of Tabernacles Sermon (John 7:1-53)
    A. The disbelief of the brethren of Christ (John 7:1-9)
        1. Their ridicule—"His brethren therefore said unto him, Depart hence, and go into Judaea, that thy disciples also may see the works that thou doest. For there is no man that doeth any thing in secret, and he himself seeketh to be known openly. If thou do these things, shew thyself to the world. For neither did his brethren believe in him" (John 7:3-5).

†*The names of Jesus' younger half brothers are recorded for us by Matthew, as is the fact that he had some younger half sisters: "Is not this the carpenter's son? is not his mother called Mary? and his brethren, James and Joses, and Simon, and Judas? And his sisters, are they not all with us? Whence then hath this man all these things?" (Matt. 13:55-56).*

      2. His response—"Then Jesus said unto them, My time is not yet come: but your time is alway ready. The world cannot hate you; but me it hateth, because I testify of it, that the works thereof are evil" (John 7:6-7).

†*Note the statement by Jesus, "My time is not yet come."*
    A. The "time" in mind here, of course, is his crucifixion. He was always acutely aware of this time and hour. Note:
        1. "Jesus saith unto her [his mother at the marriage feast in Cana], Woman, what have I to do with thee? Mine hour is not yet come" (John 2:4).
        2. "Then they [a murderous crowd in Jerusalem] sought to take him; but no man laid hands on him, because his hour was not yet come" (John 7:30).
        3. "And Jesus answered them [some Greeks who wanted to see him] saying, The hour is come, that the Son of man should be glorified" (John 12:23). (See also 12:27.)
        4. "Now before the feast of the passover . . . Jesus knew that his hour was come that he should depart out of this world unto the Father" (John 13:1).
    B. Especially important to note are the statements found in John 7:30 and 8:20. These verses teach that the servant of God is indestructible until the will of God has been accomplished in his life. (See also Rev. 11:7.)

B. The division of the temple crowds (John 7:10-30, 40-43)
    1. Some thought he was a good man (John 7:12).
    2. Some thought he was a deceiver (John 7:12).
    3. Some thought he was a demoniac (John 7:20).
    4. Some thought he was an ordinary man (John 7:27).
    5. Some thought he was a prophet (John 7:40).
    6. Some thought he was the Messiah (John 7:31, 41).
C. The disdain of the Pharisees
    1. They attempted to detain him, but were frustrated by their own officers—
      "The Pharisees heard that the people murmured such things concerning him; and the Pharisees and the chief priests sent officers to take him. . . . And some of them would have taken him; but no man laid hands on him. Then came the officers to the chief priests and Pharisees; and they said unto them, Why have ye not brought him? The officers answered, Never man spake like this man. Then answered them the Pharisees, Are ye also deceived?" (John 7:32, 44-47)
    2. They attempted to denounce him, but were frustrated by one of their own members—"Nicodemus saith unto them, (he that came to Jesus by night, being one of them,) Doth our law judge any man, before it hear him, and know what he doeth? They answered and said unto him, Art thou also of Galilee? Search, and look: for out of Galilee ariseth no prophet" (John 7:50-52).

D. The decision of the thirsty
   1. The invitation—"In the last day, that great day of the feast, Jesus stood and cried, saying, If any man thirst, let him come unto me, and drink. He that believeth on me, as the scripture hath said, out of his belly shall flow rivers of living water. (But this spake he of the Spirit, which they that believe on him should receive: for the Holy Ghost was not yet given; because that Jesus was not yet glorified)" (John 7:37-39).

† *A. The feast referred to here was the Feast of Tabernacles. It was one of the three great Jewish feasts. Josephus called it their holiest and greatest feast* (The Antiquities of the Jews *8. 4. 1). This feast, also called the Feast of Ingathering, was a time of thanksgiving for harvest. It was a happy time; devout Jews lived outdoors in booths made of tree branches for seven days as a reminder of God's provision in the desert during their forefathers' wanderings. The feast also signified that God dwells with his people.*
   B. Dr. Homer Kent of Grace Seminary suggested the following: "The custom had developed of having the priests bring a vessel of water daily during the festival from the Pool of Siloam and come with it in procession to the Temple. Here the water would be poured on the altar of burnt offering as a reminder of how God supplied Israel's need in the wilderness. On the eighth day the ceremony was omitted, signifying Israel's presence in the land. If this event occurred on the eighth day, Christ's invitation to men to come to him for living water was especially dramatic, as he claimed to be the fulfillment of the typology carried out at the feast. He was the supplier of the spiritual living water." (See also John 4:10 and 1 Cor. 10:4.)

   2. The determination—"And many of the people believed on him" (John 7:31).
SIX: The Temple Treasury Sermon (John 8:12-59)—"These words spake Jesus in the treasury, as he taught in the temple: and no man laid hands on him; for his hour was not yet come" (John 8:20).
   A. The conflict with some unbelieving Jews
      1. Their question
         a. They wanted to know who he was (John 8:25).
         b. They wanted to know who his father was (John 8:19)
         c. They wanted to know if he claimed to be greater than their father Abraham (John 8:53).
      2. His answers
         a. Concerning himself
            (1) He was the light of the world (John 8:12).

† *A. His temple treasury sermon (also known as the Light of the World Discourse) was probably the second of two preached during the Feast of Tabernacles. Here Jesus claims to be the Light of the world.*
   B. Edwin Blum wrote: "A major feature of the Feast of Tabernacles was the lighting of giant lamps in the women's court in the temple. The wicks were made from the priests' wornout garments. The light illuminated the temple area and the people gathered to sing praises and dance. The light reminded the Jewish people of how God was with them in their wanderings in the wilderness in a pillar of cloud, which turned to fire at night (Num. 9:15-23). How fitting that during the Feast of Tabernacles, when the large lamps were burning, Jesus . . . said, 'I am

*the Light of the world' (cf. 1:4, 9; 12:35, 46). The world is in darkness, a symbol of evil, sin,
and ignorance (Isa. 9:2; Matt. 4:16; 27:45; John 3:19). 'Light' in the Bible is a symbol of God
and His holiness (Acts 9:3; 1 John 1:5). Jesus is 'the light,' not merely a light or another light
among many lights. He is the only Light, 'the true light' (John 1:9) for the whole world."*
(The Bible Knowledge Commentary, *p. 303*)

---

    (2) He came to bring light and life to all (John 8:12).
    (3) He was the Messiah (John 8:24, 28).
    (4) He was sinless (John 8:6).
    (5) He was from above (John 8:23).
    (6) He would become the Lamb (John 8:28).
  b. Concerning his Father
    (1) He came from the Father (John 8:18, 42)
    (2) He was the son of the Father (John 8:19)
    (3) He was taught by the Father (John 8:28).
    (4) He was honored by the Father (John 8:54).
    (5) He spoke for the Father (John 8:26).
    (6) He would ascend back to the Father (John 8:21)
  c. Concerning Abraham
    (1) He was greater than Abraham, for he preceded Abraham—"Then said
       the Jews unto him, Thou art not yet fifty years old, and hast thou seen
       Abraham? Jesus said unto them, Verily, verily, I say unto you, Before
       Abraham was, I am" (John 8:57-58).

✝ *A. Their statement here gives us an insight concerning the awesome pressure and burden carried
   by our Lord. Here he is, barely thirty-three, and yet mistaken for nearly fifty.*
  *B. We note that Jesus did not say, "I was," but rather, "I am." Here he was simply replying
   as he once did to Moses: "And God said unto Moses, I AM THAT I AM: and he said, Thus
   shalt thou say unto the children of Israel, I AM hath sent me unto you" (Exod. 3:14).*

---

    (2) He was greater than Abraham, for he ministered to Abraham—"Your father
      Abraham rejoiced to see my day: and he saw it, and was glad" (John 8:56).

✝*When did this happen in the life of Abraham? It was probably a reference to the offering up of
Isaac. Compare Genesis 22:1-14 with Hebrews 11:17-19.*

---

  3. Their accusation
    a. That he alone bore witness of himself (John 8:13)
    b. That he was threatening suicide (John 8:22)
    c. That he was born of fornication (John 8:41)

✝*Note their sneering insinuation, "We be not born of fornication" (8:41). This is but one of
several occasions on which the Jews made snide remarks questioning the unusual circumstances*

surrounding Christ's birth. When our Lord later healed a blind man, the Pharisees refused to believe it, telling the cured man to "Give God the praise: We know that this man [Jesus] is a sinner" (John 9:24).

        d. That he was a demon-possessed Samaritan (John 8:48, 52)

    4. His defense—"Jesus answered and said unto them, Though I bear record of myself, yet my record is true; for I know whence I came, and whither I go; but ye cannot tell whence I come, and whither I go. . . . It is also written in your law, that the testimony of two men is true. I am one that bear witness of myself, and the Father that sent me beareth witness of me. . . . Jesus answered, I have not a devil; but I honour my Father, and ye do dishonour me. And I seek not mine own glory: there is one that seeketh and judgeth" (John 8:14, 17-18, 49-50).

    5. Their errors

        a. That they had never been in bondage (John 8:33)

        b. That they were the true seed of Abraham (John 8:33, 39)

    6. His correction—"Jesus answered them, Verily, verily, I say unto you, Whosoever committeth sin is the servant of sin. . . . They answered and said unto him, Abraham is our father. Jesus saith unto them, If ye were Abraham's children, ye would do the works of Abraham. But now ye seek to kill me, a man that hath told you the truth, which I have heard of God: this did not Abraham. . . . Ye are of your father the devil, and the lusts of your father ye will do. He was a murderer from the beginning, and abode not in the truth, because there is no truth in him. When he speaketh a lie, he speaketh of his own: for he is a liar, and the father of it" (John 8:34, 39-40, 44).

    7. Their rejection—"Then took they up stones to cast at him: but Jesus hid himself, and went out of the temple, going through the midst of them, and so passed by" (John 8:59).

    8. His condemnation—"I said therefore unto you, that ye shall die in your sins: for if ye believe not that I am he, ye shall die in your sins" (John 8:24).

  B. The conversion of some believing Jews—"As he spake these words, many believed on him. Then said Jesus to those Jews which believed on him, If ye continue in my word, then are ye my disciples indeed; and ye shall know the truth, and the truth shall make you free. . . . If the Son therefore shall make you free, ye shall be free indeed. . . . Verily, verily, I say unto you, If a man keep my saying, he shall never see death" (John 8:30-32, 36, 51).

SEVEN: The Good Shepherd Sermon (John 10:1-39)

    † *A. On three occasions in the New Testament Jesus is described as a shepherd.*

        1. The author of Hebrews calls him the Great Shepherd (Heb. 13:20). This corresponds to Psalm 23.

        2. The Apostle Peter refers to him as the Chief Shepherd (1 Pet. 5:4). This corresponds to Psalm 24.

        3. The Savior in this sermon describes himself as the Good Shepherd. This corresponds to Psalm 23.

    B. We are told in John 10:22 that Jesus preached this sermon during the Feast of Dedication, also called the Feast of Lights. This was not an Old Testament feast. It came to be observed after the close of the Old Testament Canon. It commemorated the purifying of the temple after its defilement by the Syrians under Antiochus Epiphanes. The feast began on the 25th of Chisleu, which in A.D. 29 was the same as our December 20. It lasted for eight days, the length of time Judas Maccabaeus, the deliverer of the city, took in purifying it. It came to be called the Feast of Lights because the city of Jerusalem was brightly illuminated for its observance.

A. Characteristics of the shepherd
   1. He does things the right way—"But he that entereth in by the door is the shepherd of the sheep" (John 10:2).
   2. He is recognized by the porter—"To him the porter openeth" (John 10:3). (Note: The porter referred to here may possibly be the Holy Spirit.)
   3. He knows his sheep (John 10:3, 14, 27)—"He calleth his own sheep by name" (John 10:3).

†*Paul the apostle amplified upon this in a later epistle: "Nevertheless the foundation of God standeth sure, having this seal, The Lord knoweth them that are his. And, Let every one that nameth the name of Christ depart from iniquity" (2 Tim. 2:19).*

   4. He is known by his sheep (John 10:4, 14, 27)—"The sheep follow him: for they know his voice" (John 10:4).
   5. He leads his sheep (John 10:3).
   6. He is the only true Shepherd—"All that ever came before me are thieves and robbers: but the sheep did not hear them" (John 10:8).
   7. He lays down his life for the sheep (John 10:17-18)—"I am the good shepherd: the good shepherd giveth his life for the sheep" (John 10:11).

†*In the Old Testament the sheep died for the shepherd. In the New Testament the Shepherd will die for the sheep. Homer Kent wrote: "Many shepherds died while defending their flocks. There were knives and clubs of robbers to be faced, as well as the attacks of wild animals. In their cases, however, death was always unintended. Christ, on the other hand, was also to die for his sheep in order to save them, but he was going to do so voluntarily. He would 'give his life.' His sheep were in danger of the greatest kind. 'All we like sheep have gone astray' (Isa. 53:6). Jesus was thus predicting his own death,sda which would occur the following spring." (Light in the* Darkness, p. 140)

   8. He takes up his life for the sheep (John 10:17-18)—"No man taketh it from me, but I lay it down of myself. I have power to lay it down, and I have power to take it again. This commandment have I received of my Father" (John 10:18).
   9. He imparts life to the sheep (John 10:9-10)—"I am the door: by me if any man enter in, he shall be saved, and shall go in and out, and find pasture" (John 10:9). "I am come that they might have life" (John 10:10).
   10. He imparts abundant life to the sheep—"And that they might have it more abundantly" (John 10:10).

11. He imparts eternal life to the sheep—"And I give unto them eternal life; and they shall never perish, neither shall any man pluck them out of my hand. My Father, which gave them me, is greater than all; and no man is able to pluck them out of my Father's hand" (John 10:28-29).

✝ A. Note the "life" and "abundant life" phrases here.
    1. *The first (life) speaks of that peace* with *God in Romans 5:1.*
    2. *The second (abundant life) refers to that peace* of *God in Philippians 4:7.*
  B. *The phrase "no man" is not found in the Greek text. It reads rather, "No thing." In other words, not even the believer himself can remove himself from the Father's hand. Paul later built a marvelous case for this. (See Rom. 8:33-39.)*

12. He is approved by the Father (John 10:15).
13. He is loved by the Father (John 10:17).
14. He is authorized by the Father (John 10:18).
15. He is one with the Father (John 10:30, 38)
16. He is the son of the Father (John 10:36).
B. Characteristics of the sheep
  1. They will not follow strangers (John 10:5, 8)—"And a stranger will they not follow, but will flee from him: for they know not the voice of strangers" (John 10:5).
  2. They are totally dependent upon the shepherd (John 10:12).
  3. They share the same fold with other sheep—"And other sheep I have, which are not of this fold: them also I must bring, and they shall hear my voice; and there shall be one fold, and one shepherd" (John 10:16).

✝*Here is a reference to the Church. Our Lord had already promised it and would soon pray for it.*
  A. *The promise—"And I say also unto thee, That thou art Peter, and upon this rock I will build my church; and the gates of hell shall not prevail against it" (Matt. 16:18).*
  B. *The prayer—"Neither pray I for these alone, but for them also which shall believe on me through their word; that they all may be one; as thou, Father, art in me, and I in thee, that they also may be one in us: that the world may believe that thou hast sent me" (John 17:20-21).*

C. Characteristics of thieves and robbers (John 10:1, 8, 10)
  1. Their words are evil—"All that ever came before me are thieves and robbers: but the sheep did not hear them" (John 10:8).
  2. Their works are evil—"Verily, verily, I say unto you, He that entereth not by the door into the sheepfold, but climbeth up some other way, the same is a thief and a robber. The thief cometh not, but for to steal, and to kill, and to destroy: I am come that they might have life, and that they might have it more abundantly" (John 10:1, 10).

✝*It was at the dawn of human history when the first thief (Cain) killed the first sheep (Abel).*

D. Characteristics of the hireling (John 10:12-13)
  1. He is unconcerned.

2. He is unprotective—"But he that is an hireling, and not the shepherd, whose own the sheep are not, seeth the wolf coming, and leaveth the sheep, and fleeth: and the wolf catcheth them, and scattereth the sheep. The hireling fleeth, because he is an hireling, and careth not for the sheep" (John 10:12-13).
E. Characteristics of the goats (John 10:19-20, 31-39)
    1. They deny the claims of the Shepherd (John 10:38)—"The Jews answered him, saying, For a good work we stone thee not; but for blasphemy; and because that thou, being a man, makest thyself God" (John 10:33).
    2. They accuse the Shepherd of demon possession—"And many of them said, He hath a devil, and is mad; why hear ye him?" (John 10:20).
    3. They accuse the Shepherd of blasphemy (John 10:33, 36).
    4. They attempt to kill him—"Then the Jews took up stones again to stone him. . . . Therefore they sought again to take him: but he escaped out of their hand" (John 10:31, 39).
EIGHT: The Mount Olivet Discourse Sermon (Matt. 24:1-31; Mark 13:1-27; Luke 21:5-28)
    A. Christ's remarks concerning the temple destruction
        1. The place involved—"And as he sat upon the Mount of Olives" (Mark 13:3a).

---

†*The Mount of Olives is directly east of the City of Jerusalem. It rises to a height of 2,743 feet above sea level, some 300 feet higher than the temple mount area.*

---

        2. The purpose involved—"And Jesus went out, and departed from the temple: and his disciples came to him for to shew him the buildings of the temple" (Matt. 24:1).
        3. The prophecy involved
           a. The what of the matter—"And as some spake of the temple, how it was adorned with goodly stones and gifts, he said, As for these things which ye behold, the days will come, in the which there shall not be left one stone upon another, that shall not be thrown down" (Luke 21:5-6).

---

†*This prophecy doubtless shocked the disciples, if for no other reason than because of the casting down of those massive temple blocks. Since 1967 the Ministry of Religious Affairs, in cooperation with the Department of Antiquities, has cleared out an ancient passage in Jerusalem which they named the Rabbinical Tunnel. Undoubtedly it dates back to the time of Christ. The tunnel runs north along the Western Wall and is more than 600 feet long. Meir Kusnetz, an American-born civil engineer, has been in charge of the project. Since 1967, more than 17,000 cubic meters of fill have been excavated. The tunnel stops just short of the northwest corner of the Temple Mount. Its starting point is in the hall under Wilson's Arch, which is directly left of the present-day men's prayer section of the Western Wall. The finished stones inside the tunnel are still beautifully preserved, and some are of unbelievable size. For example, near the beginning of the tunnel is a gigantic chiseled limestone rock 46 feet long, 10 feet wide, and 10 feet high, weighing more than 415 tons. By comparison, the largest megalith at Stonehenge, England, is a mere 40 tons, and the rocks used by the Egyptians to build the pyramids were only 15 tons. Other similar stones weighing more than 300 tons have been uncovered in the tunnel. The amazing thing is that all those massive rocks are so well cut that although there*

is no mortar holding them together, even a thin knifeblade cannot fit between their joints. (Israel at Forty, *Willmington & Pritz, Tyndale House Publishers, Wheaton, Ill., 1987, p. 63)*

---

　　　b. The who of the matter—"Peter and James and John and Andrew asked him privately" (Mark 13:3b).
　　　c. The when of the matter—"Tell us, when shall these things be? and what shall be the sign when all these things shall be fulfilled?" (Mark 13:4). "And when ye shall see Jerusalem compassed with armies, then know that the desolation thereof is nigh" (Luke 21:20).
　　　d. The program involved. Note: It appears Christ actually had two temple destructions in mind here.
　　　　　(1) The destruction of the second temple (Herod's temple) by Titus the Roman general in 70 A.D.
　　　　　(2) The destruction of the third temple (tribulation temple) by the coming antichrist in the future

---

† A. *Facts concerning the second temple:*
　　1. *The temple proper—It was the most beautiful building in the world. Herod had trained 1,000 priests in building arts and had employed 10,000 skilled masons. He then secured 1,000 wagons to haul stones from the quarries. The temple was made of beautiful marble and gold—so gleaming that it appeared from afar as a mountain of snow glittering in the sun. It could easily hold 120,000 worshipers.*
　　2. *The temple personnel*
　　　a. *The high priest*
　　　b. *The chief priests (200 highborn Jews who could trace their descent back to Zadok). They had charge of the weekly temple services, temple treasury, and maintenance of the sacred vessels.*
　　　c. *The regular priests (7,200 in number). They were divided into twenty-four priestly clans, each serving a week at a time. Their job was lighting the altar fires, burning incense, baking the unleavened bread, and sacrificing the animals.*
　　　d. *The Levites (9,600 in number). They also served one week at a time, as guards, policemen, doorkeepers, singers, musicians, and servants.*
　　　e. *The daily temple ritual required the services of 1,000 chief priests and Levites. During the three great feast days (Passover, weeks, booths) all clans were required to attend; thus, there were some 18,000 priests on hand.*
　　3. *The temple prophecy—As predicted by our Lord, the temple was destroyed by the Roman armies in A.D. 70 when Titus burned the city of Jerusalem. The soldiers pried apart those massive stones to collect the gold leaf that had melted from the fiery heat.*
　B. *Facts concerning the third temple:*
　　1. *It will (probably) be constructed by the nation Israel (Rev. 11:1).*
　　2. *It will be corrupted by the antichrist (Dan. 9:27; Matt. 24:15; 2 Thess. 2:3-4; Rev. 13:11-18).*

　B. Christ's remarks concerning the tribulation destruction
　　1. Those events to transpire during the first three-and-a-half years of the tribulation—"All these are the beginning of sorrows" (Matt. 24:8).

a. The wrath of God
   (1) Disturbances from the cosmic and natural world
      (a) Cosmic world—"And fearful sights and great signs shall there be from heaven" (Luke 21:11). "And there shall be signs in the sun, and in the moon, and in the stars" (Luke 21:25). "For the powers of heaven shall be shaken" (Luke 21:26).
      (b) Natural world: Great sea storms—"the sea and the waves roaring" (Luke 21:25); famines (Matt. 24:7); pestilences (Matt. 24:7); earthquakes (Matt. 24:7)
   (2) Deception from the religious world
      (a) False prophets—"And many false prophets shall rise, and shall deceive many" (Matt. 24:11).
      (b) False Christs—"For there shall arise false Christs, and false prophets, and shall shew great signs and wonders; insomuch that, if it were possible, they shall deceive the very elect" (Matt. 24:24). "For many shall come in my name, saying, I am Christ; and shall deceive many" (Matt. 24:5).
   (3) Destruction from the military world—"And ye shall hear of wars and rumours of wars: see that ye be not troubled: for all these things must come to pass, but the end is not yet" (Matt. 24:6). "For nation shall rise against nation, and kingdom against kingdom: and there shall be famines, and pestilences, and earthquakes, in divers places" (Matt. 24:7).
b. The witnesses of God
   (1) To be abused grievously by the devil
      (a) Arrested by the authorities—"But take heed to yourselves: for they shall deliver you up to councils; and in the synagogues ye shall be beaten: and ye shall be brought before rulers and kings for my sake, for a testimony against them" (Mark 13:9).
      (b) Betrayed by their families—"And ye shall be betrayed both by parents, and brethren, and kinsfolks, and friends; and some of you shall they cause to be put to death" (Luke 21:16).
      (c) Hated by all—"And ye shall be hated of all men for my name's sake" (Luke 21:17).
   (2) To be used greatly by the Lord
      (a) In ministering the wisdom of God—"But when they shall lead you, and deliver you up, take no thought beforehand what ye shall speak, neither do ye premeditate: but whatsoever shall be given you in that hour, that speak ye: for it is not ye that speak, but the Holy Ghost" (Mark 13:11). "For I will give you a mouth and wisdom, which all your adversaries shall not be able to gainsay nor resist" (Luke 21:15).
      (b) In ministering the Word of God—"And this gospel of the kingdom shall be preached in all the world for a witness unto all nations; and then shall the end come" (Matt. 24:14).

---

†*Many believe this task will be accomplished by the 144,000 Jewish evangelists. See Revelation 7:1-8.*

2. Those events to transpire during the last three-and-a-half years of the tribulation—"For then shall be great tribulation, such as was not since the beginning of the world to this time, no, nor ever shall be. And except those days should be shortened, there should no flesh be saved: but for the elect's sake those days shall be shortened" (Matt. 24:21-22).
   a. The defiling of the temple of God—"When ye therefore shall see the abomination of desolation, spoken of by Daniel the prophet, stand in the holy place, (whoso readeth, let him understand)" (Matt. 24:15).

†*Here Jesus seems to refer to both a historic and a prophetic event, both having to do with the defiling of the Jewish temple.*
   A. *The historic event—Daniel the prophet, writing six centuries before Christ, predicted the desolation of the second temple (Dan. 9:27; 11:31; 12:11). Some 400 years later this happened at the hands of a godless Syrian warrior known as Antiochus Epiphanes, after he captured the city of Jerusalem. On December 15, 168 B.C., his temple desecration reached its ultimate low, for on that day this Nero of the Old Testament sacrificed a giant sow on an idol altar he had made in the Jewish temple. He forced the priests to swallow its flesh, and also made a broth of it and sprinkled it all throughout the temple. He finally carried off the golden candlesticks, table of shewbread, altar of incense, and various other vessels, and destroyed the sacred books of the law. A large image of Jupiter was placed in the Holy of Holies. All this was known by the horrified Jews as "the abomination of desolation," and is referred to by Jesus in Matthew 24:15 as a springboard to describe the activities of the future antichrist.*
   B. *The prophetic event—John the apostle describes the desolation of the third temple (tribulational temple) in Scripture's final book. It has to do with the image and mark of the antichrist. (See Rev. 13:11-18.)*

   b. The destroying of the city of God—"And when ye shall see Jerusalem compassed with armies, then know that the desolation thereof is nigh. And they shall fall by the edge of the sword, and shall be led away captive into all nations: and Jerusalem shall be trodden down of the Gentiles, until the times of the Gentiles be fulfilled" (Luke 21:20, 24).
   c. The directing of the elect of God—"Then let them which be in Judaea flee into the mountains: Let him which is on the housetop not come down to take any thing out of his house: Neither let him which is in the field return back to take his clothes. And woe unto them that are with child, and to them that give suck in those days! But pray ye that your flight be not in the winter, neither on the sabbath day.... Wherefore if they shall say unto you, Behold, he is in the desert; go not forth: behold, he is in the secret chambers; believe it not. For as the lightning cometh out of the east, shineth even unto the west; so shall also the coming of the Son of man be" (Matt. 24:16-20, 26-27).
   d. The darkening of the skies of God—"Immediately after the tribulation of those days shall the sun be darkened, and the moon shall not give her light, and the stars shall fall from heaven, and the powers of the heavens shall be shaken" (Matt. 24:29).
   e. The descending of the Son of God—"And then shall appear the sign of the

Son of man in heaven: and then shall all the tribes of the earth mourn, and they shall see the Son of man coming in the clouds of heaven with power and great glory. And he shall send his angels with a great sound of trumpet, and they shall gather together his elect from the four winds, from one end of heaven to the other" (Matt. 24:30-31).

NINE: The Thursday Night Passover Sermon (John 14–16)

---

†*Assuming that Jesus was crucified at 9:00 A.M. on Friday, this sermon was given piecemeal at various locations over an extended period. It was begun in the Upper Room (John 14) and completed during a midnight walk through the deserted streets of Jerusalem en route to Gethsemane (John 15–16).*

A. Reasons for the sermon—"These things have I spoken unto you, being yet present with you" (John 14:25).
   1. That the believer might experience joy—"These things have I spoken unto you, that my joy might remain in you, and that your joy might be full" (John 15:11).
   2. That we might not stumble—"These things have I spoken unto you, that ye should not be offended" (John 16:1).
   3. That we might not forget his words—"But these things have I told you, that when the time shall come, ye may remember that I told you of them. And these things I said not unto you at the beginning, because I was with you" (John 16:4).
   4. That we might experience peace—"These things I have spoken unto you, that in me ye might have peace. In the world ye shall have tribulation: but be of good cheer; I have overcome the world" (John 16:33).
B. Relationships in the sermon
   1. Those relationships involving the Savior
      a. Christ and the Father
         (1) He declares him (John 14:7-9)—"Philip saith unto him, Lord, shew us the Father, and it sufficeth us. Jesus saith unto him, Have I been so long time with you, and yet hast thou not known me, Philip? he that hath seen me hath seen the Father; and how sayest thou then, Shew us the Father?" (John 14:8-9).
         (2) He is inseparably linked to him (John 14:10-11)—"Believest thou not that I am in the Father, and the Father in me? the words that I speak unto you I speak not of myself: but the Father that dwelleth in me, he doeth the works" (John 14:10).
         (3) He glorifies him (John 14:13).
         (4) He goes to him (John 14:2, 12, 28; 16:10, 16, 28)—"I came forth from the Father, and am come into the world: again, I leave the world, and go to the Father" (John 16:28).

---

†*Here in one verse Jesus summarizes his entire ministry.*
   A. His incarnation—"I came forth from the Father."
   B. His earthly life—"And am come into the world."

C. His ascension (following the crucifixion and resurrection)—"*Again, I leave the world.*"
D. His great high priestly work—"*And go to the Father.*"

---

    b. Christ and the Holy Spirit
        (1) He comes at Christ's prayer request—"And I will pray the Father, and he shall give you another Comforter, that he may abide with you for ever" (John 14:16).
        (2) He comes to honor and bear witness to Christ (John 15:26, 16:13-15)—"But when the Comforter is come, whom I will send unto you from the Father, even the Spirit of truth, which proceedeth from the Father, he shall testify of me" (John 15:26). "Howbeit when he, the Spirit of truth, is come, he will guide you into all truth: for he shall not speak of himself; but whatsoever he shall hear, that shall he speak: and he will shew you things to come. He shall glorify me: for he shall receive of mine, and shall shew it unto you" (John 16:13-14).
        (3) He comes to perform a threefold work for Christ (John 16:7-11).
            (a) To reprove the world of sin (John 16:8)—"of sin, because they believe not on me" (John 16:9).
            (b) To reprove the world of righteousness (John 16:8)—"Of righteousness, because I go to my Father, and ye see me no more" (John 16:10).
            (c) To reprove the world of judgment (John 16:8)—"Of judgment, because the prince of this world is judged" (John 16:11).

---

†*Note that Jesus says "sin" and not "sins." The only sin the Holy Spirit will rebuke sinners of is the sin of rejecting Christ. The reason is that this is the only sin which will eventually send a person to hell.*

---

    c. Christ and believers
        (1) He will come for them—"In my Father's house are many mansions: if it were not so, I would have told you. I go to prepare a place for you. And if I go and prepare a place for you, I will come again, and receive you unto myself; that where I am, there ye may be also" (John 14:2-3).

---

†*Note the phrase, "I will come again, and receive you unto myself." This is the only reference to the rapture in the four Gospels, and the first time in Scripture that God promises to take people from the earth.*

---

        (2) He will dwell in them—"At that day ye shall know that I am in my Father, and ye in me, and I in you" (John 14:20).
        (3) He will attach to them (John 14:20)
        (4) He will work through them in producing fruit and more fruit (John 15:2); in producing much fruit (John 15:5).

†Note the progression of this: Fruit, more fruit, and much fruit (15:1-5). This fruit can signify converts (Rom. 1:13), Christian character (Gal. 5:22-23), or conduct (Phil. 1:11; Rom. 6:21-22). Jesus then promises that this fruit will remain (see John 15:16).

---

       2. Those relationships involving the saint
         a. The believer and the Father
           (1) Indwelled by the Father—"Jesus answered and said unto him, If a man love me, he will keep my words: and my Father will love him, and we will come unto him, and make our abode with him" (John 14:23).

---

† A. Here is an amazing revelation:
    1. In Colossians 1:27 we are told that the Son indwells the believer.
    2. In 1 Corinthians 6:19 we learn that the Holy Spirit indwells the believer.
    3. Here in John 14:23 we hear Jesus saying the Father himself also indwells the believer.
  B. Note also an additional truth:
    1. In Galatians 2:20 we are told that the Son loves us.
    2. In 2 Corinthians 13:14 we learn that the Holy Spirit loves us.
    3. Here in John 14:23 (see also 16:27) we read that the Father loves us.

---

           (2) Loved by the Father (John 14:21; 16:27)—"For the Father himself loveth you, because ye have loved me, and have believed that I came out from God" (John 16:27).
           (3) Empowered by the Father—"Verily, verily, I say unto you, He that believeth on me, the works that I do shall he do also; and greater works than these shall he do; because I go unto my Father" (John 14:12).

---

†He meant "greater works" in a quantitative way and not a qualitative sense. Examples:
  A. The establishment of local churches.
  B. The spread of the gospel to the ends of the earth.

---

         b. The believer and the Holy Spirit
           (1) To be taught by the Holy Spirit—"But the Comforter, which is the Holy Ghost, whom the Father will send in my name, he shall teach you all things, and bring all things to your remembrance, whatsoever I have said unto you" (John 14:26).

---

†These words would later have great significance for three of those disciples in the Upper Room. They were Matthew, John, and Peter, all of whom were inspired by the Holy Spirit to write a portion of the Word of God.

---

           (2) To be permanently indwelled by the Holy Spirit—"And I will pray the Father, and he shall give you another Comforter, that he may abide with you for ever" (John 14:16).

†*This is a startling new revelation, for it promises the permanent indwelling of the Holy Spirit in the believer. This concept was unknown in the Old Testament.*

---

    c. The believer and other believers—"This is my commandment, That ye love one another, as I have loved you. Greater love hath no man than this, that a man lay down his life for his friends. Ye are my friends, if ye do whatsoever I command you" (John 15:12-14).

    d. The believer and persecutions

      (1) To expect many persecutions—"If the world hate you, ye know that it hated me before it hated you. If ye were of the world, the world would love his own: but because ye are not of the world, but I have chosen you out of the world, therefore the world hateth you. Remember the word that I said unto you, The servant is not greater than his lord. If they have persecuted me, they will also persecute you; if they have kept my saying, they will keep yours also. But all these things will they do unto you for my name's sake, because they know not him that sent me" (John 15:18-21). "These things have I spoken unto you, that ye should not be offended. They shall put you out of the synagogues: yea, the time cometh, that whosoever killeth you will think that he doeth God service. And these things will they do unto you, because they have not known the Father, nor me" (John 16:1-3).

      (2) To rejoice in all persecutions—"Let not your heart be troubled: ye believe in God, believe also in me. . . . Peace I leave with you, my peace I give unto you: not as the world giveth, give I unto you. Let not your heart be troubled, neither let it be afraid" (John 14:1, 27). "A woman when she is in travail hath sorrow, because her hour is come: but as soon as she is delivered of the child, she remembereth no more the anguish, for joy that a man is born into the world. And ye now therefore have sorrow: but I will see you again, and your heart shall rejoice, and your joy no man taketh from you. . . . These things I have spoken unto you, that in me ye might have peace. In the world ye shall have tribulation: but be of good cheer; I have overcome the world" (John 16:21-23, 33).

    e. The believer and fruit bearing

      (1) The source involved—"I am the true vine, and my Father is the husbandman" (John 15:1).

      (2) The steps involved

        (a) Abide in Christ—"Abide in me, and I in you. As the branch cannot bear fruit of itself, except it abide in the vine; no more can ye, except ye abide in me. I am the vine, ye are the branches: He that abideth in me, and I in him, the same bringeth forth much fruit: for without me ye can do nothing" (John 15:4-5).

---

†*Various explanations have been offered as to why Christ used the vine and branch analogy concerning the relationship between himself and his followers.*

    A. He may have seen a vine growing over the door of the Upper Room house as they were leaving.

B. *He may have pointed to the great golden vine Herod the Great had placed over a gate of the temple.*
C. *He may have called attention to the small fires on the horizon caused by the burning of dead branches.*

(b) Study the Word—"Now ye are clean through the word which I have spoken unto you" (John 15:3).
(c) Submit to pruning—"Every branch in me that beareth not fruit he taketh away: and every branch that beareth fruit, he purgeth it, that it may bring forth more fruit. . . . If a man abide not in me, he is cast forth as a branch, and is withered; and men gather them, and cast them into the fire, and they are burned" (John 15:2, 6).

---

†*If a branch fails to bear fruit, it is rejected and cast aside (15:6). There is a problem concerning these fruitless branches that are removed from the vine (15:2, 6). Three theories are offered at this point.*
A. *That the removed branches represent Christians who lose their salvation—This theory is totally refuted by various Scripture verses.*
B. *That they are Christians who commit the sin unto death as described in Acts 5:1-11; 1 Corinthians 11:27-34; 1 John 5:16—The burning, according to this theory, would be their works, as seen in 1 Corinthians 3:11-15.*
C. *That they represent mere professing Christians (religious people) who are finally severed from their superficial connection with Christ—This had already happened with Judas. (See John 13:27-30; 17:12.)*

---

(3) The success involved—"If ye abide in me, and my words abide in you, ye shall ask what ye will, and it shall be done unto you. Herein is my Father glorified, that ye bear much fruit; so shall ye be my disciples" (John 15:7-8).
(4) The stability involved—"Ye have not chosen me, but I have chosen you, and ordained you, that ye should go and bring forth fruit, and that your fruit should remain: that whatsoever ye shall ask of the Father in my name, he may give it you" (John 15:16).

---

† A. *Note the phrase, "I have chosen you." In Jesus' day the disciple would normally select his own rabbi. But this is not the case with the believer. The author of Hebrews makes this very clear: "And no man taketh this honour unto himself, but he that is called of God, as was Aaron" (Heb. 5:4).*
B. *Note also the role that the Father plays in all this. Here we are told that a fruitbearing son or daughter will enjoy a prayer-answering Father. We usually reverse the formula, assuming prayers must precede fruit.*
C. *We are the branches and Christ is the vine. The only function of a branch is to bear fruit. Branch wood makes poor firewood. No builder would think of using branch wood to construct a ship, or a house, or a piece of furniture.*

THE PRAYERS OF CHRIST

A. The occasions of Christ's prayers
1. At his baptism (Luke 3:21)
2. Before his first preaching tour of Galilee (Mark 1:35; Luke 4:42)
3. After healing a leper (Luke 5:16)
4. Before choosing his twelve disciples (Luke 6:12)
5. After the feeding of the 5,000 (Matt. 14:23; Mark 6:46; John 6:15)
6. Before hearing Peter's great confession (Luke 9:18)
7. During his transfiguration (Luke 9:28-29)
8. Upon hearing the report of the returning seventy (Matt. 11:25-27; Luke 10:21-22)
9. After visiting Mary and Martha (Luke 11:1)
10. After receiving some small children (Matt. 19:13-15; Mark 10:13-16; Luke 18:15-17)
11. Before raising Lazarus (John 11:41-42)
12. When some Greeks desired to see him (John 12:27-28)
13. After leaving the Upper Room (John 17:1-26)
14. In the garden (first prayer) (Matt. 26:39; Mark 14:35-36; Luke 22:41-42)
15. In the garden (second prayer) (Matt. 26:42; Mark 14:39; Luke 22:44-45)
16. In the garden (third prayer) (Matt. 26:44)
17. On the cross (first prayer) (Luke 23:34)
18. On the cross (second prayer) (Matt. 27:46-47; Mark 15:34-35)
19. On the cross (third prayer) (Luke 23:46)

B. A brief summary of Christ's prayers
1. What he prayed for:
a. That the Father would bless his Galilean ministry (see b above)
b. That the Father would guide him in selecting the 12 (see d)
c. That the Father would reveal the deity of the Son to Peter (see f)
d. Thanking the Father for revealing spiritual truths to the seventy (see h)
e. Thanking the Father for always hearing him (see k)
f. That the Father would be glorified (see l)
g. That the Father would glorify him (see m)
h. That the Father would keep, sanctify, unite, perfect, and gather to Christ all believers (see m)
i. That if possible, his hour of passion might pass from him (see n, o, p)
j. That his Father's will be done (see n, o, p)
k. That his enemies be forgiven (see q)

l. That he understand his sufferings (see r)
m. That the Father receive his spirit (see s)
2. Those he prayed for
   a. Little children (see j)
   b. His enemies (see q)
   c. Himself (see l, m, n, o, p, r, s)
   d. All believers (see m)
   e. The seventy disciples (see h)
3. When he prayed
   a. All night (see d)
   b. Shortly past midnight (see m, n, o, p)
   c. At dawn (see b)
   d. Early morning (see q)
   e. Late afternoon (see r, s)
4. How he prayed
   a. Lifting up his eyes to heaven (see k, m)
   b. Kneeling (see n, o)
   c. On his face (see n, o)
   d. Hanging between earth and heaven (see q, r, s)

THE SUFFERINGS OF CHRIST
A. Rejected by
1. His nation (John 1:11)
2. His hometown (Luke 4:28-29)
3. His friends (Mark 3:21)
4. His family (John 7:5)
5. The religious world (John 7:1; 9:22)
B. Tempted by Satan (Luke 4:1-2, 13; 22:28)
C. Ridiculed because of
1. His hometown (John 1:46; 7:52)
2. His background (John 8:41; 9:24, 29)
D. Threatened constantly
1. By Herod (Matt. 2:16)
2. By his hometown (Luke 4:29)
3. By the Jews
a. Because he healed on the Sabbath (John 5:16; Luke 6:10-11)
b. Because of his claims (John 8:58-59; 10:30-33)
c. Because of his sermons (John 8:40; Luke 11:53-54; Mark 12:12; Matt. 26:1-4)
d. Because of his miracles (John 11:53; see also John 12:10-11)
4. By the devil (Matt. 26:37-38; Mark 14:33-34; Luke 22:44)
E. Homeless (Matt. 8:20)
F. Betrayed by a follower (John 13:21)
G. Denied by a friend (Matt. 26:58, 69-75; Mark 14:54, 66-72; Luke 22:54-62; John 18:15-18, 25-27)
H. Misunderstood by his disciples (Matt. 15:16; 17:6-11; Mark 6:52; John 10:6; 12:16)
I. Forsaken by all (Matt. 26:56)
J. Misquoted (Matt. 26:61)
K. Illegally tried seven times
1. First trial, before Annas (John 18:12-14, 19-24)
2. Second trial, before Caiaphas (Matt. 26:57-68; Mark 14:53-65)
3. Third trial, before the Sanhedrin (Matt. 27:1-2; Mark 15:1, Luke 22:66–23:1)
4. Fourth trial, before Pilate (John 18:28-38; Matt. 27:2, 11-14; Mark 15:1-5; Luke 23:1-6)
5. Fifth trial, before Herod (Luke 23:7-12)
6. Sixth trial, before Pilate (John 18:33–19:16; Matt. 27:15-26; Mark 15:6-15; Luke 23:13-25)
7. Seventh trial, before the Roman soldiers (Matt. 27:27-31; Mark 15:16-20)

L. Indicted on false charges (Luke 23:1-2)

M. Mocked by

    1. The Roman soldiers (Luke 23:36-37; Mark 15:16-20)

    2. The watching crowd (Luke 23:35)

    3. The chief priests (Mark 15:31)

    4. The thieves (Mark 15:32; Matt. 27:44)

N. Tortured—Our Lord was

    1. Slapped (John 18:22)

    2. Blindfolded (Luke 22:64)

    3. Spit upon (Matt. 26:67)

    4. Buffeted (Matt. 26:67)

    5. Scourged (Matt. 27:26)

    6. Struck upon the head (Matt. 27:30)

    7. Pierced with thorns (Matt. 27:29)

O. Crucified (Matt. 27; Mark 15; Luke 23; John 19)

THE OLD TESTAMENT PROPHECIES FULFILLED BY CHRIST
   A. Pre-Crucifixion Prophecies
      1. That he would be born of a virgin (compare Isa. 7:14 with Matt. 1:22-23)
      2. That he would be given the throne of David (compare 2 Sam. 7:11-12; Psa. 132:11; Isa. 9:6-7; 16:5; Jer. 23:5 with Luke 1:31-32)
      3. That this throne would be an eternal throne (compare Dan. 2:44; 7:14, 27; Mic. 4:7 with Luke 1:33)
      4. That he would be called Emmanuel (compare Isa. 7:14 with Matt. 1:23)
      5. That he would have a forerunner (compare Isa. 40:3-5; Mal. 3:1 with Luke 1:76-78; 3:3-6; Matt. 3:1-3).
      6. That he would be born in Bethlehem (compare Mic. 5:2 with Luke 2:4-6; Matt. 2:5-6)
      7. That he would be worshiped by the wise men and presented with gifts (compare Psa. 72:10; Isa. 60:3, 6, 9 with Matt. 2:11)
      8. That he would be in Egypt for a season (compare Num. 24:8; Hos. 11:1 with Matt. 2:15)
      9. That his birthplace would suffer a massacre of infants (compare Jer. 31:15 with Matt. 2:17-18)
     10. That he would be called a Nazarene (compare Isa. 11:1 with Matt. 2:23)
     11. That he would be zealous for the Father (compare Psa. 69:9; 119:139 with John 2:13-17)
     12. That he would be filled with God's Spirit (compare Isa. 11:2; 61:1-2; Psa. 45:7 with Luke 4:18-19)
     13. That he would heal many (compare Isa. 53:4 with Matt. 8:16-17)
     14. That he would deal gently with the Gentiles (compare Isa. 9:1-2; 42:1-3 with Matt. 12:17-21; 4:13-16)
     15. That he would speak in parables (compare Isa. 6:9-10 with Matt. 13:10-15)
     16. That he would be rejected by his own (compare Isa. 53:3; Psa. 69:8 with John 1:11; 7:5)
     17. That he would make a triumphal entry into Jerusalem (compare Zech. 9:9 with Matt. 21:4-5)
     18. That he would be praised by little children (compare Psa. 8:2 with Matt. 21:16)
     19. That he would be the rejected cornerstone (compare Psa. 118:22-23 with Matt. 21:42)
     20. That his miracles would not be believed (compare Isa. 53:1 with John 12:37-38)
   B. Crucifixion Prophecies

1. That his friend would betray him for thirty pieces of silver (compare Psa. 41:9; 55:12-14; Zech 11:12-13 with Matt. 26:14-16, 21-25)
2. That he would be a man of sorrows (compare Isa. 53:3 with Matt. 26:37-38)
3. That he would be forsaken by his disciples (compare Zech. 13:7 with Matt. 26:31, 56)
4. That he would be scourged and spat upon (compare Isa. 50:6 with Matt. 26:67; 27:26)
5. That his price money would be used to buy a potter's field (compare Zech. 11:12-13; Jer. 18:1-4; 19:1-4 with Matt. 27:9-10)
6. That he would be crucified between two thieves (compare Isa. 53:12 with Matt. 27:38; Mark 15:27-28; Luke 22:37)
7. That he would be given vinegar to drink (compare Psa. 69:21 with Matt. 27:34, 48; John 19:28-30)
8. That he would suffer the piercing of his hands and feet (compare Psa. 22:16; Zech. 12:10 with Mark 15:25; John 19:34, 37; 20:25-27)
9. That his garments would be parted and gambled for (compare Psa. 22:18 with Luke 23:34; John 19:23-24)
10. That he would be surrounded and ridiculed by his enemies (compare Psa. 22:7-8 with Matt. 27:39-44; Mark 15:29-32)
11. That he would thirst (compare Psa. 22:15 with John 19:28)
12. That he would commend his spirit to the Father (compare Psa. 31:5 with Luke 23:46)
13. That his bones would not be broken (compare Psa. 34:20; Exod. 12:46; Num. 9:12 with John 19:33-36)
14. That he would be stared at in death (compare Zech. 12:10 with John 19:37; Matt. 27:36)
15. That he would be buried with the rich (compare Isa. 53:9 with Matt. 27:57-60)

C. Post-Cruxifixion Prophecies
1. That he would be raised from the dead (compare Psa. 16:10 with Matt. 28:2-7)
2. That he would ascend (compare Psa. 24:7-10 with Mark 16:19; Luke 24:51)

THE PREDICTIONS MADE BY CHRIST

A. Concerning the Church

    1. Its symbol—"Again, the kingdom of heaven is like unto a merchant man, seeking goodly pearls" (Matt. 13:45).

    2. Its foundation—Christ himself (Matt. 16:13-19). "And I say also unto thee, That thou art Peter, and upon this rock I will build my church; and the gates of hell shall not prevail against it" (Matt. 16:18).

    3. Its ministry (Matt. 28:19-20; Acts 1:8) "Go ye therefore, and teach all nations, baptizing them in the name of the Father, and of the Son, and of the Holy Ghost: Teaching them to observe all things whatsoever I have commanded you: and, lo, I am with you alway, even unto the end of the world. Amen" (Matt. 28:19-20).

    4. Its field of service (Matt. 28:19; Acts 1:8)—"But ye shall receive power, after that the Holy Ghost is come upon you: and ye shall be witnesses unto me both in Jerusalem, and in all Judaea, and in Samaria, and unto the uttermost part of the earth" (Acts 1:8).

    5. Its authority (Matt. 16:19; 18:18; John 20:23)—"Verily I say unto you, Whatsoever ye shall bind on earth shall be bound in heaven: and whatsoever ye shall loose on earth shall be loosed in heaven" (Matt. 18:18). "Whose soever sins ye remit, they are remitted unto them; and whose soever sins ye retain, they are retained" (John 20:23).

    6. Its persecution (Matt. 10:16-22; 23; 34; John 15:18-21; 16:1-3, 33) "Wherefore, behold, I send unto you prophets, and wise men, and scribes: and some of them ye shall kill and crucify; and some of them shall ye scourge in your synagogues, and persecute them from city to city" (Matt. 23:34). "Remember the word that I said unto you, The servant is not greater than his lord. If they have persecuted me, they will also persecute you; if they have kept my saying, they will keep yours also" (John 15:20). "They shall put you out of the synagogues: yea, the time cometh, that whosoever killeth you will think that he doeth God service" (John 16:2). "These things I have spoken unto you, that in me ye might have peace. In the world ye shall have tribulation: but be of good cheer; I have overcome the world" (John 16:33).

    7. Its discipline (Matt. 18:15-17)—"Moreover if thy brother shall trespass against thee, go and tell him his fault between thee and him alone: if he shall hear thee, thou hast gained thy brother. But if he will not hear thee, then take with thee one or two more, that in the mouth of two or three witnesses every word may be established. And if he shall neglect to hear them, tell it unto the

church: but if he neglect to hear the church, let him be unto thee as an heathen man and a publican" (Matt. 18:15-17).

8. Its removal (John 14:2-3)—"In my Father's house are many mansions: if it were not so, I would have told you. I go to prepare a place for you. And if I go and prepare a place for you, I will come again, and receive you unto myself; that where I am, there ye may be also" (John 14:2-3).

B. Concerning himself

1. His transfiguration—"Verily I say unto you, There be some standing here, which shall not taste of death, till they see the Son of man coming in his kingdom" (Matt. 16:28).

2. His betrayal by Judas

a. Predicted in Galilee

(1) First occasion—"Jesus answered them, Have not I chosen you twelve, and one of you is a devil? He spake of Judas Iscariot the son of Simon: for he it was that should betray him, being one of the twelve" (John 6:70-71).

(2) Second occasion—"And while they abode in Galilee, Jesus said unto them, The Son of man shall be betrayed into the hands of men" (Matt. 17:22).

b. Predicted in the Upper Room—"And as they did eat, he said, Verily I say unto you, that one of you shall betray me. . . . Then Judas, which betrayed him, answered and said, Master, is it I? He said unto him, Thou hast said" (Matt. 26:21, 25).

3. His denial by Peter

a. Predicted in the Upper Room—"Peter said unto him, Lord, why cannot I follow thee now? I will lay down my life for thy sake. Jesus answered him, Wilt thou lay down thy life for my sake? Verily, verily, I say unto thee, The cock shall not crow, till thou hast denied me thrice" (John 13:37-38).

b. Predicted en route to the Mount of Olives and Gethsemane—"And when they had sung an hymn, they went out into the mount of Olives. . . . Jesus said unto him, Verily I say unto thee, That this night, before the cock crow, thou shalt deny me thrice" (Matt. 26:30, 34).

4. His abandonment by the twelve—"Then saith Jesus unto them, All ye shall be offended because of me this night: for it is written, I will smite the shepherd, and the sheep of the flock shall be scattered abroad" (Matt. 26:31).

5. His sufferings

a. Predicted in Caesarea Philippi—"From that time forth began Jesus to show unto his disciples, how that he must go unto Jerusalem, and suffer many things from the elders and chief priests and scribes" (Matt. 16:21a).

b. Predicted on the Mount of Transfiguration—"Likewise shall also the Son of Man suffer" (Matt. 17:12b).

6. His death

a. The fact of his death—"I am the good shepherd: the good shepherd giveth his life for the sheep. . . . As the Father knoweth me, even so know I the Father: and I lay down my life for the sheep" (John 10:11, 15). "And they shall kill him, and the third day he shall be raised again. And they were exceeding sorry" (Matt. 17:23).

b. The place of his death—"Behold, we go up to Jerusalem; and the Son of Man shall be betrayed unto the chief priests . . . and they shall condemn him to death" (Matt. 20:18).

c. The method of his death—"And as Moses lifted up the serpent in the wilderness, even so must the Son of man be lifted up" (John 3:14). "And I, if I be lifted up from the earth, will draw all men unto me. This he said, signifying what death he should die" (John 12:32-33). "The scribes . . . shall condemn him to death . . . and to crucify him" (Matt. 20:18-19).

7. His resurrection

   a. The fact of his resurrection—"Therefore doth my Father love me, because I lay down my life, that I might take it again. No man taketh it from me, but I lay it down of myself. I have power to lay it down, and I have power to take it again. This commandment have I received of my Father" (John 10:17-18).

   b. The time element in his resurrection—"For as Jonas was three days and three nights in the whale's belly; so shall the Son of man be three days and three nights in the heart of the earth" (Matt. 12:40). "Jesus answered and said unto them, Destroy this temple, and in three days I will raise it up" (John 2:19). (See also Matt. 17:23; 20:19.)

8. His appearance in Galilee—"But after I am risen again, I will go before you into Galilee" (Matt. 26:32).

9. His ascension—"Then said Jesus unto them, Yet a little while am I with you, and then I go unto him that sent me" (John 7:33). "I came forth from the Father, and am come into the world: again, I leave the world, and go to the Father" (John 16:28).

10. His return

   a. In the air—"And if I go and prepare a place for you, I will come again, and receive you unto myself; that where I am, there ye may be also" (John 14:3).

   b. On the earth

      (1) He spoke of this as a witness to his friends—"For the Son of man shall come in the glory of his Father with his angels; and then he shall reward every man according to his works" (Matt. 16:27). "And then shall appear the sign of the Son of man in heaven: and then shall all the tribes of the earth mourn, and they shall see the Son of man coming in the clouds of heaven with power and great glory" (Matt. 24:30).

      (2) He spoke of this as a warning to his foes—"But Jesus held his peace. And the high priest answered and said unto him, I adjure thee by the living God, that thou tell us whether thou be the Christ, the Son of God. Jesus saith unto him, Thou hast said: nevertheless I say unto you, Hereafter shall ye see the Son of man sitting on the right hand of power, and coming in the clouds of heaven" (Matt. 26:63-64).

C. Concerning the resurrection of Lazarus—"These things said he: and after that he saith unto them, Our friend Lazarus sleepeth; but I go, that I may awake him out of sleep" (John 11:11).

D. Concerning the destruction of Jerusalem and the temple

   1. The destruction of Jerusalem—"For the days shall come upon thee, that thine enemies shall cast a trench about thee, and compass thee round, and keep thee in on every side, and shall lay thee even with the ground, and thy children within thee; and they shall not leave in thee one stone upon another; because thou knewest not the time of thy visitation" (Luke 19:43-44). (See also Luke 21:20, 24; 23:28-30.)

   2. The destruction of the temple—"And as he went out of the temple, one of his disciples saith unto him, Master, see what manner of stones and what

buildings are here! And Jesus answering said unto him, Seest thou these great buildings? there shall not be left one stone upon another, that shall not be thrown down" (Mark 13:1-2).

E. Concerning the death of Peter—"Verily, verily, I say unto thee, When thou wast young, thou girdedst thyself, and walkedst whither thou wouldest: but when thou shalt be old, thou shalt stretch forth thy hands, and another shall gird thee, and carry thee whither thou wouldest not. This spake he, signifying by what death he should glorify God. And when he had spoken this, he saith unto him, Follow me" (John 21:18-19).

F. Concerning Pentecost and the ministry of the Holy Spirit

1. The fact of his ministry—"In the last day, that great day of the feast, Jesus stood and cried, saying, If any man thirst, let him come unto me, and drink. He that believeth on me, as the scripture hath said, out of his belly shall flow rivers of living water. (But this spake he of the Spirit, which they that believe on him should receive: for the Holy Ghost was not yet given; because that Jesus was not yet glorified)" (John 7:37-39). "And, behold, I send the promise of my Father upon you: but tarry ye in the city of Jerusalem, until ye be endued with power from on high" (Luke 24:49).

2. The duration of his ministry—"And I will pray the Father, and he shall give you another Comforter, that he may abide with you for ever" (John 14:16).

3. The location of his ministry—"Even the Spirit of truth; whom the world cannot receive, because it seeth him not, neither knoweth him: but ye know him; for he dwelleth with you, and shall be in you" (John 14:17).

4. The nature of his ministry

   a. Regarding the Savior—"But when the Comforter is come, whom I will send unto you from the Father, even the Spirit of truth, which proceedeth from the Father, he shall testify of me. . . . He shall glorify me: for he shall receive of mine, and shall shew it unto you" (John 15:26; 16:14).

   b. Regarding the saved—"But the Comforter, which is the Holy Ghost, whom the Father will send in my name, he shall teach you all things, and bring all things to your remembrance, whatsoever I have said unto you. . . . Howbeit when he, the Spirit of truth, is come, he will guide you into all truth: for he shall not speak of himself; but whatsoever he shall hear, that shall he speak: and he will shew you things to come" (John 14:26; 16:13).

   c. Regarding the sinner—"And when he is come, he will reprove the world of sin, and of righteousness, and of judgment" (John 16:8).

G. Concerning the last days—"And as it was in the days of Noe, so shall it be also in the days of the Son of man. They did eat, they drank, they married wives, they were given in marriage, until the day that Noe entered into the ark, and the flood came, and destroyed them all. Likewise also as it was in the days of Lot; they did eat, they drank, they bought, they sold, they planted, they builded; but the same day that Lot went out of Sodom it rained fire and brimstone from heaven, and destroyed them all. Even thus shall it be in the day when the Son of man is revealed" (Luke 17:26-30). "Now learn a parable of the fig tree; when his branch is yet tender, and putteth forth leaves, ye know that summer is nigh: So likewise ye, when ye shall see all these things, know that it is near, even at the doors. Verily I say unto you, This generation shall not pass, till all these things be fulfilled" (Matt. 24:32-34).

H. Concerning the nation Israel
 1. Its blindness—"O Jerusalem, Jerusalem, thou that killest the prophets, and stonest them which are sent unto thee, how often would I have gathered thy children together, even as a hen gathereth her chickens under her wings, and ye would not! Behold, your house is left unto you desolate. For I say unto you, Ye shall not see me henceforth, till ye shall say, Blessed is he that cometh in the name of the Lord" (Matt. 23:37-39).
 2. Its rejection—"Therefore say I unto you, The kingdom of God shall be taken from you, and given to a nation bringing forth the fruits thereof" (Matt. 21:43).
 3. Its regathering—"And he shall send his angels with a great sound of a trumpet, and they shall gather together his elect from the four winds, from one end of heaven to the other" (Matt. 24:31).
I. Concerning the great tribulation—"For then shall be great tribulation, such as was not since the beginning of the world to this time, no, nor ever shall be. . . . Immediately after the tribulation of those days shall the sun be darkened, and the moon shall not give her light, and the stars shall fall from heaven, and the powers of the heavens shall be shaken" (Matt. 24:21, 29). "For these be the days of vengeance, that all things which are written may be fulfilled. . . . And there shall be signs in the sun, and in the moon, and in the stars; and upon the earth distress of nations, with perplexity; the sea and the waves roaring; men's hearts failing them for fear, and for looking after those things which are coming on the earth: for the powers of heaven shall be shaken" (Luke 21:22, 25-26).
J. Concerning the coming of Elijah—"And Jesus answered and said unto them, Elias truly shall first come, and restore all things" (Matt. 17:11).
K. Concerning the coming antichrist—"I am come in my Father's name, and ye receive me not: if another shall come in his own name, him ye will receive" (John 5:43). "When ye therefore shall see the abomination of desolation, spoken of by Daniel the prophet, stand in the holy place, (whoso readeth, let him understand)" (Matt. 24:15).
L. Concerning the Battle of Armageddon—"I tell you, in that night there shall be two men in one bed; the one shall be taken, and the other shall be left. Two women shall be grinding together; the one shall be taken, and the other left. Two men shall be in the field; the one shall be taken, and the other left. And they answered and said unto him, Where, Lord? And he said unto them, Wheresoever the body is, thither will the eagles be gathered together" (Luke 17:34-37). (See also Matt. 24:28.)
M. Concerning the resurrection of the dead—"Marvel not at this: for the hour is coming, in the which all that are in the graves shall hear his voice, and shall come forth; they that have done good, unto the resurrection of life; and they that have done evil, unto the resurrection of damnation" (John 5:28-29).
N. Concerning the future rewards—"He that receiveth a prophet in the name of a prophet shall receive a prophet's reward; and he that receiveth a righteous man in the name of a righteous man shall receive a righteous man's reward. And whosoever shall give to drink unto one of these little ones a cup of cold water only in the name of a disciple, verily I say unto you, he shall in no wise lose his reward. . . . And every one that hath forsaken houses, or brethren, or sisters, or father, or mother, or wife, or children, or lands, for my name's sake, shall receive an hundredfold, and shall inherit everlasting life" (Matt. 10:41-42; 19:29).

O. Concerning the Millennium—"And I say unto you, That many shall come from the east and west, and shall sit down with Abraham, and Isaac, and Jacob, in the kingdom of heaven. . . . Then shall the righteous shine forth as the sun in the kingdom of their Father. Who hath ears to hear, let him hear. . . . And Jesus said unto them, Verily I say unto you, That ye which have followed me, in the regeneration when the Son of man shall sit in the throne of his glory, ye also shall sit upon twelve thrones, judging the twelve tribes of Israel. . . . Then shall the King say unto them on his right hand, Come, ye blessed of my Father, inherit the kingdom prepared for you from the foundation of the world" (Matt. 8:11; 13:43; 19:28; 25:34).

P. Concerning the great white throne judgment—"When the Son of man shall come in his glory, and all the holy angels with him, then shall he sit upon the throne of his glory: and before him shall be gathered all nations: and he shall separate them one from another, as a shepherd divideth his sheep from the goats: and he shall set the sheep on his right hand, but the goats on the left" (Matt. 25:31-33). (See also Matt. 7:21-23; 13:49-50.)

Q. Concerning hell—"So shall it be at the end of the world: the angels shall come forth, and sever the wicked from among the just, and shall cast them into the furnace of fire: there shall be wailing and gnashing of teeth. . . . Wherefore if thy hand or thy foot offend thee, cut them off, and cast them from thee: it is better for thee to enter into life halt or maimed, rather than having two hands or two feet to be cast into everlasting fire. And if thine eye offend thee, pluck it out, and cast it from thee: it is better for thee to enter into life with one eye, rather than having two eyes to be cast into hell fire" (Matt. 13:49-50; 18:8-9).

R. Concerning heaven—"In my Father's house are many mansions: if it were not so, I would have told you. I go to prepare a place for you. And if I go and prepare a place for you, I will come again, and receive you unto myself; that where I am, there ye may be also" (John 14:2-3).

THE USAGE OF SCRIPTURE BY CHRIST
   A. The Old Testament events and individuals he mentioned
      1. The creation of Adam and Eve (Gen. 1:27; 2:24; Mark 10:6-8)
      2. The murder of Abel (Gen. 4:10; Luke 11:51)
      3. The corruption of Noah's day and the flood (Gen. 6–7; Luke 17:26-27)
      4. The corruption of Lot's day and the fire (Gen. 19; Luke 17:28-29)
      5. The worldliness of Lot's wife (Gen. 19:26; Luke 17:32)
      6. Moses and the burning bush (Exod. 3; Mark 12:26)
      7. Moses and the heavenly manna (Exod. 16:15; John 6:31)
      8. Moses and the brazen serpent (Num. 21:8; John 3:14)
      9. David and some shewbread (1 Sam. 21:6; Matt. 12:3-4)
      10. Solomon and the Queen of Sheba (1 Kings 10:1; Matt. 12:42)
      11. Elijah, a widow, and the famine (1 Kings 17:1, 9; Luke 4:25-26)
      12. Naaman and his leprosy (2 Kings 5; Luke 4:27)
      13. The murder of Zechariah (2 Chron. 24:20-21; Luke 11:51)
      14. Daniel and the abomination of desolation (Dan. 9:27; 11:31; 12:11; Matt. 24:15)
      15. Jonah and the fish (Jonah 1:17; Matt. 12:40; 16:4)
      16. Jonah and the repentance of the Ninevites (Jonah 3:4-10; Luke 11:30; Matt. 12:41)
   B. The Old Testament passages from which he quoted
      1. During his temptations
         a. The first temptation (in Matt. 4:4; he quoted Deut. 8:3)
         b. The second temptation (in Matt. 4:7; he quoted Deut. 6:16)
         c. The third temptation (in Matt. 4:10; he quoted Deut. 6:13)
      2. During his Sermon on the Mount
         a. In Matthew 5:21 (he quoted Exod. 20:13, the sixth commandment)
         b. In Matthew 5:27 (he quoted Exod. 20:14, the seventh commandment; also compare Matt. 5:31 with Deut. 24:1). (Note: He later quoted some of the same commandments during his talk with a rich young ruler. See Mark 10:19.)
      3. During his hometown sermon—In Luke 4:18-19 (he quoted Isa. 61:1-2)
      4. During various confrontations with Jewish rulers
         a. As he defended his associating with sinners (in Matt. 9:13; he quoted Hos. 6:6)
         b. As he expounded on marriage (in Mark 10:7-8; he quoted Gen. 2:24)
         c. As he was asked concerning the greatest of the commandments (in Mark 12:29-30; he quoted Deut. 6:4-5)

    d. As he rebuked their vain traditions (in Matt. 15:7-9; he quoted Isa. 29:13)
    e. As the Pharisees questioned his authority (in John 8:17; he quoted Deut. 17:6)
5. During his tribute to John the Baptist—In Luke 7:27 (he quoted Mal. 3:1)
6. During his triumphal entry day—In Matthew 21:16 (he quoted Psa. 8:2)
7. During his cleansing of the temple—In Luke 19:46 (he quoted Isa. 56:7)
8. During a parable about Israel—In Matthew 21:42, 44 (he quoted Psa. 118:22-23; Isa. 8:14-15)
9. During a question session in the temple—In Mark 12:36 (he quoted Psa. 110:1)
10. During his last Passover night—Predicting the world would hate the disciples as they hated him (in John 15:25; he quoted Pss. 35:19; 69:4)
11. On the cross
    a. His fourth utterance (in Matt. 27:46; he quoted Psa. 22:1)
    b. His seventh utterance (in Luke 23:46; he quoted Psa. 31:5)

THE PEOPLE CONVERTED BY CHRIST
1. Andrew (John 1:40-41)
    a. Circumstances—Saved when he left John the Baptist to follow the Lamb of God
    b. Location—Near the Jordan River
    c. Recorded testimony—"We have found the Messias."
2. Peter (John 1:41-42)
    a. Circumstances—Saved when he was brought to Christ by his brother Andrew. He had his name changed by Jesus to Cephas (a stone).
    b. Recorded testimony—None recorded at this point. (For later testimony see Matt 16:16.)
3. Philip (John 1:43, 45)
    a. Circumstances—Saved as a result of a personal visit by Jesus in Bethsaida of Galilee. Answered the call of the Master to follow him.
    b. Recorded testimony—"We have found him, of whom Moses in the law, and the prophets did write, Jesus of Nazareth."
4. Nathanel (John 1:45-51)
    a. Circumstances—Saved when he was brought to Christ by Philip. He was skeptical of Jesus at first.
    b. Recorded testimony—"Rabbi, thou art the Son of God; thou art the King of Israel."
5. Nicodemus (John 3:1-21)
    a. Circumstances—Saved in Jerusalem during a night meeting with Jesus. He was a ruler of the Jews, a teacher, a good and sincere man, but was lost.
    b. Recorded testimony—None was given at this time. (See John 7:51, given later.)
6. A Samaritan woman (John 4:29)
    a. Circumstances: Saved at Jacob's well outside a city in Samaria. She immediately gave testimony of this fact to her friends in the city.
    b. Recorded testimony—"Come see a man, which told me all things that ever I did: is not this the Christ?"
7. A nobleman (John 4:53)
    a. Circumstances: Saved in Capernaum after Jesus had healed his dying boy.
    b. Recorded testimony—None given.
8. An adulterous woman (John 8:11)
    a. Circumstances—Saved in Jerusalem after being forgiven by Christ and rescued from a mob of self-righteous Pharisees.
    b. Recorded testimony—None given.

9. A blind man (John 9:38)
   a. Circumstances—Saved in Jerusalem after receiving his sight. He witnessed boldly for Christ among the Pharisees and was thrown out of their synagogue for his testimony.
   b. Recorded testimony—"Lord, I believe."
10. Martha (John 11:27)
   a. Circumstances—Saved outside Bethany shortly after the death of her brother Lazarus.
   b. Recorded testimony—"Yea, Lord: I believe that thou art the Christ, the Son of God which should come into the world."
11. A centurion (Matt. 8:5-13)
   a. Circumstances: Saved in Capernaum after requesting Jesus to heal his beloved servant. The Master was amazed at his tremendous faith.
   b. Recorded testimony—None given.
12. Matthew (Matt. 9:9)
   a. Circumstances—Saved at his place of business in Jerusalem. He left all and followed Christ.
   b. Recorded testimony—None given.
13. A Syro-phoenician woman (Matt. 15:28)
   a. Circumstances—Saved along the Mediterranean coastline as she requested Jesus to heal her demoniac daughter.
   b. Recorded testimony—None given.
14. A Gadara maniac (Mark 5:15-20)
   a. Circumstances—Saved outside a cemetery on the eastern shoreline of the Galilean Sea.
   b. Recorded testimony—"And he departed, and began to publish in Decapolis how great things Jesus had done for him."
15. A woman with internal bleeding (Mark 5:28, 34)
   a. Circumstances—Saved in a Capernaum crowd as she touched the hem of Jesus' garment by faith for healing.
   b. Recorded testimony—"If I may touch but his clothes, I shall be whole."
16. A Galilean leper (Matt. 8:2)
   a. Circumstances—Saved during Christ's first preaching tour of Galilee as he requests healing.
   b. Recorded testimony—"Lord, if thou wilt, thou canst make me clean."
17. The father of a demoniac son (Mark 9:24)
   a. Circumstances—Saved as he meets Jesus at the base of the Mount of Transfiguration and begs for healing of his tormented son.
   b. Recorded testimony—"Lord, I believe; help thou mine unbelief."
18. Blind Bartimaeus (Mark 10:46-52)
   a. Circumstances—Saved outside Jericho as he cried out for Christ to cure his blindness.
   b. Recorded testimony—None given.
19. A paralytic (Luke 5:20)
   a. Circumstances—Saved in Capernaum as he was being lowered from a ceiling of a house.
   b. Recorded testimony—None given.
20. An immoral but heartbroken woman (Luke 7:38, 47-50)

      a. Circumstances—Saved in the home of a Pharisee as she washed Jesus' feet with her tears and dried them with her hair.

      b. Recorded testimony—None given.

21. A Samaritan leper (Luke 17:11-19)

      a. Circumstances—Saved on a country road as he returned to thank Jesus for healing him of leprosy.

      b. Recorded testimony—"With a loud voice [he] glorified God and fell down on his face at his feet, giving him thanks."

22. A publican (Luke 18:13)

      a. Circumstances—Saved as he begged for mercy in the temple of Jerusalem.

      b. Recorded testimony—None given. (Note: Even though Jesus refers to this in a parable, he very well could have had an actual case history in mind.)

23. Zacchaeus (Luke 19:8-9)

      a. Circumstances—Saved as he leaped from a sycamore tree in Jericho to meet Jesus.

      b. Recorded testimony—"Behold, Lord, the half of my goods I give to the poor; and if I have taken anything from any man by false accusation, I restore him fourfold."

24. A woman with an 18-year infirmity (Luke 13:11-13)

      a. Circumstances—Saved in a Galilean synagogue as Jesus laid his hands on her for healing.

      b. Recorded testimony—She "glorified God."

25. Mary Magdalene (Mark 16:9)

      a. Circumstances—Saved probably at the beginning of Christ's ministry when he cast seven demons from her. She is referred to in this passage.

      b. Recorded testimony—None given.

26. A centurion at Calvary (Matt. 27:54)

      a. Circumstances—Saved while watching Jesus die on the cross.

      b. Recorded testimony—"Truly this was the Son of God."

27. A dying thief (Luke 23:42)

      a. Circumstances—Saved while on a cross next to Jesus. He asked the Savior to remember him when he would establish his kingdom.

      b. Recorded testimony—None given.

**THE MINISTRY OF THE FATHER AND THE HOLY SPIRIT
IN THE LIFE OF CHRIST**

1. The ministry of the Father
    a. The Father sent his Son (John 3:16; 6:57; 8:16-18; 12:49; Gal. 4:4).
    b. He sealed his Son (John 6:27).
    c. He taught his Son (John 8:28).
    d. He anointed his Son (Luke 4:18).
    e. He honored his Son (John 8:54).
    f. He commanded his Son (John 10:18).
    g. He bore witness to his Son (John 8:18).
    h. He loved (and loves) his Son (John 10:17).
    i. He delighted in his Son (Matt. 3:17; 17:5).
    j. He heard his Son (Matt. 26:53; John 11:41; 12:27-28).
    k. He offered up his Son (John 3:16; 18:11; Rom. 8:32; 1 John 4:9-10).
    l. He raised his Son (Eph. 1:20).
    m. He exalted his Son (Phil. 2:9-11; Eph. 1:20).
    n. He glorified his Son (John 12:28; 17:1).
    o. He made his Son head of the Church (Eph. 1:22).
    p. He has committed all future judgment to his Son (John 5:22, 27; Acts 17:31).
2. The ministry of the Holy Spirit
    a. Jesus was begotten by the Holy Spirit (Luke 1:35).
    b. He was anointed by the Holy Spirit (Matt. 3:16; Heb. 1:9).
    c. He preached in the power of the Holy Spirit (Luke 4:18).
    d. He was sealed by the Holy Spirit (John 6:27).
    e. He was led by the Holy Spirit (Matt. 4:1).
    f. He worked his miracles through the Holy Spirit (Matt. 12:28; Acts 10:38).
    g. He was filled by the Holy Spirit (John 3:34; Luke 4:1).
    h. He sorrowed in the Holy Spirit (John 11:33).
    i. He rejoiced in the Holy Spirit (Luke 10:21).
    j. He offered up himself through the Holy Spirit (Heb. 9:14).
    k. He was raised from the dead by the Holy Spirit (Rom. 1:4; 1 Pet. 3:18).
    l. He commanded his apostles through the Holy Spirit (Acts 1:2).

THE ACTIVITIES OF THE ANGEL OF THE LORD AND ANGELS IN THE LIFE OF CHRIST

1. The activities of the angel of the Lord (Gabriel)
   a. He predicted the birth of Jesus' forerunner (Luke 1:11-19).
   b. He predicted the birth of Jesus.
      (1) To Mary (Luke 1:26-38)
      (2) To Joseph (Matt. 1:20-24)
   c. He announced the birth of Jesus (Luke 2:9-12).
   d. He protected Jesus from Herod (Matt. 2:13-15).
   e. He strengthened him in the Garden (Luke 22:43).
   f. He rolled away the stone from the grave (Matt. 28:2-4).
   g. He announced the resurrection (Matt. 28:5-7).
   h. He will sound the trumpet at the rapture of Christ (1 Thess. 4:16).
2. The activities of the angels
   a. They were made by and for God (Col. 1:16).
   b. They worship him (Heb. 1:6).
      (1) For his work of creation (Rev. 4:10)
      (2) For his work of redemption (Rev. 5:11-12)
   c. They rejoiced at his birth (Luke 2:13-14).
   d. They ministered to him in the wilderness (Matt. 4:11).
   e. They will accompany his second coming (2 Thess. 1:7-8).

THE ACTIVITES OF THE DEVIL AND DEMONS IN THE LIFE OF CHRIST
    1. The activities of the devil
        a. He himself tempted the Savior on three occasions (Matt. 4:1-11; Mark 1:12-13; Luke 4:1-13).
        b. He influenced the Savior's disciples on three occasions.
           (1) Causing James and John to hate the Samaritans (Luke 9:51-54)
           (2) Causing Peter to rebuke Jesus (Matt. 16:22-23)
           (3) Causing Judas to betray Jesus (John 13:27; Luke 22:3)
    2. The activities of demons
        a. They knew Jesus (Mark 3:11; Luke 4:34; Acts 16:17).
        b. They feared Jesus (Luke 8:28).
        c. They obeyed Jesus (Mark 5:13).

THE HUMANITY AND DEITY OF CHRIST
　　1. His humanity—He was as much man as if he had never been God.
　　　　a. He had a human parentage (Luke 1:31).
　　　　b. He had a human body (Matt. 26:12).
　　　　c. He had a human soul (John 12:27).
　　　　d. He had a human spirit (Mark 2:8; Luke 23:46).
　　　　e. He increased in wisdom and stature (Luke 2:52, 40).
　　　　f. He asked questions (Luke 2:46; 8:45).
　　　　g. He learned obedience (Luke 2:51).
　　　　h. He looked like a man.
　　　　　　(1) To the Samaritan woman (John 4:9)
　　　　　　(2) To the Jews (John 8:57; 10:33)
　　　　　　(3) To Mary Magdalene (John 20:15)
　　　　i. He possessed flesh and blood (John 6:51, 55).
　　　　j. He socialized (John 2:1-2).
　　　　k. He prayed (Luke 11:1).
　　　　l. He was tempted (Matt. 4:1).
　　　m. He hungered (Matt. 4:2; 21:18).
　　　　n. He thirsted (John 4:7; 19:28).
　　　　o. He ate (John 21:13-15; Luke 24:41-43).
　　　　p. He became weary (John 4:6).
　　　　q. He slept (Matt. 8:24).
　　　　r. He loved (Mark 10:21).
　　　　s. He had compassion (Matt. 9:36; 14:14; 15:32; Luke 7:13; Mark 1:41; 9:22-23; 5:19).
　　　　t. He was angered and grieved (Mark 3:5).
　　　　u. He wept (John 11:35; Luke 19:41).
　　　　v. He experienced joy (Luke 10:21).
　　　　w. He possessed zeal (John 2:17).
　　　　x. He became sorrowful (Matt. 26:37; Mark 14:34).
　　　　y. He sang (Matt. 26:30).
　　　　z. He sweated and agonized (Luke 22:44).
　　　aa. He was troubled (John 11:33; 12:27; 13:21; Mark 14:33-34).
　　　bb. He bled (John 19:34).
　　　cc. He died (Matt. 27:50).
　　　dd. He was buried (Matt. 27:59-60).
　　2. His deity—He was as much God as if he had never been man.

a. His deity was declared by angels.
   (1) By Gabriel to Mary (Luke 1:26-33)
   (2) By Gabriel to Joseph (Matt. 1:20-23)
   (3) By angels to some shepherds (Luke 2:8-11)
   (4) By angels to some women (Matt. 28:5-6)
b. His deity was declared by the Father.
   (1) At his baptism (Matt 3:16-17)
   (2) At his transfiguration (Matt. 17:5)
   (3) Shortly before his passion (John 12:27-28)
c. His deity was declared by his mighty miracles (John 20:30-31; 21:25).
d. His deity was declared by his powerful sermons (Luke 4:32; John 7:46).
e. His deity was declared by his accurate prophecies (Matt. 26:32).
f. His deity was declared by his sinless life (John 14:30).
   (1) As attested by Pilate (John 19:4)
   (2) By Pilate's wife (Matt. 27:19)
   (3) By Judas (Matt. 27:4)
   (4) By the dying thief (Luke 23:41)
   (5) By the Roman centurion (Luke 23:47)
g. His deity was declared by demons.
   (1) As he healed a maniac (Matt. 8:28-29)
   (2) As he healed a man in Capernaum (Luke 4:33-34)
   (3) As he healed many in Capernaum (Luke 4:41; Mark 3:11)
h. His deity was declared by those who worshiped him.
   (1) The shepherds (Luke 2:15)
   (2) The Wise Men (Matt. 2:2, 11)
   (3) A leper (Matt. 8:2)
   (4) A ruler (Matt. 9:18)
   (5) A Gentile mother (Matt. 15:25)
   (6) A Hebrew mother (Matt. 20:20)
   (7) A maniac (Mark 5:6)
   (8) A blind man (John 9:38)
   (9) An apostle—Thomas (John 20:28)
  (10) All apostles (Matt. 14:33; 28:9)
i. His deity was declared by Satan (Matt. 4:3, 6).
j. His deity was declared by himself.
   (1) He referred to himself as the Son of God (John 9:35; 10:36; 11:4).
   (2) He forgave sins (Mark 2:5, 10).
   (3) He is the judge of mankind (John 5:22, 27).
   (4) He is the author of life (John 5:24, 28-29).
   (5) He is to be honored like the Father (John 5:23).
   (6) He alone can save (John 10:28; Luke 19:10; John 14:6).

THE NAMES AND TITLES OF CHRIST

Bible names often give keen insight into the lives of those who bear the titles. This is especially true concerning Christ. A wealth of information concerning his Person and work can be obtained from studying some of the names and titles ascribed to him. Note some of these:

1. Adam (1 Cor. 15:45)
2. Advocate (1 John 2:1)
3. Almighty (Rev. 1:8)
4. Alpha (Rev. 1:8; 21:6)
5. Amen (Rev. 3:14)
6. Angel of the Lord (Gen. 16:9-14; Judges 6:11-24)
7. Anointed (Psa. 2:2)
8. Apostle (Heb. 3:1)
9. Author (Heb. 12:2)
10. Babe (Luke 2:16)
11. Beginning of creation (Rev. 3:14)
12. Begotten of the Father (John 1:14)
13. Beloved (Eph. 1:6)
14. Beloved Son (Mark 1:11)
15. Bishop (1 Pet. 2:25)
16. Blessed (1 Tim. 6:15)
17. Branch (Zech. 3:8)
18. Bread of Life (John 6:35)
19. Bridegroom
    a. By himself (Matt. 9:15; 25:1, 5-6, 10)
    b. By John the Baptist (John 3:29)
20. Bright and morning star (Rev. 22:16)
21. Captain (Josh. 5:14)
22. Carpenter (Mark 6:3)
23. Child (Isa. 9:6; Matt. 2:8-9)
24. Christ
    a. By Herod (Matt. 2:4)
    b. By Peter (Matt. 16:16; John 6:69)
    c. By Himself (Matt. 22:42; 23:8, 10; 24:5, 23; Luke 24:26, 46; John 20:31)
    d. By Caiaphas (Matt. 26:63, 68)
    e. By Pilate (Matt. 27:17, 22)
    f. By the chief priests (Mark 15:32)

      g. By the angels (Luke 2:11)
      h. By a dying thief (Luke 23:39)
       i. By Andrew (John 1:41)
       j. By a Samaritan woman (John 4:25, 29)
      k. By a crowd (John 7:41)
       l. By Martha (John 11:27)
25. Commander (Isa. 55:4)
26. Consolation of Israel (Luke 2:25)
27. Cornerstone (Eph. 2:20)
28. Counselor (Isa. 9:6)
29. Dayspring from on high (Luke 1:78)
30. Day Star (2 Pet. 1:19)
31. Deliverer (Rom. 11:26)
32. Desire of all nations (Hag. 2:7)
33. Door of the sheep (John 10:7)
34. Emmanuel (Matt. 1:23)
35. Eternal life (1 John 5:20)
36. Everlasting Father (Isa. 9:6)
37. Express image of God (Heb. 1:3)
38. Faithful witness (Rev. 1:5; 3:14)
39. Faithful and true (Rev. 19:11)
40. First fruits (1 Cor. 15:23)
41. Forerunner (Heb. 6:20)
42. Foundation (Isa. 28:16)
43. Fountain (Zech. 13:1)
44. Friend of sinners (Matt. 11:19)
45. Gift of God (2 Cor. 9:15)
46. Glory of the Lord (Isa. 60:1)
47. God (John 1:1; Rom. 9:5; 1 Tim. 3:17)
48. Good master (Mark 10:17)
49. Governor (Matt. 2:6)
50. Guide (Psa. 48:14)
51. Head of Church (Col. 1:18)
52. Heir of all things (Heb. 1:2)
53. High priest (Heb. 2:17; 3:1)
54. Holy child (Acts 4:30)
55. Holy One of God (Mark 1:24)
56. Holy One of Israel (Isa. 41:14)
57. Horn of salvation (Psa. 18:2)
58. I Am—He calls himself this name seven times in John's Gospel.
      a. I am the Bread of Life (John 6:35).
      b. I am the Light of the world (John 9:5).
      c. I am the Good Shepherd (John 10:11).
      d. I am the Door (John 10:9).
      e. I am the Resurrection (John 11:25).
       f. I am the True Vine (John 15:1).
      g. I am the Way (John 14:6).
59. Jehovah (Isa. 26:4)

60. Jesus
    a. By Gabriel (Matt. 1:21; Mark 16:6; Luke 1:31)
    b. By Joseph (Matt. 1:25)
    c. By demons (Matt. 8:29; Mark 1:24)
    d. By a Jerusalem crowd (Matt. 21:11)
    e. By Pilate (Matt. 27:17, 22, 37)
    f. By ten lepers (Luke 17:13)
    g. By a cured blind man (John 9:11)
    h. By some Greeks (John 12:21)
    i. By some soldiers (John 18:5, 7)
61. Judge (Mic. 5:1; Acts 10:42)
62. King (of the Jews and of Israel)
    a. By the Wise Men (Matt. 2:2)
    b. By himself (Matt. 21:5; 25:34, 40)
    c. By Pilate (Matt. 27:11, 37; Mark 15:9, 12; John 18:39; 19:14-15, 19)
    d. By some Roman soldiers (Matt. 27:29; John 19:3)
    e. By the chief priest (Matt. 27:42)
    f. By Nathanael (John 1:49)
    g. By the triumphal entry crowd (John 12:13, 15)
63. Lamb of God (John 1:29, 36)
64. Lawgiver (Isa. 33:22)
65. Lily of the valley (S. of Sol. 2:1)
66. Lion of the tribe of Judah (Rev. 5:5)
67. Living bread (John 6:51)
68. Lord
    a. By the unsaved (Matt. 7:22; 25:11, 44; John 6:34)
    b. By a leper (Matt. 8:2)
    c. By the twelve (Matt. 8:25; 26:22; Luke 9:54; 11:1; 22:49; 24:34; John 11:12; 20:25)
    d. By himself (Matt. 12:8; 21:3; 24:42; Luke 6:46; John 13:14)
    e. By Peter (Matt. 14:28, 30; 16:22; 17:4; 18:21; Luke 5:8; John 6:68; 13:6, 36; 21:15-17, 21)
    f. By the mother of a demoniac daughter (Matt. 15:22)
    g. By the father of a demoniac son (Matt. 17:15)
    h. By two blind men (Matt. 20:30)
    i. By the faithful (Matt. 25:20, 22, 37)
    j. By the angel of the Lord (Luke 2:11)
    k. By some would-be followers (Luke 9:57, 59, 61)
    l. By Mary and Martha (Luke 10:40; John 11:3, 21, 27, 32, 39)
    m. By a dying thief (Luke 23:42)
    n. By an immoral woman (John 8:11)
    o. By a cured blind man (John 9:36, 38)
    p. By John the apostle (John 13:25; 21:7)
    q. By Thomas (John 14:5; 20:28)
    r. By Philip (John 14:8)
    s. By Mary Magdalene (John 20:2)
69. Lord of Lords (Rev. 19:16)
70. Man (Acts 17:31; 1 Tim. 2:5)
71. Master (Matt. 8:19)
    a. By himself (Matt. 10:24; 23:8)

    b. By his enemies (Matt. 12:38; 22:16, 24, 36; Mark 12:19; Luke 11:45; 19:39; John 8:4)

    c. By a rich young ruler (Matt. 19:16)

    d. By Judas (Matt. 26:25, 49)

    e. By the twelve (Mark 4:38; 13:1; John 4:31; 9:2; 11:8)

    f. By the father of a demoniac son (Mark 9:17)

    g. By John the apostle (Mark 9:38; 10:35)

    h. By Peter (Mark 11:21; Luke 5:5; 8:45; 9:33)

    i. By a sincere scribe (Mark 12:32)

    j. By a carnal listener (Luke 12:13)

    k. By Martha (John 11:28)

    l. By Mary Magdalene (John 20:16)

72. Mediator (1 Tim. 2:5)
73. Messiah (Dan. 9:25)

    a. By Andrew (John 1:41)

    b. By a Samaritan woman (John 4:25)

74. Mighty God (Isa. 9:6)
75. Minister (Heb. 8:2)
76. Nazarene (Matt. 2:23)
77. Only begotten Son (John 1:18)
78. Passover (1 Cor. 5:7)
79. Physician (Matt. 9:12)
80. Potentate (1 Tim 6:15)
81. Power of God (1 Cor. 1:24)
82. Priest (Heb. 4:14)
83. Prince (Acts 3:15; 5:31)
84. Prince of Peace (Isa. 9:6)
85. Prophet (Acts 3:22)

    a. By himself (Matt. 13:57; John 4:44)

    b. By the triumphal entry crowd (Matt. 21:11)

    c. By the Pharisees (Matt. 21:46)

    d. By the citizens of Nain (Luke 7:16)

    e. By Cleopas (Luke 24:19)

    f. By a Samaritan woman (John 4:19)

    g. By the 5,000 he fed (John 6:14)

    h. By a Jerusalem crowd (John 7:40)

    i. By a cured blind man (John 9:17)

86. Propitiation (1 John 2:2; 4:10)
87. Purifier (Mal. 3:3)
88. Rabbi—On three well-known occasions he was called by this name.

    a. By Nicodemus (John 3:2)

    b. By Judas ("Master"—Matt. 26:25)

    c. By Mary Magdalene (John 20:16)

89. Ransom (1 Tim. 2:6)
90. Redeemer (Isa. 59:20; 60:16)
91. Refiner (Mal. 3:3)
92. Refuge (Isa. 25:4)
93. Righteousness (Jer. 23:6; 33:16)

94. Rock (Deut. 32:15)
95. Rod (Isa. 11:1)
96. Root of David (Rev. 22:16)
97. Rose of Sharon (S. of Sol. 2:1)
98. Sacrifice (Eph. 5:2)
99. Savior
    a. By his mother (Luke 1:47)
    b. By the angels (Luke 2:11)
    c. By the men of Samaria (John 4:42)
100. Second man (1 Cor. 15:47)
101. Seed of Abraham (Gal. 3:16, 19)
102. Seed of David (2 Tim. 2:8)
103. Seed of the Woman (Gen. 3:15)
104. Servant (Isa. 42:1; 49:5-7)
105. Shepherd
    a. The chief Shepherd (1 Pet. 5:4)
    b. The Good Shepherd (John 10:11, 14)
    c. The great Shepherd (Heb. 13:20)
    d. My Shepherd (Psa. 23:1)
106. Shiloh (Gen. 49:10)
107. Son of David
    a. By two blind men in Capernaum (Matt. 9:27)
    b. By the Syro-phoenician woman (Matt. 15:22)
    c. By two blind men in Jericho (one named Bartimaeus; Matt. 20:30; Mark 10:46-47)
    d. The Palm Sunday crowd (Matt. 21:9)
108. Son of God—Christ referred to himself by this name on only two occasions (John 9:35; 10:36), but many other people in the Gospels also called him by this name. He was called the Son of God by:
    a. Satan (Matt. 4:3, 6)
    b. Gabriel (Luke 1:35)
    c. A demon (Matt. 8:29; Luke 4:41)
    d. Disciples (Matt. 14:33)
    e. Peter (Matt. 16:16)
    f. Martha (John 11:27)
    g. Nathanael (John 1:49)
    h. A centurion (Matt. 27:54)
109. Son of man—His favorite name for himself. According to his own testimony, the Son of man:
    a. Came not to be ministered unto (Matt. 20:28)
    b. Came to save that which was lost (Matt. 18:11)
    c. Can forgive sins (Matt. 9:6)
    d. Had nowhere to lay his head (Matt. 8:20)
    e. Is Lord of the Sabbath (Luke 6:5)
    f. Would be betrayed (Matt. 17:12)
    g. Would suffer (Matt. 17:12)
    h. Would be lifted up (John 3:14)
    i. Would be three days in the heart of the earth (Matt. 12:40)
    j. Would be raised from the dead (Matt. 17:9)

    k. Will come again in the glory of his Father (Matt. 16:27; 24:30)
    l. Will send forth his angels (Matt. 13:41)
    m. Shall sit upon the throne of his glory (Matt. 19:28)
110. Son of Mary (Mark 6:3)
111. Son of Abraham (Matt. 1:1)
112. Son of Joseph—Wrongly used by:
    a. The Nazareth citizens (Luke 4:22)
    b. Philip (John 1:45)
113. Son of the highest (Luke 1:32)
114. Stone (Matt. 21:42; Mark 12:10; Acts 4:11; Rom. 9:32-33; Eph. 2:20; 1 Pet. 2:6-7)
115. Sun of righteousness (Mal. 4:2)
116. Teacher (Master) (Matt. 26:18; John 3:2; 11:28)
117. Wonderful (Isa. 9:6)
118. Word—The Apostle John's favorite name for Christ (John 1:1; 1 John 5:7; Rev. 19:13)

THE POLITICAL AND RELIGIOUS GROUPS IN THE TIME OF CHRIST
1. The Galileans
    a. They were the political "extreme right" fanatics of their day.
    b. The group arose in northern Palestine, headed up by Judas of Galilee, who led a rebellion against all foreign elements. They advocated Galilee was for Galileans.
    c. They came into violent collision with Pilate, who felt forced to slaughter a number of them on one occasion (Luke 13:1).
    d. Christ's enemies attempted to identify both him and the disciples with the Galileans (Matt. 26:69; Mark 14:70; Luke 23:6).
2. The Herodians
    a. This was a political group from the family of Herod.
    b. They derived their authority from the Roman government and favored Greek customs.
    c. They were committed to maintaining the status quo and were law-and-order advocates.
    d. They joined the efforts of the Pharisees to silence Christ.
        (1) During his early ministry (Mark 3:6)
        (2) During the middle part (Mark 12:13)
        (3) During his final week (Matt. 22:16)
    e. They regarded him as a revolutionary fanatic.
    f. Christ soundly condemned the Herodians (Mark 8:15; 12:13-17).
3. The Levites
    a. They were the descendants of Levi, Jacob's third son (Gen. 29:34).
    b. They had charge of the temple.
        (1) The Jews sent some priests and Levites to check out the desert ministry of John the Baptist (John 1:19).
        (2) Jesus used a Levite (who didn't want to become involved) in his parable of the Good Samaritan (Luke 10:32).
4. The Pharisees
    a. This group arose during the time of the Macabees under the reign of John Hyrcanus (135-104 B.C.).
    b. They were called the separatists in mockery of their enemies. This name was taken from the verb *parash*.
    c. They were the exponents and guardians of both written and oral law. In belief they were conservative, in distinction from the liberal Sadducees.
    d. They were the most bitter and hateful enemies of Christ.

(1) They condemned him for associating with sinners (Matt. 9:11; Luke 7:39; 15:2).
(2) They condemned him for healing on the Sabbath (Luke 6:7; 14:1).
(3) They condemned him for allowing his disciples to eat on the Sabbath (Matt. 12:1-2).
(4) They accused him of casting out demons through Satan's power (Matt. 9:34).
(5) They sought to kill him early in his ministry (Matt. 12:14).
(6) They demanded that he perform signs for them (Matt. 12:38; 16:1).
(7) They despised him because he refused to always follow their vain traditions (Matt. 15:1-2).
(8) They attempted to trap him on various theological issues.
    (a) Concerning marriage (Matt. 19:3)
    (b) Concerning tribute to Caesar (Matt. 22:17)
    (c) Concerning the kingdom of God (Luke 17:20)
(9) They attempted to deny his miracles (John 9:15).
(10) They cast doubt upon the legality of his birth (John 8:41; 9:24).
(11) They accused him of outright lying (John 8:13).
(12) They threatened retaliation upon all who would accept him (John 9:22; 12:42).
(13) They plotted his death (John 11:47-53)
(14) They ordered his arrest in Gethsemane (John 18:3).
(15) They demanded a guard be stationed by his tomb (Matt. 27:64).
e. They were utterly denounced by John the Baptist (Matt. 3:7-12).
f. They were utterly denounced by Jesus (Matt. 5:20; 16:11; 23:1-36; Luke 18:10).
g. The doctrine of the Pharisees would include:
  (1) An almost fatalistic concept of God's sovereignty
  (2) A belief in the resurrection of the just and the damnation of all wicked
  (3) The existence and ministry of angels
h. Nicodemus (John 3:1) and Paul (Acts 23:6) were both Pharisees by birth and training.
i. The *Jewish Encyclopedia* lists seven types of Pharisees:
  (1) The "shoulder" Pharisee, who paraded his good deeds before men like a badge on the shoulder
  (2) The "wait-a-little" Pharisee, who would ask someone to wait for him while he performed a good deed
  (3) The "blind" Pharisee, who bruised himself by walking into a wall because he shut his eyes to avoid seeing a woman
  (4) The "pestle" Pharisee, who walked with hanging head rather than observe alluring temptation
  (5) The "ever-reckoning" Pharisee, who was always counting his good deeds to see if they offset his failures
  (6) The "God-fearing" Pharisee, who, like Job, was truly righteous
  (7) The "God-loving" Pharisee, like Abraham
j. The estimated number of Pharisees in Jesus' day was around 6,000.
5. The Sadducees
  a. This group came from Zadok, the high priest, during the reign of Solomon (1 Kings 2:35).

b. They were the aristocratic and political party among the Jews and were rivals of the Pharisees.
c. The Sadducees were the modernists of the day. They denied the existence of spirits, the resurrection of the just, and immortality of the soul. They were totally anti-supernatural.
d. They came into prominence about the same time the Pharisees did. Both parties briefly set aside their differences to accomplish the common goal of murdering Christ.
e. They attempted to ridicule Christ on the subject of the resurrection, but wound up being ridiculed themselves (Mark 12:18; Luke 20:27).

6. The Samaritans
a. They were a mixed race living between the provinces of Judea and Galilee.
b. The race began in 722 B.C. when the Assyrian King Sargon II took the Northern Kingdom of Israel into captivity, leaving only the poorest and most uneducated Israelites behind. Later this group intermarried with the thousands of homesteaders who poured into the area from all over the world (2 Kings 17:24-33).
c. The Samaritans later offered to help build the Jewish temple in 535 B.C., but their offer was refused (Ezra 4:1-3).
d. The Samaritan governor, Sanballat, attempted to frustrate the building of Jerusalem's walls during Nehemiah's time (Neh. 6:1-9).
e. A complete break between the Jews and Samaritans occurred when the grandson of Eliashib the high priest married Sanballat's daughter, contrary to the statute prohibiting mixed marriages (Neh. 13:23-28). Since he refused to annul the marriage, he was promptly expelled from the priesthood and exiled. He retired to Samaria, where Sanballat built a temple for him on Mount Gerizim. This temple was destroyed by John Hyrcanus in 128 B.C. because the Samaritans had compromised with paganism under Antiochus Epiphanes IV by dedicating their temple to the Greek god Zeus.
f. By the time of the New Testament this hatred had reached its zenith (John 4:9; 8:48).
g. Christ ordered his disciples not to enter Samaria during their first preaching tour (Matt. 10:5).
h. However, just prior to his ascension he commanded them to witness for him in that land (Acts 1:8).
i. Jesus himself ministered to the Samaritans during his earthly ministry (John 4:1-42).
j. A Samaritan was the hero in one of Jesus' most famous parables (Luke 10:33).
k. On one occasion he healed ten lepers. Only one returned to thank him, and he was a Samaritan (Luke 17:16).
l. Jesus was rejected by the Samaritans during his final earthly ministry, because his face was set as though he would go to Jerusalem (Luke 9:53).

7. The Sanhedrin
a. This name comes from two Greek words: *sun* (together with), and *hedra* (a sitting place). It thus referred to a council board which sat in session.
b. The Sanhedrin was the religious and legal Jewish Supreme Court.
c. It may have come from the time of Moses (Num. 11:16-17), or have been formed during the days of King Jehoshaphat (2 Chron. 19:8).
d. The council had seventy to seventy-two members:

(1) The high priest, who was president

(2) The heads of the twenty-four priestly service divisions

(3) The scribes and lawyers

(4) The elders, who were the representatives of the laity

e. Here Christ stood during his third illegal trial (Matt. 26:65-66; 27:1-2). Here also he was blindfolded, spit upon, and beaten.

f. His trial before the Sanhedrin was a travesty of justice.

(1) They normally met in a semicircle with the prisoner standing in the midst, facing them. This was not done, for Jesus was blindfolded.

(2) Two clerks were appointed. One would record the votes for acquittal, the other for conviction. In Christ's case this was not done.

(3) The arguments for acquittal would be given first. This did not happen in Jesus' trial.

(4) If the vote was for acquittal, the prisoner was set free immediately. If the vote was for conviction, condemnation could not be pronounced until the following day. This procedure was not followed.

8. The scribes

a. They were the students, interpreters, and teachers of the Old Testament Scriptures, and the Savior's bitter enemies.

b. He denounced them for making the Word of God of no effect by their traditions (Matt. 16:21; 21:13; 23:2; 26:3; Mark 12:28-40).

c. The scribes were also called lawyers (Matt. 22:35; Luke 10:25; 11:45-52; 14:3).

THE PLACES VISITED BY CHRIST

1. Bethabara—A few miles north of Jericho, on the eastern bank of the Jordan River where John baptized Jesus (John 1:28; Matt. 3:13-17)
2. Bethany—Fifteen furlongs, or 1 3/4, miles from Jerusalem on the eastern slope of the Mount of Olives. It is on the road to Jericho. Bethany was the Judean headquarters of Jesus, as Capernaum was his Galilean headquarters.
    a. Here he raised Lazarus from the dead (John 11).
    b. Mary and Martha entertained Christ here (Luke 10:38-42).
    c. Mary anointed his feet here (John 12:1-11).
    d. It was also the home of Simon the leper (Mark 14:3).
    e. Here Christ blessed his disciples just prior to his ascension from the Mount of Olives (Luke 24:50).
3. Bethlehem—Five miles south of Jerusalem
    a. It was the birthplace of both Mary and Joseph (Luke 2:1-4).
    b. It was here that Christ was born (Mic. 5:2; John 7:42; Luke 2).
4. Bethphage—On the slopes of Mount Olivet between Bethany and Jerusalem. Here the triumphal entry began (Matt. 21:1-11; Mark 11:1-11; Luke 19:29-40).
5. Bethsaida—Located at the place where the Jordan River enters the Sea of Galilee. It means "the place of catching."
    a. It was the home of Philip, Andrew, and Peter (John 1:44).
    b. Jesus upbraided this city, along with others, for its unbelief (Luke 10:11-14; Matt. 11:21).
    c. Here he also healed a blind man (Mark 8:22-26).
6. Bireh—Located fifteen miles north of Jerusalem and the first stopping place for caravans going from Jerusalem to Galilee, Bireh is thought to be the place where Jesus was found to be missing during his visit to the temple at age twelve (Luke 2:41-45).
7. Caesarea Philippi—Situated at the base of Mount Hermon, northeast of the Galilean Sea. This was doubtless the farthest point north traveled by our Lord. Here he heard Simon Peter's great confession (Matt. 16:13-16).
8. Cana—Four miles northeast of Nazareth, on the road to Tiberias
    a. It was the hometown of Nathanael (John 21:2).
    b. Here Jesus performed his first miracle, that of turning water into wine (John 2:1-11).
    c. Here he also worked his second miracle, the healing of the nobleman's son (John 4:46-54).
9. Capernaum—Located along the northwest shore of Galilee, 2 1/2 miles from where the Jordan River enters the lake

a. This became the Galilean headquarters of his earthly ministry (Matt. 4:13; 9:1).

b. Here he chose Matthew (Matt. 9:9).

c. Here he delivered his great Bread of Life sermon (John 6:24-71).

d. Here he performed nine of his recorded miracles.

    (1) Healing of the centurion's servant (Matt. 8:5-13)

    (2) Healing of Peter's mother-in-law (Matt. 8:14-15)

    (3) Healing of a demoniac (Mark 1:21-27)

    (4) Healing of a palsied man who was lowered from the roof (Mark 2:1-5)

    (5) Healing of a woman with a bloody issue (Matt. 9:22)

    (6) Healing of Jairus' daughter (Matt. 9:25)

    (7) Healing of two blind men (Matt. 9:29)

    (8) Healing of a dumb demoniac (Matt. 9:33)

    (9) The miracle of the tribute money (Matt. 17:24-27)

10. Chorazin—Two miles north of Capernaum. Christ pronounced judgment upon this city for its unbelief (Matt. 11:21-23).

11. Emmaus—About 7 1/2 miles west of Jerusalem. Here Christ appeared to two disciples after his resurrection and revealed himself to them at the supper table (Luke 24:13-31).

12. Gergesa—Located on the northeastern shore of Galilee, where Jesus healed the demon-filled maniac of Gadara (Mark 5:1-21).

13. Gethsemane—Located across the Kidron Valley from the golden gate of Jerusalem. It was the garden place where he prayed just prior to his betrayal and arrest (Matt. 26:36-56; John 18:1-14).

14. Jenin—Twenty-four miles north of Samaria, where some believe Jesus healed the ten lepers (Luke 17:11-19).

15. Jericho—Located seventeen miles northwest of Jerusalem near the Jordan River.

a. Here Jesus healed a blind man named Bartimaeus (Luke 18:35).

b. Here Zacchaeus met Christ (Luke 19:1-10).

c. Jesus used this city to help illustrate his Good Samaritan parable (Luke 10:30-37).

16. Jerusalem—The capital of God's world. It is situated on a rocky prominence about 2,500 feet above the Mediterranean and 3,800 feet above the Dead Sea. It is 33 miles east of the Mediterranean Sea and 14 miles west of the Dead Sea.

a. Jesus was dedicated here (Luke 2:1-38).

b. He attended the Passover at age twelve (Luke 2:41-50).

c. He cleansed the temple (John 2:13-17).

d. He spoke to Nicodemus (John 3:1-16).

e. He healed a thirty-eight-year-old invalid (John 5:8).

f. He preached on the Holy Spirit during the feast of the tabernacles (John 7:10-39).

g. He forgave an adulterous woman (John 8:1-11).

h. He preached on the devil and his children (John 8:33-59).

i. He healed a man born blind (John 9:7).

j. He preached a sermon on the Good Shepherd (John 10:1-18).

k. He made his triumphal entry (John 12:12-15).

l. He cursed the fig tree (Matt. 21:19).

m. He utterly condemned the wicked Pharisees (Matt. 23:1-36).

n. He preached the Mount Olivet discourse (Matt. 24—25)

o. He wept over Jerusalem (Luke 19:41; Matt. 23:37-39).

p. He conducted the service in the Upper Room (John 13—14).

q. He preached on the vine and branches (John 15—16).

r. He prayed his great high priestly prayer (John 17).

s. He was arrested in Gethsemane (Matt. 26:47-56).

t. He restored a severed ear (Luke 22:51).

u. He was condemned to death (Matt. 27:26).

v. He was crucified (Matt. 27:27-50).

w. He was buried (Matt. 27:57-60).

x. He rose from the dead (Matt. 28:1-10).

y. He visited the Upper Room for the first time following his resurrection (Luke 24:36-43; John 20:19-23).

z. He visited the Upper Room for the second time (John 20:24-29).

aa. He visited the Upper Room for the third and final time (Mark 16:14-18; Luke 24:44-49).

bb. He ascended into heaven (Acts 1:4-11).

17. Jordan River—It begins at the base of Mount Hermon, about 1,700 feet above sea level. From there it goes to the waters of Merom, some 12 miles down course. From there it flows the 5 miles to the Sea of Galilee, some 682 feet below sea level. Finally, it proceeds the 65 miles to the Dead Sea, 1,300 feet below sea level. Thus, during its 82-mile course, the Jordan River drops 3,000 feet. It was in the Jordan River that our Lord was baptized (Matt. 3:13-17).

18. Kidron—A valley, about 2 3/4 miles long, located immediately east of the wall of Jerusalem between the city and the Mount of Olives. Jesus crossed this valley en route to Gethsemane (John 18:1).

19. Magdala—Located three miles north of Tiberias on the western shore of the Galilean Sea (Matt. 15:39). This was the home of Mary Magdalene (Luke 8:2; Mark 16:9).

20. Mount Hermon—Located some 17 miles north of the Galilean Sea. It is by far the highest mountain in all Palestine, reaching 9,101 feet. Many believe this to be the "high mountain" of Matthew 17:1 where Christ was transfigured.

21. Mount of Olives—Located due east of Jerusalem, across from the Kidron Valley. Its height is 2,641 feet.

a. Here Christ wept over Jerusalem (Luke 19:41-44).

b. Here he delivered his great sermon on prophecy (Matt. 24—25).

c. Here he walked after the Passover in the Upper Room (Matt. 26:30; Mark 14:26; Luke 22:39).

d. From here he ascended into heaven (Luke 24:50-51; Acts 1:6-12).

22. Mount Tabor—Located 5 1/2 miles southeast of Nazareth. Its height is 1,843 feet above sea level. Some believe this was the mount of transfiguration instead of Mount Hermon. However, the text prefers the latter.

23. Mount Zion—The height which rises close to the southwest corner of the old walled city. Here was located the Upper Room (Mark 14:12-16; Luke 22:7-13; John 13—14).

24. Nain—A city some ten miles southeast of Nazareth, where Jesus raised the dead son of a sorrowing widow (Luke 7:11)

25. Nazareth—Located about midway between the Sea of Galilee and the Mediterranean Sea

a. Both Joseph and Mary received the news from Gabriel concerning the virgin birth here (Luke 1:26; Matt. 1:18-25).

    b. Here Jesus grew into manhood (Luke 2:39-40, 51-52).

    c. Here he preached two sermons.

       (1) After the first, on Isaiah 61, the citizens attempted to kill him (Luke 4:16-30).

       (2) After the second, he was totally rejected by the citizens (Matt. 13:53-58; Mark 6:1-6).

26. Sea of Galilee—This inland sea lake is 13 miles long, 7 1/2 miles wide, and 32 miles in circumference. It is 700 feet below sea level, and its greatest depth is 200 feet.

    a. Beside this body of water, Jesus fed the 5,000 (John 6:1-14).

    b. On the Mount of Beatitudes, he gave the Sermon on the Mount (Matt. 5–7).

    c. Here he calmed the wild stormy sea waters (Matt. 8:23-27).

    d. Here he walked on the water (John 6:15-21).

    e. Here 2,000 hogs were drowned after he healed a maniac (Mark 5:1-21).

    f. Here he performed his last miracle (Mark 14:28; 16:7; John 21).

27. Sychar—Located some 25 miles due north of Jerusalem in Samaria. Here Jesus met the Samaritan woman at Jacob's well (John 4).

28. Tyre—A city located on the Mediterranean Sea, some 20 miles due west of Caesarea Philippi. Jesus healed the Syro-phoenician woman's daughter is this area (Mark 3:8; Luke 6:17).

29. Wilderness of temptation—The exact spot is unknown. However, some feel it may have been southeast of Jerusalem in the Dead Sea area (Matt. 4:1).

INDEX

IMPORTANT EVENTS
IN THE LIFE OF CHRIST

NOTES

NOTES

NOTES

NOTES

NOTES

NOTES

NOTES

NOTES

NOTES

NOTES

NOTES

NOTES

NOTES

NOTES

NOTES

NOTES

NOTES